Nuclear Age Literature for Youth

The Quest for a Life-affirming Ethic

Nuclear Age Literature for Youth

The Quest for a Life-affirming Ethic

By
MILLICENT LENZ

American Library
Association
Chicago and London 1990

Designed by Charles Bozett

Composed by Central Photo Engraving
in Palatino on a CCI 400

Printed on 50-pound Glatfelter,
a pH-neutral stock, and bound in
10-point Carolina cover stock by
Edwards Brothers, Inc.

PN1009
.A1
L47
1990
cop. 2

The paper used in this publication meets the minimum requirements of American National Standard for Information Sciences—Permanence of Paper for Printed Library Materials, ANSI Z39.48-1984. ∞

Library of Congress Cataloging-in-Publication Data

Lenz, Millicent.
  Nuclear age literature for youth: the quest for a life-affirming ethic/Millicent Lenz.
    p. cm.
  Includes bibliographical references.
  ISBN 0-8389-0535-8 (alk. paper)
  1. Children's literature—History and criticism. 2. Young adult literature—History and criticism. 3. Atomic bomb in literature. 4. Nuclear warfare in literature. 5. Ethics in literature. 6. War in literature. 7. Mythology in literature. 8. Children—Books and reading. 9. Young adults— Books and reading. I. Title.
PN1009.A1L47 1990
809'.93358—dc20   90-497
                                                                                    CIP

94 93 92 91 90 5 4 3 2 1

for Robert Gilson

Contents

Acknowledgments

I wish to thank the University at Albany, State University of New York, Office of Research, for a FRAP grant to assist me in the initial work on the manuscript;

Richard S. Halsey of the School of Information Science and Policy at the University, for unflagging moral support;

the library staff of University Libraries for assistance in obtaining vast quantities of materials;

Joseph E. Milosh, Jr., for wise mentorship in years past;

Paul Brians of Washington State University, Pullman, for incisive, constructive criticism of an early version of the manuscript;

H. Bruce Franklin, Becky McLaughlin, and Elise Harvey, for their permission to use previously unpublished materials;

students in my literature courses at the University at Albany, whose lively intellects are a constant challenge and delight;

the staff of ALA Publishing, especially Bettina MacAyeal, for her fine balance of enthusiasm and critical insights as an editor; Helen Cline, whose expertise and unerring sense of style guided the manuscript through production; and Ellen Faist and Ruth Ann Jones, for their role in reaching the book's readership;

and most of all, Robert Gilson, my husband, whose contributions surpass enumeration.

Introduction

Once upon a time, goes a Chinese fable, the cats ruled the world. For centuries, they enjoyed the status of dominant species. In the spirit of *noblesse oblige* they tried to solve the ethical problems life inevitably poses. Finally, having tried without success to find solutions to the dilemmas of existence, they despaired of the effort. The cat philosophers decided to give up the governance of the world to a lesser species, one "optimistic enough to believe that the mortal predicament could be solved and ignorant enough never to learn better." This, says the narrator of William Faulkner's *The Reivers*, is "why the cat lives with you, is completely dependent on you for food and shelter, but lifts no paw for you and loves you not; in a word, why your cat looks at you the way it does."[1]

Unlike the cat philosophers, our semi-optimistic and multiply ignorant species has persisted over centuries in its effort to solve the riddles of the human condition. Today one of our most challenging dilemmas is to find an ethic adequate to forestall the global catastrophe that seems likely to occur from one of two causes: irreparable damage to the ecosystem, stemming from the "greenhouse effect," or thermonuclear disaster, arising from accident, war, or dementia. We dare not, like the cat philosophers, abandon the quest to find solutions, because the very fate of the earth depends upon finding a value system equal to the demands of our nuclear and global age.

Such value systems traditionally have been embodied in culture heroes, larger-than-life figures whose lives express the ideals of a given society. One of our problems is the lack of such an admirable yet believable mythic figure. The warrior-hero, so long dominant in our culture,

1. William Faulkner, *The Reivers* (New York: Random House, 1962), p. 122. Joseph Meeker relates this anecdote in *The Comedy of Survival: In Search of an Environmental Ethic*, foreword by Konrad Lorenz, introduction by Paul Shepard, illustrated by William Berry (Los Angeles: Guild of Tutors Press, 1980), p. 119. First published by Charles Scribner's Sons, 1974.

has become an anachronism; our literature is populated by antiheroes, with whom we can more comfortably identify. Yet some feel a void where they would like to find heroic patterns.

The Need for Heroic Patterns

Who can be heroic in a nuclear age? Who can even believe seriously in the concept of heroism? Some would say nuclear arms have made heroism obsolete, or that true heroism today would lie in achieving the dream of world peace or perhaps in the corollary aim of freeing the world from the threat of ecological disaster. In an interconnected, nuclear world, cynics argue, we are all at once potential executioners and certain victims. Are not the mushroom clouds over Hiroshima and Nagasaki final punctuation marks, endstops to traditional notions about so-called heroic action in war? The threat of destruction, this argument goes, now impersonal and unimaginable in scale, makes the hero outdated. No more Hector versus Agamemnon, no St. George versus the dragon, no Joan of Arc against the infidel. Thermonuclear bombs reduce human heroics to absurdity. Ursula Le Guin, skeptical of hero myths that force Nature into opposition with humanity, said several years ago that she would like to "lose the hero myths so that I can find what is worth admiration."[2] In our darker moments we all feel it is hard to find much worthy of admiration in contemporary life.

Yet the evolving human being in transition from youth to adulthood still needs models to emulate, believable examples of how life may be not just lived out but lived well, with grace and gusto. In traditional societies puberty rites and education have sought, as Joseph Campbell says in *Myths to Live By*, to switch "the response systems of adolescents from dependency to responsibility."[3] The transformation of a youth from dependent child to responsible adult, never easy in any context, becomes virtually impossible in a cultural setting where the traditional patterns of human excellence have been lost, where there exists no living mythology to provide archetypal models, no culture heroes to whom the young may look for inspiration, no clear articulation of a life-affirming ethic.

Archetypes, in Carl Jung's meaning, provide "deep and abiding patterns in the human psyche that remain powerful and present over

2. Ursula LeGuin, "Heroes," in *Dancing at the Edge of the World: Thoughts on Words, Women, Places* (New York: Grove Press, 1989), p. 174.

3. Joseph Campbell, *Myths to Live By*, foreword by Johnson E. Fairchild (New York: Viking, 1972; Bantam, 1973), p. 46.

time." As Carol S. Pearson observes in *The Hero Within: Six Archetypes We Live By*, they appear in art, literature, and myth, and we can recognize them in our own lives and in those of others. They may exist in the "collective unconscious" or be "coded into the makeup of the human brain." Archetypes differ from stereotypes in an important way, for whereas "the stereotypes are laundered, domesticated versions of the archetypes from which they derive their power," archetypes nourish the psyche, providing "life and power."[4] Brought to consciousness, they can enrich our self-awareness and psychic energies.

An urgent need exists today for archetypal mythic figures invested with vibrant energy capable of informing the consciousness of the young and leading them forward into the future—as mythologies are meant to do—and away from the jejune dependencies of childhood. The lack of viable mythic models manifests itself in the current dearth of what some call cultural literacy.

Just fifty years ago, playwright Arthur Miller in his essay "Tragedy and the Common Man" made an eloquent plea for a tragic figure based upon the experience of the "common" twentieth-century individual as distinct from the kingly figure of traditional tragedy. Today the need is for a mythic figure who embodies an ethic that can support survival in a world threatened with total destruction. There are telling distinctions between Miller's common man and the proposed survivor figure central to this study, differences reflecting the changes wrought by the past five decades in the ways we perceive ourselves and our world. Miller saw the essence of the tragic figure as the capacity to invoke a certain emotional response, the emotion felt "when we are in the presence of a character who is ready to lay down his life to secure one thing—his sense of personal dignity."[5]

In the context of literature of nuclear disaster, a protagonist suffers under conditions different from those of Miller's tragic hero. Securing personal dignity can no longer take center stage as the foremost concern. Life itself—the life of the planet, the species, the individual, and all plants and animals—is at risk. The fate of the entire biosphere of Earth, one living entity reinvoked under the ancient name of the goddess Gaia, teeters in the balance.

4. Carol S. Pearson, *The Hero Within: Six Archetypes We Live By.* (San Francisco: Harper and Row, 1989), pp. xxi, xv. See also the section "Archetypes" in Harry A. Wilmer, *Practical Jung: Nuts and Bolts of Jungian Psychotherapy* (Wilmette, Ill.: Chiron Publications, 1987), pp. 55–133, for a helpful, basic discussion.

5. Arthur Miller, "Tragedy and the Common Man," *New York Times*, February 27, 1949, Sec. 2, pp. 1, 3; reprinted in *The Theater Essays of Arthur Miller*, ed. with an introduction by Robert Martin, foreword by Arthur Miller (New York: Viking, 1978), p. 4.

The Biophile as Heroic Figure and the "Enemy" Redefined

Under the looming mushroom cloud, we collectively face a new form of disaster. Miller describes the disaster essential to tragedy as the experience of "being torn away from our chosen image of what and who we are in this world," in finding the cosmos antithetical to our personal interests. Herein however lies the significant difference: The cosmos seen by Miller as antithetical to the tragic protagonist and hostile to that figure's dignity is the very entity we now seek to befriend and preserve. In Miller's frame of reference, the "wrong" perceived by the tragic figure is "the condition which suppresses man, perverts the flowing out of his love and creative instinct," the force that stifles human "freedom."[6] Today, the exact nature of this "condition" or force that blocks the flow of human freedom, this "enemy" of life, needs careful redefinition. The survivor figure can no longer be primarily concerned with the luxury of claiming his or her "due" as an individual in a total struggle of will set on affirming personhood. Instead, the ethic of survival in the nuclear world will demand that the heroic individual surrender certain self-aggrandizing ego claims, affirming the value and dignity of all beings—in short, express a life-affirming ethic in his or her mode of being.

To express this more humble ideal, I have coined the word *biophile* to mean a lover of the *bios*, or total life system. The biophile epitomizes what I see as the most essential quality of the admirable mythic figure in our age of impending global catastrophe. Only a person endowed with holistic vision and reverence for the totality of life on Earth can, I believe, go beyond personal limitations and point the way to a future where the Earth might be free of nuclear arms and the biosphere free of lethal pollutants—a condition some believe to be the closest we can come to a contemporary vision of paradise.

An emerging biophile as protagonist can be found in some of the best nuclear literature available for youthful readers. Rarely, however, does the word *hero* seem applicable. For one thing, the word itself has become suspect. For decades serious literature has favored the anti-hero, a character more akin to Willy Loman than to Beowulf. Even when an admirable character of larger-than-life proportions is depicted, the heroic nature of the person's action is rarely articulated. Just as Arthur Miller found it necessary to redefine tragedy for the mid-

6. Miller, "Tragedy and the Common Man," p. 5.

twentieth-century audience, I believe a new heroic voice must be found to address the human predicament meaningfully in a world permeated by fear of global catastrophe. Survival itself is now the first condition, yet mere physical survival cannot suffice. We need to survive with our specifically human qualities of choice, love, and reverence for the dignity of life still intact if life is to continue to be worth living. Indeed, there are those who believe that survival with humanity intact may be intrinsically heroic in the face of what sometimes seem to be overwhelming odds against the continued existence of life. Albert Einstein was once asked what he believed to be the most important question facing humans in the twentieth century. His studied reply was this: "Is the universe a safe place?" The question posed here expands on Einstein's: Is the universe a safe place for human beings to thrive as a peaceable, creative, life-enhancing species? Moreover, may it be that human beings themselves are making their only known habitable space in the universe unsafe not only for themselves but for all life? Further, since life is, as poet John Keats said, a "vale of soul-making," where can we look for the mythic/heroic models to shape and sustain the resilient sort of soul needed by the biophile?

Erik Haugaard, whose historical fiction for youth has never shied away from portrayals of the dark netherworld of the human psyche, and who in *The Little Fishes* starkly images the tragedy of children caught in the jaws of war, affirms that survival coupled with the persistence of the ability to love is heroic:

> I conceive of my fellow men as individuals: lonely figures trying to understand the dilemma they were born into. To live, to survive, is to me an heroic task but not necessarily a tragic one: victory is possible, at least on an individual level. The possibility of love and friendship exists: it is not a matter of chance but of choice.[7]

Haugaard's remarks are addressed to the timeless, universal human condition, not specifically to the nuclear era. Even so, he offers hope that in unimaginably terrible circumstances, there is still a way out available to those who continue to affirm their human capacity for choice and, unlike the Chinese cats, do not shrink from confronting the dilemmas.

Nuclear fear, some might argue, is only a contemporary version of the innate anxiety of the human predicament. Fear has always been a factor in life and hence always an element in literature for young and old alike,

7. *Twentieth Century Children's Writers*, ed. D. L. Kirkpatrick, with a preface by Naomi Lewis, 2d ed. (New York: St. Martin's, 1983), p. 582.

but nuclear fear has its own peculiar nature, more fully explored in the following chapter. Myth and other forms of symbolic meaning, literary or artistic, traditionally have been important means of dealing with fear. The dilemma now is that traditional mythic patterns of Western literature seem impotent to cope with the fear of possible total death of the world. It is appropriate to consider, as background to the quest for a new heroic pattern, the strengths of the traditional mythic model familiar to many of us through the writings of Joseph Campbell.

Revising Traditional Perspectives on Heroism

Campbell traces the progress of the traditional mythic culture hero through three stages: (1) "separation [anxiety-producing]; (2) initiation; and (3) return," a pattern he calls "the nuclear unit of the monomyth."[8] We may compare analyst Carol S. Pearson's description of the hero's journey in *The Hero Within* as a lonely quest, demanding a confrontation with dragons and a discovery of the true self, leading to the reward of a "sense of community" and the gift of new life to one's world.[9] Her formulation corresponds well to the tripartite Campbellian scheme. In Campbell's view, the hero is the individual who has faced the "ogres"—"the nursery demons of his local culture"—and discovered and assimilated the archetypal images of ritual, mythology, and vision that come "pristine" from the unconscious. In *The Hero with a Thousand Faces*, Campbell affirms that these archetypes provide "the primary springs of human life and thought . . . eloquent, not of the present, disintegrating society and psyche, but of the unquenched source through which society is reborn."

Faced with disintegration, the labyrinth of our current nuclear society needs such a hero, an Ariadne who can spin the symbolic thread needed to guide the human spirit forward, away from fixation on unexorcised images of terror, so that, as in a successful heroic adventure, there may be an "unlocking and release again of the flow of life into the body of the world."[10]

Campbell's mythic hero succeeds in transcending fears and ordeals and returns to the community with something new to offer, which may be a needed boon, a synthesizing vision, or, to use anthropologist Gre-

8. Joseph Campbell, *The Hero with a Thousand Faces*. Bollingen Series (1949; Princeton, N.J.: Princeton Univ. Pr., 1972), p. 30.

9. Pearson, *The Hero Within*, p. 1.

10. Campbell, *Hero with a Thousand Faces*, pp. 17, 20, 40.

gory Bateson's words, "a pattern which connects."[11] The mythic hero may, however paradoxically, triumph through becoming the sacrificial victim, then arising from death triumphant, as in the myths of the vegetation gods. These mythic paradigms, to the extent they persist in today's nuclear literature, call for reinterpretation to address the present concerns of young readers.

There are compelling reasons, however, why Campbell's formulation of the monomyth needs some modification before it can serve the needs of contemporary youth. Campbell himself remarks that the traditional Western heroic model, being exclusive and ethnocentric, cannot supply the "inward instruction" that comprises the pedagogical function of myth. As he notes, psychic integration and a resultant clear vision of one's place in life and the cosmos have been withered away by the values of Western industrial society, values prizing the democratic, rationalistic, and commercial above the intuitive and spiritual. Democratic, rationalistic, and commercial values being hostile to the "dream web of myth," we have lost the pattern which connects and become in consequence alienated from self, from other beings, and from the planet itself.[12] The sense of this loss has prompted thinkers from many disciplines—general systems theory, Buddhist metaphysics, cybernetics, humanistic and archetypal psychologies, philosophy, women's studies—to seek a countervision of connectedness, a sense of solidarity with the whole.

We shall never recover "the lost Atlantis of the integrated soul" and a communion with other beings until we can heal our alienation from our own spiritual natures. This can happen, Campbell maintains, not through the power of the will but only by means of a "transmutation of the whole social order" and its myths, which today must encompass the "community" of "the planet, not the bounded nation."[13]

The Indian philosopher Yogananda in 1946, just one year after the atomic devastation of Hiroshima and Nagasaki, similarly spoke of the urgency of a transformation of both the individual and collective psyches through "energies greater than those within stones and minerals, lest the material atomic giant, newly unleashed, turn on the world in mindless destruction."[14]

Campbell asserts in another essay that "ethnocentric historicism,"

11. See "The Pattern Which Connects: Gregory Bateson," in Fritjof Capra, *Uncommon Wisdom: Conversations with Remarkable People* (New York: Bantam, 1988), pp. 71–89.

12. Campbell, *Hero with a Thousand Faces*, p. 388.

13. Ibid., pp. 388, 390.

14. Quoted in *Facing Apocalypse*, ed. Valerie Andrews, Robert Bosnak, and Karen Walter Goodwin (Dallas: Spring Publications, Inc., 1987), p. 3.

exemplified in the idea of a Chosen People, "is poor spiritual fare" for our global age. Divisive, exclusive mythologies are archaic. "Dividing horizons have been shattered. We can no longer hold our loves at home and project our aggressions elsewhere; for on this Spaceship Earth there is no 'elsewhere' anymore." No mythology that holds to "elsewheres" and excludes "outsiders" can meet today's requirements: "Our mythology now, therefore, is to be of infinite space and its light, which is without as well as within." Unhappily, the works of creative artists have been inadequate in mirroring the era since World War II, the era of "the greatest spiritual metamorphosis in the history of the human race."[15] I contend, nonetheless, that writers of science fiction, and more specifically nuclear fiction, are beginning to fill the mythology gap. They are beginning to give us viable mythic patterns that can perform the established function of myth, which is, as Claude Levi-Strauss points out, to provide logical models capable of overcoming the contradictions always inherent in human life, contradictions now compounded in our situation of a complex, interconnected world facing the likelihood of total doom.[16]

Mythology and the Space Age

In place of disintegrating mythologies, Campbell proposes that we might find new "symbolic heroes" for our era in the astronauts, "our splendid moonmen."[17] The moonwalk and space exploration have immeasurably and irreversibly transformed our view of our place in the cosmos. This can be seen in the view Campbell and many others have drawn from contemporary science, a view of human beings as the sentient system of a living Earth, a view given fresh and eloquent expression with spiritual overtones in Thomas Berry's *The Dream of the Earth.* Later in this study the Gaia concept that undergirds this view will be articulated in more detail as a key emergent myth reflected in a number of nuclear fictions. Briefly, this concept of Earth as an organic sentient being, rooted in ancient myth (hence the name, from *Ge*, the Earth goddess), undergirds Campbell's perception of humans as "the functioning ears and eyes and mind of this earth," or "the mind of space." Campbell notes the link between contemporary scientific theories and

15. Campbell, *Myths to Live By*, pp. 49–50, 274, 275.

16. Claude Levi-Strauss, *Structural Anthropology*, Trans. Claire Jacobsen and Brooke Grundfest Schoepf (New York: Basic Books, 1963), p. 229.

17. Campbell, *Myths to Live By*, p. 257.

the ancient mythologies that depict the Earth as "peopling."[18] The Gaia or planetary perspective, which sees Earth as an organic web of interlacing life and energy, is not a new or unnatural view but has re-emerged from centuries of obscurity, reintroduced into consciousness by the image of Earth as seen from space.[19] The Gaia myth will be seen to connect intimately with the goddess mythologies.

Campbell points out our lack of a "properly operating" mythology to fulfill four and possibly five pedagological functions:

1. To awaken and maintain a "sense of awe and gratitude" about the mysteries of the universe; in William Blake's metaphor, to cleanse "the doors of perception" so that we may discover the "wonder" of life
2. To offer a cosmology in accord with the scientific knowledge of the time
3. To "validate, support and imprint the norms of a given moral order"—the one the person presently inhabits
4. To guide the person through the developmental stages of life, from birth to death (which is the final " 'yielding' of the world or self").

In the global space age, a possible fifth function is

5. To awaken individuals to their identity not just as "egos fighting for place on the surface of this beautiful planet" (cf. Miller's tragic hero's struggle) but "equally as centers of Mind at Large," Aldous Huxley's term for the One, the cosmic intelligence.[20]

The pedagogical functions of myth can be made still more specific to the needs of the psyche in a nuclear age. I would distinguish three additional roles myth can play in relation to our nuclear anxieties:

1. To supply "countermyths" to demythologize the bomb, which has assumed mythic proportions (a revitalized story of Gaia is an example of such a countermyth and a possible basis for a new, working cosmology)
2. To help individuals achieve a balance of self-esteem and humility, perhaps a natural consequence of seeing Spaceship Earth as a glo-

18. Ibid., pp. 253, 254, 274.
19. Joseph Campbell, *The Inner Reaches of Outer Space* (New York: Van Der Marck Editions, 1985), p. 124.
20. Campbell, *Myths to Live By*, pp. 6–7, 221, 222, 266, 275.

rious yet small and fragile globe suspended in the immensity of the universe
3. To enrich the variety of images available to individuals for the choice of personal patterns or models by which to order consciousness. One such means of ordering consciousness is through the Eastern use of the personal mandala—a map of a psychic state. (The connections between the mandala and the "ringed atom" are noted in Spencer R. Weart's *Nuclear Fear: A History of Images* and will be explored in detail later.)[21]

The moment is ripe for the restructuring of mythic paradigms, not only because of what Campbell terms the "inner reaches of outer space" but because we live in an era of the destructuring and questioning of all assumptions. William Irwin Thompson, philosopher and sociologist, noted that "when you are living in a period of destructuring, the unconscious projects mythologies of destruction" that, by means of the process of symbolic transformation, prepare the way "for the senescent civilization to be replaced by another, perhaps more vigorous and less decadent."[22] Such mythologies of destruction were apparent in the best visionary and speculative writings of 1945–50. In *By the Bomb's Early Light: American Thought and Culture at the Dawn of the Atomic Age*, Paul Boyer says of the imaginative writings of that time:

> At a time when many opinion-molders were arguing briskly that with intelligence, planning, and goodwill the atomic threat could be controlled and atomic energy made a great blessing to mankind, science-fiction writers and the authors of speculative fiction were offering a countervision almost unrelieved in its bleakness and despair.[23]

The bleak and despairing countervision of so many nuclear narratives can paradoxically, by raising our level of awareness, clear the way for a "restructured" vision. This revisioned myth may prove to be a mythology of peace potent enough to enhance our chances of survival.

21. Spencer R. Weart, *Nuclear Fear: A History of Images* (Cambridge, Mass.: Harvard Univ. Pr., 1988), pp. 404–6.
22. William Irwin Thompson, *Darkness and Scattered Light: Four Talks on the Future* (Garden City, N.Y.: Doubleday, 1978), p. 74.
23. Paul Boyer, *By the Bomb's Early Light: American Thought and Culture at the Dawn of the Atomic Age* (New York: Pantheon, 1985), pp. 264–65.

Mythologies of War and Mythologies of Peace

Heroic literature since the time of Homer and earlier has featured the theme of war. War easily engages the passions of writers, some of them veterans of its horrors who wish to exorcise their own demons of memory. Portrayals of war can of course raise the desire for peace: Think of Homer's Hecuba mourning her children in the *Iliad* or of Penelope at her loom in the *Odyssey* (an archetypal relative, incidentally, to the feminine "peace weaver" figure of Old English poetry, the woman given in marriage to seal a treaty of nonaggression between previously warring tribes). In contrast, peace rarely serves as a main theme in literature. One searches long and hard through critical and historical surveys of young people's literature for index entries under "peace," and it is virtually impossible to find mention of "heroes of peace." A well-established text, Kenneth L. Donelson and Alleen Pace Nilsen's *Literature for Today's Young Adults* lists no index entries for "peace" (nor is there one for "ecology") but does list "war" and "heroes—in war." Chapter 7, "Life Models: Of Heroes and Hopes," cites Mollie Hunter's *Horn Book Magazine* article, "A Need for Heroes." Heroes are classed as "Quiet Heroes," such as Butler Craig of Alice Childress's *A Hero Ain't Nothin' But a Sandwich*; "Heroes in Biographies and Autobiographies," such as Christopher Nolan, whose story is told in *Under the Eye of the Clock*; "Heroes in Death"; "Heroes in Sports"; "Heroes in War"; and "Heroes of the Holocaust" (not, in this case, nuclear holocaust). The atomic bomb dropped on Hiroshima is mentioned in the context of "retribution for Pearl Harbor." Recognition is given to John Hersey's *Hiroshima* as more important today than it was when it first appeared in the *New Yorker* in 1946, "celebrating/lamenting that horror."[24] Rodney Barker's *The Hiroshima Maidens* is noted as the historical account of the "Maiden's Project" in which twenty-five *hibakusha* (atom bomb affected) women were brought to the United States to receive therapy and restorative plastic surgery. Donelson (who wrote this chapter) presents a fine array of titles for teenagers on other aspects of World War II and many additional titles on the Vietnam war. The importance assigned to quiet heroes as distinct from "the grandiose heroes of old" may suggest heroes of peace, but peace is not mentioned. "Romanticized" pictures of war are re-

24. *Literature for Today's Young Adults*, ed. Kenneth L. Donelsen and Alleen Pace Nilsen, 3d ed. (Glenview, Ill.: Scott, Foresman, 1989), p. 242.

jected as "dishonest and offensive" to most contemporary readers. Nevertheless, at one point, in commenting on Henry James's statement, "life is a slow march into enemy territory," Donelson adds, "Maybe being a hero means marching onward without making peace with the enemy, no matter what or who that is," an observation that gives credence to the "life is war" metaphor.[25]

The neglect of explicit and positive portrayals of peace can be seen in other sources, and this lack is a major theme of Winifred Kaminski's 1987 article, "War and Peace in Recent German Children's Literature." Kaminski subscribes to the literary stance of many German writers since World War II who have sought a rationale for political and social morality and have critiqued children's literature as designed either (1) to indoctrinate the young in the ideas of "the dominant class(es)" or (2) to instruct them in resistance to the powers that be. Kaminski tries to establish criteria for evaluating peace literature, beginning with the established aesthetic ones—coherence, subtlety, vividness, an engaging protagonist, psychological depth, narrative force—but points out how these qualities inevitably intertwine with the "political," committed view of a given author.[26]

Four difficulties or shortcomings of portrayals of peace in antiwar books are noted: (1) peace may seem merely negative—the absence of war; (2) peace may be sentimentalized, static rather than purposive (Gudrun Pausewang's *Die letzten Kinder von Schewenborn* is cited as a notable exception, presenting the full horrifying details usually deemed unsuitable for children, thus indicating peaceful coexistence as the only alternative to nuclear catastrophe); (3) peace may be treated with naiveté and oversimplification; and (4) stress on the sufferings of war victims can leave the reader overwhelmed by feelings of powerlessness, thus preempting action. Admitting the difficulties of making peace as "exciting and viable" as war and of portraying realistic means to achieve peace, Kaminski calls on authors nonetheless to be more inventive in dramatizing peace as a literary theme.[27]

Some children's literature texts, curiously enough, give more attention to peace, ecology, and nuclear war themes than do the texts for young adult literature. Berneice E. Cullinan's *Literature and the Child* devotes a section to education for peace and lists bibliography entries

25. Ibid., p. 219.
26. Winifred Kaminski, "War and Peace in Recent German Children's Literature," trans. and adapted by J. D. Stahl in *Children's Literature: Annual of the Modern Language Division on Children's Literature and the Children's Literature Association* (Princeton, N.J.: Princeton Univ. Pr., 1987), p. 55, note.
27. Ibid., pp. 61–62, 65.

on "Living Together in a World of Peace."[28] A brief section, "The Nuclear Threat and Hiroshima," analyzes *Hiroshima no Pika* and *Wolf of Shadows*, emphasizing in both cases the persistence of "compassion and concern" amidst desperate injury and soul-scarring horrors.[29] Several pages are devoted to "survival" in the context of "nuclear scenarios," with Louise Lawrence's *Children of the Dust* and Robert C. O'Brien's *Z for Zachariah* the featured titles. Cullinan gives science fiction credit for developing "flexibility of imagination."

An older text, *Now Upon a Time: A Contemporary View of Children's Literature* by Myra Pollack Sadker and David Miller Sadker, provides helpful though dated chapters "Spaceship Earth: Ecology in Children's Literature" and "War and Peace."

Carolyn T. Kingston in *The Tragic Mode in Children's Literature* gives a section to books on themes of war, pointing out her belief that youngsters must be given an honest portrayal of the cruelties of war yet not be overwhelmed by its large-scale horrors, difficult claims to reconcile where nuclear war is concerned. She includes a detailed analysis of one example of nuclear catastrophe (reflecting the rarity of the theme in children's books of several decades ago)—Karl D. Bruckner's *The Day of the Bomb.*

Though for the most part neglected in mainstream Western education, mythologies of peace exist and could contribute significantly to the restructuring of heroic paradigms. Like all mythologies, the peace mythologies have their roots in religious beliefs. In addition to the familiar war mythologies of Homer's *Iliad*, Joseph Campbell's chapter "Mythologies of War and Peace" in *Myths to Live By* surveys *The Persians* (Aeschylus), the Old Testament, and Zoroastrian beliefs as well as the peace mythologies of the New Testament, the Jain religion of India, Buddhist thought, the writings of Lao-tzu, and Confucianism. Among the peace mythologies, emphasis is given to the Taoist philosophy as described in the *Tao Teh Ching,* or "Book of the Virtue of the Tao," popularly known as the *I Ching.*

Campbell's discussion draws certain basic contrasts between mythologies of peace, which forbid the killing of any sentient creature, and mythologies of war, which affirm the necessity to prey on others as a fact of nature, a "given," essential to survival. Mythologies of peace deny that killing is a precondition of life and, in their purest form, require their adherents to practice vegetarianism. Yet humans are noth-

28. Berneice E. Cullinan, *Literature and the Child,* 2d ed. (New York: Harcourt Brace Jovanovich, 1989), pp. 619–25.
29. Ibid., pp. 621–22.

ing if not inconsistent, and even in countries where many people hold spiritual beliefs forbidding the killing of animals, as in India, the mythology of war may reign. India, for example, has governed its international relations for centuries by the *matsya nyaya*, the "law of the fish," whereby "the big ones eat the little ones and the little ones have to be smart."[30]

Campbell's claim that all primitive mythologies depict the affirmation of warfare and the killing of animals must be weighed against Riane Eisler's opposite assertions in *The Chalice and the Blade: Our History, Our Future*, based on her research into the Minoan culture of Crete, which spanned the period from 2000 to 1500 B.C.E. She convincingly documents the primacy of a mythology of peace over myths that depict the "hero as killer" and "the Other as Enemy."

Whether carnivorous peoples have an edge over vegetarians when it comes to survival is debated by anthropologists. Campbell chooses his evidence in favor of the survival value of carnivorousness from the proto-humans or hominids who lived 18,000 or more years ago in East Africa. L. S. B. Leakey found the line of the vegetarian *Zinjanthropus* to be extinct today, whereas the "killer" species, *Homo habilis* (meaning "able or capable man"), a carnivore and tool and weapon maker, seems to be the ancestor of the present human species. Allowing that Leakey and Campbell may be correct in their theorizing that vegetarians fare poorly in the process of natural selection, is it too much to hope we might evolve beyond our "killer" origins?[31]

The two most influential mythologies of war in the Western tradition have been dramatized in the *Iliad* and the Old Testament. Both assume a two-story world, Earth below, the domain of divine beings above, a hierarchical cosmos. In the Greek cosmos, wars raged both in the pantheon of gods and among mortals. In the Israelite world view, Jehovah was "a single minded . . . deity" whose sympathies were restricted to one side, and this exclusivity was mirrored at Earth level by the viewing of the "enemy" as an "It" rather than a "Thou." Campbell calls the Old Testament "one of the most brutal war mythologies of all time" (referring specifically to Deut. 7:1–6). He notes also, however, that Isaiah, chapter 45, provides an "ideal of an ultimate and universal peace" where the lion and lamb live in harmony—the mythical motif of the Peaceable Kingdom. (Even this peace, however, was to be based on the servitude and subjugation of 'foreigners.') Cyrus the Great of the gentiles is depicted as the forerunner of the "King of

30. Campbell, *Myths to Live By*, pp. 175, 205.
31. Ibid., p. 175.

Kings," foreshadowing, in Campbell's opinion, the peace mythology of the New Testament. Cyrus, who conquered Babylon in 539 B.C., did not seize empire as an excuse to massacre enemies but wished instead to restore peoples to their places and their gods and to govern them through subordinate kings.[32] Given the norms of his time, his policies were liberal.

Campbell stresses how the mythology of peace in the New Testament demands a radical transformation of the Old Testament apocalyptic theme of the coming of a Messiah who would bring about the reign of justice in this world. Jesus disappointed messianic expectations when he made the locus of the apocalypse not in a future time but in a "psychological present." In short, he taught that the Kingdom of Peace can be found in the here and now, within the hearts of those who can see it. The last lines of the Gnostic Gospel According to Thomas proclaim this truth. Unhappily for the history of the world, this spiritual teaching of peace was distorted by his followers into yet another "doctrine of the Holy War, *jihad*, or crusade."[33]

Other mythologies of peace have been similarly debased from the ideal. The Jains of India, whose teacher Mahavira was a contemporary of Buddha, forbade killing any living thing, plant or animal, and, carrying this to a logical extreme, aimed to quench "the will to life" itself, since life subsists by "hurting and murdering things." Those holding to this belief could obviously not proliferate. Buddhist belief relates to Jainism, but aims at the quenching of one's "ego" rather than one's life. Mythologies of peace requiring such absolute purity and "rule of virtue" pose the dilemma raised as well by pacifism: How far can the "absolute pacifist" go to defend "absolutely no one and nothing but his own so-spiritual purity?"[34] Examples would be the pacifist who torches himself in the cause of peace, the nuclear arms protester who bombs an arsenal, or the conscientious objector who refuses to use force even if necessary to save the life of a child.

Other mythologies of peace, such as those of Taoism and Confucianism, find the basis for universal harmony in an all-suffusing natural balance of the principles of active/passive, light/dark, heavenly/earthly, yin/yang (feminine and masculine principles, respectively). The "Way," or the Tao, permeates nature, manifesting itself as the alternation of opposites. To be in accord with the Tao equals peace. *Yoga*, meaning "yoke," consists in the even-mindedness of the one whose

32. Ibid., pp. 179–81, 187–89.
33. Ibid., pp. 193, 195.
34. Ibid., pp. 196–97.

consciousness is at peace, who has achieved "non-attachment" and the attendant self-control. The Taoist sees arms and all implements of conflict as "unblessed," to be used by the wise person only as a last resort.[35]

In contrast to Taoist teaching, there exist two "Machiavellian" Chinese works that endorse war and approve of murder for political gain. These war manuals date from the era of the Warring States (453–221 B.C.) and are known as *The Book of the Lord Shang* and Sun Tzu's *The Art of War.*[36]

Mythologies of war and mythologies of peace, Campbell concludes, have existed as diametrically opposed symbolic systems throughout the history of civilization. A mirroring of the conflict between the two in children's literature, also illustrating the reign of the war mentality, is brought out poignantly in Haugaard's *The Little Fishes* at the point where Anna, heartsick over the impending death of her little brother Mario, invokes "Our Lady's mercy, . . . for She is a woman" and will, Anna thinks, pity her grief; but the monk informs her that "God rules the world and He will not listen to Our Lady; and that is why we have war."[37]

A third mythological system, aspiring to a time when wars would cease, can be seen in Persian Zoroastrian eschatological myth, where the transformation comes through a "cosmic crisis," "when the laws of nature would cease to operate," time and change would halt, and no life as we know it would come into being. This belief in apocalypse was assimilated to Christian and Muslim thought. Campbell adds one final tradition, wherein peace might come about through "a law of nations based on ethical, not jungle, principles," on the realization that it is of "rational mutual interest." This idea grew from the writings of the seventeenth—century Dutch legal philosopher Grotius, whose *The Rights of War and Peace* appeared in 1625. Our American eagle, with an olive branch grasped in its right talon, a bundle of arrows in its left, and its head turned toward the olive branch, reflects symbolically the eighteenth century ideal of peace as "the proper civilized norm."[38]

35. Ibid., pp. 197, 202.

36. Yang Kung-sun (d. 338 B.C.), *Book of the Lord Shang*, trans. J. J. L. Duyvendak, with introduction and notes (San Francisco: Chinese Materials Center, 1974), I.8, 10–12; Sun-Tzu, *The Art of War*, trans. with an introduction by Samuel B. Griffith, foreword by B. H. Liddell Hart (New York: Oxford Univ. Pr., 1963), I.1–9. See Campbell, *Myths to Live By*, p. 198.

37. Erik Haugaard, *The Little Fishes* (Boston: Houghton Mifflin, 1971), pp. 188–89.

38. Campbell, *Myths to Live By*, p. 205.

Pearson has pointed out the adherence to the Warrior archetype with its hero/villain/victim myth as the basic myth informing our "secular belief system." It can be seen wherever the winner/loser, race, or crusade, models are active—in sports, business, religion, the economic system, the educational system, politics, the legal system, and even what might be called our thought system in its concern with winning arguments by marshaling "facts." The logical consequences of the Warrior myth and life viewed as contest are "world hunger, environmental devastation, racial and gender inequality, nuclear war, and, at the very least, the waste of the talents of all those who see themselves as losers."[39]

Moving toward an Archetype of Peace: The Role of the "Hera"

The challenge to writers today is to create or unearth a mythology of peace that can surpass and overshadow the inherent excitement of the mythologies of war. The appeal of the latter may indeed rest upon our submerged desire to punish ourselves, or, as Martha Bartter says in *The Way to Ground Zero: The Atomic Bomb in American Science Fiction*, our need to externalize "our internal war" and open the door (at least in fantasy) to a new start, "if anything is left to start from."[40]

Contemporary challenges to mythologies of war and a counter-movement toward mythologies of peace have been spurred by myriad influences: the desire to avert nuclear conflagration, the women's movement and its related resurgence of interest in goddess mythologies, and a reawakening of sensitivity to the fragility of the Earth and its interwoven life-support systems. There are related movements toward holistic perspectives and "systemic" thinking observable in many fields of human inquiry.

Women's studies provide a rich source for myths of peace that may prove to be ancient myths reborn. Motifs from Eisler's *The Chalice and the Blade* and Merlin Stone's *Ancient Mirrors of Womanhood: A Treasury of Goddess and Heroine Lore from Around the World* and from a sampling of female literary theorists, will be contrasted here to the view of woman in the traditional Western mythic pattern represented by Campbell.

39. Pearson, *The Hero Within*, pp. 77–79, 81.
40. Martha Bartter, *The Way to Ground Zero: The Atomic Bomb in American Science Fiction* (New York: Greenwood Press, 1988), p. 218.

Campbell's heroic paradigm leaves little room for female heroes. In *The Hero with a Thousand Faces* he states, "Woman, in the picture language of mythology, represents the totality of what can be known," that is, the world and life. The heroic male's marriage with the cosmic goddess "represents the hero's total mastery of life; for the woman is life, the hero its knower and master." In this framework, mother and daughter figures represent "the mastered world." In the myths Campbell chooses to emphasize, woman symbolizes "life energy" to be released by the hero.[41]

Thus the traditional hero is a primary character, a charismatic leader who requires followers and can exist without a heroine, whereas the traditional heroine is secondary, a follower who falls into line and cannot exist without the hero, as Lee R. Edwards notes in *Psyche as Hero: Female Heroism and Fictional Form*. The hero "dances in the spotlight. The heroine is eclipsed." Yet it is role, not sex, that distinguishes the two.[42]

Despite Campbell's sensitivity to the necessity of an inclusive mythology, he seems oddly to have exiled half the human race from eligibility for hero-hood. The unhappy result of this male-privileging paradigm can be seen in Sylvia Plath's Esther Greenwood (*The Bell Jar*), who could not accept the status of secondary human being—the place from which the arrow takes off—and yearned against the culture's discouragement of her hopes to be the arrow itself or, in mythological terms, the questing hero, not the supporting heroine. In the traditional mythological model, woman is assigned important roles—Cosmic Mother, the Virgin, Helen of Troy, Beatrice, Gretchen, the helpful (or hateful) old crone, the fairy godmother, the temptress, and, above all, the hero's prize, the bride—but typically she is a protector or subordinate figure, not the aspiring, central consciousness—not the knower but the known.

Merlin Stone, sculptor and art historian, questioned the assumption that the heroic role belongs automatically to man while woman is "relegated to the role of ever-patient helper." Though assured by many that this is the natural state of affairs, she dared to doubt, embarking on years of assiduous scholarship, searching obscure archeological texts and studying countless artifacts to glean material about early female deities. Two major studies are the fruit of her Arachne-like labors: *When God Was a Woman* and *Ancient Mirrors of Womanhood: A Treasury of Goddess and Heroine*

---

41. Campbell, *Hero with a Thousand Faces*, pp. 116, 120, 136, 342.
42. Lee R. Edwards, *Psyche as Hero: Female Heroism and Fictional Form* (Middleton, Conn.: Wesleyan Univ. Pr., 1984), pp. 5–6.

Lore from Around the World. The first study documents the change from the religion of the Near and Middle Eastern Goddess—known by many names (Astarte, Isis, Ishtar)—to the patriarchal religion of Judeo-Christian cultures. Stone's searching critique of the story of Adam and "fallen" Eve, evidently designed by the Levites to suppress goddess religion, casts doubt upon the patriarchal mythological tradition per se. The second book gathers over one hundred portraits of goddess and culture heroines from records as diverse as the *Prose Edda* and the *Shan Hai Ching.* The stories she records reveal women as strong, determined, "wise, courageous, powerful, adventurous, and able to surmount difficult obstacles to achieve set goals." Stone dedicates *Ancient Mirrors* to the twenty-three women who compiled *The Woman's Bible* (Stanton), which as Stone notes contains information that "has been completely ignored in our educations, and in popular literary themes." Knowledge of goddess mythology, with its diversity and range of women's roles and images in many cultures, has been denied to women for centuries. Stone associates this loss of women's heroic heritage, especially the loss of the interconnections between reverence for the Goddess and reverence for "the sanctity of nature," with the threats of nuclear weapons, the pollution of land, sea, and air, the extinction of many species, and indeed the endangerment of all life on Earth. She admonishes, "We might do well to examine the rituals, parables and spiritual beliefs" that regarded certain aspects of nature as sacred and inviolable. Survival of life on the planet may depend on a recovery of wonder and respect for natural life.[43]

Stone's words mesh with those of ecologist Roy Rappaport, who once remarked "Knowledge will never be able to replace respect" in our dealings with "ecological systems."[44]

Others anticipated Merlin Stone in heralding a reawakening of woman's heroic consciousness. Rachel Blau DuPlessis in "Psyche, or Wholeness" critiques the assumptions underlying Erich Neumann's *Amor and Psyche: The Psychic Development of the Feminine, a Commentary on the Tale by Apuleius.* DuPlessis's reinterpretation of the Amor and Psyche myth, retold by Apuleius in *The Golden Ass,* disagrees with Neumann's assertion that "the feminine manner of defeating the dragon is to accept it."[45] Neumann's thinking is obviously in line with Campbell's, relegating the

43. Merlin Stone, *Ancient Mirrors of Womanhood: A Treasury of Goddess and Heroine Lore from Around the World* (Boston: Beacon Press, 1979), pp. 3, 18.

44. Stewart Brand, *II Cybernetic Frontiers* (New York: Random House/Bookworks, 1974), epigraph.

45. Erich Neumann, *Amor and Psyche: The Psychic Development of the Feminine, a Commentary on the Tale by Apuleius,* trans. from the German by Ralph Mannheim (Princeton, N.J.: Princeton Univ. Pr., 1956), p. 121.

feminine to a passive role. Instead Duplessis presents, through a brilliant analysis and rethinking of Psyche's quest, the interpretation of Psyche as *wholeness*. This interpretation lays the groundwork for a concept of *hera* (the feminine of *hero*). The hera does not sacrifice her quest for developed consciousness and knowledge to the need to preserve her "femininity" and the hero's love; rather, she seeks *gnosis*, not *eros* alone. Daringly, she breaks the rules (the first law of seeking knowledge), demonstrating "the generative failure to follow instructions." By challenging the taboos, lighting the lamp to see the face of Eros, she brings "consciousness to her sensual experience." Her four tasks or quests, assigned by Aphrodite, portray the trials she must undergo in the creation of her soul. Whereas the typical plot so often ends with marriage, the story of Psyche as DuPlessis expounds it encompasses quest—"the quest within marriage, the quest as an act of marriage, and self-marriage: wholeness, psyche. Marriage contains quest, quest contains marriage." Passing beyond marriage, the "third plot" is birth—to give life, to be born, that is, to become a whole person.[46]

This concept of the generative mythic hera, who brings latent creative powers to consciousness, actualizing wholeness, and "stealing" life from death, bringing the self to birth and transforming the potential into the actual, is an extremely important one, and I shall return to it repeatedly.

Psyche's heroism in DuPlessis's interpretation stems from her growth in consciousness, her success at four seemingly impossible tasks—sorting a hopeless jumble of seeds, gathering hair from the sheep of the sun, capturing water from a raging mountain stream in a crystal vial, journeying to the underworld—before completing her quest for love. As Marleen S. Barr notes, Psyche's special accomplishment is her synthesis of the quest for knowledge with the quest for love. Barr discusses how speculative fiction by women writers such as Octavia Butler, Pamela Sargent, Ann Maxwell, Cynthia Felice and Connie Willis, Jacqueline Lichtenberg, and Marcia J. Bennett portrays female protagonists who, by synthesizing these two quests, succeed in saving their fictional world. Their synthesis of the quests for love and knowledge brings together the tasks traditionally split between the hero and the heroine: the hero (male) seeking knowledge, the heroine (female) seeking love, a division Barr and many others regard as obsolete.[47] The fully developed human psyche needs, obviously, both to love and to know.

46. Rachel Blau DuPlessis, "Psyche, or Wholeness," *Massachusetts Review* 20 (Spring 1979): 90–91.

47. Marleen S. Barr, *Alien to Femininity: Speculative Fiction and Feminist Theory* (New York: Greenwood Press, 1987), pp. 62–63.

Other literary theorists who have expounded related views include Alice Walker, whose concept of the "womanist" in her *In Search of Our Mother's Gardens* comprises a female heroic pattern; and Lee R. Edwards, whose idea of heroism blends action and knowledge and is meant to be "read and understood" as "a human necessity, capable of being represented equally by either sex. Edwards promotes a woman hero who will transcend both traditional hero and heroine, who, like DuPlessis's Psyche uses "both physical and mental powers to change the sense and substance of reality itself," and whose "new world" is no longer structured on the patriarchal model. This new world validates the hero's (male or female) public role as well as private love relationship. The aggressivity and conquest inherent in war mythologies is transformed into "affiliation" without hierarchy, to "render life not an endless battle but a celebration." The values Psyche has learned in her long oppression under patriarchal rule are used in the "larger world" to create new human communities.[48] Life is not, as in the patriarchal heroic paradigm, an obstacle course to be mastered, but a gift to be used with humility and gladness.

Pearson's *The Hero Within* also embraces a feminine heroic by illuminating and expanding upon Campbell's monomyth. Her six archetypes portray developmental stages that coordinate with the separation/initiation/return pattern but refine and extend it. The archetypes, which are to be understood not as a linear progression but as a spiraling one, are those of the

1. Innocent, who dwells in paradise, a "prefallen state of grace," a pre-heroic stage
2. Orphan, who confronts the "Fall" (Campbell's separation)
3. Wanderer, who undertakes a solitary quest for selfhood
4. Warrior, who struggles to defend the self and change the world
5. Martyr, committed to love and serve, ready to sacrifice self for the sake of others
6. Magician (Shaman), an ancient archetypal mode, whose "magic" consists of knowing how to "move with the energy of the universe" and inner wisdom, to trust the self, to view life as a gift, and to view "tragedy" as failure to develop and use one's gifts to the fullest.[49]

48. Edwards, *Psyche as Hero*, pp. 11, 145, 148–49. Edwards refers to the sense of *communitas* as given by Victor Turner in *The Ritual Process: Structure and Antistructure* (Hammondsworth, England: Penguin/Pelican, 1974), where it means "a vision of community in its spiritual sense" (not administrative or geographical), where its participants know one another directly. See Turner, pp. 114, 119.

49. Pearson, *The Hero Within*, pp. 4–5.

Just as the Orphan mode in Pearson's scheme parallels Campbell's stage of separation, the Wanderer and Warrior archetypes correspond to Campbell's initiation stage, and the Martyr and Magician epitomize much that Campbell includes under the return. Typically, as Pearson explains, the male in his heroic journey may be pushed into the Warrior mode and become stuck there, for it is the Warrior our secular world prizes most. Long reserved primarily for white men, this mode was defined by kings, princes, and their poets, and it belonged exclusively to the elite (i.e., the class of knights and nobles) until the rise of equalitarian ideals. White men then claimed it as theirs, and today women and minority men are claiming it also. As this is happening, many men of the privileged classes are becoming alienated from the Warrior archetype and are, ironically, opting for the Wanderer or Magician modes.[50]

Females on their heroic journey, on the other hand, may be deprived of the Wanderer and Warrior modes and move from Orphan directly to Martyr. Women who assume the Warrior mode are construed as Amazons by traditional society, yet the "truly liberated" woman has an affinity with the Magician and the process of "transformation of human consciousness." It is important to remember, however, that every person's experience is unique, and all the archetypes teach important knowledge. As Pearson says, "We go to school with each archetype many times in our lives."[51]

The positive, loving facets of the Martyr are emphasized in Pearson's analysis to counter the negative connotations of the word, especially in feminist theory. A parallel to DuPlessis's Psyche emerges in Pearson's concept of woman's heroism as consisting of a *state* of "integrity" (wholeness), not in the act of slaying dragons. She further notes that in women's experience, the dragons are often the people who entrap them by insisting they "forgo their own journeys to serve others."[52]

In place of the old heroic Warrior pattern with its "hero-kills-the-villain-and-rescues-the-victim plot," Pearson proposes a plot allowing the heroic nature of all humans to blossom—a hero/hero/hero structure. This can come to be only as both men and women conceive of heroism as "becoming more and more fully themselves at each stage of their development." Her new heroic paradigm defines heroism as "not only *moving* mountains but *knowing* mountains," implicitly priz-

50. Ibid., p. 2.
51. Ibid., pp. 9, 13.
52. Ibid., p. 4.

ing *gnosis*, like DuPlessis, for females as well as males.[53] Pearson's Magician archetype brings knowledge and love into harmony, just as DuPlessis's Psyche balances *eros* and knowledge.

Riane Eisler's *The Chalice and the Blade* poses a creative challenge to the received myths of "hero as killer" and "other as Enemy," myths based on the assumptions of an androcratic society. She affirms "new myths" of "gratitude" and "celebration" of life and love, and a concept of education as "a lifelong process for maximizing flexibility and creativity at all stages of life." The "chalice" refers to the power of actualization and symbolizing, the "blade" to the power of domination. Eisler proposes "chalice power" as the basis for a "partnership" model of society, "in which neither half of humanity is ranked over the other and diversity is not equated with inferiority or superiority." She presents evidence for the existence of such a partnership society in the Crete of the Minoan period, 2000–1500 B.C.E., characterized, as shown by ancient artifacts, by a reign of "a spirit of harmony between men and women as joyful and equal participants in life." The symbolic motif of the Goddess Mother of the universe and life, representing our oneness with nature, presents a theme Eisler deems "prerequisite for ecological survival" today. Minoan art exhibits no statues of rulers, no scenes of battle or hunting, nor any investment of life energies in technologies of destruction. There is evidence of a shift to a warrior society and its attendant mythology of war when the Old European culture of sedentary horticulturalists, who worshipped the Mother creatrix, was forced to protect itself from barbaric invasions by the Kurgans, whose mythology glorified the blade. Unlike the Goddess-centered Old Europeans, the Kurgans valued the taking more than the giving of life.[54] Eisler draws on the archaeological and anthropological research of scholars such as Marija Gimbutas.

Some Creative Responses to Global Crises: The Gylanic Model

Our global crises evoke in Eisler's estimation four possible responses: (1) a return to the old "religious" world view (as seen in the increase in fundamentalist beliefs, both Christian and Muslim), mak-

53. Ibid., p. 10.
54. Riane Eisler, *The Chalice and the Blade: Our History, Our Future* (San Francisco: Harper and Row, 1987), pp. 28, 31, 36, 202–3.

ing the next world the way out and the locus of reward or punishment; (2) indulgence in the escape of nihilism, drugs, mechanical sex, or entertainment; (3) a return to an imaginary better past before women and other oppressed peoples challenged their secondary status in the social order; or (the alternative Eisler favors) (4) a movement to actualize the principles of equality and freedom for all through a postpatriarchal paradigm exemplified in Eisler's partnership model.[55] This shift forward is at the same time a recapturing of the ancient ways of love for life and nature, of sharing and caring rather than oppressing, which never died out but were devalued by the process of "alienation of caring labor" whereby the nurturing tasks so largely done by women go unrecognized in the economic system.[56] The fundamental economic and political transformation heralded by the partnership model would integrate this caring labor into the mainstream—and recognize and reward its value.

Eisler's vision of the partnership society presents a new mythic model. In her reimaging of the world, change can come about only through the transformation of personal relationships, especially those between men and women. She coins the word *gylanic* to describe the new values that underlie the partnership relationship. *Gylanic* comes from *gy*, Greek *gyne* (woman); *an*, Greek *andros* (man); and *l*, from both English "linking" (of both halves of humanity) and Greek *lyein* or *lyo*, meaning "to solve or resolve or to set free." The gylanic model, as an alternative to the ranking, dominator model, frees "both halves of humanity from the stultifying and distorting rigidity of roles imposed by domination hierarchies inherent in andocratic systems." Eisler makes a further useful distinction between domination hierachies and actualization hierarchies, the latter being organic, "systems within systems."[57] Like those of the Baha'i faith, Eisler ascribes to an ideal of world peace based upon "the achievement of full equality between the sexes."[58]

Eisler's new mythical paradigm harmonizes well with the theories of Jean Baker Miller (*Toward a New Psychology of Women*) and Carol Gilligan (*In a Different Voice: Psychological Theory and Women's Development.*) Both believe present differences in the socialization of the sexes, with

55. Ibid., pp. 159, 169.

56. Eisler acknowledges Hilary Rose, "Hand, Brain, and Heart: A Feminist Epistemology for the Natural Sciences," *Signs* 9 (Autumn 1983): 81, as her source for this term.

57. Eisler, *The Chalice and the Blade*, pp. 105–6.

58. Eisler refers to *The Promise of World Peace* (Haifa: Baha'i World Center, 1985), pp. 11–12, and the 1985 Statement of the Baha'i Universal House of Justice, presented to world heads of state. See Eisler, p. 170, note.

women encouraged to overidentify with others' welfare on the one hand, and men fearing affiliation as a threat or danger on the other, are a source of psychic distortion for both sexes. The partnership model holds promise of restoring the balance.

Essential to restoring the balance is the removal of psychic distortions rooted in language. The assumptions underlying the words *hero* and *heroine* have been scrutinized as problematical because of the connotations of active/passive and primary/secondary, respectively, and *hera* is adopted in this discussion as the alternative term for a female hero. Without sensitivity to the linguistic devaluation of the female, writers can easily and unconsciously commit blatant gaffes. A case in point is the approving use of a passage from Jerzy Kosinski's *The Devil Tree* to illustrate the nature of the hero in Donelsen and Nilsen's *Literature for Today's Young Adults*. Kosinski's character remarks:

> Of all mammals, only a human being can say "no." A cow cannot imagine itself apart from the herd. That's why one cow is like any other. To say "yes" is to follow the mass, to do what is commonly expected. To say "no" is to deny the crowd, to be set apart, to reaffirm yourself.[59]

Conceptually, the character reiterates Campbell's heroic paradigm wherein separation is the first step on the heroic journey and in the process of heroic identity formation. Unhappily, the language of Kosinski's character singles out the female of the bovine species (why not *bull* or better yet *cattle*, which would have been gender-inclusive?), thereby tacitly approving on some deep level the secondary status of the female as nonheroic, one of a herd. The passage alerts a perceptive reader to the justice of Judith Fetterley's plea for a "resisting" reader—one who rejects mere passive assent and perpetually questions assumptions of a given text.[60]

Nuclear Fiction and a Life-affirming Ethic

Nuclear fiction, by nature speculative and a source of alternate worlds, is a fine ground for exploration of both new mythical paradigms and new language. Its best writers raise metaphysical ques-

59. *Literature for Today's Young Adults*, p. 220.
60. Judith Fetterley, *The Resisting Reader* (Bloomington: Indiana Univ. Pr., 1978).

tions, often making readers confront unconscious sociopolitical assumptions by projecting them as public myths. Martha A. Bartter points out how a basic technique of science fiction writers, "creative violation of tacit assumptions" (which she identifies with what Darko Suvin calls "cognitive estrangement"), inevitably makes science fiction an intellectual genre where mindplay (a delight in speculation) is directed toward the critical evaluation of the problems of the world. In this respect it is consciously didactic, and it deals not just with change as is often observed, but with "the power of humans to effect radical, historically significant change."[61] Bartter points to Mary Shelley's *Frankenstein, or the Modern Prometheus* as an example of a myth about a human being trying to deal with his or her creation (in this case technology) and "the combined power and responsibility that ensues."[62] In her chapter "The Hero and Society: Sturgeon vs. Heinlein," she uses the stories of Sturgeon to highlight a "transactional" model of human relationships that may offer hope for positive, creative social change through individuals. Sturgeon's characters, she maintains, express a "possibilist" view; he does not claim to know what can be done to save society, "aside from intraspecies [relationships?] and communication and emotional openness."[63] Bartter's study admirably demonstrates the woeful inadequacy of the peculiarly American heroes Superman and The Lone Ranger as mythic models for the nuclear age.

It is evident why a traditional archetypal/mythical approach to much of nuclear fiction is bound to yield less-than-satisfying results. Somehow, the traditional categories for analyzing literature are inadequate: The atom bomb has changed everything, to expand upon Albert Einstein, including our mythic requirements. A writer who approaches the topic of the possible death of the world in the spirit of bitter satire can succeed in convincing the audience of the stupidity of the human race, but where are a myth and a hero/hera who can lead us toward a livable future—as myth is meant to do? Scenarios that attempt to show people carrying on their lives after a nuclear holocaust seem hollow, unconvincing, and lacking in a viable ethic. After such horror, what desire can there be to continue life? Would humanity not simply repeat its errors, invent the bomb again, and destroy itself repeatedly in an endless cycle of death/rebirth—a spectacle to fill the thoughtful

61. Bartter, *The Way to Ground Zero*, p. 42, note 5. Bartter refers to Darko Suvin, *Metamorphoses of Science Fiction* (New Haven: Yale Univ. Pr., 1979), p. 4, where he speaks of "the literature of cognitive estrangement." See also Bartter, p. 47.

62. A recommended recent edition with notes is that published by Orchises, Washington, D.C., 1988.

63. Bartter, *The Way to Ground Zero*, pp. 7, 10, 202.

with despair? This scenario in fact is played out in Walter M. Miller, Jr.'s *A Canticle for Leibowitz*.

Such despair may be permissible in literature for seasoned, cynical adults, but children demand better. In their moral universe, the villain must pay. But who is the villain in the tale of nuclear disaster? Since all are victims, even the most culpable, who shall play judge or executioner? Who shall bring all humanity before the bar of justice on one hand, and who shall escape the collective guilt on the other for what amounts not only to suicide but *ecocide?*

Approaching nuclear literature with these questions in mind, one cannot fail to be struck by the quality of narratives of the actual atomic catastrophes of Hiroshima and Nagasaki, which are more life-honoring, more inspiring to the human spirit, than any nuclear fiction yet invented. Few if any of the fictional treatments written for younger readers seem adequate to their topic. For example, Raymond Briggs's *When the Wind Blows* might be suitable fare for jaded adults but hardly for the child who must have hope to live. Betty Jean Lifton's *A Place Called Hiroshima* and John Hersey's *Hiroshima*, rooted in actual history, grapple more acceptably with the topic. Neither diminishes the persons it depicts by casting them as mere victims on the one hand or by deluding the readers with pseudo-heroics on the other. In the shock of such a catastrophe, the *hibakusha* (bomb-affected) seem to have intuited the organic unity of life, knowing in their innermost being that the Earth can be sustained only through respecting the global weave of life—the integrity of the total biosphere.

A Possible Life-affirming Ethic, Ecology-Biology Based

The Comedy of Survival: In Search of an Environmental Ethic by Joseph W. Meeker illuminates the urgency of restoring the consciousness of life as sacred. Meeker's insights are crucial in trying to arrive at a survival ethic and in critiquing the "widely spread cultural ideology which has contributed to our contemporary ecological crisis."[64] He explains how the same sort of cultural ideology that endangers our ecology underlies our nuclear madness.

Meeker finds the root of our problems in what he calls "the tragic view of man" (cf. Arthur Miller's view of tragedy at the opening of this chapter). He sets forth a number of brilliant arguments to demonstrate

64. Meeker, *The Comedy of Survival*, p. xv.

how literary tragedy, and its close partner, humanism, have "flattered the human ego while jeopardizing the survival of our species." He insists on a distinction between tragedy and disaster, the latter being our present condition. Whereas tragedy depends on an event of "moral consciousness" and a context of good versus evil, disaster stems from physical, biological events "which pose problems of endurance and survival." In the situation of impending disaster, we do well to worry less about trying to transform the world or establish anyone's moral purity, and rather to try to adapt—"to change ourselves to fit the world that surrounds us."[65] This mode of behavior, I would add, corresponds well to how the *hibakusha* actually continued to carry on their lives in the aftermath of atomic catastrophe.

Though at first glance it may seem strange to mention comedy in the same breath as nuclear catastrophe, I believe Meeker's call for a "comic" vision of life may provide one component of a survival ethic to illuminate nuclear literature. Meeker's insights relate well to the biophile, the figure I propose as a possible hero/hera. The "comic perspective," Meeker points out, is intimately related to health and stems from a philosophy of

> immediacy of attention, adaptation to rapidly changing circumstances, joy in small things, the avoidance of pain whenever possible, the love of life and kinship with all its parts . . . It permits people to accept themselves and the world as they are, and it helps us to make the best of the messes around us and within us.[66]

In times of danger and fear of disaster, the recognition of the kinship of all life, and a large, inclusive view of humanity and the world— the perspective of comedy—make creative action possible.

Meeker spends considerable time pointing out how "megalomania" (a word that invokes the mindset of both the hubristic tragic hero and Dr. Strangelove) and visions of "perfection" bring calamities on the world, both in literary tragedy and in everyday experience. In contrast to the self-aggrandizement of the tragic hero, the central comedic figure displays "humility before the earth and its processes . . . [the quality] necessary for the survival of our species." Our current crisis of consciousness is attributable to "a widespread recognition that many important models of reality inherited from the human past [and especially from war mythologies] are inadequate, irrelevant, or destructive when applied to present cir-

65. Ibid., pp. 8, 10.
66. Ibid., p. 11.

cumstances.''[67] In short, a new model of reality is urgently needed: the biophile may, in my belief, supply one. The biophile displays a quality of mind different from that of the traditional hero, as the literature will reveal.

Despite our need for a new heroic pattern, much of mainstream literature as well as some science fiction continues to perpetuate inadequate myths. What Meeker calls literary ecology, or the "study of biological themes and relationships which appear in literary works," may hold the key to our attainment of a mythology we can live with.

An example may be helpful here. A fictional figure who relates to the biological world with respect and humility is Ann Burden in Z for Zachariah by Robert C. O'Brien. She seeks harmony in her relationships to the natural world and to the one other surviving human with whom she comes into contact (a crazed man who tries to exploit and enslave her). It is because of her enduring respect for life that she is able to set out at the end of the book in hope of discovering another "ecological enclave" (a place where the health of the natural world has been naturally preserved from atomic radiation) and people motivated like herself by the desire to make the Earth a better, more fruitful, and happy place, a garden instead of a battlefield.

Some correspondences remain, nonetheless, between the biophile and his or her literary ancestor. Obviously, not every protagonist in nuclear fiction, by any means, fits the biophile mold. Just as the traditional hero was on a quest for self-completion, revelation, or epiphany, the same can be said of certain main characters in nuclear fiction. The central character of Tim O'Brien's The Nuclear Age resembles Campbell's monomythic hero in facing separation (through his near-madness) and trial (the temptation to despair and die), and achieves a return in his choice to overcome the negations of the "hole" and live by a vision of the "whole"—even though he recognizes that his choice is an absurd one, given the likelihood that the world will be blown up. The full-fledged biophile goes beyond a return of this kind, achieving a holistic vision, becoming a shaper of meaning, a cleanser of language and symbol, a healer of the dream, like Snake in Vonda McIntyre's Dreamsnake. The hero/hera of the twenty-first century will be, I believe, the one who goes beyond self-knowledge to seeing the unity and wholeness of life: a visionary, a seer in the old sense of see-er, a restorer of the hope and an illuminator of the truth that all life is interdependent and reality is in relationship.

67. Ibid., pp. 18, 22, 28.

Campbell's heroic paradigm expresses important truths. First, the heroic individual's illumination of life, rendering its experiences "transparent to transcendence," is needed today as never before.[68] The maverick, who challenges the received tradition or system, fills a perennial need for the iconoclast (cf. the "gadfly" of Socrates). The new heroic model differs, however, in significant ways. In metaphors derived by Matthew Fox, the Dominican priest who wrote the *Manifesto for a Global Civilization* and *A Spirituality Named Compassion and the Healing of the Global Village, Humpty Dumpty, and Us*, the new paradigm rests upon the rediscovery of the "Sarah's Circle" approach to life rather than an adherence to the "Jacob's Ladder" syndrome. Sarah's Circle is a metaphor representing life as a spiral-like weave of interconnections, in contrast to the restrictive, elitist, and hierarchical Jacob's Ladder model.[69]

In terms familiar through the storyteller's tradition, the hero/hera makes the *peopledom* possible through the communion of myth and symbol and keeps the community whole and healthy. (The term *kingdom* would seem inappropriate, as would *queendom*.) Traditionally, this preservation of the well-being of the realm is a prime responsibility of the storyteller or mythmaker. The function can also be phrased in metaphysical terms, as the process connecting the individual to a "larger self." An anecdote told by Jungian analyst Jean Houston about her visit as an eight-year-old to the ventriloquist Edgar Bergen, for whom her father wrote scripts, is instructive. The child Jean enjoyed conversing with Charlie McCarthy, Bergen's dummy, who was friendly to her (though not to Bergen's daughter, Candace, with whom there existed some "sibling rivalry"). On this occasion, Mr. Bergen was deep in conversation with Charlie and did not hear the knock on his door. Jean and her father could hear the ventriloquist asking the dummy such philosophical questions as "What is the meaning of life?" "What is the nature of love?" Charlie was answering with insight and wisdom. After several moments, embarrassed to be eavesdropping, Jean's father coughed, alerting Bergen to his guests. Shamefacedly, he greeted them, acknowledging that the two had caught him talking to "Charlie . . . the wisest person I know." When Jean's father protested that it was after all Bergen's voice and mind "coming out of that dummy!" Bergen replied, "Yes, Jack, I suppose it is. . . . And yet,

68. Campbell, *The Inner Reaches of Outer Space*, p. 20.
69. Matthew Fox, *A Spirituality Named Compassion and the Healing of the Global Village, Humpty-Dumpty, and Us* (San Francisco: Harper and Row, 1979), pp. 44–45. At this writing, Father Fox has been silenced by the Vatican for a year because of the controversial nature of his creation theology. See Sam Keen, "Original Blessing, Not Original Sin: A Conversation with Matthew Fox," *Psychology Today*, June 1989, pp. 54–58.

when he answers me, it is so much more than I know." Bergen's "dummy" had become his avenue to his "larger self."

For Jean, the experience was revelatory; she knew in a flash that she must follow a career that could enable her to reach that "so much more" that lies within all, rarely tapped. She began her lifelong quest to help people "inhabit more levels of themselves."[70] The historical moment seems ripe to explore how myth, as understood in archetypal, Jungian psychology and as manifested in the speculative fiction of nuclear disaster, can help us find our way forward into the twenty-first century. The interest in Jung's thought is abounding, as the author of *A Guided Tour of the Collected Works of C. G. Jung* can attest. Robert Hopcke proposes that the "slavish devotion to rationality," itself a pseudomyth, has waned, with a consequent decline in the influence of Freud. The enchantment of Jung's work on myth comes at a time when "the threat of global extinction . . . may at last [have] forced upon human beings an inward turn of the intellect, a penitential soul-searching, in order to understand ourselves and find the courage and hope we need to survive our own aggression."[71]

In what follows, we shall survey the achievements of some of the key mythmakers of the nuclear age in their efforts to access the larger self on its own ground, the transtemporal, transspacial home of the archetypes, the realm of the Great Story.[72]

70. Jean Houston, *The Search for the Beloved: Journeys in Sacred Psychology* (Los Angeles: Jeremy P. Tarcher, Inc., 1987), p. 92.

71. Robert Hopcke, *A Guided Tour of the Collected Works of C. G. Jung,* foreword by Aryeh Maidenbaum (Boston: Shambhala Publications, 1989), p. 2.

72. See Mircea Eliade, the historian of religions, in *Cosmos and History,* trans. Willard R. Trask (New York: Harper, 1959), pp. vii–viii.

CHAPTER 1

The Role of a New Heroic Model

The Fear of Fissioning

In Pat Frank's *Alas Babylon!*, a late 1950s novel about a Florida community struggling to resurrect itself in the aftermath of a nuclear attack, two children, Ben and Peyton, decide to go fishing, more for food than for pleasure, since fish are now the mainstay of their diet. As they are returning home, Randy, who chances to see them from the upstairs window of their house, asks what they have caught. Ben gloats over his catch of fifteen fish, adding that Peyton, his girl companion, has only one. She, annoyed at Ben's arrogantly competitive attitude, replies angrily, "Who cares about fish? *If I grow up*, I'm not going to be a fisherman!" [Italics added.] Randy and Helen, his companion, are appalled, for they have never before heard a little girl say "*If* I grow up." Helen adds that Peyton's doubt of reaching maturity "gives me the creeps."[1]

This example is fictional, but research documents the reality of nuclear fears among the young. A major report by two medical doctors, William Beardslee and John Mack, "The Impact on Children and Adolescents of Nuclear Developments" in *Psychosocial Aspects of Nuclear Developments: A Report of the Task Force on Psychosocial Aspects of Nuclear Developments of the American Psychiatric Association*, includes a review of the major studies of children's nuclear anxieties through the late 1970s. Phyllis LaFarge in *The Strangelove Legacy: Children, Parents and Teachers in the Nuclear Age* offers a survey of studies updated through 1986.[2]

---

1. Pat Frank, *Alas! Babylon* (Philadelphia: Lippincott, 1959), p. 182.
2. See especially the chapters "Knowing and Feeling: Nuclear-Age Education" and "The Question of Impact."

These two sources provide valuable evidence of the effects of nuclear age fears on the ways children visualize their futures.

Sibylle Escalona, a child psychiatrist at Albert Einstein Hospital in the Bronx, conducted one of the first investigations into children's nuclear fears in the early 1960s. Her "Children and the Threat of Nuclear War" used an indirect approach, interviewing 311 youngsters between the ages of ten and seventeen. More than 70 percent *spontaneously* mentioned the possibility of nuclear war. From her findings, she went on to speculate on how the children's fears affected the development of aspects of their personalities. She concluded from the data that "profound uncertainty" about the future "exerts a corrosive and malignant influence upon important development processes in normal and well-functioning children." Beardslee and Mack add their paraphrase of Escalona, "If the future seems in doubt to the child, and if adult models appear to feel inadequate to cope with the dangers of nuclear war, and hence unable to ensure a future . . . where is the pull for maturity?"[3]

In short, what happens to the child's desire to become an adult in a world where adults seem unable to cope with the nuclear threat and maintain the peace? The young person's sense of time becomes contaminated by the sense that the ticking clock is sweeping the world toward inevitable destruction. This sense of time as destructive rather than as a medium of growth and creativity can be seen in much nuclear fiction, where countdown to doomsday defaces the future. If fiction stops at this, the reader's natural incentive to move into the future with confidence and hope is gravely diminished.

Another important study of the early 1960s was carried out by Milton Schwebel of the School of Education at New York University. His "What Do They Think about War?" in *Children and the Threat of Nuclear War* reported the responses of three thousand children, elementary through senior high school age, to questions on the likelihood of nuclear war, their degree of apathy toward it, and how they felt about fallout shelters. On the chances of a war occurring, 45 percent of the junior high youngsters felt it was likely, with older children being slightly less pessimistic. Almost all expressed their concern about the risks to life. Forty-eight percent of these junior high students favored shelters, whereas 78 percent of senior high students opposed them—possibly reflecting the older students' greater appreciation of the futility of shelters to protect people from wholesale thermonuclear explosions. LaFarge points out that Schwebel

---

3. William Beardslee and John Mack, *Psychosocial Aspects of Nuclear Developments: A Report of the Task Force on Psychosocial Aspects of Nuclear Developments of the American Psychiatric Association* (Washington, D.C.: The Association, 1982), p. 69.

was researching children's fears at the time when Governor Nelson Rockefeller was supporting the establishment of bomb shelters. Schwebel and his colleagues felt, on the basis of their research, that plans for bomb shelters presented the wrong "adult" model for children, serving to increase their anxieties rather than to allay them.[4]

Schwebel's findings were also published in "Nuclear Cold War: Student Opinions and Professional Responsibility," in which he proposes that children's insecurities about the future could engender two possible responses: They might (1) "face the facts of war and live with the 'erosive effects' of fear," or (2) "avoid the facts and *deny* the thought and understanding processes." As neither alternative is desirable for mental health, Schwebel suggested their fears could be countered by "an active involvement toward effecting peace."[5]

Beardslee and Mack also sum up the findings of a study done by N. Law for the Association for Childhood Education International in 1971. Law gave particular attention to school curricula and concluded that organized warfare was still being presented as a "natural" and perhaps even "noble" human experience.[6] Equally disturbing is the outcome of a study done by T. Buergenthal and J. Torney in 1976, which revealed that children tend to see peace not as "an active process of conflict resolution and cooperation" but as *"an absence of war"* and for many, war is "inevitable, necessary, and likely.'"[7] The mythology of war is alive and well in today's schools and in society at large.

LaFarge reports on an ongoing study begun in 1975 by Jerald G. Bachman and Lloyd Johnston of the Institute for Social Research at the University of Michigan, entitled *Monitoring the Future*. This study is particularly important for its nationally based sample of the responses of high school seniors to questions about their concern over nuclear war. In 1975, the first year of the study, 7 percent reported worrying often about the risks of nuclear war; by 1982 one-third believed that the human race would be annihilated by nuclear or biological warfare during their lifetimes; and by 1984 the number that worried often about nuclear war had increased to almost 30 percent.[8]

---

4. Phyllis LaFarge, *The Strangelove Legacy:Children, Parents and Teachers in the Nuclear Age* (New York: Harper and Row, 1987) pp. 24–25.

5. Quoted in Beardslee and Mack, *Psychosocial Aspects of Nuclear Developments*, p. 70.

6. N. Law, *Children and War* (Washington, D.C.: Association for Childhood Education International, February 2, 1973), p. 232. Quoted in Beardslee and Mack,*Psychosocial Aspects of Nuclear Developments*, p. 71.

7. Summarized in Beardslee and Mack, *Psychosocial Aspects of Nuclear Developments*, p. 71.

8. Summarized in LaFarge, *The Strangelove Legacy*, pp. 27–28.

The study that seems to have had the most public impact is that of
Beardslee and Mack. Their findings, reported in 1980 and published in
1982, detail the chief concerns of children about threats of nuclear war.
They give representative responses to ten questions put to about
seventy-five tenth-, eleventh-, or twelfth-grade students in the Boston
area. The question most pertinent to this discussion is number nine,
"Have thermonuclear advances influenced your plans for marriage,
having children, or planning for the future?" The nine representative
answers quoted by Beardslee and Mack range from one response of
"Not in the least" to five that indicated a reluctance to have children.
One response typical of these five stated "I don't choose to bring up
children in a world of such horrors and dangers of deformation." Two
others seemed to take a *carpé diem* (seize the day) view, saying threats
of nuclear war intensified their desires to live fully; for example, one
student replied that thermonuclear realities had "made me live a little
more day to day knowing any time I might not be around."[9] Merely
surviving in a nuclear world seems to this youngster to be the only possible "heroic" act.

Beardslee and Mack illuminate the impact of nuclear developments
on "the very structure of personality itself in adolescence," particularly on the development of the "ego ideal" and "impulse manage-
ment." They recognize that it is difficult to factor out the effects of nuclear technology from effects of other changes, such as the presence of
pollution, computers, and the pervasive images of calamity on the
nightly television news. However, they find that the building of a
healthy ego ideal, which depends heavily on a "stable and enduring"
present and "a future upon which the adolescent can, at least to some
degree, rely," has become much more difficult than it once was. The
ego ideal (cf. the heroic archetype) is threatened by an uncertain future
and the perception that the adults of society, from whom the young
ought reasonably to expect leadership, are seen as incompetent and
less than admirable. Further, uncertainty over the future

> is readily perceived to be [the result of] the folly or "stupidity" of the
> adults around the adolescent who, because of perceived incompetence,
> greed, aggressiveness, lust for power, or ineffectualness can leave their
> children no future other than a planet contaminated by radiation and on
> the verge of incineration through the holocaust of nuclear war. In such a
> world, planning seems pointless, and ordinary values and ideals seem
> naive. In such a context, impulsivity, a value system of "get it now," the
> hyperstimulation of drugs, and the proliferation of apocalyptic cults that

9. Beardslee and Mack, *Psychosocial Aspects of Nuclear Developments*, p. 84.

try to revive the idea of an afterlife while extinguishing individuality or discriminating perception, seem to be natural developments.[10]

Many young people who suffer intensely from the experiential sense of impending doom perceive adults to bear the blame for destroying their possibilities of a desirable future. In this kind of emotional environment, who dares to introduce the concept of an "heroic" paradigm?

Perhaps the most sobering point made by Beardslee and Mack is their belief that adults, caught up in their own denial of nuclear fear, "have entered into a kind of compact with ourselves not to know."[11] LaFarge calls this same phenomenon "The Pact of Silence," the title of the third chapter of her book. Even for well-intentioned adults, it seems simpler to pretend the fears do not exist than to respond to them with truth and the kind of objective knowledge that alone could enable young people to prepare to participate in the public debate over nuclear issues and to develop some sense of control over their own destinies. The need for education on the realities of nuclear weapons and nuclear energy is heavily underscored by the implications of Beardslee and Mack's studies. Never has H. G. Wells's observation that "human history becomes more and more a race between education and catastrophe" been more applicable. Peter Kropotkin's advice to today's students is apt: "Think about the kind of world you want to live in. What do you need to build that world? Demand that your teachers teach you that."[12] Speculative fiction offers rich resources for teachers who wish to respond to this challenge.

The Atom Bomb and the Death of the Future

The subjective human experience of time has been drastically altered by the awareness of mass death as an imminent possibility. Awareness of time and transience, perennial themes in literature (and the basis of the *ubi sunt* motif—"Where are the snows of yesteryear?"), helps to define our humanness. The radical difference in the human

10. Ibid., pp. 89–90.

11. Ibid., p. 91.

12. Both Wells and Kropotkin are quoted by Michael N. Nagler in *Education for Peace and Disarmament: Toward a Living World*, ed. Douglas Sloan (New York: Teachers College Press, 1983), p. 102. See also *Harvard Educational Review* 54 (August 1984), a special issue on "Education and the Threat of Nuclear War," for an overview of the topic.

experience of time today rests on what Edwin S. Schneidman, former professor of medical psychology and director of the Laboratory for the Study of Life-Threatening Behavior at UCLA, has called in chapter 15 of his *Deaths of Man*, entitled "Megadeath: Children of the Nuclear Family," the "psychological fallout from yet unexploded bombs," resulting in "a chronic low-grade psychic infection throughout the world."[13] Megadeath, mass death on an unprecedented scale, perhaps even the death of the entire biosphere, is a new element in the psychic landscape. The traditional heroic challenge of time—expressed in the desire to live on through fame—is negated. Ambition is discouraged when people feel even their best efforts may amount to no more than rearranging the deck chairs on the *Titanic*. Schneidman refers in his discussion to Kenneth Keniston, author of *Young Radicals*, for his insight into the way the bomb has "set the tone" for youth of this era, even for those who have tried not to think of it. As Keniston said, is there anyone among us who, on seeing a bright flash or hearing a faraway sonic boom, has not wondered, at least for an instant, is this "It"?

A couple of literary examples are pertinent here. In his introduction to *Writing in a Nuclear Age*, Jim Schley speaks of "that sensation so common to our time: a ripping sound inside, a shadow that falls on some daily experience, as we weed the tomatoes, ride to work, or tie a child's shoelaces."[14] Such flashes of fear figure significantly in Tim O'Brien's popular *The Nuclear Age*, whose protagonist, William Cowling, is hounded by the question "Am I crazy?" to be so concerned that the bombs are *real* and there is no escape from them? He digs a hole in his backyard, a place to hide, even though he knows his act is absurd. He stoically bears his twelve-year-old daughter's accusation that he is "pretty nutto." He hates the solemnity of his feeling of responsibility, for he "would prefer the glory of god and peace everlasting, world without end, a normal household in an age of abiding normalcy. It just isn't possible."[15] The daughter's blasé attitude toward his obsession may mask a denial that is more damaging in its subtle, long-term effects than Cowling's direct confrontation of his anxieties.

Cowling's anxieties drive him to the brink of insanity, to the point

13. Edwin S. Schneidman, *Deaths of Man*, foreword by Arnold Toynbee Quadrangle/New York Times Books, 1973; (Baltimore, Md.: Penguin Books, 1974), pp. 180–83.

14. Jim Schley, *Writing in a Nuclear Age*, ed. Jim Schley (Hanover, N.H.: University Press of New England, 1984), Introduction. *New England Review and Bread Loaf Quarterly* 5, no.4 (Summer 1983).

15. Tim O'Brien, *The Nuclear Age* (New York: Alfred A. Knopf, 1985), pp. 3, 7.

where he is ready to kill his family to save them from nuclear holocaust. Yet he is more in touch with the reality of the tremors from Los Alamos and Hiroshima than are his apathetic fellows. Listening is an important metaphor in the book, betokening full awareness, the antithesis of the "pact of silence" noted by LaFarge. As Cowling says, "Listen, listen hard, because you'll get one hell of an answer. If you hold your breath, if you have the courage, you'll hear the soft drip of a meltdown, the ping-ping-ping of submarine sonar, the half-life of your own heart." "Half-life of the heart" captures beautifully the alienation and vacuousness that grow out of denial. Cowling valiantly refuses to ignore the real, though few in "this nation of microchips," as he says, really care. The apathy, the absence of caring, is to him "the stunner."[16]

Cowling's dilemma will be returned to later. His psychic paralysis from nuclear fear serves as a negative example, a road the reader is cautioned not to take, for that way madness lies. Another alternative must be found. Cowling's particular predicament, however, underscores an important truth, namely, that though fear of mass death or *total death* has been an imaginative possibility for centuries (as seen in the myths of the end of the world in so many cultures), total death as a real possibility is a new phenomenon produced by twentieth century violence.[17]

This era, Schneidman argues, is a "fulcrum time," with life and death poised on a see-saw, "life teetering in the balance," and young people angry and disrespectful of their elders, whom they blame for creating the current mess. Schneidman goes further, attributing the "dangerous rage" in our cities, schools, and prisons to "atomic fear." The feeble attempts to assuage this rage through social measures, such as desegregation, improved public housing, and so on, "are from youth's point-of-view, a sardonic band-aid on a hemorrhaging wound." He theorizes that inner rage is at the root of youth's psychological investment in mere excitement to the detriment of traditional values. Paradoxically, the young may risk death, as in their experimentation with drugs, because they fear mass death (cf. psychiatrist Robert J. Lifton's contention that the quest for high psychic states originates in this same fear, as discussed below).[18]

Admittedly, it oversimplifies the situation to ascribe the inner rage of young people to nuclear fear alone, and it is obvious that young peo-

16. Ibid., pp. 7–8.
17. The term *total death* comes from Gil Elliott, *Twentieth Century Book of the Dead* (New York: Charles Scribner's Sons, 1972), and is quoted by Schneidman, *Deaths of Man*, p. 182.
18. Schneidman, *Deaths of Man*, pp. 187–88.

ple enduring the everyday violence of our inner cities face more tangible threats of annihilation than that of the Bomb. Psychiatrist Robert Coles, in *The Moral Life of Children*, reports his findings from a six-year study that indicate economic status is a major factor in whether children feel nuclear bombs to be a "morally compelling" issue. The children of the affluent are most likely to be anxious about nuclear catastrophe, for the poor tend to be "overwhelmed by different issues," such as hunger and day-to-day survival. Coles points out the precarious, politically explosive situation that results when "educated, well-intentioned" citizens are "fatally separated from millions of working people" with different priorities.[19] The situation is a sure recipe for social violence. Nuclear fear among children is revealed in Coles' discussion as largely a luxury of the young of the middle and upper socioeconomic classes.

In this climate of ephemeralism and inner rage, conventional modes of heroic experience become meaningless and, in the words of Alice Childress's title, *A Hero Ain't Nothin' But a Sandwich*. (The book belies the title, giving an example of quiet heroism in the beleaguered stepfather, Butler Craig, as noted earlier.) With little or no chance to experience through viable cultural myths any sense of the "larger self" accessible through living, meaningful myth and ritual, how could children feel otherwise?[20]

A further difficulty is the disruption of the *timing* of the individual's introduction to concepts of massive death, primarily through exposure to mass media at an early age. Such "age-inappropriate" knowledge may seriously disrupt the maturation process. Experiences that come too early create a heavy psychological burden. It is premature, Schneidman says, for seven-year-olds to become aware of giant city-killing bombs; such early awareness causes them to grow up thinking about death, "an orientation discordant with their time of life."[21] The ancient wisdom of Ecclesiastes speaks of a "time to be born, a time to die." There is similarly a time to learn about mass death, and a time to be sheltered from the dark reality of nuclear madness. Without this time of haven from threat, there is no chance to nurture the sense of life

---

19. Robert Coles, "Children and the Bomb," adapted from his *The Moral Life of Children* (Atlantic Monthly Press, 1986), in *New York Times Magazine Section*, December 8, 1985, pp. 44–50, 54, 61–62. Coles notes George Orwell's "The Road to Wigan Pier" as prophetic of the consequences of this split among classes. See *The Complete Works of George Orwell* vol. 5 (London: Secker and Warburg, 1986).

20. Jean Houston, *The Search for the Beloved: Journeys in Sacred Psychology* (Los Angeles: Jeremy P. Tarcher, 1987), pp. vii–viii.

21. Schneidman, *Deaths of Man*, p. 197.

as a medium of creative possibilities, no chance for the growth of the creative imagination and instilling of the enduring universal human values. Thus, "ripeness is all," and the timing of discussion of nuclear fear needs to correlate with a given child's readiness. A rule of thumb is to listen for the rumblings of nuclear anxiety, and to respond appropriately.

Nuclear Fear and the Denial of the Real

In 1967, two noted psychiatrists contributed to the literature concerning the effects of nuclear weapons on children's thoughts and feelings. Jerome D. Frank in *Sanity and Survival: Psychological Aspects of War and Peace* highlighted the underlying psychological factors in human aggression, noting also how children are socialized for aggression rather than cooperation. (In times when warriors were our heroes, socialization for aggression may have made good sense, but it is outmoded today.) Robert Jay Lifton considered the effects of nuclear weapons on the human psyche in *The Broken Connection: On Death and the Continuity of Life*. Lifton's work examined how the modes of "symbolic mortality" have been damaged by nuclear anxieties; he coined the phrase *new ephemeralism* to describe the sense that, since nothing is lasting, all claims to achievement are questionable.

A summary of Frank's thought in "Psychological Determinants of the Nuclear Arms Race" notes how all people have difficulty grasping the magnitude and immediacy of the threat of nuclear arms and this psychological unreality is a basic obstacle to eliminating that threat.[22] Only events that people have actually experienced can have true emotional impact. Since Americans have escaped the devastation of nuclear weapons on their own soil and "nuclear weapons poised for annihilation in distant countries cannot be seen, heard, smelled, tasted, or touched," we find it easy to imagine ourselves immune to the threat. Albert Camus had the same phenomenon in mind when he wrote in his essay *Neither Victims nor Executioners* of the inability of most people really to *imagine* other people's death (he might have added "or their own"). Commenting on Camus, David P. Barash and

22. Jerome D.Frank, "Psychological Determinants of the Nuclear Arms Race," *Directions in Psychiatry*, Lesson 28 (New York: Hatherleigh Company, 1981). Write *Directions in Psychiatry*, 420 East 51st Street, New York, NY 10022. See also "The Face of the Enemy," *Psychology Today* 2 (1968): 24–29.

Judith Eve Lipton observed that this distancing from death's reality is yet another aspect of our insulation from life's most basic realities. "We make love by telephone, we work not on matter but on machines, and we kill and are killed by proxy. We gain in cleanliness, but lose in understanding."[23] If we are to heed Camus's call to refuse to be either the victims of violence like the Jews of the Holocaust, or the perpetrators of it like the Nazi executioners of the death camps, we must revivify the *imagination* of what violence really entails. It is here, of course, that the literature of nuclear holocaust can play a significant role.

Without either firsthand experience or vivid imagining, it is natural, as Frank points out, to deny the existence of death machines and their consequences. In psychiatric usage, *denial* means to exclude them from awareness, because "letting [the instruments of destruction] enter consciousness would create too strong a level of anxiety or other painful emotions."[24] In most life-threatening situations, an organism's adaptation increases chances of survival, but ironically, adapting ourselves to nuclear fear is counterproductive: We only seal our doom more certainly. The repressed fear, moreover, takes a psychic toll.

The Obsolescence of Violence and Aggression

The human "propensity to violence" is yet another aspect of psychology Frank takes into consideration, but, as he points out,

> to claim that because man is innately violent, war is inevitable would be like saying that because he is innately violent, human sacrifice in religious rites is inevitable. Social institutions wither away when they cease to perform useful social functions. In my opinion, nuclear weapons are destroying the usefulness of war[25]

Like the institution of slavery in the American South more than a century ago, war has become obsolete and demonstrably a suitable target for a new abolitionist movement. Frank notes also how the propensity to violence may not be as dangerous as the deeply ingrained human behavior of obedience—and the willingness to sacrifice the

23. David P. Barash and Judith Eve Lipton, *The Caveman and the Bomb* (New York: McGraw-Hill, 1985), p. 225.
24. Jerome D.Frank, "Psychological Determinants of the Nuclear Arms Race," p. 3.
25. Ibid., p. 4.

individual to preserve the group. He gives the example of soldiers in a bunker or on a nuclear submarine, whose greatest temptation might be to succumb to the desire to banish boredom by firing a nuclear weapon on command.[26] (The fictional examples of the fatal obedience of the bomber pilots in Eugene Burdick and Harry Wheeler, Jr.'s *Fail-Safe* and the psychologically disastrous boredom of X-127, the underground push-button operator in Mordecai Roshwald's *Level 7*, both to be discussed later, spring to mind.)

A further factor recognized by Frank as seemingly innate to human nature is the ethnocentric tendency to "overvalue" our own group and "disparage and distrust members of other groups" (what Joseph Campbell would call loyalty to one's tribal "monad"). Groups in conflict readily develop a negative "image of the enemy." Each side attributes virtues to itself and vices to the enemy. " 'We' are trustworthy, peace-loving, honorable, and humanitarian; 'they' are treacherous, warlike, and cruel." The "enemy" image acts as a self-fulfilling prophecy, for "in combatting what it perceives to be the other's cruelty and treachery, each side becomes more cruel and treacherous itself." The enemy image becomes a "distorting lens" through which information that confirms the image is exaggerated, whereas information that is incompatible with it is minimized or suppressed. In the old adage, we see what we want to see, namely that which is consistent with our foregone conclusion about those whom we have defined as the enemy. Frank points out how the enemy's atrocities are "evidence of his evil nature," whereas "ours are portrayed as regrettable necessities." The distorted perception of the enemy also leads us to fail to see that there may be courses of action that would be beneficial to both the enemy and us; both the United States and the Soviet Union, for instance, could win by mutual reduction of arms.[27]

Thinking about nuclear weapons is further distorted by what Frank terms the "primitivizing effects of emotions." Fear exaggerates our feelings of vulnerability and suspicions of treachery on the part of the enemy. Deterrence rests on the attempt to control the actions of the other by threatening punishment should the other perform a forbidden act. But if the other, the enemy, calculates that the potential benefits of the forbidden act outweigh the probable costs, or if emotional tensions reach an unbearable pitch, caution will be thrown to the

26. Jerome D. Frank, "Sociopsychological Aspects of the Nuclear Arms Race," in *Psychosocial Aspects of Nuclear Developments: A Report of the Task Force on Psychosocial Aspects of Nuclear Developments of the American Psychiatric Association*, Task Force Report 20 (Washington, D.C.: American Psychiatric Association, 1982), pp. 4–5.

27. Frank, "Psychosocial Determinants of the Nuclear Arms Race," pp. 4–5.

winds. Frank notes Bertrand Russell's observation that there is a point at which "the desire to destroy the enemy outweighs the desire to stay alive oneself." In the grip of primitivized emotions, "there is nothing harder . . . than to do nothing."

Frank finds grounds for hope in three new technologies that could serve to heighten worldwide consciousness of the dangers, reduce mutual fears, and create "an international consensus supportive of eventual world governmental structures." The three technologies are international electronic communications, international rapid mass travel, and the exploration of outer space; the latter in particular "is a particularly effective way to enhance the realization that we are all inhabitants of a small and fragile world."[28]

Threats to Symbolic Immortality

Robert J. Lifton wrote the premier study of the Hiroshima *hibakusha*, the "atom bomb–affected," *Death in Life: The Survivors of Hiroshima*, and has written extensively about the impact of the threat of extinction on human attitudes and behavior. His studies have led him to conclude that there are certain patterns that suggest a profile for the young man and woman of the nuclear age, manifest in their attitudes toward the bomb.

In Lifton's essay "The Psychological Impact of the Threat of Extinction," he identifies the beginning of a pattern with "amorphous death anxiety in early childhood." This stage can be illustrated by the results of bomb drills held in schools in the 1950s (the infamous "duck-and-cover" drills) and the resultant anxiety over an amorphous threat of a bomb so powerful it could blow up the world. Youngsters in this stage experience visions of extinction and fantasies of desperate searches for shelter or for other family members.

The next stage, numbing, starts later, perhaps in the early teen years, when there is little "remembered awareness of the bomb," though there may be "fantasies of unlimited sex play in the shelters." Terrifying dreams sometimes signal the fact that the imagery of extinction is only barely submerged in the young person's consciousness.

The third stage in Lifton's paradigm, occurring in late adolescence or early adulthood, is characterized by a broad continuum of response, from obsessive anxiety to the claim that nuclear fears have had no impact. Nonetheless, on further psychological probing of an individual,

28. Ibid., pp. 5–6.

Lifton invariably found "powerful images having to do with nuclear holocaust or other forms of annihilation." Typical examples were the expectations that one's life would end prematurely or that one's children would not have a chance to grow up, a vacillation between numbness toward the topic and periodic anxiety, or a vague sense of living under a nuclear "shadow."[29]

As Lifton describes his own discussions with young adults in *The Broken Connection*, he observes that "the bomb had always been part of their landscape. They had known no world in which it did not exist, and it was just one of their dubious legacies from my generation and its predecessors." On deeper probing, they would recall striking and perhaps terrifying images; they might relate the bomb to cynicism about their life plans, to their politics, or to involvements with drugs or meditation.

The recurring themes identified by Lifton are (1) the equation of one's personal death with "collective annihilation" (i.e., no one will survive); (2) the sense of "the unmanageability of life," that nothing will last, leading to what Lifton terms the new ephemeralism, which images the destruction of books, artworks, libraries, museums—in short, "a vision of hell for the intellectual";[30] (3) the perception of the absurdity of the world where implicitly suicidal weapons are made, stockpiled, and used; and (4) the theme of the "double life": "We all go about our lives as if these dangers did not exist."[31] The psychic cost of sustaining this double life is inestimable and demands the maintenance of a chasm between thinking and feeling. To go about business as usual, it is necessary to deaden one's feelings and compartmentalize one's personality.

Lifton analyzes the anxieties of youth today in terms of the damage done by the "flash" image of Hiroshima (*pika* in Japanese) to the modes of symbolic immortality. These modes traditionally have been (1) the *biological*, seeking fulfillment in the continuation of life through one's offspring; (2) the *creative*, achieving some impact on the world through one's writings, influences, teachings, and so forth; (3) the *theological*, which may be an actual life after death or a belief in a level of spiritual attainment; (4) the *natural*, the sense of becoming once again a part of eternal nature, returning to Mother Earth; and (5) *experiential transcendence*, "the classical mode of the mystics," dramatically rediscovered by our culture in recent years.

29. Robert J. Lifton, "The Psychologic Impact of the Threat of Extinction,"' '*Directions in Psychiatry*, Lesson 27 (New York: Hatherleigh Company, 1981), pp. 2–3.

30. Robert J. Lifton, *The Broken Connection: On Death and the Continuity of Life* (New York: Basic Books, 1979), pp. 338-41.

31. Lifton, "The Psychologic Impact of the Threat of Extinction," pp. 3–4.

All of these modes have suffered injury because of nuclear fear. The biological mode is directly threatened, for no one can be certain that posterity can live on in a nuclear world. Similarly, the achievement of immortality through the creative mode becomes improbable: Who will be around to read the writings, to carry on the influences, or to remember the teachings?

Attitudes of youth toward work display a paradoxical bipolar response to nuclear threat. At the one pole are some who have become ever more frenetic workers, anxious to have it all before the bomb goes off, and at the other are those inclined to reject unsatisfying work as increasingly ephemeral and meaningless.

The theological mode of immortality has been profoundly wounded, making religious symbolism, as weighed against the idea of "total annihilation or extinction," both more sought after and more inadequate.[32] Nuclear peril has created a religious "crisis within a crisis" and negated the comfort religion once offered to assuage death anxieties.

The mode perhaps least susceptible to the threat of extinction, that of experiential transcendence, is being made to bear a greater weight. It is characterized by the quest for high psychic states, states so intense that time and death are forgotten or disappear.[33] Young people today seek such states through a variety of means, among them drugs, meditation, even disciplined exercise (cf. the "jogging high.")

As for the natural mode, imagery of nature has taken on increasing and very special significance. Lifton mentions Nigel Dennis's novel *A House in Order* as an example of the urge among ordinary people to "make things grow" despite nuclear peril, an idea one can link to the resurgence of interest in gardening as a hobby, to Voltaire's advice at the conclusion of *Candide* to "cultivate your own garden," and to the biophile as a timely paradigmatic figure. It is important to remember, however, that no pastoral paradise will be spared in the event of thermonuclear war, and that the biophile cannot simply withdraw and let the rest of the world spin on to doomsday. In today's intricately interconnected world, involvement cannot be avoided.

Lifton's overriding concern is the necessity to maintain awareness of the nuclear threat, however uncomfortable, for only through such awareness can we resist the chance of nuclear annihilation. What Frank called denial and adaptation seems to be subsumed in Lifton's thought under the term *numbing*. These natural psychological defenses

---

32. Ibid., pp. 5–6.
33. Lifton, *The Broken Connection*, pp. 345, 348.

now seem dangerous to survival. A delicate but difficult balance is demanded, a kind of "ideal level of tension . . . that neither excludes threatening perceptions nor immobilizes us with anxiety."[34]

The Imagery of Nuclear Winter

Any consideration of the face of the future today must recognize the current form of the wasteland metaphor—the image of nuclear winter, fittingly described by Lewis Thomas as the "long, sunless, frozen night" that would follow in the wake of nuclear cataclysm. In this dread scenario, there would be

> a settling of nuclear soot and dust, and . . . a new, malignant kind of sunlight with much of its ultraviolet band, potentially capable of blinding many terrestrial animals. The ozone in the atmosphere, which normally shields the Earth from dangerous ultraviolet radiation, would be substantially depleted.[35]

For his details, Thomas draws on the seminal study of climatic effects of multiple nuclear explosions, named the "TTAPS" paper from the initials of its authors' surnames.[36] Nuclear weapons are, he notes, "not really weapons at all but instruments of pure malevolence," the very existence of which threatens irreparable injury to the "whole, lovely creature" Earth. In the introduction to Thomas's book, Donald Kennedy notes that any analysis of the risks from a major nuclear exchange (an unfortunate euphemism that makes it sound like a bartering of goods) must be measured in *years*: "No longer is it acceptable to think of the *sequelae* of nuclear war in terms of minutes, days, or even months. That would be like evaluating a toxic chemical, in this day and age, in terms of what it did to one after five minutes."[37]

Jonathan Schell creates yet another vivid image for the wasteland that would prevail after multiple thermonuclear explosions in the initial chapter of *The Fate of the Earth* with his chapter title, "A Republic of

34. Lifton, "The Psychologic Impact of the Threat of Extinction," p. 6.

35. Lewis Thomas, Foreword to *The Cold and the Dark: The World after Nuclear War*, Conference on the Long-term Worldwide Biological Consequences of Nuclear War, Washington, D.C., 1983 (New York: Norton, 1984), p. xxi.

36. R. P. Turco, O. B. Toon, T. P. Ackerman, J. B. Pollack, and Carl Sagan, "Nuclear Winter: Global Consequences of Multiple Nuclear Explosions," *Science* 222 (December 23, 1983): 1283–92. See also the same authors' "The Climatic Effects of Nuclear War," *Scientific American* 251, no. 2 (August 1984): 33–43.

37. Thomas, *The Cold and the Dark*, pp. xxiv, xxxi.

Insects and Grass." Novelist Walker Percy presents a similarly vivid metaphor for the malaise that stems from nuclear fear in the title of his *Thanatos Syndrome, thanatos* being the perverse love of death, the antithesis to *eros*, life-sustaining passion.

Young people themselves are the most abundant source of imagery of future catastrophe. From grammar school to college age, they show in interviews a tendency to image the world as (1) out of control, (2) having no future, and (3) in the hands of adults who are powerless to bring about positive, life-sustaining change. Their response at the college level is often some form of "Grab it while you can because it may not last!" A frequently encountered image is that of life as "a train, without an engineer, hurling forward into the darkness, over a track that leads inexorably to a cliff. We do not know when we shall plummet over the edge, but we know our plunge into death is inevitable, and there's no way to avert the catastrophe."[38]

These are but a few samplings of the imagery of the future available to youth today. The dangers of psychological fallout from Hiroshima were perceived by our most sensitive writers and artists immediately after the explosions, yet it has taken over forty years for nuclear imagery to become a subject of much concern. In 1948, Joseph Barth wrote in *The Art of Staying Sane* that "for imaginative and for informed minds, the atom bomb has already fallen with a sickening prolonged explosion in their hearts."[39] The poet Milton Kaplan even earlier had intuited the phenomenon of psychic numbing in "Atomic Bomb," where he wrote of people as being "cocooned" and having "insulated" minds, denying the sight of others "gnawed . . . to residual bone," so long as they could distance themselves from the catastrophe, crying "not me!, not me!"[40]

From Credicide to Nuclearism

Where among these comfortless images can young people of sensitivity and imagination find consolation and even minimal hope for a fulfilled future? Some have tried the route of religious cults, too often a dead end. William Wagar, author of *Terminal Visions: The Literature of Last Things*, presents the bleak theory that the present climate offers little or no sustenance for the human spirit. He coins the term *credicide* to de-

38. My paraphrase of group discussions related by Professor Barbara Glaser of Skidmore College in a presentation at the State University of New York at Albany, May 1987.
39. Joseph Barth, *The Art of Staying Sane* (Boston: Beacon Press, 1948; Freeport, N.Y.: Books for Libraries Press, 1970), pp. 184–85.
40. Milton Kaplan, "Atomic Bomb," *Commentary* (March 1948): 262.

scribe the historical phenomenon of "the destruction of the will and power to believe," a process he traces in the thought of "bourgeois intellectuals" since the time of Voltaire. Credicide is in his estimation "a killing much more tremendous than deicide." It results from moral relativism and logical positivism, which holds all statements about the beautiful, good, true, and real to be no more than language games. The climate of unbelief created by these negativistic forces has created the context for "presentiments of extinction" and the expectation that the world is nearing "end-time."[41] Wagar's study surveys the mythic archetypes of end-time in speculative fiction. Nuclear war, for Wagar, is a metaphor for end-time, which may or may not be brought about through the use of nuclear weapons but is nonetheless a psychological reality, a present condition of human thinking.

The mythology of end-times is, of course, nothing new in human history: The Greek gods went through cycles of killing and replacement of deities, Nordic mythology has its Ragnarok, Indian philosophy has its cycles of creation and destruction emanating from the dance of the god Shiva. What is new, however, is the expectation of young people that civilization will last "no more than a century or two"; one class of ninety-four students at The University of California at Los Angeles (UCLA) expressed their belief that it will last no more than twenty-five years.[42] The crisis of traditional religions seems to have created a kind of vacuum that is to some extent being filled by individuals inventing their own personal myths, stories that, like the myths of old, explain "the meaning and goals of their lives." In so doing, as a number of researchers have demonstrated, they "match—quite unwittingly—the characters and themes" of the ancient stories.[43] Another individual, more self-aware, may consciously set out to construct his or her own personal mandala, or symbolic circular design representing a personal relationship to the cosmic order. Joseph Campbell calls the process of making a mandala a "discipline for pulling all those scattered aspects of your life together, for finding a center and ordering yourself to it. You try to coordinate your circle with the universal circle."[44] Young people

41. Warren Wagar, *Terminal Visions: The Literature of Last Things* (Bloomington: Indiana Univ. Pr., 1982), pp. xi–xiii.

42. Ibid., pp. 5, 33. The first recorded appearance of the *Ragnarok* was in the Icelandic *Volospa*, "The Sibyl's Prophecy," of the tenth century (Ibid., p. 44).

43. Daniel Goleman, "Personal Myths Bring Cohesion to the Chaos of Each Life," *New York Times Science Times*, May 24, 1988, pp. C1, C11–12. Carol S. Pearson's *The Hero Within: Six Archetypes We Live By* (San Francisco: Harper and Row, 1989) shows the contemporary fascination with personal myth.

44. Joseph Campbell, *The Power of Myth*, with Bill Moyers, ed. Betty Sue Flowers (New York: Doubleday, 1988), p. 216.

stranded spiritually by credicide and nuclear fear may well turn to such individual methods of salvaging meaning from the chaos of experience. Another feature of the contemporary mythological environment that emanates from the bomb is nuclearism, the worship of nuclear weapons as unacknowledged deities, the "bombaholic" addiction to destructive power, inevitably intermixed with elements of apocalyptic thought. The most extensive study of this kind of thinking and symbolization is Ira Chernus's *Dr. Strangegod: On the Symbolic Meaning of Nuclear Weapons*. Chernus finds the bomb a complex symbol combining the ideas of annihilation, "power without limit" (hence its ability to evoke the emotion of the "sublime"), "omnipotence—and hence of numinous mystery." It has become, perhaps because the power of a nuclear explosion seems to echo the Big Bang of creation as well as the explosion ending the world, "our prime symbol of the alpha and omega of the universe and the whole span of time in between."[45] In 1962 Gunther Anders had noted the fascination of feeling identified with the "omnipotent power of the Bomb," and concluded that modern man no longer looks to a god or nature for the "infinite," but rather to his own power to create and destroy: "*creatio ex nihilo* . . . once the mark of omnipotence, has been supplanted by its opposite, *potestas annihilationis* or *reductio ad nihil*."[46] There is a terrible appeal, Dionysian in nature, in the idea of "the *big whoosh*—the total annihilation of structure and the permanent release from self." Chernus also points out the affinities between nuclear war and theatrical arts—evident in the expression "nuclear theater."[47] This bombaholic mentality is vividly satirized in the film *Dr. Strangelove, or How I Learned to Stop Worrying and Love the Bomb*.[48]

The parallel Chernus draws between nuclear war and the ancient tradition of the sacrificial feast is especially revealing. He refers to Gaston Bouthoul's suggestion that war has "all the characteristics of a feast"—and its principal function, according to Emile Durkheim, is "to unify the group." The hidden sacrificial appeal of nuclear weapons has much in common with the appeal of martyrdom and with a kind of perverse "imitation of Abraham's sacrifice"—for it too in-

45. Ira Chernus, *Dr. Strangegod: On the Symbolic Meaning of Nuclear Weapons* (Columbia: Univ. of South Carolina Pr., 1986), pp. 15, 26.

46. Gunther Anders, "Reflections on the H-Bomb," in *Man Alone*, ed. Eric and Mary Josephson (New York: Dell, 1962), p. 288.

47. Chernus, *Dr. Strangegod*, pp. 23, 76. See also Bonnie Marranca, "Nuclear Theater," *Village Voice* June 29, 1982, p. 103.

48. Chernus, *Dr. Strangegod* Chap. 2.

volves "the most abominable of immoralities—the sacrifice of our children."[49]

Another illustration occurs in the novel *Fail-Safe* when the general whose mission is to drop the bomb over New York City in a bizarre move to placate the Russians for the accidental destruction of Moscow imagines himself to be akin to Abraham (the last chapter is entitled "The Sacrifice of Abraham"), for his own family is in the zone of destruction, and he is willingly "making the biggest sacrifice" any human can make.[50] At the moment of detonation, he kills himself with his suicide kit.

The recognition of the addictive quality of nuclear weapons, an addiction given the name *nuclearism*, is scarcely new. Jerome D. Frank in 1967 remarked that "nuclear armaments have become for nations what alcohol is for the alcoholic."[51] The law of technology, like the law of alcoholism, is "more, more, and ever more." Thus the appropriateness of the term *bombaholic*, which can be found in Amory B. Lovins and L. Hunter Lovins' *Energy/War: Breaking the Nuclear Link.*[52] In a similar thought, sardonic in tone, Kurt Vonnegut has spoken of the need for an organization called "War Preparers Anonymous," modeled after Alcoholics Anonymous, where compulsive War Preparers can admit to their "disease" and, with the help of their peers, begin the long trek of Western civilization back to "sobriety."[53]

Chernus recognizes that the bomb as a religious symbol operates, like other primary religious symbols, to reconcile opposites; it is both a "source of utter extinction" and "a symbol of new life" (presumably the new life to follow Armageddon). As a symbol of new life, it has associations with the "rebirth of the apocalyptic hero," who will overcome the "enemy" and purify the world. However, such thinking perpetrates a cruel hoax, for it seduces us to accept Death as god:

> To flow up into the great mushroom cloud; to be filled with the unbelievable power of the atom; to explode the oppressive structures within us and around us; to take the final plunge, along with all humanity, into a cosmic unity; to return to the source from which all began. These are the deeply buried symbolic images that seduce us into following the

49. Ibid., pp. 109, 116.

50. Eugene Burdick and Harry Wheeler, Jr., *Fail-Safe* (New York: McGraw-Hill, 1962; Dell, 1969), p. 283.

51. Jerome D. Frank, *Sanity and Survival: Psychological Aspects of War and Peace* (New York: Random House, 1967), p. 34.

52. Quoted in Barash and Lipton, *The Caveman and the Bomb*, p. 172.

53. Kurt Vonnegut, "War Preparer's Anonymous" [speech] *Harper's* 268, no. 1606 (March 1984): 41.

Bomb, our modern God, down the path to the martyrdom of mutual suicide.[54]

Chernus criticizes the movie *Star Wars* for its mesmerization of our culture's youth with a "simplistic apocalyptic plot."[55] His view is diametrically opposed to Joseph Campbell's belief that *Star Wars* may provide a myth meaningful for today, universal in its applications, not limited to a "specific historical situation." Its "monster masks . . . represent the real monster force in the modern world," namely, "the unformed individual," a "bureaucrat" with no personal identity.[56] Chernus attributes the enthronement of the Bomb, representing death, to the desire in contemporary technological society to eliminate "disorder and death," repressing them into the unconscious and by so doing making them the Enemy.[57] This misleading apocalyptic myth acts as a barrier to eliminating nuclear weaponry; it gives credence to the thanatos syndrome in a politico-historical context and falsely encourages the idea that a phoenix will arise from the nuclear ashes. In previous times, as horrible as the carnage of war has always been, the heroic myths attached to it offered to some a form of escape from mundane temporality into "the time of beginnings" when the gods participated directly in human affairs.[58] Heroes in a certain kind of war mythology gained access at death to a timeless realm and quasi-godlike status as mythical beings. Nuclear conflict has none of this mythological allure, having become impersonal, automated, and unwinnable—simply suicidal.

A heroic vision in this framework becomes the ability to visualize and *communicate*, through language, symbol, and myth, the new model of global awareness, based on an intuited knowledge of the unity and value of all forms of life. The new hero/hera is not the one who slaughters the external monster, the Grendel that lurks in the terrible mere, or the threatening external dragon, but one who can move us to hold in check our own inner dragon—the destructiveness within—and to turn its energies to creative purposes—form-making rather than form-demolishing. Such a creative transformation of energies is the origin of a life-affirming ethic of survival.

54. Chernus, *Dr. Strangegod*, p. 132.
55. Ibid., pp. 98, 136, 142.
56. Campbell, *The Power of Myth*, pp. 144–45.
57. Chernus, *Dr. Strangegod*, p. 143.
58. Mircea Eliade, *Cosmos and History*, trans. Willard R. Trask (New York: Harper, 1959), pp. vii–viii.

Mythmaker and Storyteller in a Nuclear World

The artist, the poet, the seer, the traditional form-makers are still the "shapers," even in this era of nuclear fear. The challenge to the shaper of speculative fiction is to visualize a new wholeness for the Earth and help restore the weave of life in all its interconnectedness in order that the contemporary sense of fragmentation, alienation, and a seemingly closed future can be transcended. Such a vision can respond to Peyton's plaintive phrase, quoted at the opening of this chapter, "*If* I grow up!" The great potential of speculative fiction lies in its capacity to bring nuclear fears to light and provide a counter-vision of alternate futures. If the shadow of peril is buried or denied, as it is by Cowling's daughter in *The Nuclear Age*, it will break out, as Carl Jung knew, in ways destructive to the psyche. Emily Grosholz writes in "Arms and the Muse: Four Poets":

> Probably the hardest thing for us to admit in our attempts to be moral is that the violence we most fear lies within all of us already, in the midst of everyday life. The poets who depict violence in its ordinary manifestations help us to recognize and live with it, exploiting its energy, guarding against its dangers, mourning its excesses . . . let us think and feel through dour deep fascination with and revulsion against it.[59]

Through the "catharsis of pity and terror," she adds, we can "confront our own destructiveness, and reaffirm our intention to keep it within bounds."[60] Literature to help us confront the shadow within, a time-honored theme of fantasy, is needed today more than ever. Exposing the roots of destructiveness within can be a route to affirmation of life in the face of perils within and without. The poet Terence Des Pres notes that rejecting nuclear threat demands "a vehement Yes to life and value," yet cynicism and despair have made it hard for writers to "make a language to match our extremity."[61] Poet John Elder in "Seeing Through the Fire" calls on imaginative writers "to communicate our common danger and to invent a vocabulary of response."[62]

Spencer Holst's "The Zebra Storyteller" explains in metaphorical

59. Emily Grosholz, "Arms and the Muse: Four Poets," in *Writing in a Nuclear Age*, p. 211.
60. Ibid.
61. Terrence Des Pres, "Self/Landscape/Grid," in *Writing in a Nuclear Age*, p. 11.
62. John Elder, "Seeing Through the Fire," in *Writing in a Nuclear Age*, p. 223.

guise how the story-making function relates to survival. Once upon a time, we are told, a Siamese cat pretending to be a lion succeeded in mastering "Zebraic," the language "whinnied" by zebras—the "striped horses of Africa." By means of this talent the cat startled unsuspecting lone zebras, astounding them so severely that they were "fit to be tied." The smart feline then tied up the zebras, killed them, and (still pretending to be a lion), carried the best parts of the carcasses back to his "den." In this way the cat successfully dined on "filet of Zebra" for months, also making neckties and belts of the better hides, and boasting over the tokens of his prowess. Meanwhile, the zebras, with their delicate sense of smell, knew there was no *real* lion about, but the deaths of so many of their fellows made them avoid the region. In their superstitious fear they began to believe the woods were haunted by the ghost of a lion. One day, the storyteller of the zebras was strolling about, thinking of plots for stories that would delight the others. Suddenly his eyes lighted up, and he said to himself, "That's it! I'll tell a story about a Siamese cat who learns to speak our language! What an idea! That'll make 'em laugh!" Just then the Siamese cat appeared before him and said in Zebraic, "Hello there! Pleasant day today isn't it?" The zebra storyteller was not fit to be tied by this pretender who spoke his own language, because he had been imagining just such a cat. He took a good look at him, and something about his looks displeased him, so he kicked with a hoof and killed him. And, the story concludes, "that is the function of the storyteller."[63]

There it is in a nutshell—the "cognitive alienation" through which speculative fiction captures the imagination (making the familiar strange and the strange familiar);[64] the transcending through imaginative creation (of a story of a fabulous Siamese cat) of life-threatening fear aroused by the old, destructive myth (of the deadly "ghost" of the lion); and the making of renewed, fear-purged life possible—in short, being imaginatively fortified to meet the Shadow.[65]

63. Spencer Holst, "The Zebra Storyteller," in *Fantastic Worlds: Myths, Tales and Stories*, ed. with commentaries by Eric S. Rabkin (New York: Oxford Univ. Pr., 1979), pp. 460–61. Originally published in *The Language of Cats and Other Stories* by Spencer Holst (New York: E. P. Dutton, 1971).

64. The term *cognitive alienation* is basic to the theory of science fiction presented by Suvin Darko, *Metamorphoses of Science Fiction: On the Poetics and History of a Literary Genre* (New Haven, Conn.: Yale Univ. Pr., 1979).

65. "The Zebra Storyteller" is also a marvelous example of what Jungian psychology terms the *principle of synchronicity*, "a meaningful relationship with no possible causal connection between a subjective experience within the human psyche and an objective event which occurs at the same time but at a distant place in the outer world of reality"—a principle often manifested in the lives of creative artists. See Harry A. Wilmer, *Practical*

This survey of nuclear fiction looks at the shadow of nuclear fear as portrayed in literature, from the picture book to the popular adult novel, defining how a variety of writers express "the common danger," identifying the language and symbol by which they address the specter of fear, and gauging their success in creating, out of stories of threat and death, new, life-affirming myths for young people today.

Jung: Nuts and Bolts of Jungian Psychotherapy (Wilmette, Ill.: Chiron Publications, 1987), pp. 169–72.

CHAPTER 2

Narratives of Life Lived in the Nuclear Shadow

The threat of nuclear holocaust, of what Roger Sperry calls in *Science and Moral Priority* ''that impending final fatal flare of fission fireworks,''[1] lends itself to a savagely satirical exposé of human foibles, as in *Cat's Cradle* by Kurt Vonnegut or *Dr. Strangelove, or How I Learned to Stop Worrying and Love the Bomb*, Terry Southern and Stanley Kubrick's widely known film tour de force. On the other hand, narratives of the common nuclear danger may use a realistic mode, treating the characters with compassion rather than scornful ridicule. Both modes have value, but the latter kind of narrative has more practicality because it calls on readers to find a way to live humanly and hopefully despite the ''balance of terror,'' in Herman Kahn's vivid phrase. The books to be considered in this chapter provide examples of both types of narrative. I shall look at them with these questions in mind: What literary means—tone, language, symbol, metaphor—are employed to express nuclear fear? Are there elements in the story to counter the fear? Does the narrative portray a heroic ideal in any sense or present an archetype of the hero/hera and, if so, what is deemed admirable in this person? What life-affirming ethic, if any, does the story convey to the reader?

The Butter Battle Book

The Butter Battle Book by Dr. Seuss exemplifies a world where life is lived in tension between terror of disaster and frustrated desires for

---

1. Roger Sperry, *Science and Moral Priority: Merging Mind, Brain and Human Values* (New York: Columbia Univ. Pr., 1983), p. 44.

peace. Seuss's outlandish fantasy creatures, the Yooks and the Zooks, engage in their version of an arms race—competing for ever more sophisticated weapons. Finally, the two adversaries compete in a "Big-Boy Boomeroo" (note the resemblance to "Little Boy," the atom bomb's nickname) and the last picture portrays the unresolved suspense over the question, who will drop it first?? Without ever mentioning nuclear weapons, Seuss creates a parable about the psychology of the Enemy (cf. Jerome D. Frank's insights in chapter 1). On its deliberately modest scale, Seuss's picture book is in the tradition of Swiftian satire, for the triviality of the cause of hostilities between the Yooks, who believe in eating their bread butter side up, and the Zooks, who insist on eating theirs butter side down, recalls Jonathan Swift's satire on the "Big-Enders" and "Little-Enders" in *Gulliver's Travels*, whose hostilities stemmed from the debate over which end of the egg was the proper one to crack.

In his review article, "Some Leading, Blurred, and Violent Edges of the Contemporary Picture Book," John Cech points to several difficulties with the book from a critical perspective: first, the "shifting narrative point-of-view" is problematical—the Grandfather who finds the Yooks and Zooks's dispute absurd is swept nonetheless into the combat; second, the poetry does not possess Seuss's "usual fresh zing"; and third, the open-endedness leaves anxieties and does not supply the "narrative closure" important for young children. Nonetheless, Cech believes the book's theme and purpose transcend these faults, leaving the reader, whatever age, with "an intergenerational work that courageously brings a serious problem to the attention of the general public."[2]

Through its satirical technique, the book offers a "cautionary tale" approach to the topic and implies the need for overcoming the competitive, bombaholic addiction to weapons and finding a nonlethal means of conflict resolution. The text transcends the mythology of war by implication, for it is obvious that if the Yooks and Zooks remain stuck in the archetypal Warrior mode, holding to the Enemy psychology, they are doomed. It is left to the reader, however, imaginatively to supply a solution to the problem of the "balance of terror."

2. John Cech, "Some Leading, Blurred, and Violent Edges of the Contemporary Picture Book," *Children's Literature: The Annual of the Modern Language Association Division on Children's Literature and the Children's Literature Association* 15 (1987): 200–201. A discussion of the difficulties in the narrative time frame of Seuss's *Butter Battle Book* may be found in Harry Eiss, "Materials for Children about Nuclear War" (Paper presented at the 18th Annual Meeting of the Popular Culture Association, New Orleans, March 23–26, 1988). Available as ERIC document ED 297 339.

Nobody Wants a Nuclear War

In contrast, a simple, unpretentious picture book dealing realistically with fear of nuclear war from a child's perspective is Judith Vigna's *Nobody Wants a Nuclear War*. The children build a crude shelter in a cave to protect themselves from nuclear attack, an idea that suggests seeking a way out of peril through reverting to a simpler (non-technologically advanced) and comforting relationship with the natural world. When the mother discovers what they have done, she identifies with their fear: "I know how scared you must feel. . . . Lots of children worry about nuclear war. Grownups worry, too. But you don't need to hide by yourselves." Reassuring the children that they are loved, she tells them that adults are working to make the world safe. The children take action on the level available to them: using a picnic blanket, they devise a banner emblazoned with the words "Grownups for a Safer World to Grow Up In," and mail it to the president. The cave, representing a retreat to a womblike refuge, is temporarily associated with a safe feeling and furnished with blankets, water, and canned goods, but it is shown to be an unsatisfactory choice because it provides no real safety (a rejection of the survivalist shelter mentality, which belongs to the archetypal mode of the Lone Ranger). The alternatives to denial and nuclear fear prized in this story are commitment to a sense of community and the taking of decisive action to promote peace. The book weaves together the themes of nuclear fear, of the archetypal Orphan who rediscovers the peace/Mother Nature link, and an activist perspective (the archetypal Warrior's energies transformed into the pursuit of peace) on the most fundamental level. The "Nobody" of the title implies the inverted statement: All humans are of one family in their desire to forestall nuclear war. Though not presented as "heroic," the children's simple actions are admirable and imply a life-affirming survival ethic that includes acting responsibly in accord with one's convictions. Archetypally, they relate well to the biophile and hark forward to the Peace Pilgrim (see chapter 4).

If Winter Comes

Lynn Hall's novel for young adults, *If Winter Comes*, gives a teenage perspective on nuclear fear. It captures poignantly the responses of a young man and woman to being targeted by missiles. Anyone who lived through that near-approach to nuclear war known as the Cuban missile crisis will appreciate Hall's capturing of the emotional qualities of the experience. The book is about the psychological tension between the life instinct and the death wish rather than about nuclear conflict itself. In Hall's story, Meredith McCoy learns on a Friday afternoon in May through the television screen in her classroom that the United States faces a nuclear crisis: Vendura, a small country in the Caribbean, has issued an ultimatum demanding the withdrawal of all U.S. troops by 8:00 P.M. Saturday, or missiles already aimed at our country will be fired. The people are assured that United Nations negotiators are working frantically to avert disaster. As they await the outcome of the external crisis, Meredith and her boyfriend Barry become aware of the depth of their private terrors. The insights that come to both during this, their possibly last weekend on earth, are of a kind that only a life-and-death crisis engenders. The clock of countdown to doom ticks loudly in the background as Meredith draws closer to the dearest adults in her life for mutual spiritual self-searching. Her mother and farmer father live separately but still love each other. Barry's family situation is also complicated but much different. He has a cold, demanding attorney father and a mother stupefied by tranquilizers (her psychic bomb shelter, one might say), neither of whom pays any heed to Barry's emotional needs. Finding no parental support, he must look within himself for strength to meet the crisis.

Barry seems ready to succumb to his strong thanatos syndrome, to "engineer his own exit" rather than survive and face the hideous suffering of nuclear winter. His death wish becomes a death wish for the entire earth: "I wish they'd go ahead and fire the damn rockets and get it over with. Wipe the planet clean and let's start from scratch."[3] (Ira Chernus, in *Dr. Strangegod*, calls this the desire to experience the "sublime . . . Big Whoosh!" that appeals as a "sacrifice" that releases "cosmic power" hitherto missing in our lives.[4]) Barry is prepared to resign himself to *geocide*, to letting Earth revert to the wasteland; in this frame of mind he is the antithesis of the biophile and the unconscious exemplar of the "bombaholic" mentality.[5]

3. Walker Percy's novel, *The Thanatos Syndrome* (Farrar, Straus, and Giroux, 1987), is the source of the phrase. For Barry's attitudes, see Lynn Hall, *If Winter Comes* (New York: Charles Scribner's Sons, 1986), pp. 4, 20.

4. Ira Chernus, *Dr. Strangegod: On the Symbolic Meaning of Nuclear Weapons* (Columbia: Univ. of South Carolina Pr., 1986), pp. 107–08.

5. Although Barry's wish seems disdainfully naive and bordering on the psychopathic, it is important to realize that beneath the superficial fears of many people there lies "evidence of a growing desire to experience the Bomb." Dean MacCannell, in "Baltimore in the Morning . . . After: On the Forms of Post-Nuclear Leadership," *Diacritics* 14

Meredith plays the part of Friend of the Earth. She shows her strong life instincts when she rescues a scraggly cat from being "put down" and, glancing at the scarred head, feels that saving even one life is worthwhile, though she has no power to protect the macrocosm, the world of budding trees and flowers. Later, alert to the missiles, she and Barry watch the moon from a car at night, and she feels overcome by a disturbingly impersonal desire to conceive a child, as though this new life could challenge the threat to all life, "the nuclear winter that had the power to end the human race."[6] Meredith counters Barry's death wish with an awareness of the fragility and preciousness of life. Similarly, Mrs. Johnson, an old woman who is building a "park" in a Chicago slum, is a biophile who tells Barry he is "lazy" for considering suicide:

> Life ain't over till it's over, and if you throw away what you got, you're a fool. You could wipe yourself out, sure. Or you could spend your life being so scared of losing it that you'd be just as well off if you did lose it. But those are *choices*, boy. You make 'em, you live with them. But they're *your* choices. That's not some fool in some foreign country blowing your life out of your hands, it's [you] this fool right here.[7]

---

no. 2 (Summer 1984): 33–46, argues that a close examination of social policies betrays a willingness to allow our inner cities, so largely inhabited by "the mass of disadvantaged people," to become targets of nuclear holocaust. The deterioration of our inner cities, MacCannell believes, has become acceptable to the collective unconscious of the policy-makers, whose true attitude is betrayed in language such as that of James Conant, who has referred to the people of the slums (largely black) as "inflammable material" (see Conant, *Slums and Suburbs* [New York: McGraw-Hill, 1961]). MacCannell reaches the dismal conclusion that unconsciously our policymakers have allowed the transformation of our whole society into "a new kind of enormous strategic weapon of which our nuclear arsenal is only a part" (MacCannell, *Baltimore in the Morning*, p. 45) One comes away from his essay with a new understanding of the significance of the term *economic violence*. Martha A. Bartter in "Nuclear Holocaust as Urban Renewal," *Science Fiction Studies* 13 pt. 2 (July 1986): 148–58, expresses a similar theory. She laments the lack of fiction offering a "new vision" of alternatives to the deterministic "cycle of city, holocaust, wilderness, city (as portrayed so vividly in *A Canticle for Leibowitz*)." Readers need, she argues, creative fiction with the power to present a compelling "new vision of peace," something mere rhetoric cannot do. If MacCannell and Bartter are correct, the collective unconscious has succumbed to a death wish for the disadvantaged that seems to be the societal expression of the fictional death wish explicitly expressed by the teen-aged Barry in *If Winter Comes*. In the novel, the death wish is overcome. The question remains, can it be overcome in the real world? In relation to the notion that nuclear holocaust equals slum clearance, I suggest a possible subconscious link between *mushroom* and *muchroom*.

6. Hall, *If Winter Comes*, p. 32.
7. Ibid., p. 88.

Hall uses Mrs. Johnson as a "mentor" figure (what Hemingway called the "tutor"), who belongs to the archetype of the Sage. Meredith's father plays the part of Devil's Advocate, observing that if insects inherit the earth, "Who's to say that some future form of insect might not do a better job of husbanding this planet than *Homo sapiens* has been doing this past sixty-five million years? Maybe it's time to give someone else a turn at the wheel."[8]

The crisis passes—the Venduran missiles are disarmed and peace is restored. The book has been criticized by some as too bland, too muted as well as stereotypical in its portrayal of emotions. The *angst* of encountering death so closely seems missing—or does it? In such a crisis there is often a denial at work, a suspension of overt emotion, that Hall has captured rather well. The creative response of the hera-protagonist, Meredith McCoy, who manages to sustain a life wish against the impending forces of catastrophe, marks her as a biophile, along with Mrs. Johnson, and both illustrate the human prerogative of *choice*. The human race can *not* destroy itself.

The Nuclear Age

Tim O'Brien's tour de force, *The Nuclear Age*, is a popular adult book that teenage readers with an appreciation of irony will find intriguing. The narrator, William Cowling, tries to cope with his terror of nuclear war by digging a hole in which to hide with his wife, Bobbi, and daughter, Melinda. This latter-day Noah, ridiculed like his prototype for being "wacko," has suffered from nuclear fear since childhood, when "nuke fever" made him hide under the ping-pong table. He has vivid erotic dreams about Sarah Strouch, his onetime sweetheart and partner in peace activist efforts. Bobbi, a poet, sublimates both his and her own nuclear fear through writing, as in her poem "Balance of Power," where the metaphors of a "high-wire man" and "the Man in the Moon . . . divorced from Planet Earth" yet bound to her "by laws of church/ and gravity," symbolize the fragility and madness of the human nuclear predicament.[9]

Cowling's adult perspective is interesting to consider here for the way it may mesh or fail to mesh with his perspective as a youngster. O'Brien masterfully paints the growth of Cowling's terror of nuclear destruction from his childhood feelings of isolation and powerlessness to his eccentric adult fantasies of escape. As a boy he resists adults' de-

8. Ibid., p. 65.
9. Tim O'Brien, *The Nuclear Age* (New York: Alfred A. Knopf, 1985), pp. 64–65.

nial mechanisms, their "secret codes and secret meanings," and feels outrage at Dr. Crenshaw, called to examine him and find the basis for his supposedly irrational fears. His intuition that "the world wasn't safe" manifests itself in brilliant technicolor scenarios of nuclear disaster, wherein he sees nature become a "molten stream that roared outward into the very center of the universe," engulfing all. As an adolescent, he "hid" in mediocrity, finding "a comfortable slot for myself at the dead center of the Bell-Shaped Curve." Like all adolescents, he feels sometimes alien, an outsider, but his case is exaggerated and he believes there is a "short-circuit" in the "wiring that connected me to the rest of the world." The potency of his doomsday vision influences his therapist, Charles C. Adamson, in a comic reversal, to become depressed himself and to renounce astronomy, the science he had once exalted: "Frozen oceans! Frozen continents! *Doom*, that's the lesson of astromomy."[10] The stars remind us of the fault within ourselves.

Cowling recognizes how our lives "are shaped in some small measure by the scope of our daydreams. If we can imagine happiness, we might find it. If we can imagine a peaceful, durable world, a civilized world, then we might someday achieve it. If not, we will not."[11]

Adulthood finds him disillusioned, seeking disengagement and retreat. He wonders what has happened to bring on such endemic spiritual ennui,

> the loss of energy, the slow hardening of a generation's arteries. What *happened*? Was it entropy? Genetic decay? Even the villains are gone. . . . No more heroes, no more public remorse, no more public enemies. Villainy itself has disappeared, or so it seems, and the moral climate has turned mild and banal. . . . And who among us would become a martyr, and for what?[12]

The lack of heroes *and* villains signals our spiritual *acidia*, to use the medieval term. There is a parallel between O'Brien's insight into the spiritual climate of our time and the philosopher Allan Bloom's perception of "The Death of Longing" among the young.[13]

For William Cowling, the hole he digs becomes the major symbol of spiritual and emotional emptiness. Language and metaphor, which

10. Ibid., pp. 30–31, 34–35, 52.
11. Ibid., p. 70.
12. Ibid., p. 127.
13. Bloom remarked on the television feature "Firing Line" with William Buckley that this was the title he had wanted to give his book, *The Closing of the American Mind: How Higher Education Has Failed Democracy and Impoverished the Souls of Today's Students* (New York: Simon and Schuster, 1987), but the publisher did not like the title.

should vivify reality and provide myths to nurture the spirit, instead are used as the "opiate of our age." It would be better, he believes, if people expressed their fears rather than burying them: "Nobody's scared. Nobody's digging. They dress up reality in rhymes and paint on the cosmetics and call it by fancy names"—his judgment also of Bobbi's poetry. The apathy is incomprehensible. "Why do we tolerate our own extinction? Why do our politicians put warnings on cigarette packs and not on their own foreheads?" The hole takes on a personality and speaks to its creator, in a surreal apocalyptic fantasy:

> I am Armageddon! I am what there is when there is no more. I am nothing, therefore I am all. . . . I am sackcloth, the empty promise, the undreamt dream, the destroyer of worlds. . . . I am safe.[14]

Later, close to the end of the novel, the hole pontificates on its theme of negation, mocking Cowling's question "Where on earth is the happy ending?" and his self-supplied answer "Love," with an amazing recital of all manner of holes, from "keyhole" to "black hole" to "the ovens at Auschwitz," revealing its identity with the nay-saying Devil bent on persuading William Cowling to dynamite his world, to commit suicide in order to escape suffering.[15] Cowling's state of mind is like Barry's in *If Winter Comes*, but more extreme. He has unwittingly become his opposite—the crusader for peace transformed into the bombaholic, in a fine fictional example of the Jungian phenomenon of "enantiodromia," the psychic process by which all things turn into their opposites— "shadow to hero and hero to shadow, trickster to redeemer, and good to bad."[16] Cowling in the novel's final scene cowers in the hole with his captive daughter, the terrified Melinda, who is fully aware of her father's madness. He is almost overcome by a desire to push the yellow button (which will set off the dynamite that will explode a nuclear device). In the strange clarity of his psychic distortion, he wants to "know what the hole knows," recognizing that "the hole is where faith should be. The hole is what we have when imagination fails." In a flash of psychotic insight, he says "The hole, it seems, is in my heart."

This glimpse into hell, the abyss of negation, almost leads to murder and suicide, but the situation is saved when Cowling sees that Melinda has grasped the firing device away from him, holding their fate in her precarious grasp. Her yell "Stop it!" restores him to his senses. He chooses

14. O'Brien, *The Nuclear Age*, pp. 124, 205, 300.

15. Ibid., pp. 298–99.

16. Henry A. Wilmer, *Practical Jung: Nuts and Bolts of Jungian Psychotherapy* (Wilmette, Ill.: Chiron, 1987), pp. 112–16.

life, for even though "to live is to lose everything, which is crazy . . . I choose it anyway, which is sane. It's the force of passion. It's what we have."[17]

O'Brien takes his antihero to the brink of disaster and then pulls him back with a child's extended arm. Cowling resolves to take his place

> happily, without hesitation . . . in the procession from church to grave, believing what cannot be believed, that all things are renewable, that the human spirit is undefeated and infinite, always. I will live my life in the conviction that when it finally happens—when we hear that midnight whine, when Kansas burns, when what is done is undone, when fail-safe fails, when deterrence no longer deters, when the jig is at last up—yes, even then I will hold to a steadfast orthodoxy, confident to the end that E will somehow not equal mc^2, that it's a cunning metaphor, that the terminal equation will somehow not quite balance.[18]

Cowling's wish that the equation representing atomic energy will fail when actually put to the test may be reminiscent of the belief by a U.S. general that the atomic bomb would fail to explode over Hiroshima (even though it had exploded on a platform in desert tests in Nevada). Cowling also experiences insight into the parallel between the senselessness of the nuclear age and the absurdities and uncertainties of love. He is convinced of two inevitabilities: the world will be lost and his wife will leave him. His enchantress Sarah represents unfulfilled possibilities, and the temptation to follow her into death (she has died of encephalitis but continues to reappear to Cowling in quantum leaps of his imagination) is expressive of his present suicidal state of mind. The noteworthy feature of the novel for present purposes is the triumph of the choice of life over the temptation to self-destruct, and the fact that this choice comes about through the power of relationships—Cowling's love for his wife and child. Though hardly a conscious biophile, he preserves life in spite of himself, triumphing over nuclear fear with the help of a clear-sighted child.

"The Pride of the Peacock" and the Mentoring of Life

Yet another example of nuclear fear and triumph over it occurs in Stephenie Tolan's *The Pride of the Peacock*. The young protagonist,

17. O'Brien, pp. 306, 310.
18. Ibid., p. 312.

Whitney Whitehurst, an emotionally intense fourteen-year-old who is devastated by nuclear fear, finds a "life-mentor" in an older woman, Theodora Bourke, a famous sculptor who is renovating a nearby estate. Whitney has read Jonathan Schell's *The Fate of the Earth* and becomes possessed by despair. Tolan's graceful prose images the fears and the hopes of the characters and develops a Demeter/Persephone motif through Theodora's association with the garden and gardening; as gardener she is identified with Demeter, goddess of fertility and vegetation. As the archetypal Demeter saved Persephone from all-year banishment to Hades, Theodora (no stranger to loss herself, having lost her artist husband to murderers in New York City) rescues Whitney from the underworld of despair.

Images of fear and despair are counterbalanced with images of faith in life and love. Whitney's fear tenses her muscles like "a rubber band . . . twisted . . . 'round and 'round and 'round until it coiled on itself and got shorter and shorter," ready to snap at any moment. She reverts psychologically to the womb, curling herself up into "a tight ball," and in her desperate dreams sees the entire human race becoming extinct, with "wispy ghost babies stretched in a long line, waiting to be born" but forever denied the chance for life. In contrast, Whitney's sister Kate keeps a diary that becomes an image of hope for the future—"four fat volumes, each a different color," and writes poetry. Whitney questions, what is the use of writing if the world is going to blow up? Whitney wishes for a dog, because the animal life might give her comfort:

> a big, shaggy, bumbling idiot of a dog whose name would be Fred, and he would sleep on her bed with her, his warm body against hers. . . . Having a warm body against her, hearing something breathing, might help her stop shivering. It might help her believe that life would go on and on, eons and eons of it.[19]

The touch images, implicitly associated with the life force, are posed against images of death elsewhere in the narrative. At one point Whitney imagines Earth as a dead skeleton, "a bare, dead, poisoned planet whirling around in the darkness and loneliness of space," and again, "a little blue ball floating through the silent, cold darkness of space, with no eyes to see it happening, no mind to feel sorry, no heart to mourn all the birds and animals and plants and stupid humans." Phrased in the language of an adolescent, this is an expression of a ho-

19. Stephanie Tolan, *The Pride of the Peacock* (New York: Charles Scribner's Sons, 1986), pp. 3, 4–5.

listic, "Gaia" vision that sees the Earth as worthy of inhabitation by human beings who, by beholding it, participate in its creation. The death of intelligent, sentient life means the death of the entire biosphere.[20]

Paul, Whitney's young friend, finds the sole hope for humanity's future in escape to other planets, presumably through time travel, an idea he has borrowed from science fiction. His implausible extraterrestrial source of hope contrasts with the insights gained by Whitney through the tutelage of Theodora, whose name, meaning "lover of god," hardly seems incidental.[21]

The peacock of the title, Raj, becomes the major symbolic expression of the persistence of beauty and hope despite the threats of outrageous fortune. Raj displays a tail as beautiful as "a burst of fireworks that kept on, that didn't fade and disappear." In a later passage, Theodora quotes from the poet William Blake, "The pride of the peacock is the glory of God," and affirms her belief that "whoever or whatever designed peacock tails and roses also makes some of us want to create beauty ourselves. . . . I believe that's all 'the glory of God." As Theodora's own emotional wound begins to heal, she reaffirms her identity as a sculptor. To Whitney she says, "I began to suspect that avoiding who you are is a kind of suicide. It's siding with death." Theodora sides with life, as shown in her "finding a wife for Raj" and in practicing her art, for "every day I spend refusing to do my work is a day I side with chaos and violence and death." Through Theodora's influence, Whitney decides to work with groups dedicated to bringing about a nuclear freeze. In response to the older woman's declaration, she asks, "[you mean] every day I don't join those people working against nuclear war is a day I side with war?" and realizes the answer is undebatably yes.[22] Whitney exemplifies, as does Theodora, the biophile's perspective. Though hers is not the traditional heroic quest, such dedication to the cause of peace wins her, in my estimation, a contemporary kind of hera-hood.

"Countdown": Personal Culpability for Nuclear Peril

The previous examples have centered on characters who feel no *personal* responsibility for the dilemma posed by nuclear weapons. In con-

20. Ibid., pp. 22, 45.
21. Ibid., p. 153.
22. Ibid., pp. 100, 183–84.

trast, Kate Wilhelm's short story "Countdown" gives a perspective that involves the recognition of personal culpability. The husband in the story works as an administrator at Cape Canaveral and is involved in launching a nuclear military satellite. His wife has recently given birth to a child and, through the story's symbolic logic, a bizarre parallel is developed between the child and the nuclear weapon loosed from its "umbilical" cable. As H. Bruce Franklin observes, the administrator and his colleagues have released the "beast" from its umbilical cable and the Bomb is in orbit when "a colleague turns to him in horror and blurts out, 'My God . . . what have we done?' " When the father "returns home to his wife, whom he considers 'a good kid,' he begins to comprehend the domestic consequences of his professional act: One day, he knew . . . her eyes would slide past him to fasten on the baby and she would also ask, 'What have we done?' "[23] He cannot escape his guilt over helping to militarize space: "Above them, above the earth in a nearly circular orbit whose aphelion and perihelion didn't vary more than seven miles, rode the nose cone of the rocket, and inside it, just one push of a finger away, nestled the Bomb."[24] Wilhelm refuses to allow the individual to disown a personal share in our collective responsibility for the nuclear peril.

23. Kate Wilhelm, "Countdown," in *The Downstairs Room and Other Speculative Fiction* (New York: Doubleday, 1968), p. 110. In an unpublished paper, "The Bomb in the Home: Stories by Japanese and American Women Experts on Nuclearism" (presented at the Modern Language Association Conference, New Orleans, December 28, 1988), H. Bruce Franklin discusses this story and others, all by women, contained in two paperback anthologies, *The Crazy Iris and Other Stories of the Atomic Aftermath*, edited by Kenzaburo Oe, and *Countdown to Midnight:Twelve Great Stories about Nuclear War*, edited by Franklin, to illustrate how "a number of Japanese and American women have created an antithetical form of discourse: fiction that dramatizes the domestic, human reality invisible to the nuclear arms-makers and strategists who speak of 'delivery systems' for the 'exchange' of thousands of 'clean' hydrogen bombs, each up to a thousand times more powerful than 'Little Boy' and 'Fat Man'," the "cutesy" names given to the bombs that ravaged Hiroshima and Nagasaki. (Used with permission.)

24. Wilhelm, "Countdown," p. 110.

CHAPTER 3

Voices from Hiroshima and Nagasaki

Who Can Be Heroic Today?

When teenagers were asked to identify someone they admire or consider to be a hero or heroine, many of them named a real-life individual, in some cases a family member, in others, a person of worldwide renown, such as Anne Frank or Mahatma Gandhi. Asked to name a fictional hero, they displayed greater reluctance, and some raised objections to the word *hero* itself on the principle that a book character is not "real."[1] This resistance to accepting a fictional heroic pattern relates to the decay of the old mythologies. Rather than seek a heroic model in traditional myth, therefore, we may find that the nonfictional stories stemming from Hiroshima and Nagasaki provide a more acceptable basis for an exemplary contemporary hero/hera figure.

The accounts of those who endured the inferno of nuclear holocaust in Japan in 1945 may be the best source for a nuclear-age survival ethic. A secondary source, valuable for gaining insights into the mythological dimensions of nuclear literature, is *fictionalized* accounts based on the actual events. This chapter considers both factual and fictionalized stories from the perspective of the *hibakusha*, properly translated not as "survivors," but as "bomb-affected" persons.[2] The link between the experiences of actual *hibakusha* and a holistic survival ethic, as epito-

---

1. Results of a poll of teenagers conducted through a graduate class in young adult literature, State University of New York at Albany, Spring 1988.

2. *Hibakusha* is thus defined in Peter Goldman et al., *The End of the World That Was: Six Lives in the Atomic Age* (New York: New American Library, 1986), p. viii. The dedication of the book is "to the *hibakusha* —all of us." Goldman's narratives bear out his contention that all of us are bomb-affected.

mized in the biophile, will be shown, with connections to the holistic emphasis in current environmental and psychological thought.

"Shallow Imaginations": The Root of Nuclearism

A character in Helen Clarkson's *The Last Day: A Novel of the Day After Tomorrow* tells us why we need to listen to the voices from Hiroshima and Nagasaki. As painful as it may be to do so, we need to imagine our own extinction. Clarkson's Dr. Joel, witness to nuclear devastation on American soil, seeing many of the children he had attended at birth die of nuclear radiation, knows his own death is imminent. He questions *why* nuclear catastrophe has been allowed to happen and finds four contributing causes: the loss of belief in immortality, which made life seem meaningless and contemptible (cf. Lifton's loss of "symbolic immortality"); paranoia over the threat of Soviet aggression and the subsequent arms race (cf. Frank's psychology of the Enemy); boredom, an even more fatal thing than fear; and, most important, the lack of imagination—the inability to imagine our own extinction. The world portrayed in Clarkson's novel will soon be dead because people succumbed to an "automatic amnesia for the unbearable"[3] (cf. Lifton's "psychic numbing").

One corrective for this lack of ability to imagine our personal extinction was recommended to Pentagon officials: It was proposed that part of the code necessary to launch American nuclear missiles be implanted inside the body of a volunteer, with the code card so designed that only the heat of this person's burning flesh could activate the chemicals necessary to decipher the code.[4] The president would have to see one human being burn to death before initiating the launch that would incinerate tens of millions. The bureaucrats were aghast. They maintained that such a horrible spectacle could "affect the president's judgment."[5] A less extreme remedy for shallow imaginations, proposed here, is the scrutiny of the works of those artists, illustrators, and writers who can visually and verbally bring us vivid scenes of the annihilation that occurred in Hiroshima and Nagasaki.

3. Helen Clarkson, *The Last Day: A Novel of the Day After Tomorrow* (New York: Dodd, Mead, 1959), pp. 161–63.
4. *Education for Peace and Disarmament: Toward a Living World*, ed. Douglas Sloan. (New York: Teachers College Press, 1983), pp. 240–54.
5. Ibid., p. 247.

Demystifying the Unbearable

The question of making the unbearable the locus of attention raises aesthetic dilemmas; the section later in this chapter on the art of Iri and Toshio Maruki will take up this question in detail. However tempting it is to turn away from actual or imagined images of nuclear devastation because we find them too painful, this kind of escapism is self-defeating: It means a refusal to admit the existence of objective danger. Artists must, if they are to be socially responsible, risk aesthetic failure, for depiction of the infernos caused by nuclear weapons serves a purpose similar to Dante's journey into a literary Inferno with his guide, Virgil: namely, to allow us to behold the landscape of hell vicariously, as pilgrims of the imagination, not permanent residents. The hope of emergence from the intolerable can keep us going. It is erroneous to accept the commonly voiced objection"I don't want to think about nuclear war—it's too depressing!" As Robert Musil says, "If we are successfully to educate about nuclear war, we must do as the verb *educare* says: lead our students out of this mess." But the first step is to "demystify nuclear weapons and policy planning, and pierce the veil of secrecy and obfuscation" surrounding the topic. [6]

Demystification can take place through fiction or nonfiction; both serve their own specific purposes. Although ultimately, there can be no substitute for political activism, such activism needs to be informed. The process of informing the imagination can be carried out in the classroom and library, where students and teachers can ferret out, confront, probe, and weigh the images of massive destruction with an eye to disarming and uprooting them, so the images of the Peaceable Kingdom may thrive in their place. "Where you cultivate a rose, a thistle cannot grow," says Frances Hodgson Burnett in *The Secret Garden*. The abolition of fascination with technologies of destruction (the thistles) can clear the way for the ascendancy of the rose, heralding a new structuring of relationships based on the biophile's inclusive and global ethic of survival.

Children of Hiroshima

Children do not usually, with the exception of certain precocious individuals such as Anne Frank, record their own experiences of war; their sufferings are most often an "untold tale." Adults, however,

6. Ibid., p. 95.

have elicited and preserved children's memories of their sorrows, and the children, grown to adulthood, have authored reminiscences. In his *Children of Hiroshima*, Arata Osada has preserved the words of many of these children, fulfilling the dying wish of their teachers who lost their lives in an effort to rescue their students. The children remembered their teachers' wish that "every child, without exception, become the kind of person who would help to build a peaceful community . . . [and] would hold the establishment of peace on earth to be the highest morality of a human being." Both students and teachers died in the atomic bombings and their aftermaths, but as responsible adults the teachers, who had suffered injuries themselves, attempted to rescue their charges. Those who lived to tell of these efforts spoke of the teachers' belief, even in the face of impending death, that education held the power to "train the spirit" of human beings so they might triumph over the psychological state of mind conducive to war.[7] Like Einstein, these doomed educators called for a "new way of thinking."

Many of the *hibakusha* children remembered the dark silhouettes of human forms emblazoned on buildings at the moment of the flash. One such shadow appeared on the stone wall and steps leading to an entrance of a bank, where a nameless man was caught at the moment of his vaporization, sitting in a pose resembling that of Rodin's *The Thinker*. A university student, reflecting on his own experience of the explosion, said time was powerless to heal injury to "the marrow of our being. In the blood that flows through me there is a black undercurrent that ebbs and flows, sometimes with great pressure, sometimes gougingly," making him feel out of control. This man's words reflect the inner, emotional pillaging mirroring the devastated natural environment. Others expressed their memories of feeling victimized; one little boy became convinced that "terrible things came out of the sky" and began to fear looking up, though his older sister told him the stars were still beautiful. A girl who suffered a *pikadon* (flash-boom) scar on her face and was taunted and teased about it by unmerciful schoolmates, felt such grief that she could only express the wish she had died *with* the bomb.[8] These children fit the Orphan archetype, translated into the extremity of the nuclear landscape, where their feelings of separation from the natural world and from human comfort are intensely magnified.

Other children responded philosophically, asking the metaphysical questions "What is war? What is peace? Why must we make terrible

7. Arata Osada, ed., *Children of Hiroshima* (Tokyo: Publishing Committee for "Children of Hiroshima," 1980; London: Taylor and Francis Ltd., 1981), passim, pp. xv–xxvi. Originally published as *Gembaku no ko* (1951).

8. Ibid., pp. 182, 259, 329–30.

atom bombs to maintain peace? Why is it that humanity and science don't advance the same?" This from a ninth grade boy who was in third grade at the time of the disaster. A tenth grade boy raised moral questions: "There is no escape from the law of retribution. Those haughty in their wealth, who take pride in their power, and glory in their arms must fall before the power of the next generation."[9] Though this may sound like a desire for vengeance, this particular youngster renounced a war mythology and determined to work for world peace.

Many of the children longed so much for peace and life that their words transcend negations. They draw upon the natural world, especially water and vegetation, for images of life's power of renewal. A ninth grade boy (in third grade at the time of destruction) remembers seeing

> a tree already beginning to bud by a dead body with no face. It seemed like a symbol of the city of Hiroshima making progress against indescribable difficulties and miseries. I found in the tree a symbol of the strong will of Hiroshima people for reconstruction—a will which even the 4,000 degree heat of the atom bomb could not melt.[10]

Two other children, expressing the comfort of the healing presence of nature, sound like unconscious biophiles. An eleventh-grade boy tells how now, six years after the event, he cleansed suffering from his heart by imaginatively identifying with the "limpid" waters of the River Ohta. The plants that sprang up in the "scorched remains" were his image for "strength of life. They grew up against all obstacles— bricks, tiles, debris. . . . I want to live like these plants" (cf. *Barefoot Gen*, later in this chapter.) An eleventh- grade girl, looking back six years to a time when her severe suffering tempted her to commit suicide, creates a lovely fountain metaphor to explain how she resisted becoming a warped, twisted person. If we persist along life's "thorny mountain path . . . a beautiful and clear fountain will appear before us. We must walk forward until we are able to scoop this clear fountain water with our own hands. Such is life."[11]

The overriding images radiating from the memories of these children express the making of a peace mythology: a spirit of triumph over suffering, a desire for peace, aversion to the very word *war*, and a consciousness of choices. A twelfth-grade girl says, "In the right hand, we have penicillin and streptomycin; in the left the atom bomb and the hydrogen bomb. Now is the time for the people of the world to consider more rationally this

9. Ibid., pp. 111, 166.
10. Ibid., p. 149.
11. Ibid., pp. 189, 211.

contradiction."[12] These *hibakusha* children display the qualities Phyllis La-Farge finds in the "invulnerable" child, who displays incredible strength, typically in the absence of strong adults on whom to lean.[13]

A Place Called Hiroshima

Another haunting documentary and monument to the courage of the children of Hiroshima is Betty Jean Lifton's *A Place Called Hiroshima*. Lifton's previous book, *Return to Hiroshima*, published in the late sixties, documented what the atomic bomb had done to the city and its people. Fifteen years later, mindful of the pall cast by the nuclear arms race over the planet's future, Lifton and photographer Eikoh Hosoe revisited Hiroshima to create a graphic record of the changes since their first visit. They found a bustling, prosperous new city, and many people—mostly settlers who came from other locations after the war—who are comfortable, well dressed, and unburdened by personal memories of the nuclear holocaust.

The aging A-bomb–affected people can still be found, however, suffering physically and mentally from delayed effects of radiation. The book highlights the Children's Monument in Peace Park, dedicated to the memory of Sadako Sasaki, whose story has been mythologized in fiction (see the section "Sadako: The *Hibakusha* Experience in Picture Books," later in this chapter). Sadako's monument is ambiguous in its iconic significance, for the form of the youngster with arms upraised suggests at once a crucifixion scene and a victorious gesture of praise.[14] In the latter aspect the monument portrays the life-affirming stance of the biophile. In another section of the book, far from being triumphant, the child is presented as victim, or archetypal Martyr, in no uncertain terms through the description of "The Mushroom Club" for families of microcephalic children.

Hersey's "Hiroshima"

John Hersey's *Hiroshima* has possibly been the book most influential in shaping attitudes of many U.S. citizens toward our nation's use of

12. Ibid., p. 265.

13. See Phyllis LaFarge, *The Strangelove Legacy: Children, Parents, and Teachers in the Nuclear Age* (New York: Harper and Row, 1987), pp. 168–69.

14. Betty Jean Lifton, *A Place Called Hiroshima*, photos by Eikoh Hosoe (Tokyo and New York: Kodansha, 1985; distributed by Harper), p. 46.

the atomic bomb against Japan. Those who came of age with the entrance of the Bomb into Western collective consciousness have internalized this book's images.

Children in Hersey's narrative repeatedly question what was happening. Mrs. Nakamura cannot answer Myeko's questions—"Why is it night already? Why did our house fall down? What happened?"—for the situation is incomprehensible even to an adult. The natural curiosity of youngsters was not quelled by their sickness and suffering; they were curious about everything that was happening. When one of the city's gas-storage tanks went up in a burst of flame, the children were as delighted as if it were a massive display of fireworks. Father Kleinsorge, one of Hersey's witnesses, tells of meeting two engaging children who had become separated from their mother when she turned back to try to retrieve extra food and clothing. The five-year-old boy and the thirteen-year-old girl found it hard to "sustain the sense of tragedy," but "occasionally they stopped suddenly in their perfectly cheerful playing and began to cry for their mother."[15]

Regardless of the horrors buried deep within the children's minds, Hersey found "their recollections, months after the disaster, were of an exhilirating adventure." Toshio Nakamura's essay, done in a child's matter-of-fact style for his teacher at Nobori-cho Primary School, serves as an illustration:

> The day before the bomb, I went for a swim. In the morning, I was eating peanuts. I saw a light. I was knocked to little sister's sleeping place. When we were saved, I could only see as far as the tram. My mother and I started to pack our things. The neighbors were walking around burned and bleeding. Hataya-*san* told me to run away with her. I said I wanted to wait for my mother. We went to the park. A whirlwind came. At night a gas tank burned and I saw the reflection in the river. We stayed in the park one night. Next day I went to Taiko Bridge and met my girl friends Kikuki and Murakami. They were looking for their mothers. But Kikuki's mother was wounded and Murakami's mother, alas, was dead.[16]

The child's observations conclude Hersey's original edition. Critic Peter Schwenger in his "Writing the Unthinkable" has noted how, except for the injured neighbors and Murakami's mother being (alas!)

15. John Hersey, *Hiroshima* (New York: Knopf, 1946; Bantam Books, 1959), pp. 26, 63, 68. A new edition was published by Knopf in 1985, with "The Aftermath," a final chapter written forty years later, chronicling the lives of six who survived severe radiation exposure. Originally published in the *New Yorker*, 1946.

16. Ibid., pp. 115–16.

dead, the boy's expression has the rhetorical tone of straight reporting, showing the childish inability to distinguish between the tragic and the inconsequential, yet naively juxtaposed is his implicit conviction that life continues. Comparing Hersey's book to James Kunetka and Whitley Strieber's *Warday, and the Journey Onward*, Schwenger finds *Hiroshima* "more honest about the inadequacies of its form, as can be seen in a comparison of the two endings." Whereas the amelioristic Kunetka and Strieber moralize—"If only we have gained wisdom from the fire. If only we can accept how alike we all are, one and another"— Hersey lets the ingenuous simplicity of the boy's words mirror "the inadequacy of *any* words to evoke a full emotional comprehension of this subject."[17] The archetypal Innocent cannot comprehend the ancient mysteries of evil and unmerited suffering.

The mythic import of the images of the child presented in Hersey's book centers around the contrast between the child victims and invulnerable children (who transcend their suffering to find incredible strength), yet all become finally inarticulate in the face of unfathomable evil. In the responses of those who seem invulnerable, one may see a perspective similar to that described as comedic by Joseph W. Meeker in *The Comedy of Survival: In Search of an Environmental Ethic*. By "comedic" Meeker means a perspective characterized by an "immediacy of attention, adaptation to rapidly changing circumstances, joy in small things, the avoidance of pain," and an ability to affirm life despite whatever disasters it may offer. Instinctively these youngsters transcended the hell of their experience by their psychological participation in the state Meeker calls purgatory (as distinct from hell, where no change is possible), for they displayed an eagerness to "discover what else there is in the world besides themselves."[18] They were not bound within the more limited perspective common to adults, who typically suffer from hardening of the attitudes.

"Barefoot Gen"

Several kinds of illustrated accounts of the *hibakusha* experience are available. There are photographic records and drawings (in *Barefoot*

17. James Kunetka and Whitley Strieber, *Warday, and the Journey Onward* (New York: Holt, Rinehart, and Winston, 1984), p. 374; Peter Schwenger, "Writing the Unthinkable," *Critical Inquiry* 13, no. 1 (Autumn 1986): 36.

18. Joseph W. Meeker, *The Comedy of Survival: In Search of an Environmental Ethic* (Charles Scribner's Sons, 1974; Los Angeles: International College Guild of Tutors Press, 1980), pp. 11, 137.

Gen, cartoon drawings), paintings by survivors, the imaginative renderings made by professional artists, the illustrations of these events done for children, and illustrations of imagined future nuclear holocausts.

The largely autobiographical *Barefoot Gen: A Cartoon Story of Hiroshima* by Keiji Nakazawa is a translation of *Hadashi no Gen*, the initial illustrated eyewitness account of the atomic devastation of the city. It first appeared in serialized form in 1972–73 in *Shukan Shonen Jampu*, Japan's largest weekly comic magazine, with a circulation of over two million. Appreciated by both children and adults and widely acclaimed for its graphic, moving portrayal of the atomic bombing and its aftermath, the material was anthologized in four paperback volumes and later made into a three-part film. Nakazawa subsequently expanded the story to include the U.S. occupation of Japan and the events of the 1950s.[19] Though the book is available, few libraries seem to have acquired it; hence, a detailed summary will be given here.

Barefoot Gen, volume 1 describes the life of the Nakaoka family in the days leading up to the bombing of Hiroshima. The hardships suffered by all Japanese civilians—the stresses of fear, air raids, lack of food, coercion from the military government—are aggravated for the Nakaokas because Gen's father has spoken out against the war. Such resistance was rare; few people dared to question the authorities. The family of seven finds life oppressive: The eldest son, Koji, to counteract the label of "traitors" given to his family, joins the Imperial Navy's Air Corps but is soon disillusioned with the inadequacies and brutalities of its Youth Training Program (a fellow recruit is beaten into a successful suicide attempt, which is covered up by the military and called an accident). Akira, a second son, is evacuated to the country (purportedly to protect him from the war but in fact for something close to slave labor); Eiko, the single daughter, Gen, and Shinji, the youngest son, stay in the city with their father and their pregnant mother. Gen, a second-grader in primary school, is the indomitable hero of the story, whose courage in the face of hunger and injustice helps to sustain the family.

Author and cartoonist Keiji Nakazawa was seven years old and in second grade when Hiroshima was destroyed. He explains his choice of the name *Gen* (pronounced with a hard G), meaning roots or source, for his main character:

19. Keiji Nakazawa, *Barefoot Gen: A Cartoon Story of Hiroshima,* 3 vols. (Philadelphia: New Society Publishers, 1988 and 1989.) Originally published Tokyo: Project Gen, 1978–80, Call 1-800-333-9093 for ordering information.

> I named my main character Gen in the hope that he would become a root or source of strength for a new generation of mankind—one that can tread the charred soil of Hiroshima barefoot, feel the earth beneath its feet, and have the strength to say ''no'' to nuclear weapons. . . .I myself would like to live with Gen's strength—that is my ideal, and I will continue pursuing it through my work.[20]

The strength the Earth gives to Gen through his bare feet and the centrality of the root metaphor for the renewal of life suggest the survival principle of the biophile. *Barefoot Gen* has a dynamism of feeling and a certain bluntness of visual and verbal qualities that give it a special impact. Westerners will find its comic format peculiar. Dadakai, the group of translators, point out that in Japan comics are read by all the people, ''from elementary schoolchildren to company presidents,'' and that *Barefoot Gen* is in no sense ''the property of an isolated subculture.'' There were special problems in translating the cartoons, for the sequence had to be reversed for Western readers, and the body language and expressions sometimes called for ''altering or expanding the information available'' so the English reader would not misunderstand. Further, the number of incidents of personal violence—people striking or slapping each other—needs explanation: ''Violence is a form of exaggeration commonly used in the Japanese comic idiom for dramatic effect''; not surprising, it also reflects ''tensions in people's lives at the time.''[21]

Gen's father, Eiko, and Shinji are burned alive in the fires after the blast. Volume 2 of *Barefoot Gen* tells of the struggle of Gen, his mother, and her newborn baby to survive. They face ''the nightmare of total destruction, starvation, radiation sickness, and social breakdown'' that ensued. Though full of images of the inexpressible suffering caused by mutilation and radiation sickness, of mental anguish and insanity, of cruel ostracism (the other Japanese feared contamination from the dreaded *hibakusha*), there are also shining moments of love, compassion, and, above all, perseverance. Gen's unflagging spirit is better understood as mythic (in the manner of the hero of a folktale) than judged by realistic standards, for by the latter he is indeed too good to be true.

The imagery of almost unremitted horrors expresses the worst fear of the *hibakusha* —the desecration of their humanity. The very artlessness of the cartoons and the accompanying banalities of the text allow no aesthetic distancing to cushion the effect on the reader. In a striking

20. Ibid., vol. 1, Introduction, unp.
21. Ibid. 2:xiii.

instance, Gen is revolted to see the badly burned body of a man, with his mouth still moving, loaded onto a truck full of corpses as if he were no more than a piece of rubbish. When Gen protests, the clean-up crew worker says it doesn't matter—the man will soon be dead.[22] Such scenes can be compared to nothing but the photographed atrocities of the Jewish Holocaust.

Nakazawa's images can be broadly classed into those that have to do with the sufferings of the flesh and those that depict the pain of the spirit. A particularly vivid instance of the former occurs when the starving Gen, searching for rice for himself and his family, is distracted by a "pop" sound. Looking to the river, he sees that the noise comes from the stomachs of the dead, swollen up from the pressure of gas inside until they burst like balloons. There are further hellish images of unbearable stench, flies, maggots, exposed bones, and even of pow-dered bone made from the remains of victims in accordance with the folk belief that powdered bone has medicinal value.

As for spiritual and psychological torments, one of the worst was the harsh treatment received from more fortunate Japanese. The homeless Gen and his mother are called "dirty beggars" as they are rejected by landlords fearing for their own safety and profit. The mother, Kimi, speaks of such selfishness as "wretchedness," which makes people trample others who are weak. Fear and cupidity rule those who feel threatened themselves. The worst example of rejection of the weak occurs when Seiji, an artist who has been monstrously burned, finds his family cannot bear to have him in their presence. Only through the patient care and love of Gen is Seiji reclaimed, trans-formed, and made able to live and paint again.

Two other instances of Gen's ability to nurture and sustain life can be cited: Gen helps the grotesquely burned Natsue and saves her from committing suicide in her despair. Similarly, he persuades his mother to let Ryuta (a boy who has been surviving by leading a gang of thieves) live with them because they see in him a resemblance to the dead Shinji.[23]

The central image of nurturance in the story, however, centers around Gen's baby sister, born at the close of volume 1 amid the fire following the blast, a kind of human phoenix from the ashes. She is named Tomoko, a combination of the words for friend (*Tomo*) and child (*Ko*). With her smiling, laughing face, unaware of the tragedy and pain around her, she is the archetypal Innocent, a reminder of a different

22. Ibid. 2:21.
23. Ibid. 2:51, 65ff., 240, 313ff.

(and in this Wasteland a much-needed opposite) reality—that of simple *joie de vivre*.

The primary image of the will to live, aside from Tomoko and Gen, is in the symbolic rendering of wheat. In the book's opening, the reader is explicitly told that wheat, though trampled, "sends strong roots into the earth, endures frost, wind and snow, grows straight and tall . . . and one day bears fruit." Later, Kimi tells Gen and Shinji they must grow up, as their father always tells them, "like wheat. Get stepped on, again and again, but grow up strong, get stepped on, bear the wind and snow, and grow TALL and STRONG like wheat."[24] Noboru Nishio, of the Research Institute on Energy and Environment in Tokyo, implies this image when he says *Gen* portrays the "history of the common people whose lives have constantly been trampled on."[25] *Barefoot Gen* provides an exemplar of the biophile's faith and strength as the basis of a survival ethic.

"Unforgettable Fire"

Barefoot Gen was followed in 1977 by *Unforgettable Fire: Pictures Drawn by Atomic Bomb Survivors*, a translation of *Goka o mita*. The stunning pictures, with accompanying commentary by the illustrators, convey in a way more personal and graphic than that possible through cartoons or photographs the heart-wrenching memories of their creators. One particularly striking image was recalled by Mikio Inoue (aged 72 when he did his drawing): the picture of an acquaintance, Professor Takenaka, who had tried in vain to rescue his wife trapped under a burning roof beam. Urged by her to escape with his own life, he was remembered standing dazed at the foot of Miyuki Bridge, clad only in shorts, with a rice ball in his right hand. Mikio Inoue speculates, "But I wonder how he came to hold that rice ball in his hand? His naked figure, standing there before the flames with that rice ball looked to me as a symbol of the modest hope of human beings."[26]

Kinzo Nishida, 82 years old, remembered "a stark naked man standing in the rain with his eyeball in his palm. He looked to be in great pain but there was nothing I could do for him. . . . I wonder what became of him."[27] Many of the explanatory statements accompanying

---

24. Ibid. 1:48.
25. Ibid. 2:viii.
26. *Unforgettable Fire: Pictures Drawn by Atomic Bomb Survivors*, ed. the Japan Broadcasting Corporation [NHK] (New York: Pantheon Books, 1981), p. 46.
27. Ibid., p. 48.

the pictures ended with the words *gashoo* or *gashoonembutsu* —meaning praying hands or folded hands in prayer for the dead. This signifies that the survivors wished by drawing these pictures ''to make amends individually for the people who died that day and to relieve the anguish of their souls." The desire to make a symbolic restitution suggests the phenomenon of the guilt of the survivor, the guilt suffered by those who are inexplicably spared when those around them are catastrophically destroyed. Such guilt manifests itself in the tormenting memory of being unable to answer the cries for help (especially, again and again, the cry for water), as well as the pain of the question "Why did I survive when so many others died?" The desire of the *hibakusha* that others understand the truth of their experiences and remember them in perpetuity is vividly portrayed.[28]

"The Hiroshima Murals" and "Hiroshima no Pika"

Iri and Toshi Maruki, Japanese artist-illustrators, created the murals collected in *The Hiroshima Murals: The Art of Iri Maruki and Toshi Maruki*, which depicts the scenes burnt into their memories when they arrived in Hiroshima a few days after the devastation of August 6, 1945. The original Hiroshima Murals and later paintings by the Marukis are on permanent display at the Maruki Gallery for the Hiroshima Panels (Maruki Bijutsukan), northwest of Tokyo in Saitima Prefecture.

Toshi Maruki has also created the picture book for children, *Hiroshima no Pika* (Hiroshima, the Flash). Her afterword tells us it is "written . . . for grandchildren everywhere." The picture book relates the events of August 6, 1945, when the crew of the U.S. Air Force bomber *Enola Gay* dropped an atomic bomb on the city of Hiroshima. In simple prose, Toshi Maruki expresses how one small Japanese girl and her family were affected. Horrors are not spared: "Then it happened. A sudden, terrible light flashed all around. The light was bright orange—then white, like thousands of lightning bolts all striking at once."[29] The stylized illustrations are powerfully surrealistic in feeling yet also earthy. A stark red scene of the city burning contrasts sharply with the

28. Ibid., p. 108; Afterword, "The Pictures of the Atomic Bomb: An Appeal of the Citizens."

29. The light image of the flash may be contrasted with Gary Paulsen's use of the sound *click* followed instantaneously by a blinding flash as the harbinger of nuclear annihilation in his *Sentries* (New York: Bradbury, 1986), pp. 164–65.

scene of the river to which people flee. The little girl, Mii, clutches her chopsticks throughout. Her father dies slowly, Mii fails to grow, and the brain damage she suffers keeps her perpetually a child. Years later the mother is still picking slivers of glass out of the child's scalp. The mother's words at the close are meant to offer hope: "It can't happen again if no one drops the bomb." As an antiwar and anti–nuclear weapons statement, the book has few equals.

For that very reason, however, and for aesthetic ones as well, the book is highly controversial. Maruki has powerfully visualized what Natalie Babbitt in her review of the book called "only a nightmare of fire, nakedness, and death." Babbitt believes it is "not a cautionary tale wherein if one is good one can escape disaster, but a tale wherein there is no escape, no matter what one does."[30] Thus she argues the book's inappropriateness for the usual picture book readers, who are not yet ready for the complexities of nuclear warfare, the "moral instability of humans" being still beyond their ken. Placing this book in children's hands, Babbitt believes, is morally equivalent to hanging Picasso's *Guernica* in the nursery. Moreover, she considers the book "far too incomplete" for any reader over the age of ten.

Babbitt's criticism of the inappropriateness of *Hiroshima no Pika* for both children and adults signifies the difficulty of finding any adequate means of expression—visual or verbal—for the fact of Hiroshima. One reply to Babbitt can be found in the words of Dorothy Briley, who made the decision to publish the book. Briley stresses how the book's very simplicity transcends anger and the implication of "collective or individual guilt," and she views it as a plea simply to "listen." Thinking back to her own childhood in World War II, Briley concluded that children need to know the full horror wrought by the use of nuclear weapons, and she views the book as essentially cautionary. The violence of the book, moreover, is occasionally countered by what critic Barbara Harrison calls "compassionate and courageous action," as when a mother saves her husband from a fiery death and flees with him and their child to seek shelter.[31]

The debate over offering this picture book to young children is polarized: On the one hand it can be argued that the horror is too strong,

30. Natalie Babbitt, review of *Hiroshima no Pika*, by Toshi Maruki, *New York Times Book Review*, October 10, 1982, p. 24.

31. Dorothy Briley, "*Hiroshima no Pika*" (Paper presented at Simmons College Institute, "Do I Dare Disturb the Universe?", Boston, Mass., July 18, 1983; quoted by Barbara Harrison, "Howl Like the Wolves," *Children's Literature: Annual of the Modern Language Association Division on Children's Literature and the Children's Literature Association* 15 (1987): 79, 80.

too overwhelming, too potentially stupefying to the emotions. On the other, it can be maintained equally well that the "unthinkable" event can be stemmed only if we name and visualize the terrors—face the reality of the horror. Since the destructive jinni is out of the bottle, our hope to control it lies in calling it by its true name and painting it in its ugliest guise. The question is not *whether* the young child should confront the truth of the horror, but *when*, and through what medium. The debate over when the child is ready to confront what one writer has called a "Garden of Terrors" is sure to continue.[32]

The Aesthetic Dilemma Posed by Atrocities: The Marukis

A reflection of Briley's thinking may be found in what Iri and Toshi Maruki say about their reasons for painting the *Hiroshima Murals*. They were compelled to do so:

> After the war, many of our artist friends in Tokyo decided that we should try to paint healthy, cheerful portraits of Japan at peace. We tried to do this. . . . But somehow, inexplicably we ended up painting grief-stricken faces. No shining light came from within.[33]

The wounds from Hiroshima cried out for visual expression, and though Toshi and Iri sincerely wanted "to create optimistic bright paintings," they realized they must first "communicate the nature of the darkness that kept encroaching on our work." This meant painting Hiroshima and the atomic bomb not for humanitarian motives but because its reality demanded expression. The Marukis were already mavericks, "different" in their way of thinking about the world, socialists, and pacifists. Toshi sees the painting of the Murals as part of a whole life-process, the groping for meaning followed by an unfolding, like the answer to a riddle.

The Marukis' 1985 mural *Hell* represents no particular historical incident but rather the reality of the world we inhabit, where people kill other people, an atrocity many times more terrible than any imaginable devils could inflict because it is treachery to one's own kind. Iri says,

---

32. The title of Maya Pines's review of *The Strangelove Legacy: Children, Parents, and Teachers in the Nuclear Age,* by Phyllis LaFarge, *New York Times Book Review*, March 22, 1987, p. 38.

33. Iri and Toshi Maruki, *The Hiroshima Murals,* ed. John W. Dower and John Junkerman (Tokyo: Kodansha International Ltd., 1985), p. 123.

"It is a reality. But we don't paint this reality so that people will rethink things, or so we can create a world that is not so hellish." They disclaim didactic purposes, but simply wish to paint "reality": "If people happen to learn something from the painting, that is wonderful; if they don't, that's all right too. The point is that all of us, all living human beings, are living in that reality. We paint that reality."

In the *Hell* mural, Toshi has portrayed the *gaki*, "the beasts that are neither human nor animal, that are invisible but are always present and are eternally hungry," and who add to the torments of the infernal world. *Gaki* exist among the living, also, where they "make this world into hell, and it is hard to escape them." The Marukis painted themselves as falling into hell "because we do not have the strength to stop war." They felt for a time they should leave God out of hell, even though in Nagasaki "the bomb exploded right above Urakami Cathedral; in Hiroshima, the bomb was dropped over a Buddhist temple, which was blown to smithereens." Finally, as they neared the end of the painting, they added the Christian cross, which, like all symbols, can be variously interpreted—as the failure of hope, or as hope abiding even in the inferno.[34]

The Marukis refusal of any doctrinaire ideas, their use of symbolic and mythic perspectives, radiates a "holistic" and self-questioning perspective: Hope seems to lie in facing the reality of the hell of war. Joseph W. Meeker's concept of Hell as a place of ecological disaster, the wasteland hostile to life, reeking in moral and biological pollution, parallels well with the Marukis' artistic conceptualization.[35]

The terrible images of the Hiroshima Murals group themselves into a kind of grotesque typology. They are categorized here because they provide the realistic basis for images used by many writers of fiction. Most haunting are the eye images: a maggot in a dead man's eyeball, causing the lifeless pupil to move weirdly in a sickening imitation of life; the eyeballs of Korean corpses being devoured by crows (for the corpses of the Korean forced laborers were the last to be disposed of in the mopping up after the blast). Bird images also abound, visualizations of poignant helplessness: birds rendered incapable of flight, having had their wings burnt off. There are monster images, portrayals of the victims themselves, horribly transformed and disfigured by their wounds and suffering. Whereas in the old Buddhist scroll paintings of Hell, monsters tormented the victims, the new victims of this technologically created Hell are a torment to themselves and others. The im-

---

34. Ibid., pp. 125, 127–28.
35. Meeker, *The Comedy of Survival*, pp. 137, 139.

ages of the scorching and mutilation of the human form are too numerous to tally. *Pika-don*, a booklet filled with black-and-white illustrations done by the Marukis, was suppressed by the American occupation authorities because it featured such "icons" of the devastation of Hiroshima and Nagasaki as "severed legs still standing upright, dead soldiers turned into recognizable statues of ash." People who had been skinned alive were painted as a procession of ghosts with arms held in front of them, hands dangling—like the living dead of traditional iconography in both Japanese and Western art.[36] The mentality that censors these realities of war is akin to the spirit of economic exploitation that markets GI Joe "dolls" without making sure that some of them are depicted as amputees.

Ironic inversion occurs repeatedly in the Murals. The Madonna becomes a mother cradling a dead child, a sight called by the Marukis "the twentieth-century image of . . . despair." Water, traditionally a symbol of the source of life, becomes the agent of death when victims are drowned in their efforts to escape the burning city. Similarly, gnarled trees—ancient symbols of longevity in Oriental art—are reduced to "the debris of a blasted landscape, their twisted forms echoed by the broken bodies of schoolchildren lying alongside them." In a like manner, bamboo, an established image of the qualities of grace and resilience, becomes permanently bent and broken in the seventh mural. Inversion occurs again in a literal fashion in the Nagasaki mural, where the Marukis depict the Christ crucified upside down.[37]

The twelfth mural, *Floating Lanterns,* mirrors the paradoxical qualities in the ritual observance of the *Bon* holiday, the Feast of Lanterns traditionally celebrated in mid-August, when the dead are commemorated by floating lanterns inscribed with their names upon the rivers at dusk. As the lanterns move gently away into the darkness, the souls seem visibly to return to the other world. When the occupation ended in 1952, the Japanese began to float lanterns on August 6 in memory of the bomb victims and as a supplication for peace. John W. Dower comments: In the Marukis' painting, as in the ritual observance itself, the floating lanterns offer a nearly perfect counterpoise of beauty and creativity set against war and brutalization. Aesthetically and spiritually, the atomic-bomb experience is transcended.[38]

Since 1975, the two artists have painted other scenes of war and destruction of twentieth century: the Rape of Nanking, Auschwitz, the

---

36. Maruki, *The Hiroshima Murals*, pp. 14, 39, 83.
37. Ibid., pp. 16–17, 24.
38. Ibid., p. 20.

Minamata mercury poisoning. Enriched by both Asian and Western traditions, their artistic vision transcends its subject matter—the horrors of "militarism, war, and nuclear devastation" as well as "racism and the destruction of the environment." As Dower says, "Their work represents both an act of consecration of the dead and an affirmation of life. As such, the Maruki paintings stand in direct opposition to the horrors they depict." The influence of these powerful visual images on the way both Japanese and non-Japanese will remember these decades of the twentieth century remains incalculable.

Perhaps because of the Marukis' insistence on stark reality, they have not been exempt from censorship. The Japanese Ministry of Education in 1981 refused to give its approval to a textbook containing the two central panels of the mural *Relief*, declaring the sight to be "'too cruel' for young people—a euphemism, as critics saw it, for being too politically sensitive."[39]

"The Original Child Bomb"

The perspectives of the *hibakusha* contrast ironically with those of the people who, in their political, scientific, or military roles, made nuclear devastation happen. *The Original Child Bomb: Points for Meditation to Be Scratched on the Walls of a Cave*, with text by Thomas Merton and illustrations by Emil Antonucci, defies comparison in its understated, "primer" style of expression and its artwork reminiscent of Rorschach blobs. Despite its picture-book format, its biting irony makes it suitable for adults. Since few libraries hold copies, it will be described in detail here.

The illustrations, splotches of black ink on a white background, seem to expand in the manner of a lethal mushroom cloud—in angry, explosive shapes of visual turmoil. The page opposite the last page of text is done in a mottled black that recalls the "darkness visible" of Milton's Hell. Merton's spare text uses sustained metaphor to work out a parallel between the Bomb (personified throughout the book) and the Christ Child. "Original Child" was the name given to the bomb by the Japanese, "who recognized that it was the first of its kind." To carry out the child metaphor, Merton notes how others had spoken of the bomb as a new birth: When the results of the July 16, 1945, test in the desert at Alamogordo, New Mexico, were reported to President Truman, then in Potsdam, the commander in chief left the

39. Ibid., pp. 8, 25.

conference with a "jaunty" mood and "light step"; later that same day, July 21, Stimson reported to Winston Churchill the coded message, "Babies satisfactorily born." On August 1, the bomb was assembled on the island of Tinian. "Those who handled the bomb referred to it as 'Little Boy.' Their care for the Original Child was devoted and tender." The bomb was "tucked away in the womb of Enola Gay" (the name of the pilot's mother), and the crew "were as excited as little boys on Christmas Eve."

Merton believes, along with a number of historians, that the use of the bomb against the Japanese to end the war was militarily unnecessary. Moreover, the pleas of sixty scientists who signed a petition urging the president not to use the bomb were ignored. The president's own committee, appointed to study whether the bomb would work, and if so, what to do with it, was split: Some felt its use "would jeopardize the future of civilization." Others wanted its power to be demonstrated, possibly on an unpeopled, forested area. Still others believed that if it were used "just once or twice, on one or two Japanese cities, there would be no more war. They believed the new bomb would produce eternal peace." The religious awe surrounding the experience of the desert test in Alamogordo became a theme woven into the later events. Admiral Leahy, cast by Merton into the role of Doubting Thomas, insisted up to the day of the bombing that the weapon would not explode when dropped from a plane over a city.

To illustrate the religious euphemisms employed to mask the weaponry from the start, Merton notes the code names of the Alamogordo test—"Trinity"—and the island of Tinian—"Papacy." Merton anticipated Ira Chernus's insight that the bomb became a perverse object of worship, a *deus otiosus*.[40]

In Merton's understated, devastating little book, the president from Missouri seems dwarfed and overcome by the fateful web of events in which he was caught up. Merton uses Truman's own words to sum up his philosophy: "We found the bomb . . . and we used it." He parodies attitudes toward this new technology of destruction as typical of American pragmatism and "business" values: "Lucky Hiroshima!"—chosen because it had not yet suffered bombing and would therefore make a clearer demonstration of the power of the new weapon. It would be destroyed in a single day—what efficiency! To save time is to save money! Merton's sardonic style fits the portrait of human blindness and error, and his bitter ending twist calls the entire future of the

40. Ira Chernus, *Dr. Strangegod: On the Symbolic Meaning of Nuclear Weapons* (Columbia: Univ. of South Carolina Pr., 1986), p. 18.

world into question: "Men seem to be fatigued by the whole question" of what is going to happen to the world now that so many bombs have been "found." The implication is that we shall blunder into disaster more out of sheer weariness than from perversity or recklessness, and meet our end with an exhausted whimper rather than a bang. "Found" suggests the skirting of responsibility for the use of so terrible a weapon. Merton sees us as a people diminished, deluded, and demoralized, lost amidst moral complexities too overwhelming to contemplate, actors in an inscrutable drama of destruction brought about through our collective adherence to a concept of power as the license to dominate rather than the responsibility to serve. In Merton's view, the human race seems dead set on destruction. His bleak book dramatizes our sore need for a survival ethic and for what Riane Eisler calls "gylanic" relationships (see the Introduction to this book).

The World as Nuclear-armed Camp: An American Childhood Remembered

A remarkable autobiographical account of an American child growing up in the nuclear shadow, written from the perspective of thirty years later, comes from Scott Sanders in "At Play in the Paradise of Bombs." Sanders grew up on the grounds of the Ohio Arsenal, where his family moved in 1951 when he was six. His father's company supervised the production lines for artillery shells, land mines, and bombs. His "birth sign," he feels, was the mushroom cloud. Like Musil (see the following section, "An American Perspective from the Sixties"), he was "bomb-affected." The military milieu combined elements of the armed camp and a Nazi concentration camp. People one hundred years from now, Sanders predicts, will see our time "through the cross-hairs of memory" as "like the Arsenal, a fenced wilderness devoted to the building and harboring of instruments of death."[41]

Surrounding the Arsenal was a forest, "a tangled, beast-haunted woods stretching for miles in every direction," and to the children it seemed a place of adventure in contrast to the "charmed circle" of human habitation. Only later did Sanders know how the lethal environment entered his "bone marrow," where

41. Scott Sanders, "At Play in the Paradise of Bombs," *North American Review* 268, no. 3 (September 1983): 53.

I carry traces of the poison from that graveyard of bombs, as we all carry a
smidgen of radioactivity from every atomic blast: perhaps at this very moment one of those alien molecules, like a grain of sand in an oyster, is irri-
tating some cell in my body, or in your body, to fashion a pearl of cancer.[42]

The child here is the Innocent betrayed by the very society that pro-
fesses to protect him. Sanders was introduced to killing, to the fact that
life feeds on life (what Joseph Campbell calls life's "voraciousness")
through the annual deer kills. He importuned his father to allow him to
work as a "beater," whose role it was to find the deer and herd them
into easy range so the generals could gun them down, a practice reminiscent of the buffalo kills described in *Bless the Beasts and Children* by Glendon Swarthout. The sight proved so sickening that he "never again
asked to work as a beater, or to watch the grown men shoot, or to
hunt."[43]

Fear had always affected the personnel of the Arsenal, driving Army
wives to drink and drugs. After the Soviets launched *Sputnik*, however, fear gripped people in more obvious ways. The children were
sleepless. To a child it seemed that the only salvation was in running
away, because adults offered no protection from the terror. The "wild
things" had usurped his home. His fantasies of escape to "fresh, un-
poisoned planets" were frustrated by the realization that only a handful of people could escape to the stars, and, further, he could not bear
to abandon a beloved Earth. For the twelve years he lived within the
Arsenal, it was official practice to detonate outmoded bombs at evening mealtime, and their sound, like "the muttering of local gods,"
consistently ruined his appetite for supper. The family at last left the
Arsenal, but the Arsenal could never leave the boy, for its fences
"stretched outward until they circled the entire planet. I can never
move outside, nor can you.'"[44] The barbed wire fences are permanently
installed in the psychological landscape.

Sanders's recollections present the child primarily as victim, able to
escape only through fantasies, forever after carrying the "cancer cell"
of fear or possibly of actual radiation in his bone marrow, forever after
imaging his world as an armed camp. The one element of hope grows
from Sanders's adult ability to distance himself from the experience, to
reorder it through writing it down and giving it form. In this way he
prefigures the survival ethic exemplified in the hero/hera as artist or
journalist, the subject of a later chapter.

42. Ibid., p. 54.
43. Ibid., pp. 54, 56.
44. Ibid., p. 58.

An American Perspective
from the Sixties

Several real-life examples of how consciousness of atomic weapons affected sensitive young people in the United States can give a global perspective on the ''bomb-affected.'' The first example comes from Robert Musil, who relates his experience of nuclear fear during the Cuban missile crisis in his essay ''Teaching in a Nuclear Age.'' As a student at Yale in October of 1962, Musil watched in horror as John Kennedy announced on television, ''We do not seek worldwide thermonuclear war. The fruits of victory would be but ashes in our mouths. But neither will we shrink from it at any time it must be faced.'' This is how Musil imagined nuclear war:

> Images of collapsing buildings, fireballs, dead and injured students and faculty, family and friends flooded my mind. My response—appropriately absurd in retrospect—was to contemplate changing my major. Suddenly, the works of Shakespeare, Milton, Chaucer that I was studying seemed futile and ridiculous, a future as a college professor absurd. I decided briefly to be an opthalmologist—images of melting eyeballs, of blinded victims needing help haunted me for days.[45]

Musil's images mirror those of John Hersey's *Hiroshima*. He was later to realize the misguided nature of his contemplated change of major and the reality that he could take action to ''do something concrete about the arms race itself.'' In retrospect Musil also understood that ''it was partly because of my interest in literature that I felt the Cuban Missile Crisis so deeply.'' Literature, more than any other discipline, awakens imagination and empathy. As he says, ''My own initial reaction to abandon literature and the arts as trivial in the face of nuclear terror was not only absurdly inappropriate—it was also wrong.''[46]

The memoirs of Musil and Sanders show how the *hibakusha* experience has become globalized on the level of psychological fallout. The universalized, sinister presence of nuclear arms in our world finds embodiment in Peter Goldman's documentary, *The End of the World That Was: Six Lives in the Atomic Age*. Called by its author a nonfiction novel, the book traces the effects of the bomb on the lives of six people, several of them citizens of the United States. The latter are people who were

45. Robert Musil, ''Teaching in a Nuclear Age,'' in *Education for Peace and Disarmament*, p. 88.
46. Ibid., pp. 88–89.

involved in the production or launching of the weapons. In one case, a relative—the stepdaughter of an armaments officer who helped load the bomb on Tinian Island—is today a peace activist devoted to challenging the views of her beloved but in her view mistaken stepfather. The stories of these individuals raise the reader's consciousness of the intricate intertwining of lives in our nuclear global village.

Sadako: The Hibakusha Experience in Picture Books

Sadako and the Thousand Paper Cranes by Eleanor Coerr is based on the actual girl (mentioned in Lifton's *A Place Called Hiroshima*) who lived in Japan from 1943 to 1955 and who died ten years after Hiroshima as a result of radiation exposure. In this picture-book retelling, Chizuko explains to Sadako the meaning of the story of the crane: "It's supposed to live for a thousand years. If a sick person folds one thousand paper cranes, the gods will grant her wish and make her healthy again."[47]

Sadako is encouraged to begin making cranes, and Masahiro, her brother, promises to hang them from the ceiling for her. The book draws on the tradition of *O Bon*, when spirits of the dead are believed to return to the earth to visit those they loved. When Sadako realizes she will die, cranes notwithstanding, she asks her mother to put her favorite bean cakes on the altar for her spirit on the *Bon* holiday. The distraught mother urges Sadako to make "only a few hundred more cranes." Attired in her new silk kimono adorned with cherry blossoms, Sadako makes her last paper crane. Her final vision is an epiphany:

> She looked at her flock hanging from the ceiling. As she watched, a light autumn breeze made the birds rustle and sway. They seemed to be alive and flying out through the open window. How beautiful and free they were! Sadako sighed and closed her eyes.
> She never woke up.[48]

Even as the wingless, burnt birds haunted the memories of Hiroshima survivors, the paper cranes stir hope of spiritual transcendence. The ceremonial launching of paper cranes on the anniversary of the Hiroshima bombing is observed by peace groups, both in Japan and

47. Eleanor Coerr, *Sadako and the Thousand Paper Cranes*, illus. Ronald Himler (New York: G. P. Putnam, 1977), p. 34.

48. Ibid., pp. 56, 63.

the United States Elise Harvey was inspired by Sadako's story to write the song "Sadako's Wish"; she wrote another in memory of Samantha Smith (the New England girl who has passed into legend for her courage in visiting the USSR on a mission of peace). Both songs may be found at the end of this chapter.

Sadako's Story for Middle and Upper Grades

Karl Bruckner's *The Day of the Bomb* also relates Sadako's story, fictionalizing the experiences of her family, the Sasakis. Bruckner depicts their harsh lives preceding the event, particularly the suffering and hunger of Sadako and her small brother, Shigeo, who must fend for themselves while their father is at war and their mother is at work in a factory. The narrative shifts from the Hiroshima scene to give a glimpse of the thoughts of the American crew whose dire assignment was to drop the bomb; this change in perspective seems designed to help the young reader appreciate the moral complexities of the situation. The remainder of the story tells how the Sasakis endure the opportunistic exploitation perpetrated by their more fortunate fellows and their worst trial, the onset of the deadly bomb sickness in Sadako.

The strength of the story lies in Sadako's courage and dignity, her full "living" of her dying. As her life finally ebbs and ends, despite her brave persistence in folding cranes, she is portrayed by Bruckner as illuminated by a light of mysterious origin, a hint of her "saintly" nature. Despite the way war typically twists humanity "into one jellied mass, burying the individual, or wrenching him out of his customary shape," in Carolyn Kingston's words, Sadako survives as an archetypal Martyr, possibly even a Magician figure, a hera and biophile in her creative attitude toward life up to its final moment.[49]

"The Miracle Tree"

An illustrated, fictionalized treatment of the consequences of radiation sickness is *The Miracle Tree* by Christobel Mattingly. The story of a husband, wife, and the wife's mother, who become separated at the time of the explosion of the atom bomb over Nagasaki, is remarkable

---

49. Carolyn Kingston, *The Tragic Mode in Children's Literature* (New York: Teachers College Press, 1974), p. 94.

for its aesthetic distancing. The audience is cushioned from the impact of the catastrophe by the lapse of time since the bombing (the events of the book encompass a period of twenty years). Taro, a gardener, searches in vain after the bombing of Nagasaki to find his beautiful young wife, Hanako. The couple is alienated from Hanako's mother (known throughout only as "the woman with the bent back") because she was angered when they married before obtaining her permission (not willfully, but owing to the pressures of wartime). In a fit of rage the mother tore up the slip of paper that bore Taro's last name; consequently, she does not know her daughter's married name. The paths of Taro and his unknown mother-in-law cross through their shared devotion to a tree planted by Taro adjacent to the site of the church flattened by the bomb. Though it takes twenty years, the reunion of the family occurs on Christmas Day through their mutual love of the "miracle" tree. The folktale mode of the story transcends the improbabilities of its plot.

The power of this simple contemporary myth of the healing, restorative power of love and of nature centers around the image of the tree as an analogue of the human form. Hanako's beauty, before suffering disfigurement, is described in terms reminiscent of a fairy-tale princess: skin like "a camellia petal," hair "as shiny as a crow's wing," eyes sparkling "like pools in the sun." The description of the pine's appearance echoes hers: needles "smooth as a camellia petal, with a sheen like a crow's wing." The post–atom-bomb Hanako (now called Shizuka to signify her transformation) has "skin as ridged as pine bark and hair as tufty as unplucked pine needles." The metaphorical identity is extended throughout the book, and in the recognition scene Taro experiences a "tree of promise" opening within himself:

> Taro felt as if a hundred thousand seeds were springing into blossom in his brain and a million leaves were unfolding all about him, cool and green and full of promise.[50]

The imagery of rebirth of life and hope, on the very site of inconceivable suffering and destruction, expresses the survival ethic as based on reverence for the Earth and all its beings.

The second key image in the book is that of the paper cranes folded by Hanako-Shizuka from the paper on which she has written poems. When Taro, Hanako, and her mother enter the church to lay the cranes

50. Christobel Mattingly, *The Miracle Tree*, illus. Marianne Yamaguchi (Australia: Hodder and Stoughton, 1985; San Diego: Harcourt Brace Jovanovich, Gulliver Books, 1986), unp.

in the creche of the Christ Child as an offering for peace, the accompanying illustration shows the Christ Child covered with paper cranes so arranged that in a trompe l'oeil effect they also constitute a crown of thorns, thus paradoxically fusing suffering and joy. Hanako's heart at that moment yearns for "the baby she would never have," symbolically replaced by the Christ Child into whose "outstretched empty hands she placed her cranes, patterned with pain and love, suffering and rejoicing." Through these images the story conveys a vision of wholeness and the reconciliation of the opposites of pain and joy. Transcending suffering, the bomb-affected attain a vision of peace based on harmonious linking with one another and with the natural world, in the mode of the biophile.

The Hibakusha Story for Mature Readers: "Black Rain"

One of the most distinguished pieces of nuclear literature is Masuji Ibuse's *Black Rain*, an example of a "documentary novel" much praised for its realism. Paul Brians calls it more valuable than "all the fantasies of the future lumped together" for those seeking insight into the "facts" about human repercussions of nuclear conflict.[51] Incorporated into Shigematsu's personal diary, which forms the narrative, are the diaries of his niece Yasuko; the diary of Shigeko, Shigematsu's wife, kept during Yasuko's illness; and the diary of a physician who describes a highly unexpected recovery from A-bomb effects. The book's central theme, according to Robert J. Lifton's analysis, explores the scope of human responsibility: Shigematsu's feelings of responsibility to Yasuko (as closest male relative) to give her the traditional assistance in finding a suitable husband; to himself and his community, devastated by the bomb; to the dead (reverence of ancestors being an important part of Japanese cultural values); and finally to history.[52] The setting is the village of Kobatake, one hundred miles east of Hiroshima. "Black rain" refers to the shower of polluted rain that fell on Hiroshima shortly after the detonation of the bomb, to which Yasuko was exposed. Her misfortune makes her a virtual pariah in the eyes of potential suitors and their families.

51. Paul Brians, *Nuclear Holocausts: Atomic War in Fiction 1895–1984* (Kent, Ohio: Kent State Univ. Pr., 1987), p. 25.

52. Robert J. Lifton, *Death in Life: The Survivors of Hiroshima* (New York: Random House, 1967), p. 544. The Appendix gives a fine appreciation of Ibuse's novel.

Yasuko, though an outcast who has been victimized by the effects of the bomb, displays a heroic will to live against overwhelming odds. Nevertheless, the close of the novel leaves the reader certain she will die of the effects of radiation (contrast Sadako, immortalized in Coerr's and Bruckner's retellings of her story).

Children, who always fare even worse than adults in war, are also presented as victimized, first by the damage inflicted at the bomb's impact and second by the panic of the mobs trying to flee its terrors. Shigematsu remembers an anonymous boy of about seven whom he encountered wandering alone after the bombing. Wrapped in his own pain, Shigematsu tries to evade responsibility by passing him off to a woman—also a stranger. The boy has a mind of his own and, seemingly with a destination in mind, goes off ahead of the woman, heading in the direction from which he had come, an abandoned, pathetic figure. In a second instance, Shigematsu sees a woman with her belongings and child loaded on a baby carriage "engulfed in a sudden wave of humanity that crushed the baby carriage and felled her on top of it."[53]

Children are also portrayed as martyrs to a hypocritical educational establishment, corrupted by government policy, which stoops to alter even traditionally venerated poetry to fit the conditions of war. Ibuse gives the example of a line of poetry by Kenji Miyazawa that in its original form in traditional textbooks had said, "To each his four *go* / Of unhulled rice a day," unscrupulously altered (to fit conditions of famine) to "three *go* " to correspond to the actual diminished ration.[54] The child, of course, was in no position to detect the fraud.

Even adults like Shigematsu are reduced by the bomb to a childlike state of dependency and helplessness. Paradoxically, the life-and-death crisis may endow them with a new, childlike clarity of vision. Shigematsu's moment of vision comes when, as the neighborhood association house collapses and becomes silent, he sees his life in a new perspective: all the hours of firefighting drill "come to nothing now. Not a single lookout posted. . . . Suddenly, all the things we had done up to now seemed to me so much children's play, and my own life, too, a toy life." He decides that if life is no more than "kid's play," he will nonetheless throw himself into it wholeheartedly.[55]

In another of his moments of lucid vision, Shigematsu rejects the mythology of war represented by a heroic poem that praised the worm

53. Masuji Ibuse, *Black Rain* (Reprint. Palo Alto: Kodansha International, 1969; New York: Bantam, 1985), pp. 6, 54, 58. Originally *Kuroi Ame*, published in *Showa*, January 1965–September 1966.

54. Ibid., p. 65.

55. Ibid., p. 88.

as a friend and glorified death as ''brave and moving.'' He realizes that peace, regardless of who claimed victory, would be preferable to a ''just'' war.[56]

In the closing passage of the story, Shigematsu spontaneously reverts briefly to a childlike faith in animistic magic. He fantasizes that Yasuko will miraculously become well: ''If a rainbow appears over those hills now, a miracle will happen,''—not a ''white'' rainbow, which would betoken calamity, but ''one of many hues.'' ''Adult'' common sense triumphs, however, and the reader is told he knows this particular miracle will not come to pass.[57]

Because they fall into victim or martyr roles, the children of *Black Rain* stand in contrast to the adults who, like Shigematsu, can partially transcend their experience of the A-bomb by writing about it (see the further discussion of writing as a means of survival in chapter 7).

Another Novel for Mature Readers: ''The Clock at 8:16''

Edwin Lanham's adult novel, *The Clock at 8:16: A Novel of Hiroshima*, is a starkly absurdist contrast to *Black Rain*. The symbolic clock of the title represents the ''freezing'' of time for the *hibakusha* at the moment of the atomic blast over Hiroshima. The basic romantic plot of the love affair between the American Eli Dean, a medic involved in the Vietnam War, and Kamiko, the young Japanese woman, is overshadowed from the start by the specter of the bomb. Kamiko's brother Takeo was left grossly disfigured, scarred facially in a gridlike pattern on the right side, with a ''keloid mass'' on the other that ''twisted his mouth in a lupine snarl.''[58] He is scarred in spirit as well, having been cruelly mocked as the ''Pikadon Monster.'' To survive spiritually, he creates a fantasy self in the letters he writes to his American pen pal, Dean. In his dream Takeo becomes all that he might wish to be but cannot—a dashing ladies' man, a connoisseur of the arts, a man of the world. When Dean writes from Vietnam that he will visit Takeo in Japan on his leave, Takeo panics and goes into hiding to avoid letting Dean see the truth that is written on his face.

The stopped clock metaphorically represents Takeo's inability to

56. Ibid., pp. 161–62.

57. Ibid., p. 300.

58. Edwin Lanham, *The Clock at 8:16: A Novel about Hiroshima* (Garden City, N.Y.: Doubleday, 1970), p. 16.

participate any more in the creative flow of life, or in terms of this study, to survive heroically. Kamiko compares him to the "living dead" she saw at the time of the *pikadon*, the "flash-boom" that struck the people below like "little ants . . . when they are stamped dead by one tremendous foot." For Kamiko time has not stopped but is wounded, and runs "with the slow tick of a mainspring wound too tight, needing an occasional shake to keep it going."[59]

Dean too has been spiritually injured by his experience of battle in Vietnam where, despite his intent to save lives as a medic, he has been forced to kill in self-defense. He fantasizes that the Vietnamese baby he helps an impoverished peasant woman deliver might somehow redeem him from guilt for the man he killed, a man "with a small boy's bewildered face." He is cruelly disillusioned when the baby turns out in fact to be abnormal, spastic and probably mongoloid, as though to mock his presumption that atonement could be so easily found.[60]

Lanham foreshadows the tragic end to the romance between Dean and Kamiko from the start and creates a parallel between the flash-boom of the atomic bomb and the circumstances of Dean's death in Vietnam, when a lightning flash silhouettes him, making him an easy target for the Viet Cong. This repetition of the flash-boom metaphor demonstrates how no human can find immunity from the *hibakusha* experience.

The abnormal child, the spiritual as well as physical scars of Kamiko and Takeo, and Dean's aborted life express the failure of redemption from the destructive cycle wrought by war. There is little in the story to suggest a survival ethic; instead, it presents a picture of life stunted by the failure of idealism to cope with forces that oppose life. Lanham's vision is ironic in mode, conveying life's preciousness by portraying its vulnerability to tragedy.

Short Stories by Hibakusha: "The Crazy Iris"

Award-winning Japanese author Kenzaburo Oe has collected seven short stories by Japanese writers in *The Crazy Iris and Other Stories of the Atomic Aftermath*. Chronicling the impact of the atomic bombings on the lives of ordinary people, the narratives powerfully stir "our imaginative powers to consider the fundamental conditions of human existence" and our inescapable common movement toward an "unknowa-

59. Ibid., pp. 95, 151, 188.
60. Ibid., pp. 29, 31.

ble future." The fundamental condition of postatomic life, says Kenzaburo Oe, is to be "assailed by overwhelming fear," yet we must "rebuild hope, however difficult, in defiance of that fear."[61]

The title story, "The Crazy Iris" by Masuji Ibuse (author of *Black Rain*,) portrays the abnormal blooming of an iris out of season, in defiance of nature's cycles, as a parallel to the abnormality of man's inhumanity to man in the use of nuclear weapons. Other stories included are "Summer Flower" by Tamiki Hara, reflecting this masterful writer's personal experience of the bombing during his return to Hiroshima, his hometown, to place the ashes of his wife in his family's ancestral tomb. Hara's poetic "The Land of Heart's Desire," left behind when he committed suicide in despair over rumors that the atom bomb might be used again during the Korean War, uses the image of a lark transformed in a scorching blue sky into a "shooting star" to symbolize his "heart's desire"—expressed in the picture of life flaring up beyond the "limits of the living." He desires that his life might be "a splendid blaze of beautiful moments lived to the full."[62] "Human Ashes" by Katsuzo Oda represents the work of nonprofessional writers who base their often starkly realistic stories on childhood memories. "The Colorless Paintings" by Ineko Sata depicts the depression of a painter who ceases to paint in color after her A-bomb experience. "The House of Hands" by Mitsuharu Inoue treats the fears of aftereffects of radiation disease through the story of an A-bomb survivor who, grown to womanhood, faces a difficult childbirth.

The remaining stories, "The Empty Can" by Kyoko Hayashi, "Fireflies" by Koko Ota, and "The Rite" by Hiroko Takenishi, all women who survived the A-bombing of Japan, illustrate the domestic effects of the devastation. H. Bruce Franklin sees these works as ascribing the genesis of atomic weapons, at least in part, to society's male domination and American fantasies of power.[63] In "The Empty Can," five Japanese women of middle age, all but one childless, reminisce about their school days and the intervening years. They remember a desolate classmate who brought a mysterious, seemingly empty can to school every day. The can, as they finally discover, contains the bones of the girl's mother and father. The narrator realizes how her entire life has been haunted by the memory of her classmate's desolation. The "Fire-

61. Kenzaburo Oe, ed., *The Crazy Iris and Other Stories of the Atomic Aftermath* (New York: Grove Press, 1985), p. 16.

62. Tamiki Hara, "The Land of Heart's Desire," in *The Crazy Iris*, p. 61.

63. H. Bruce Franklin, "The Bomb in the Home: Stories by Japanese and American Women Experts on Nuclearism" (Paper presented at the Modern Language Association Convention, New Orleans, December 28, 1988). Used by permission.

flies'' tells of the return visit of the author to Hiroshima in 1952, when she met Mitsuko Takada, the most hideously scarred of the *hibakusha*, and came to accept and love him. She comes to see the ''real monsters'' as those who used the bombs because ''they were afraid of losing their military balance of power with the Soviet Union.''[64] ''The Rite'' involves a woman survivor of Hiroshima who yearns to participate again in life, to marry and have children, but who cannot find any ritual to free her of her abominable death-obsessed memories.

Fictional Hibakusha: ''Hiroshima Joe''

In *Hiroshima Joe* by Martin Booth, antihero and *hibakusha* ex-POW Joseph Sandingham, broken by his experience of World War II, ekes out his existence in a cheap Hong Kong hotel room. Occasionally he meditates in a Buddhist monastery, visits a bargirl, or ''chases the dragon,'' a euphemism for visiting an opium den. Pitied and condemned by those who regard him as crazy, this man, shattered by the horrors of twentieth-century warfare and the death of his beloved comrade-in-arms, Bob, amazes the reader by the persistence of his compassion and will to survive. Caught finally between two kinds of death—from his worsening radiation disease and the threat of assassination by criminal thugs (as revenge for his killing of a mob boss and his mistress), Hiroshima Joe stoically chooses to terminate his life on Christmas Eve, 1952.

Joe vacillates between seeing himself as a pure, unworldly martyr, a refugee from materialistic European values, and a failure who has sinned by neglecting to act for the good of others. The abbott of the Trappist monastery to whom he confesses tells him he is good, for he displays ''concern for life'' by his persistence in trying to overcome the ''hornet'' of negativity. Joe's sexual attraction to a young boy resident at his hotel plays an important part in the story; the boy reminds him of his lover, lost in the ''filthy'' war, which Joe views as ''a disease upon the nature of men.'' The boy does not fully comprehend Joe's behavior toward him, knowing only that his parents and others consider the man dangerous and evil. Years later, it is the boy, grown to adulthood and a successful executive, who puts the memory of Joe in perspective by honoring his grave with an epitaph: ''He saw what no man should be made to see; he died fearing what we all must

---

64. Koko Ota, ''Fireflies,'' in *The Crazy Iris*, p. 100.

fear.''[65] *Hiroshima Joe* offers mature young adult readers insight into the existential dilemmas of an individual isolated from society by his grief over the terrors of war and his inability to make peace with himself. Booth's ironic vision, like Lanham's in *The Clock at 8:16*, elicits compassion for the protagonist's failure to find any sustaining life-affirming ethic.

These works of fiction and nonfiction telling the stories of the *hiba-kusha* can keep us from succumbing to amnesia for the unbearable, from becoming the victims of our own emotional defense mechanisms. The psychological fallout is there whether we wish to admit it or not. As William Dickey wrote in his poem "Armageddon," describing a student of twenty,

> for to him it is already there
> like the underwear that he puts on in the morning.
> It is with him all the time, as his shadow is.[66]

Readers of Jung or of Hans Christian Andersen do not need to be reminded how perilous it is to deny the shadow. The books that vivify the experiences of the *hibakusha* help us confront the shadow and move beyond it. Franz Kafka in one of his letters once likened poetry to an ax whose function it is to break up the frozen sea within us: to keep us from freezing emotionally, to make us aware of the choices.[67] It is up to us to look, to see, and—in the ancient injunction—"choose this day life or death." It is up to us in our roles as educators to clarify the choices for young people. Visualizing nuclear doom and alternatives to it are processes we can encourage and bring to fruition in those young people whose destiny it is to live at this crossroads in human history where the choice of futures is still possible.

Hibakusha as Harbingers of a Paradigm Shift

Many of the accounts considered here have featured *hibakusha*, actual or fictional, whose actions accord with Eisler's gylanic values, that

65. Martin Booth, *Hiroshima Joe* (Boston: Atlantic Monthly Press, 1985), pp. 95, 107, 114, 190–91.

66. William Dickey, "Armageddon," in *Writing in a Nuclear Age*, ed. Jim Schley (*NER/BLQ: New England Review and Bread Loaf Quarterly* 5, no. 4 (Summer 1983); reprint, Hanover, N.H.: University Press of New England, 1984), p. 43.

67. See "Anne Sexton," in *Contemporary American Poetry*, ed. A. Poulin, Jr. (Boston: Houghton Mifflin, 1971), p.381.

is, with awareness of and respect for their links with other human beings, and a consciousness, often implicit rather than articulated, of the fragility and preciousness of the totality of life, the total ecosystem. Eisler points out how in Western society, based as it is on "andocratic" assumptions about the nature of power as "domination" of the weaker by the stronger, the "feminine" view of "power as responsibility," requiring caring rather than oppressing, has been devalued, relegated to a secondary place.[68] Yet it is these qualities that characterize the "survivor ethic" of the *hibakusha*, who have been forced by incredible suffering to recognize that true strength lies in linking, not in vanquishing. Their recognition represents a paradigm shift to a more "feminine" perspective on human suffering that views all persons as having inherent worth, regardless of race, gender, nationality, genetic purity, or any other basis on which people have throughout history been oppressed or excluded from sympathy. Those who share this vision are the mythic champions of a global compassion. They locate the Enemy not in others or in nature, but in whatever blocks human potential for lives of dignity, self-fulfillment, and service.

The life-affirming ethic of the *hibakusha* relates not just to Eisler's gylanic values but also to Joseph W. Meeker's prizing of the comedic approach to life in *The Comedy of Survival: In Search of an Environmental Ethic*. Aldo Leopold's "Land Ethic" is pertinent as well: the principle that "a thing is right when it tends to preserve the integrity, stability, and beauty of the biotic community."[69] As the thought of these three thinkers and many others shows, the time is ripe for the global adoption of the ethic of empathy, stemming from the recognition of the underlying unity of all life.

Cynics will dismiss this way of thinking as naive nonsense; skeptics will rightly question how such a view of things can cope with the Shadow, the dark side of human nature. An answer lies in certain concepts from archetypal psychology, where the Enemy lurking within, no longer supposed to be external, is no longer projected on others. As Arnold Mindell, author of *Coma: Key to Awakening*, remarked in an interview, we must each "work at our own edges,"[70] meaning the edges of the abyss within ourselves. In mythological terms the dragon within represents bondage to one's own ego. Medieval thinkers called this internal dragon "cupiditas." It is possible at least to imagine a world

68. Riane Eisler, *The Chalice and the Blade: Our History, Our Future* (San Francisco: Harper, 1987), pp. 104–05.

69. Aldo Leopold, *A Sand County Almanac* (New York: Oxford Univ. Pr., 1966), pp. 224–25. Leopold redefines "community" through this concept.

70. Arnold Mindell, *Coma: Key to Awakening* (Boston: Shambhala, 1989).

where "war" could be confined always to the discipline of our own inner conflicts, contained and resolved on an intrapersonal level. In such a context, each must be master of himself or herself, allowing no external rulers to lead us into conflict against others. This may be the essential qualification of today's hero or hera. Such self-mastery is ultimately the only viable basis for true global harmony. It may be that our species can survive the nuclear peril only as we individually evolve in spiritual insight, self-rule, and compassion. Thereby it may be possible to overcome the fear of personal annihilation that makes us annihilate others.

The actions of the *hibakusha* suggest that technologies of destruction might ultimately be defused by the individual's transformation of consciousness to a recognition of connections between human beings, other forms of life, and ultimately all creation. Collective hostilities rest on fear, and fear can be cast out only by those strong enough to risk themselves in loving relationships. These relationships in turn rest upon attention to, dialogue with, and questioning of others.

Milan Kundera, a Czech novelist, writes in *The Book of Laughter and Forgetting* that "love is a constant interrogation."[71] Commenting on this concept of love as a questioning of the Other, David Barash and Judith Eve Lipton note that inquiry can lead to "genuine knowledge and intimacy, because the loved one feels valued enough to be heard." They believe the process can be effective with "enemies" as well, helping the Other become real—"not a projection of self or self-interest." They go on to assert, "If the nations of the world are to survive, we must replace easy, longwinded, self-serving answers with sympathetic questions," and instead of "intimidating" others, relate to them.[72]

The relational art of questioning—of seeking dialogue rather than debate—has inestimable survival value. Poet Allan Ginsberg plumbed the problem of fragmented, splintered relationships when he remarked that all human beings have a deep longing and grief within them, largely unrecognized (almost certainly by others and often even by themselves), and that recognition of and dialogue concerning these needs in each other would go a long way to reducing hostilities.[73] He was speaking in the context of interpersonal relationships, yet his insight has global pertinence as well.

71. Milan Kundera, *The Book of Laughter and Forgetting*, trans. from the Czech by Michael Henry Heim (New York: Penguin Books, 1981), p. 163.

72. David P. Barash and Judith Eve Lipton, *The Caveman and the Bomb* (New York: McGraw-Hill, 1985), p. 225.

73. Allan Ginsberg, interview, June 12, 1988, National Public Radio, WAMC, Albany, New York.

In a word, the post-Hiroshima world demands compassion. It also requires a mythology of peace that can entice us to shed our outmoded mythologies of war. Myth and symbol, with their power to transform consciousness, and stories mythologizing the *hibakusha* may hold the key.

Ancient myth can also provide images of a "linking" cosmic order. As Andrew Bard Schmookler points out, King Arthur's Roundtable provides a model for envisioning "a cosmic order in which all are accepted," for in its circle shape it expresses "the shape of peace and abundance." Seated in a circle, "each [person] feels special, sitting at the head of his own banquet."[74]

Schmookler sees the struggle for domination, which informs the Warrior's mentality, as motivated by a need to erect armor around the "feminine" within himself. A similar psychology undergirds "sexual possessiveness" and an insistence upon the "veiling" of the female. Personal relationships, particularly those between men and women, establish the prototypes for the way people deal with larger social and political relationships. The key to a *novo order secolorum* lies in recovery of the ancient wholeness and balance of masculine and feminine. Schmookler finds a model for this wholeness in the "bio-civisphere," defined as a biosphere governed by a consciousness that "transcends boundary." Such a consciousness can overcome the "structural fragmentation of our macrosystems" and generate peace, humility, and a tolerance for diversity.[75]

A contemporary student of shamanism, Joan Halifax has pointed out that the Warrior metaphor itself is in need of revisioning. In *The Way of the Warrior*, she speaks of the "warrior" who does battle with the self, who "defends the future against the aggressor still lurking in his own psyche."[76] As the venerated Krishnamurti once said, "The only battleground is the self." This is a truth that transcends all considerations of race, class, and gender. The portrayals of the *hibakusha* provide an exemplary pattern of a means whereby the psychic "aggressor" within, whose natural impulse is to strike out in anger and revenge, may be quelled for the sake of establishing a compassionate relationship to others. I propose that the *hibakusha* may serve for us all as exemplars of Einstein's "new manner of thinking," a thinking not divorced from feeling and intuition. As such, they show the life-affirming ethic in action.

74. Andrew Bard Schmookler, *Out of Weakness: Healing the Wounds That Drive Us to War* (New York: Bantam, 1988), p. 191.

75. Ibid., pp. 170, 311.

76. Joan Halifax, *Way of the Warrior* (San Francisco, Calif.: New Dimensions, n.d.). Sound cassette.

Appendix

Sadako's Wish

I dreamed I saw a thousand cranes
All flying in the sky,
The cranes affirmed Sadako's wish
That she would never die,
That she would never die.

"The legend says you'll have your wish
Sadako," she was told,
"Your wish comes true, my little one,
When a thousand cranes you fold,
A thousand cranes you fold."

Sadako, two in forty-five
Grew ill in fifty-three,
'Twas then she started folding cranes,
Now it's up to you and me,
It's up to you and me.

She folded cranes until she made
Six hundred forty-seven.
She didn't fold a thousand cranes
Before she went to heaven,
Before she went to heaven.

But that little girl made many friends
Who loved her deep and true.
They said, "We'll fold your thousand cranes,
It's up to me and you,
It's up to me and you."

They built Sadako a monument
Where all of us can bring
The cranes we fold, the dreams we hold,
The songs we have to sing,
The songs we have to sing:

Of peace on earth, and life for all,
And love under the sun.
Please fold your cranes and pray for life,
And know we all are one,
And know we all are one.

I dreamed I saw a thousand cranes
All flying in the sky,
The cranes affirm Sadako's wish
That she would never die,
And she will never die.

—Elise Harvey

Samantha's Wish

I dreamed I saw two little girls,
With hands across the world,
Singing songs of peace and love,
With every boy and girl,
With every boy and girl.

Samantha Smith to Andropov
A letter she did write:
"God made the world for us to live
In peace, and not to fight,
In peace, and not to fight."

We all can make a difference,
Samantha showed the world.
Please write and speak what you believe,
Every boy and girl.
Every boy and girl.

The children teach the older folks
Sincere and simple truth,
Folding cranes in peace and love,
The lessons of our youth,
The lessons of our youth.

I dreamed I saw a thousand cranes
All flying in the sky.
The cranes affirm Samantha's wish
The world would never die,
And the world must never die.

—Elise Harvey

Poems reprinted by permission: "Elise Harvey thanks all the children who sing those songs and fold peace cranes."

CHAPTER 4

The Peace Pilgrim as Hero/Hera

In *Peace Pilgrim: Her Life and Work in Her Own Words*, the narrator tells a parable for our time. It is worth quoting here in full:

This Strange Creature Called Man

An outsider might view this strange creature called Man this way:

A Being from another world parked his spaceship in an isolated spot. The next morning he passed a military camp, where he saw men sticking knives fastened to odd-looking poles into bags of straw. "What is this?" he asked a uniformed youth. "Bayonet practice," answered the youth. "We're practicing on dummies. We have to learn to use the bayonet a certain way to kill a man. Of course we don't kill many men with bayonets. We kill most of them with bombs." "But why should you want to learn to kill men?" exclaimed the Being, aghast. "We don't," said the youth bitterly. "We are sent here against our will and we don't know what to do about it." That afternoon the Being passed through a large city. He noticed a crowd gathered in a public square to see uniformed youth being decorated with a medal. "Why is he being decorated with a medal?" inquired the Being. "Because he killed a hundred men in battle," said the man beside him. The Being looked with horror upon the youth who had killed a hundred men and walked away. In another part of the city the Being heard a radio announcing loudly that a certain man was soon to be executed. "Why is he to be put to death?" asked the Being. "Because he killed two men," said the man beside him. The Being walked away bewildered. That evening, after the Being had thought the matter over, he opened his notebook and wrote: "It seems that all youths are forced to learn how to kill men efficiently. Those who succeed in killing a large number of men are rewarded with medals. Those who turn out to be poor killers and succeed in killing only a few men are punished by being put to death." The Being shook his head sadly and added a postscript: *It looks as though this strange creature called Man will exterminate himself very quickly.* [1]

The real-life Peace Pilgrim, who crossed the United States on foot six times between 1953 and 1981, vowed to walk as a witness for her cause, and to remain a wanderer until humankind learned the ways of peace. On her seventh crossing, as she was being escorted by a friend to a speaking engagement in Indiana, she was killed instantly in a head-on collision. Peace (as she preferred to be called) was motivated by her deeply felt belief that the "way of peace" was to "*overcome evil with good, and falsehood with truth, and hatred with love.*" Homeless, penniless, and simply clothed in a blue tunic, slacks, and tennis shoes, she spoke of peace to all who would listen at all levels: between nations, among groups, between individuals, and, most important, within, for only inner peace can ultimately banish war. She believed the discovery of nuclear energy heralded a new era, which "calls for a new renaissance to lift us to a higher level of understanding so that we will be able to cope with the problems of this new age."[2] It was characteristic of her positive outlook that she referred to nuclear energy, not nuclear weapons.

Like many others who have developed spiritual insight, Peace found her inspiration in a mountaintop experience.[3] Out walking in a beautiful natural setting early in the morning, she experienced a spiritual awakening: "I knew *timelessness* and *spacelessness* and *lightness*." Everything seemed transformed; all things wore a halo, and every flower and bush emanated light. Flecks of gold floated in the air. The most striking part of the "illumination," however, was "the realization of the oneness of all creation"—and she felt a "*oneness with that which permeates all and binds all together and gives life to all.*"[4]

Peace Pilgrim's story can be read in more detail in the sources cited. She provides a model of living one's conviction as well as a real-life

1. *Peace Pilgrim: Her Life and Work in Her Own Words,* comp. some of her friends (Santa Fe, N.Mex.: Friends of Peace Pilgrim, 1983), pp. 106–7. Reprinted with permission.

2. *Steps toward Inner Peace: Suggested Uses of Harmonious Principles for Human Living: A Discourse by Peace Pilgrim* (Hemet, Calif.: Friends of Peace Pilgrim, n.d.), unp. This 32-page booklet is available at no charge from Friends of Peace Pilgrim, 43480 Cedar Avenue, Hemet, CA 92344. Also available are a "Peace Pilgrim Cassette Tape," a 90-minute audiocassette of her speeches before audiences, and (for loan) "A Day in the Life of a Pilgrim,"a VHS videotape made for the "PM Magazine"television show.

3. See Dolores LaChapelle, *Earth Wisdom,* photographs by Steven J. Meyers, drawings by Randy LaChapelle (Los Angeles: Guild of Tutors Press, 1978), chaps. 3, 4, "Sacred Mountains."

4. *Peace Pilgrim,* p. 21.

paradigm of the biophile. To those who would dismiss her as a starry-eyed idealist, she replied, "In this nuclear age the idealists have become the only realists. . . . The nuclear bomb says to you, 'Make peace or perish!'"[5]

Despite the lack in mainstream literature of a strong mythology of peace and models of the peacemaker as a heroic figure, certain narratives depict a peace pilgrim type of protagonist who sometimes fits the definition of the biophile. As seen in the previous chapter, literature depicting life in the shadow of the bomb sometimes features a character who grows into a peace pilgrim–biophile role. Here I shall consider three related themes: the discovery of the "peace child" who sees through the sham of a war mythology and a falsely heroic tradition of war; the peace–inner peace–nature link; and the growth of the biophile into a peace activist, a "witness" in the Quaker sense, who devotes energies to forestalling the inherently suicidal arms race or the proliferation of nuclear power plants.

Each of the three themes I have identified relates to peace, yet they are played out against a background world in precarious balance on the brink of nuclear disaster. This threatened world calls on the hero to live humanly and hopefully despite the "balance of terror," in Herman Kahn's vivid phrase. The first theme, the discovery of the child, or the "inner child", pictures the clarity of the child's vision in contrast to the astigmatic, myopic vision of jaded adults. Typically the child sees the value of preserving life rather than clinging to a falsely heroic war mythology. This theme often merges with the second theme of a harmonious relationship to the natural world, a relationship children intuitively experience. Within this framework, the biophile is the ideal or heroic kind of human being. A third theme presents the life-affirming hero as a peace activist.

The Discovery of the Child: Nature as a Link to Inner Peace

A number of picture books in various languages from a variety of countries feature the themes of peace and a harmonious relationship to the natural world from a child's perspective. Concern over the destructive capacities of nuclear power and stockpiled weapons are often interwoven with concern over nuclear war. The books to be surveyed here link the biophile to these related themes.

5. *Peace Pilgrim*, pp. 106,108.

A survey article by Ruth Kath, "Nuclear Education in Contemporary German Children's Literature," analyzes a number of key titles. Kath explores three picture books on the issue of the impact of nuclear power on ecology, an issue with "long-term and very crucial implications for the quality of life that coming generations, including young readers of children's literature, can hope to experience as adults."[6] Three German-language picture books are examined closely: Erich Kastner's *Die Konferenz der Tiere* (The Conference of the Animals); Walter Schmogner's *Das neue Drachenbuch* (The New Dragonbook); and Colin Thiele and Mary Milton's *Die Ttupak! (Die Kaputt!)* (originally published as *The Sknuks/The Skunks)*. Gudrun Pausewang's *Die letzten Kinder von Schewenborn* (The Last Children of Schevenborn), called by Kath a *Lord of the Flies* about nuclear winter, is given brief attention along with several other titles.[7] Though Kath analyzes primarily the issue of nuclear power, not nuclear war, the epigraph to Kath's article suggests the broad context of peace education: She quotes Mahatma Gandhi's often-cited statement: "If we are to reach real peace in this world, and if we are to carry on a real war against war, we shall have to begin with the children."

Das neue Drachenbuch by Schmogner tells a fantasy tale of a red-green polka-dotted dragon who undertakes a journey, accompanied by his animal friends, in search of a place where nature is unspoiled by pollution. Their pilgrimage is reminiscent, particularly in the illustrations, of the quest of the animals for a home in the traditional folktale "The Musicians of Bremen." The dragon, his mouse friend, a dog sickened from auto exhaust, a bee fleeing the poisoned leaves of plants, a cow, a pig, and a chicken, similarly disgruntled, are joined by a bird, a butterfly, and a snake in search of a poison-free environment. When they find the lovely looking pond, they believe their troubles are over, but then the doomsaying Frog warns them not to trust appearances. The pond has become deadly, filled with radioactive waste from the nuclear power plant nearby. In a splendid touch of irony, Schmogner depicts a factory aptly named "Future, Ltd." His most striking image conveys his vision of nuclear winter: a defoliated tree (shades of *Waiting for Godot* by Samuel Beckett?) with its

6. Ruth Kath, "Nuclear Education in Contemporary German Children's Literature," *The Lion and the Unicorn: The International Scene* 18 (1986): 31.

7. Gudrun Pausewang's book is discussed in chapter 5. Kath also includes Georg Bydlinski and Hans Domenego's *Macht die Erde nicht kaput!* (Freiburg: Herder, 1984), dealing with pollution, and Frank Ruprecht's *Jakob's Traum* (Stuttgart: Otto Maier, 1983), a portrayal of the arms race in a manner "much like the American Dr. Seuss's *Butter Battle Book,* but less graphic, more subtle." See Kath," Nuclear Education," pp. 38–39.

trunk terminating in a death's-head, and a dead bird at its feet. As Kath points out, Schmogner's closing hortatory words are aimed at adults: The animals plead, in chorus, "Why don't you love us? Why do you only think of yourselves? You can't live without us!" And again, "Stop destroying the world . . . for us and for the sake of your children!"[8]

Kastner's *Die Konferenz der Tiere* (The Conference of the Animals) portrays a revolt by animals disgusted with the ineffectuality of human "peace" conferences, which, as Kath notes, produce "abundant press releases, but no peace." The elephant's lament bemoans many human ills ("enough to drive me crazy"): refugee problems, the atom bomb, strikes, hunger in China, and the human propensity for "destruction." "Whenever they want to construct something, it turns into the Tower of Babel!" The elephant's sympathies are with the children. The close of the book is utopian—animals and reason triumph, an international peace treaty is signed, military forces are dissolved, and the world is freed of "shooting and explosive weapons."[9] Winifred Kaminski calls this an enduring fable that avoids the pitfall of sentimentality by the author's modeling of a process of achieving peace through "nonhierarchical" interrelationships (cf. the partnership model) and jargon-free communication.[10]

Die Ttupak! (Die Kaputt!), the German translation of Colin Thiele's *The Sknuks/The Skunks*, is the most striking of the books surveyed and may be called a contemporary vision of paradise lost. It describes the glory of the Sknuks' original home in shimmering prose:

> one of the most beautiful planets in the universe. It was a place of sparkling water and green grass and golden flowers. There were birds like rainbows and fish like arrows of fire. There were animals swifter than sunlight and butterflies softer than mist. There were rubies, opals, and sapphires, silver like beads of frost, and copper like sheets of sunshine. There were caverns of coal and brooding mountains of iron. There was everything the Sknuks could wish for.[11]

The snake in this paradise is uncontrolled greed, which leads the Sknuks to plunder their lovely Earth, waste its resources, foul its envi-

8. Kath, "Nuclear Education," p. 34.
9. Ibid., p. 35.
10. Winifred Kaminski, "War and Peace in Recent German Children's Literature," trans. and adapted by J. D. Stahl, *Children's Literature: Annual of the Modern Language Division on Children's Literature and the Children's Literature Association* 15 (1987), p. 62.
11. Colin Thiele, *The Sknuks/The Skunks*, illus. Mary Milton (Rigby, Ltd., 1977; distributed by Weldon Publishing, 372 Eastern Valley Way, Willoughby, NSW68, Australia), unp.

ronment, and make war on the wise and friendly visitors from outer space who wish to help them. The Sknuks are described as "greedy" and "ruthless," and without conscience. Thiele's most dramatic image juxtaposes a deadly cobra and a thread to dramatize the risks of playing with atomic power: "'They even played games with the centres of atoms—it was like walking a cobra on a leash made of string." The fruits of the Sknuks' cupidity and false pride are dire: They make a "waste-land" of their home and bring about their own demise. Here we can see the familiar mythic theme of the Fall from innocence and the archetype of the Orphan who becomes the Wanderer, exiled from paradise because of folly and betrayal of natural law.

Throughout the narrative Thiele makes use of inverted spelling— *Htrae* for Earth', *nam* for a father Sknuk, *dik* for a little Sknuk, and so on—an orthographic reflection of the Sknuks' inverted values. Since this is a story for those of tender years, Thiele allows a few Sknuks to survive high in the mountains, led by "an old Sknukish prophet . . . half as old as Time." The aged wise man, implicitly a biophile, teaches a new but really ancient wisdom:

> Learn—and be speedy—
> Not to make wars,
> Not to be greedy
> And break natural laws.
> Listen, and learn well,
> Every last day
> If you hope to survive
> On the good planet Htrae.

The insistent didacticism of the tale is lightened and redeemed by Thiele's delightful poetic prose and Milton's splendid artwork. Unhappily the book is out of print in English; it would be a valuable reissue for children of the United States and England, comparable in theme to Bill Peet's *The Wump World* and Dr. Seuss's *The Lorax* but surpassing both in visual and verbal beauty.

Nuclear education tends, as Kath's article shows, to emphasize the perils of nuclear power plant pollution of the environment and to teach, either directly or by implication, the values epitomized in the biophile's love for the Earth. The terrors of nuclear disaster and possible total annihilation implied by the mushroom cloud are held at a distance, presumably out of respect for the emotional delicacy of the young. These books stress instead the responsibility for choice in determining human destiny, and in Kath's opinion they agree in showing that "the awesome responsibility for the use of nuclear power is in the hands of a race with such abominable track records for tolerance and self-preservation." If the authors/illustrators seem despairing about the ability of adults to remedy the precarious position of the human race, their act of addressing their works to children nonetheless suggests their belief that the young might "rectify" the "foolish and potentially deadly" acts of their elders.[12] The new generation holds the key to the achievement of a worldwide survival ethic.

Young Activists as Peace Pilgrims

Certain other novels portray young people as peace activists. In these books, the young protagonists rally behind the cause of peace or the health of the Earth, energetically protesting the arms race or the operation of nuclear power plants.

"The Peace Book" and "The Peace Child"

In *The Peace Book* by Bernard Benson, a scientist-inventor turned peace activist, the storyteller-narrator relates a tale intended to inculcate "the imagination of peace." It is a fable urging nuclear disarmament, wherein the young child protagonist (whose father is a nuclear weapons researcher) puzzles over the stupidity of power-hungry adults.

The child's precocious vision of peace is posed against the stupidity and linguistic dishonesty of grown-ups. A good example of the latter is the acronym TLD, used by bureaucrats to mean "tolerable level of destruction." The only way to peace, as the wise child sees, lies in protecting our neighbors from ourselves, or, as someone once observed, we will make no progress until "they" become "we." The child urges the adoption of the "Rule of the World," the principle that "protecting ourselves from our neighbors is the path of arms and leads to WAR!" whereas "protecting our neighbors from *ourselves* is the path of disarmament, and leads to PEACE!"

Reviewed as adult fiction by *Booklist*, Benson's book was roundly faulted for its "cloying" and "precocious" tone and "sticky-sweet" line drawings.[13] From a literary point of view, these are weighty objec-

12. Kath, "Nuclear Education," p. 38.
13. Review of *The Peace Book*, by Bernard Benson, *Booklist* 79, no. 7 (December 1, 1982): 466.

tions, but they need to be balanced by the thematic value of the author's indictment of the deadening and deadly rhetoric of euphemisms and acronyms that pollute public discourse on nuclear topics. Though it is doubtful that any child will read the book spontaneously, it has possibilities as a read-aloud to spur discussion.

The Peace Book debuted as a drama with the title *The Peace Child,* an adaptation by David Woollcombe, a British playwright who produced it in London in 1981. Since that time there have been more than 260 performances of the play in the United States and elsewhere. Like the book from which it was adapted, *The Peace Child* reflects Benson's quest for a "new kind of truth," a search that began when he abandoned his work on missile guidance systems and turned to the study of Tibetan Buddhism. He believes the Tibetan culture to be more steeped than any other in the understanding of the human mind. Benson describes his vision as closely connected with spirituality and with the capacity of inventive genius to keep seeing things fresh, including the ability to see that the emperor, although in this case bearing arms, is naked.[14]

The play, like the book, has been ridiculed as a "tract," but despite its heavy-handedness, we do well to remember, as Phyllis LaFarge says in her commentary on Benson in *The Strangelove Legacy: Children, Parents and Teachers in the Nuclear Age,* that *Uncle Tom's Cabin* by Harriet Beecher Stowe was similarly derided, along with many "other books that have helped change consciousness."[15]

"The Fragile Flag"

Jane Langton's *The Fragile Flag* also presents the child as a peace pilgrim, the victor in a crusade against nuclear arms. Georgie, a nine-year-old girl, leads a children's march from Massachusetts to Washington D.C., to protest the launching of a new doomsday machine the president calls, in a linguistic twist typical of nuclear misnomers, "The Peace Missile." Georgie becomes acquainted with the celebrated psychic child actress, Veronica, who joins the crusaders enroute. When Veronica falls into a trance in Temple Beth Tikvah, she envisions the Earth catching fire and turning to ashes.[16] The fragile flag, borne by fragile children, becomes the potent peace symbol that effects a change in consciousness on the part of the country's commander in chief.

14. Benson is quoted in Phyllis LaFarge, *The Strangelove Legacy: Children, Parents and Teachers in the Nuclear Age* (New York: Harper and Row, 1987), p. 147.
15. LaFarge, *The Strangelove Legacy,* p. 150.
16. Jane Langton, *The Fragile Flag* (New York: Harper and Row, 1984), pp.7, 175–76.

On seeing the flag the president reenacts Veronica's visionary experience, seeing the nation he leads in a new way—not composed of Republicans, Democrats, soldiers, sailors, fighter pilots, and so on but of

> a mighty swarm of children . . . kids in their heyday, their springtime, their green prime, hungry for the good things of earth that were their due. . . . They were spinning seeds exploding from the tree of the present moment, sent whirling into the future as far as the winds would blow. They were careless and hopeful and greedy, they were grinning and expectant, healthy and strong, and altogether worthwhile.[17]

In mythological terms, the president sees the children in their essential Being, as expressions of the One; they become "transparent to transcendence." The nature imagery—green things in their prime, the "spinning seeds" of life, and the wondrous expectancy of youth—all work their magic on his imagination. But this fantasy-celebration of life is followed by a "flash of blinding light"—like the *pika* over Hiroshima. Struck by psychic lightning, he is converted to the mind of peace. He cancels the "Peace Missile" plan, having seen its true demonic nature. His decision brings into relief the two epigraphs of the novel:

> The flag of our nation stands for a strong
> defense in a dangerous world.
> > James R. Toby, President of the U.S.
> > The White House, Washington, D.C.

> The flag means American people being friends with all the other people.
> > Georgie Hall, Grade 4, Alcott School
> > Concord, Massachusetts

The president sees that the strength the flag symbolizes is meaningless unless it grows from friendship among all peoples on the Earth. He has achieved the holistic vision natural to Georgie.

"It Can't Happen to Me"

Arnold Madison's *It Can't Happen to Me* presents the child as a questioner, a seeker, and a choice-maker rather than an overt peace activist through the story of a community under threat of a radiation leak from a nuclear power plant. The title alludes to the mentality of denial that made the Nazi persecution of the Jews possible—the "it can't happen

17. Ibid., pp. 264–65.

here'' syndrome. This is made explicit in the book at several points, for example, in the parallel drawn between the enforced evacuation of the townspeople and the historic evacuation of the Jews to concentration camps. Sandy Farrell, a teenager who lives near the Rocky Falls Nuclear Power Plant, tells the story. Her difficulties with her boyfriend Bryan's controlling and possessive approach to their relationship parallel on a human level the misuse of power implicit in subjecting nature to a potentially destructive technology. The opening paragraph describes the power plant exhaling its steam ''like a tired, old man, resigning himself to his outdated views and expectancies,'' effectively conveying the tone of disdain for nuclear power.

Sandy has two mentors in the novel—Mr. Woods, a teacher who insists his students think for themselves and act on their own convictions, and Marta, Sandy's strong, self-assured friend who has the internal freedom and strength Sandy covets for herself.

When Sandy's class in Problems of Democracy learns that their local media probably suppressed the truth about the danger of radiation leaking from the plant, they decide as concerned citizens to write a guest editorial in the *Rocky Falls Gazette*, protesting the failure to render ''prompt, truthful reporting of information'' and the consequent undermining of ''the basic tenets of democracy and the people's faith in public agencies.'' Against Bryan's wishes, Sandy signs the letter, challenging her boyfriend's contention that Mr. Wood is using the class for his own political ends. Mr. Wood has helped Sandy distinguish between being ''for oneself'' in a positive sense (directing our lives in the direction of our ''bliss,'' to use Joseph Campbell's term), and the ''sick'' use of others to gain our selfish ends. She is prepared to affirm her identity through his observation, ''Just keep in mind that sometimes other people become shocked when we follow our own route rather than the one they anticipated we would travel.''[18] In mythic terms, she separates from the mass, defining her integrity—moving toward psychic ''wholeness.''

The role of language in the manipulation of others in both public and personal relationships is an important theme, seen in the radio announcement on the power plant crisis, a classic example of doublespeak:

> Officials today announced that they would have a statement tomorrow morning about the problem at the nuclear power facility. Dr. Edward Rask did admit the plant experienced a small event early Satur-

18. Arnold Madison, *It Can't Happen to Me* (New York: Scholastic, 1981), pp. 100, 102, 105.

day morning, but that there was no radiation leak now. Whatever it was, has been contained.[19]

Whereupon the newscaster goes blandly on to sports events, implicitly reducing the "small event" to the status of fun and games.

As Sandy takes control of her own life, Bryan learns to do the same, transcending his previous false identity as a mouthpiece for his father's convictions. Sandy galvanizes his energies by sharing with him the three questions Marta has posed to her as a guide to her own existential quest: "Who am I? Where am I going? How do I get there?"[20] Through dramatizing this existential dilemma, the novel provides teenagers with a strong heroic model of young people empowered to find their "centers" and make authentic choices. Although Sandy does not engage in activism as such, she reaches a state of mind where action on her own convictions becomes possible.

"Band of Angels"

Band of Angels by Julian Thompson resembles the novels of Robert Cormier in depicting adult treachery against children. In this thriller five teenagers become the unwitting prey of secret agents bent on destroying them to insure against a possible threat to national security.

Eric and Sweets, the two FBI men, are assigned to find Jordan Paradise (born Amos Goodspeed, Jr.), son of two researchers who many years ago developed a supervirus coveted by the government as a weapon. Realizing the dangers of their invention and unwilling to contribute to germ warfare, the elder Goodspeeds destroyed the virus and the records of their research and then committed suicide, first making certain their infant son would be cared for by a friend, Dorothy Simon, who has assumed the name Karen Archibald. For years Karen and Jordan have lived on the run, eluding their pursuers, but as the novel opens Karen is killed by a hit-and-run driver, leaving Jordan, in true gothic tradition, an orphan with a mysterious past. From Orphan, he develops into the Wanderer, finding a friend—and eventually a sweetheart—in Riley Roux, daughter of affluent parents suitably kept in the background throughout the melodrama, cultivating their svelte figures at a "fat farm."

The novel presents an interracial romance (Jordan is black, Riley white), depicts nudity and premarital sex as natural, and displays a

19. Ibid., p. 46.
20. Ibid., p. 169.

predilection for androgyny.[21] The five angels of the title are energetic peace pilgrims, multiethnic and global in their human sympathies, clear-eyed in their view of the nuclear threat as the "dragon" of our times, and confident of their ability to bring about a significant change in consciousness, thereby salvaging the future. As Michael says of himself, he is a true futurist, one who wants to "be there when it [the future] happens," not to succumb to the "reverse lemming effect"— the process whereby endangered people deny the nuclear threat and "feed on one another's ostrich-headedness."[22]

Jordan, Riley, and Michael begin their quest at Jettison City, seeking Jordan's admission to study, where they are joined by two more seekers of adventure sympathetic with their cause—David Gracey and the precocious fifteen-year-old Lisa. The band journeys on toward Shangri-La, a wilderness preserve owned by Riley's parents. Their peace pilgrim energies are aroused when, at a rally of the Futurists of America on the university campus, the war mythology of Alan Mason clashes with Jordan's belief in the abolition of nukes. Inspired by his love of Riley, Jordan believes "kids" worldwide could be persuaded to sign a pledge stating "I . . . a free human being, will never willingly take part in the manufacture, transport, or use of a nuclear weapon." Whereas the traditional hero may have faced a fire-breathing dragon, these young people face the dragons of our time—nuclear warheads and the mentality that engenders them. Nuclear war is the issue of the eighties, says Michael—"what civil rights was to the sixties." Awareness of a satirical, comic, antiwar literary tradition breaks through when Lisa remarks that a "date" strike by girls between the ages of twelve and sixteen might help win a moratorium on nuclear weapons. The intellectual Michael alludes to the similar strategy of the women in ancient Greece, though Euripides' *Lysistrata* is not explicitly named.[23]

Riley adds another idea, the wearing of buttons declaring NEVER by kids worldwide to signify their having taken "the pledge." Here is a nice parallel between resisting bombaholic mentality and the Alcoholics Anonymous approach of pledging abstinence. To make this seem less naive, Thompson is careful to express opposing viewpoints, as when Michael points out the likelihood that the pledge would be considered "stupid, immature, or even disloyal" by adults, who

21. An example occurs when Riley's father lightly boasts of having raised his two daughters "like boys with tits" (p. 68), a statement Thompson leaves unexplored, though it seems disturbingly insensitive to the reality of masculine and feminine principles.

22. Julian Thompson, *Band of Angels* (New York: Scholastic, 1986), p. 28.

23. Ibid., pp. 159, 236, 244–45.

would "blow kids away with so-called 'facts' and 'information' that they'd claim to have." David counters with the statement that it is the adults who have messed up, and they are the "stupid" ones.

The novel's portrayal of adults as almost unremittingly corrupt or fatuous raises the question of fairness and balance. Karen Archibald, Jordan's protector, is an exception, but she is killed in the first chapter of the book. Riley's parents seem shallow and conceited despite the fact that they have managed to raise two decent, even admirable, teenagers. The resident faculty advisor (a sociology professor who calls himself an "untenured *peon*") proves despicable when he offers temporary shelter to the band and proceeds to attempt to break into the young women's room. Sweets, one of the FBI agents, begins as reprehensible but undergoes a transformation when he experiences a vision of the five youngsters as "a band of angels."[24] There may, Thompson suggests, be some hope for adults after all.

In a hair-raising dénouement, Eric, the other FBI agent, meets a fate befitting a villain, the band of teenagers escapes with the help of a mysterious "wild survivalist," and they never know of the plot to kill them. The lasting impression in a reader's mind may well be the image of confident, clear-sighted, purposeful peace pilgrims, all the more appealing to a youthful audience because depicted as far superior to adults. They relate in a gylanic, partnership fashion, and archetypally fall into the Wanderer and Peace Warrior categories. Although their pilgrimage into a natural setting parallels their concern with peace, Thompson does not portray them as conscious biophiles.

"Children as Teachers of Peace"

There is much to be learned from children, as G. G. Jampolsky, editor of *Children as Teachers of Peace*, has demonstrated. The book gives numerous examples of children's completions of the sentence opener, "Peace is . . ." Many of the youngsters voice fears of nuclear destruction and anger at adult obtuseness: Typical of these is Caitlin, age ten, who says to her senator,

> You probably won't pay any attention to me but I would like you to know one thing. I want to live! I want to be able to grow up and have a family! I want to have a job and be happy! But all I have to look forward to is being killed by a nuclear bomb.[25]

24. Ibid., pp. 117, 239, 241, 124–25, 254.
25. G. G. Jampolsky, *Children as Teachers of Peace*, foreword by Hugh Prather (Millbrae, Calif.: Celestial Arts, 1982), p. 83.

The circle—universal metaphor of wholeness and unity—appears in the comment of Bill, age eleven, who imagines teaching world leaders to refrain from quarreling (note the echo of the typical adult addressing children), to be silent and look around so they could see

> a circle, A circle of peace, a circle of people.
> They would find that they had stumbled upon,
> The fact that peace is togetherness, all nations one.[26]

The imaginations of children offer much wisdom in the quest for peace and healing. Novelist Walker Percy expresses this truth in *The Thanatos Syndrome* as Father Smith recounts what the Blessed Virgin said to six Yugoslavian children when she appeared to them in a vision:

> you must not lose hope . . . Because if you keep hope and have a lov-
> ing heart and do not secretly wish for the death of others, the Great
> Prince Satan will not succeed in destroying the world. In a few years this
> dread century will be over [in which God 'let Satan have his way with
> men for a hundred years']. Perhaps the world will end in fire and the
> Lord will come—it is not for us to say. But it is for us to say . . . whether
> hope and faith will come back into the world.[27]

If we could become as little children in clarity of perception and humility, we could enter into the mode of consciousness conducive to world peace.

Sometimes the perceptions of poets are congruent with those of children in their clarity and freshness. Not long after the atomic bomb was dropped on Hiroshima, the American poet Hermann Hagedorn wrote a pedestrian, 57-page poem, *The Bomb That Fell on America*, a hortatory Whitmanesque production that urged Americans to "grow/ up overnight, or make the world one final Hiroshima."[28] Though verbose in contrast to the succinctness of most children's expressions, Hagedorn's poem deserves credit for intuiting the truth of the Bomb's psychological fallout affecting all humanity. Instead of urging us to grow up, however, he might better have urged us to recapture some of the child's intuitive vision of what controversial Catholic theologian Matthew Fox calls "original blessing" (the inherent goodness of creation) and the child's faith in the

26. Ibid., p. 77.
27. Walker Percy, *The Thanatos Syndrome* (New York: Farrar, Straus, and Giroux, 1987), p. 365.
28. Hermann Hagedorn, *The Bomb That Fell on America* (Santa Barbara, Calif.: 1946), p. 34.

possibility of sweeping away the old destructive patterns of thought and behavior and opening the imagination to the mythology of peace.

"Protest and Survive"

The importance of protest in relation to a survival ethic is the subject of E. P. Thompson's 1981 "Letter to America," in *Protest and Survive*, a publication written as a "counterblast" to the 1980 classified British civil defense pamphlet, "Protect and Survive," designed for distribution in the event of a nuclear attack. When the pamphlet was leaked, the public was scandalized. Thompson, an eminent historian and outspoken critic of British nuclear policy, responded with a document that "became the rallying cry for the peace movement in England and Europe."[29] (Raymond Briggs gave us his satiric, artistic response to this instance of bureaucratic fatuousness in *When the Wind Blows*.) Thompson, a staunch supporter of the campaign for European Nuclear Disarmament, embraces protest as "the only realistic form of civil defense," given the fact that the deterministic, degenerative logic used by advocates of nuclear arms must be challenged.[30] Protest has a chance of being effective only if it is informed, yet nuclear education to prepare students to discuss the issues intelligently continues to be forestalled by opponents who argue variously that it is unpatriotic (presumably because it opens national policies to debate), that it increases fear and anxiety, or that there is a dearth of competent teachers. There is little empirical evidence of the intellectual, emotional, and behavioral effects of nuclear education, but evidence favors the conclusion that "it is possible to teach about nuclear weapons issues in a responsible way that empowers students, without indoctrinating them and without inciting fear." It is interesting to note that *teachers* of nuclear education units are more likely to become activists as a result.[31]

"The Dark of the Tunnel"

Phyllis Naylor's *The Dark of the Tunnel* relates the theme of coping with the personal experience of death to that of civil defense prepara-

29. "A Note from the Publisher," in *Protest and Survive*, ed. E. P. Thompson and Dan Smith, drawings by Marshall Arisman (New York: Monthly Press Review, 1981), unp. In this U.S. edition, some essays from the United States replace several of those in the original British edition.

30. E. P. Thompson, "A Letter to America," in *Protest and Survive*, p. 47.

31. Daniel J. Christie and Linden Nelson, "Student Reactions to Nuclear Education," *Bulletin of the Atomic Scientists* 44, no. 6 (July/August 1988): 22–23. No attempt was made to measure student activism.

tions to survive a nuclear attack. Craig, a high school senior, becomes a peace activist after he observes the futile nature of planning for a civil defense drill and simultaneously suffers through the death of his mother: It is as though personal experience of the loss of a loved one sensitizes him to the need to counter the planetary thanatos syndrome. In contrast, there is Craig's uncle, the county civil defense chief responsible for planning futile evacuation drills, a misguided peace activist who has been traumatized by the loss of his brother in the Vietnam War; this man sacrifices his life in a blast that destroys the tunnel, the proposed ''shelter.'' The irony of the peacenik meeting a violent end (a good instance of enantiodromia, the Jungian reversal of opposites) is not lost on the reader, nor is the symbolism of the dark tunnel— representing the tunnel vision that puts its confidence in the ability to ''protect and survive'' so scathingly pilloried in E. P. Thompson's book. Craig grows in insight into the value of the creative vision and its relationship to inner peace: Pondering the unknown writers of the woefully inadequate and misleading civil defense leaflets, he thinks

> Maybe the wrong people had been hired. Maybe, instead of technicians, they ought to hire playwrights or painters or poets—someone with enough imagination to see the things that weren't yet there.[32]

Craig intuits the gulf between tracts such as ''Protect and Survive'' and imaginative visions such as Raymond Briggs's *When the Wind Blows* in expressing the essence of ''the things that weren't yet there.''

Education for Peace Pilgrims

Peace education goes hand-in-hand with nuclear education, and both can be immeasurably enriched by the use of speculative fiction, for its imagined scenarios of nuclear devastation are a basis for contrasts with alternative futures, worlds not yet realized, thus presenting the range of choice. Writing from an educator's perspective, Roger I. Simon has remarked that it is a goal of education to encourage individuals to

> take risks, to struggle with ongoing relations of power, to critically appropriate forms of knowledge that exist outside of their immediate ex-

---

32. Phyllis Naylor, *The Dark of the Tunnel* (New York: Atheneum, 1985), pp. 87–88.

perience, and to envision versions of a world which is "not yet"—in order to be able to alter the grounds upon which life is lived.[33]

Practical and factual resources for the peace activist are also essential and continue to grow in number, with several timely examples for teenage readers being Milton Meltzer's *Ain't Gonna Study War No More: The Story of America's Peace Seekers,* Melinda Moore and Laurie Olsen's *Our Future at Stake: A Teenager's Guide to Stopping the Nuclear Arms Race,* and Sarah Pirtle's *Outbreak of Peace.*

Metta L. Winter's "Nuclear Education Update" gives a valuable survey of the issues and resources. She notes the need to recognize "complexity" as central to developing educational approaches; certain recurring themes, such as "a holistic approach that includes facts, values, and feelings," a "tolerance for diversity," "contextualizing information," and the "exercise of the imagination," are just a few examples.[34]

Overt activism is, of course, not the only route open to the peace pilgrim. The priority of an inner, personal quest to define one's own values is appreciated by Joanna Rogers Macy, author of *Despairwork: Awakening to the Peril and Promise of Our Time* and *Despair and Personal Power in the Nuclear Age.* Macy espouses the walk and the peace camp as ways people can enhance their inner resources and "spin webs of relationship that do not evaporate once they return home." As an exponent of Eastern spiritual traditions, Macy stresses the need for all of us to look inward, to face our despair over the dire fate of our planet, experiencing "pain for the world" as evidence of our webs of relationship with it and with one another. She identifies three stages in the process—Despairwork, Turning, and Empowerment, leading to a sense of "solidarity with other beings and the planet itself."[35]

Moral Imagination
and the Dream of Peace

The process of imagining a world without weapons, today's "utopian" model, can become an exercise in "moral imagination." Mary

---

33. Roger I. Simon, "Empowerment as a Pedagogy of Possibility," *Language Arts* 64, no. 4 (April 1987): 375.

34. Metta L. Winter, "Nuclear Education Update," *School Library Journal* (January 1986): 23.

35. Joanna Rogers Macy, "Learning to Sustain the Gaze," in *Facing Apocalypse,* ed. Valerie Andrews, Robert Bosnak, and Karen Walter Goodwin (Dallas: Spring Publications, Inc., 1987), pp. 165–67.

Watkins, a clinical and developmental psychologist, writes in her essay, "'In Dreams Begin Responsibilities': Moral Imagination and Peace Action," of the need to go beyond mere dreaming to action.[36] She traces the history of the demoralizing of the imagination from the time of Adam Smith and Percy Bysshe Shelley, when it was viewed as "the great instrument of moral good," to its devaluation in twentieth-century psychology, where it has become focused on the self, psychologically, spiritually, and physically, losing its component of action.[37]

Imagination, as Watkins points out, can be used for good (imagining the United Nations) or for ill (imagining Auschwitz), it can be self-indulgent or empathetic, passive or active. In Watkins's experience, Harvard students in the early 1970s demonstrated the lack of active, moral imagination for, whereas 90 percent of them believed nuclear war would come within ten years, only 5 percent were active to avert the danger. Their imaginations of disaster were not counterbalanced by an imagination active enough to create what the Romantic poets called "a heterocosm—a world other than this one—which, once alive imaginally, can inspire action."[38]

A technique emerging from Watkins's groupwork with people ranging in age from seventeen to sixty-five reveals the differing "voices" of responses to the imagining of global nuclear peril. Watkins identifies two main groups: the voices of the psychically "numbed," who seek to insulate themselves from disaster, and the voices of the "aware," who prefer to confront and scrutinize their anxieties. The numb voices fall into six "characters": (1) the Child, who avoids the horror, finding it "impossible to imagine"; (2) the "specialist," who anesthetizes the imagination with workaholic behavior (here, interestingly enough, Watkins finds the Scholar who believes the immersion in intellectual pursuits grants a "special dispensation" from involvement in world problems); (3) the "nature enthusiast," who flees the peopled world hoping to find "peace" in the woods; (4) the isolated suburbanite, wrapped up in "family, work, and friends," to the exclusion of activism; (5) the "hedonist," who seizes the present moment, rationalizing indulgence in pleasure

36. The title of Watkins's essay quotes Delmore Schwartz's short story, "In Dreams Begin Responsibilities" (originally published by New Directions, 1938). Schwartz also wrote a cycle of poems, "The Dreams Which Begin in Responsibilities."

37. See Shelley's "Defense of Poetry." Watkins refers for further elucidation of this concept to Patricia M. Ball, *The Central Self: A Study in Romantic and Victorian Imagination* (London: Athlone Press, 1968), p. 14.

38. Mary Watkins, "In Dreams Begin Responsibilities," in *Facing Apocalypse*, pp. 72, 74, 75.

by the fatalistic belief that the world will end anyway (cf. Lifton's "new ephemeralism"); and (6) the "gray lifers," who see life as "desperate" and "unsalvageable," and who may even view the prospect of massive destruction as a "relief."

The aware voices, on the other hand, are of three kinds: (1) the "victim," whose awareness only leads to overwhelming despair; (2) the "activists," divided into the young "peace activists"—attractive, hip, busy, optimistic that social problems can be solved—and the "inner activists," whom Watkins characterizes as "pessimistic, non-escapists," very likely to "burn out"; and (3) the "mother" and "teacher" types, who resist numbing because of a *particular* love for nature, children, and all beings, and whose love motivates "feeling action."[39]

Watkins documents the positive results from involving the numb voices in a dialogue with the aware voices: If carried on with sensitivity and empathy, this sort of conversation can succeed in moving the numb person to identify what he or she treasures enough to work to protect. Failed dialogues result if people are taken at face value, "as indifferent, uncaring, self-centered," for their deeper feelings must be tapped, and this can be accomplished only by finding a common ground of concern, a shared humanness.[40]

Chances of finding this common ground between the United States and the USSR have improved with the recent moves toward more relaxed relationships between these superpowers, plus the demolishment of the Berlin Wall. Cooperative ventures, such as the timely article co-authored by Vladimir Gakov and Paul Brians, "Nuclear War Themes in Soviet Science Fiction: An Annotated Bibliography," are encouraging as evidence of meaningful intellectual exchange. Gakov, an author of science fiction, and Brians, noted for his contributions to scholarship on nuclear fiction and much consulted for the present study, examine Soviet science fiction about nuclear catastrophe and fears of nuclear holocaust in order to reveal Soviet attitudes on these topics. They document a shift in mindset from an "unspoken taboo" on nuclear war themes to considerable attention to the subject from young writers. This new body of Soviet nuclear fiction actually anticipated and perhaps facilitated the drastic changes in Soviet society now defined by the two magic words, *perestroika* (restructuring) and *glasnost*

39. Ibid., pp. 80–88.
40. Ibid., pp. 88–90. Watkins observes that all the "mother" and "teacher" voices in her groups were from women; not a single man "spontaneously entertained a female character" as an imagined voice, though over half of the women imagined one or more of their "voices" as male. She concludes that "many men may indeed be cut off from the feminine voices in dealing with 'the numb one' " (n.21).

(openness).[41] Their findings demonstrate how fiction can play an important part in exercising the moral imagination.

Since exerting one's moral imagination in the furthering of peace can be an emotionally draining process, it is well to remember Watkins's recommendation that the peace pilgrim do two things to avoid burnout: first, take a fishing holiday from the struggle in order to relax and refresh, and second, cultivate his or her own "obnoxious" inner opponent, the inner gadfly, with whom to carry on an interior, self-questioning dialogue.[42] The challenge to "come to peace" with this inner voice of doubt can keep us in delicate balance, save us from the psychic "reversal" that can turn the peace pilgrim into the battle-fatigued bombaholic. Obsessiveness, even in so worthy a cause, distorts the heart and mind and, through the phenomenon of enantiodromia, bends the best intentions to an opposite effect.

41. Vladimir Gakov and Paul Brians, "Nuclear War Themes in Soviet Science Fiction: An Annotated Bibliography," *Science Fiction Studies* 16, pt. 1 (March 1989): 68,70.

42. Watkins, "In Dreams Begin Responsibilities," in *Facing Apocalypse*, pp. 92–93.

CHAPTER 5

Scenarios of End-Time

The Wise Woman telling Odin (Wotan) of his doom in the *Poetic Edda:*

> Brothers shall fight and fell each other,
> And sisters' sons shall kinship stain;
> Hard it is on earth, with mighty whoredom;
> Ax-time, sword-time, shields are sundered,
> Wind-time, wolf-time, ere the world falls.
> —Joseph Campbell *The Hero with a Thousand Faces*

Stories of the end of the world have existed since ancient times. With the nuclear age, however, they have undergone a genre change from improbable fantasies to believable predictions of an all-too-possible end-time. Myths of many cultures envision the world's end as part of a cycle of renewal and regeneration. Mircea Eliade, noted scholar of comparative religions, observed how in early mythic traditions "the end of the world is never absolute; it is always followed by a new, *regenerated* world."[1] The likelihood of nuclear holocaust presents us with a different prospect, namely that humanity may succeed in bringing on an absolute end to human life, canceling all chance of renewal for our species. Scientists theorize that there have been, in the earth's history, cycles of destruction and renewal, such as the apparent extinction of anaerobic life-forms by the introduction of oxygen into the atmosphere, an event that, of course, made it possible for mammalian species to become dominant.[2]

1. Mircea Eliade, *Dreams and Mysteries,* trans. Philip Mairet (New York: Harper and Row, 1975), p. 243.
2. Pertinent discussions of past extinctions of entire species include these articles easily accessible to high school students: James Trefil, "Stop to Consider the Stones That Fall from the Sky," *Smithsonian* 20, no. 6 (September 1989): 80–92, on how asteroids may have caused the extinction of dinosaurs and "cleared the way for the rise of mammals"

The present concern, however, is with the destiny of human life. As Mike Perlman observes, "In some versions of the most recent stories of the end of the world—predictions of a nuclear winter—humankind succeeds in doing itself in," with "no New Creation to follow."[3] Stories of biocide or total geocide are the theme of this chapter.

End-of-the-World Fiction: Traditional Structure

In "The Remaking of Zero: Beginning at the End," Gary Wolfe has outlined five stages of action in most fiction depicting the world's end: (1) experience of the cataclysm; (2) the journey through the wasteland; (3) establishment of a new community; (4) the emergence of the wilderness as "antagonist"; and (5) a decisive "struggle to determine which values shall prevail in the new world."[4] This is the well-established cyclic structure of the end merging into a new beginning. With few exceptions, the novels to be considered here are not cyclic in nature; rather, they depict only the first stage, with Earth either dying a permanent death or suffering a terminal illness. These novels, in short, resist the pattern of established apocalyptic fantasies that allow a few elite to survive to begin a New Adam and New Eve scenario. Novels that build upon the New Eden pattern, an extremely popular one, will be discussed in chapter 6.

Kopit's "The End of the World"

Before discussing the archetypal patterns in these novels of ecocide, I wish to look briefly at one writer's dramatic working through of the

---

(p. 92); Rick Gore, "Extinctions," with photographs by Jonathan Blair, *National Geographic* 175, no. 6 (June 1989): 662–99, focused on the loss of species, from the dinosaurs to the vanishing life-forms of today; and Bill McKibben, "Reflections: The End of Nature," *New Yorker*, 11 September 1989, pp. 47–105, a more generalized discussion of the probable consequences of global warming, popularly known as the greenhouse effect. I am indebted to Bettina MacAyeal for pointing out the pertinence of these sources to my discussion.

3. Mike Perlman, "When Heaven and Earth Collapse: Myths of the End of the World," in *Facing Apocalypse*, ed. by Valerie Andrews, Robert Bosnak, and Karen Walter Goodwin (Dallas, Tex.: Spring Publications, 1987), p. 172.

4. Gary Wolfe, "The Remaking of Zero: Beginning at the End," in *The End of the World*, ed. Eric S. Rabkin, Martin H. Greenberg, and Joseph D. Olander (Carbondale: Southern Illinois Univ. Pr., 1983), p. 8.

question, why are we so fascinated by stories of the world's destruction? Arthur Kopit's play *The End of the World* is based on his real-life experience of being prevailed upon to write a dramatization of the end of the world, and it incorporates his interviews with Jonathan Schell, Freeman Dyson, Herman Kahn, and similar experts on nuclearism.

Michael Trent, the fictional playwright, is commissioned by Philip Stone, a wealthy backer, to write a drama on the theme of nuclear weapons proliferation. Trent's literary agent, Audrey Wood, encourages him to do the play on the grounds that it might forestall global doom. Trent, however, finds the topic impervious to language: The more he learns about the realities of nuclear conflict, the more he finds the topic eludes the limits of imagination. Despite the purported inadequacies of language, Kopit's play expresses vividly the two real blocks to ending the arms race: the perverse attraction of death-dealing power, thrilling to the human heart (thus the appeal of the "worship" of nuclear arms); and the denial of actual peril that anesthetizes us to our anxieties (what Robert J. Lifton calls "numbing").

Stone's soliloquy late in the play explains the emotional roots of his obsession with the "glitter" of nuclear weapons. He had witnessed the atomic bomb tests on Christmas Island and the horrible spectacle of flying albatrosses consumed by radiation, wheeling in fantastical contortions, smoking from the intensity of the heat. In an apocalyptic flash, he saw how it will be *"at the end of time. . . And we all felt . . . the thrill of that idea."*[5] He saw into the Mephistophelean depths of his own heart and felt an abominable *schadenfreude* at the prospect of the human power to annihilate the world as we know it.

Trent finds this evil thrill within himself as well. He confesses to Stone that he had known this emotion when, standing by the window of his twentieth-floor apartment and holding his newborn son, he had experienced the terrible temptation to let the child drop to his death. The seductiveness of the power to destroy the "tiny creature" had almost overwhelmed him. He had been fascinated at the thought that "I will be *unable to get him back."*[6] (This is, incidentally, an excellent example of the phenomenon of enantiodromia, whereby the fear becomes the desire.)

Happily, Trent escapes the temptation by simply backing away from the window. Kopit as playwright brings his audience and Trent face-to-face with the demonic and shows that humans have the power to refuse the destructive impulse.

5. Arthur Kopit, *The End of the World* (New York: Hill and Wang, 1984), p. 93.
6. Ibid., pp. 94–95.

The astute reader-viewer will see the parallel with the nuclear pre-dicament: The choice is there—and we can *not* destroy our world. At the same time, Kopit has given a fine example of what has been called the "nuclear sublime," the psychological attraction to nuclear annihi-lation, a manifestation of the "egotistical sublime" that desires to be rid of the burden of existence.[7] Yet another applicable term for this phe-nomenon is "nuclear fascination," explicated in Robert Mielke's "Imaging Nuclear Weaponry: An Ethical Taxonomy of Nuclear Repre-sentation."[8]

Kopit's play satirizes nuclear fascination and leaves us convinced that we must look within to find the root of evil objectified in the mush-room cloud. To prevent emotional numbing from the gravity of the topic, Kopit uses ample humor, as when one of the two Paramount Studio representatives, absurdly comic figures, informs Trent's liter-ary agent that "Paramount will only consider projects about nuclear war if there's an upbeat ending." The agent aptly retorts that for such a plot there is "no ending whatsoever." The other Paramount agent finds Trent's assertion that nuclear conflict will doom our civilization distressing, and he asks, "Does he mean the West Coast, too?"[9]

Kopit also portrays the manipulation of language by those who play with war scenarios, as when Stone explains the "ion curtain" concept—an "invulnerable window shade" to allow our missiles out but prevent any from coming in—as a device to allow us time to "*take care of things,*" that is, to annihilate the Enemy.[10]

Paradoxically, Kopit's play on the topic of the impossibility of find-ing adequate language to portray nuclearism succeeds admirably in convincing us that nuclear proliferation must be stopped to forestall geocide. It also suggests that this can be accomplished only by over-coming the "heart of darkness" lurking within us all, but it remains for the audience to find the means of doing this. The play thus stands as a cautionary tale that does not tell us what steps we must take to avoid wiping ourselves out.

In the survey of novels to follow, I shall sum up the main features of their scenarios of ecocide or geocide, discuss the symbolic and mythic means used by the authors to express their visions, and try in each case to articulate the "message," in most cases a cautionary one. Since

7. Frances Ferguson, "The Nuclear Sublime,"*Diacritics* 14 (Summer 1984): 9.

8. Robert Mielke, "Imaging Nuclear Weaponry: An Ethical Taxonomy of Nuclear Representation," *Northwest Review: Warnings, an Anthology on the Nuclear Peril* 22, nos. 1, 2 (1984): 164–80.

9. Kopit, *End of the World*, p. 22.

10. Ibid., pp. 89–90.

these are antiheroic stories by definition (no hero or hera survives to bring new life to the community), I shall pose the question, is any survival ethic *implied?* Some of the novels are bitterly satirical; others are less caustic, gentler cautionary tales. The novels will be approached chronologically. All of these fictions portray the probable future— really a "future impossible"—if humanity collectively fails to find a life-affirming survival ethic to meet the challenges of the nuclear age.

"On the Beach": The Death of the Earth

Much of the power of Nevil Shute's *On the Beach* grows from his use of the "terminal" beach image, fraught with echoes of the dead souls of classical literature embarking on the River Acheron or River Styx enroute to the underworld. Quite possibly Shute's novel and the film version have had more impact than any other work of nuclear fiction on the collective imagination of readers and viewers worldwide. The epigraph comes from T. S. Eliot's "The Hollow Men":

> In this last of meeting places
> We grope together
> And avoid speech
> Gathered on this beach of the tumid river.

Shute alludes to another famous use of the beach image, Matthew Arnold's "Dover Beach," in which the speaker contemplates not the end of the world but the end of an era of faith and the ascendancy of an era of ugly warfare.

On the Beach is set after a worldwide nuclear war, with the Earth slowly dying from the effects of radiation. In Australia, the central locale, people are waiting to die. Individual reactions vary: some engage in passive denial, making believe life will go on (planting flowers and vegetables that will never bloom); others, like John Osborne, race cars in a frenzied attempt to feel more alive while waiting for the end. The main characters are Peter Holmes (a member of the submarine crew), his wife, Mary, their daughter, Jennifer, and John Osborne, the scientist who accompanies the submarine crew on a voyage to measure the intensity of radiation. The submarine's commander, Dwight Lionel Towers, becomes involved in a doomed romance with Moira Davidson, and their bittersweet relationship serves as a contrast to the domestic love of the Holmeses.

The prominence of the beach metaphor encourages an interpretation drawing upon marine biology. Recently a professor of biology from Tufts University, Dr. Edward S. Hodgson, identified three "trouble" areas for the human species: sustenance, sex, and signaling.[11] In the manner of the ecologist, Hodgson directs us to nature for "mentorship" in solving these problems, specifically to the plants and animals of the coral reefs. Inhabitants of the coral reefs have shown innate abilities to function successfully in all three areas: the coral polyp is "solar powered" (its energy source is renewable); it does not overbreed its ecological constrictions ("no teenage pregnancy problem"); and it uses signaling to minimize aggression (living cooperatively with other species, such as the clownfish and sea anemone).

Taking my cue from Joseph W. Meeker's ideas on literary ecology, I shall apply the tri-part schemata of sustenance, sex, and signaling to *On the Beach* (with some expansions to make the categories applicable to humans). Sustenance has been threatened by radiation; the world's former energy sources can no longer support life. On the human level, physical sustenance must be supplemented by provision for psychological and spiritual needs (cf. Maslow), but fulfillment of these is curtailed by the absence of any future. Sex, the second term in Hodgson's schemata of current threats to survival, must be humanly expanded to encompass love; both are still powerful forces in the novel (as in Moira's passionate attraction to Towers, blocked by his emotional tie to a certainly dead wife and family: His denial is strong). In proper fifties fashion, abstinence rules over desire. The movie version, however, grants the two a night of love before the end. Love in all its aspects—*eros, philia,* and *agape*—is treated ironically, as a manifestation of the life force still trying to function in an impossible situation.

The most poignant image in the book represents the failure of signaling, Hodgson's third term. In the earlier part of the story there is a slight hope that the indecipherable radio signal coming out of Seattle might betoken surviving intelligent life. It is found, however, to emanate from a Coke bottle, caught in a broken window shade blowing in the breeze, periodically striking a telegraph key. Moreover, it was the breakdown of signaling that set off the nuclear conflagration: After Albania instigated hostilities between the Arabs and Israelis, the superpowers could not identify the point of origin of nuclear bombs, and in their fear and ignorance they used their massive powers on each other, acting out the scenario of Mutually Assured Destruction.

11.   Edward S. Hodgson, "Education from Eden: Crucial Lessons from Coral Reefs," speech at dinner meeting of Phi Beta Kappa, April 30, 1988, Desmond Americana, Colonie, N.Y.

At the close of the narrative the sea, traditionally a symbol of the source of life, becomes the medium in which all hope for life is drowned, as Moira watches Towers head the *Scorpion* out of the harbor on his last mission, under orders to sink the vessel. Moira then prepares to take a fatal pill as she sits in her car, in full view of the beach. Her last words are "Dwight, if you're on your way already wait for me."[12] Her love for him becomes the desire to join him in death, and thanatos wins out over eros. The implied cautionary message in this ecological interpretation is that the human race would do well to heed the wisdom of the coral reefs and to apply its energies and imagination to solving its severe problems of sustenance, sex, and signaling rather than to stockpiling weapons.

"The Last Day"

Helen Clarkson's *The Last Day* shares with Shute's *On the Beach* a vision of the total extinction of human life from the poisoning of the biosphere by radiation. Clarkson probes the sicknesses of society that lead to nuclear war through Lois, a character whose feminine, domestic perspective presents a strong challenge to what H. Bruce Franklin calls the "cult of superweapons." Resisting the mentality of "messianic anticommunism," Lois sees clearly the enormity of imbalance in a culture where "love is 'dirty' and a hundred-megaton bomb is clean," and affirms life against another character's implication that "mothers are a lunatic fringe, a minority group" who should be prevented from rallying against nuclear testing and the worship of weapons.[13] Her sympathies with mythologies of peace (she is a pacifist who advocates the doctrines of Gandhi[14]) and her view of nuclear war as the ultimate child abuse plus her instinctive biophilic stance contrast strongly to the "hawk" mentality of the island's reactionary oldtimers, incipient bombaho-

---

12. Nevil Shute, *On the Beach* (New York: William Morrow, 1957), p. 238.

13. H. Bruce Franklin, unpublished essay. Used with permission.

14. Paul Brians in his *Nuclear Holocausts: Atomic War in Fiction, 1895–1984* (Kent, Ohio: Kent State Univ. Pr., 1986) notes Clarkson's advocacy of the "doctrines of Gandhi" and her insights into the senselessness of "the usual clichés about dying for one's country" when "one's government is engaged in ensuring the death of its own citizens and the destruction of its territory" (p. 38). He credits her analysis of the distinct differences between nuclear war and traditional war as anticipating many of Jonathan Schell's ideas in his *Fate of the Earth*. Brians adds, significantly, "But rarely in these liberal works do pacifists succeed in gaining power. That happens mainly in the nightmare of conservatives," the "pacifist dystopias" discussed by Brians in Chapter 4 of his work.

lics who welcome apocalypse as God's just punishment of those who indulge in "a guilty state of Babylonian luxury."[15]

Lois, the teller of the tale, and Bill, her husband, are on vacation on Selsea Island when nuclear bombs strike the United States. Their daughter, Eunice, is away in France, and the couple is looking forward to a pastoral idyll in their habitual vacation spot. Nearby are Eric and Sally Linden, long-time friends. There is a new resident, an unpleasant woman called Frisky, whose jarring presence provides an avenue for the exploration of child abuse. Frisky's own inner tortures cause her to mistreat her daughter, Jean. Thus, Clarkson provides a microcosmic instance of child abuse to parallel the macrocosmic abuse wreaked by the use of nuclear weapons.

Early in the narrative Clarkson makes mythological links to Greek tradition and the Bible through Sally, a prescient character called "Cassie" by Bill (an allusion to the Greek prophetess Cassandra, whose warnings were fated to go unheeded). Sally responds to rumors of war on the daily radio news broadcasts by drawing a parallel between "Lot's wife" and the similarly improvident humans of today, who ignore warnings of the "Fire" from heaven and the injunction to "Escape for thy life . . . look not behind thee . . . lest thou be consumed." Sally goes on to criticize Americans for being seduced by the "cult of the happy ending . . . the most dangerous American tradition," leading us collectively to suppose, subconsciously, that we can afford to make mistakes because we are conditioned to believe the "plot" will inevitably end happily for us. Sally sees the need to stop creating the "enemy" through "newspaper vilification." Verbal disarmament, she argues, would be almost as good an alternative as physical disarmament. "Wars, like everything else, begin in the mind. An arms race leads to war largely because of its psychological effect." Bill speaks to the same point in calling the "jungle of hostility" outside ourselves less fearful than the "hell within . . . where nightmares are born" and where the true "devils" dwell.[16] The characters who provide perspective in Clarkson's novel are not numbed into denial: They have not bought the cult of the happy ending.

Clarkson is prescient as an author, anticipating the idea of contemporary physics that an "observer" is needed to "create" the universe by perceiving it (an idea that has an analogue in the ancient mythological thought of Hinduism). Two instances may be cited. While waiting for the sound wave from the nuclear blast, Lois hears the measured tick

15. Helen Clarkson, *The Last Day* (New York: Dodd, Mead, 1959), p. 70.
16. Ibid., pp. 31, 55–56.

of the clock, loud in the unnatural stillness, and thinks of time as dying. With no human consciousness surviving to perceive time, she wonders, will the world even exist? Later, she thinks "only living eyes see certain waves as light and color. Only living eyes see the dance of electrons as form. Soon there would be no form, no color, no light—only a vast, monstrous pulsation of electric and magnetic forces without purpose or future."[17] For Helen, it is difficult to imagine how, given no consciousness to behold it, the world can be said to exist. (A dissenting view should be noted, for there are those who would argue that if human consciousness is a part and parcel of the Earth—Gaia—then it cannot logically be ascendant over her. Hence, the idea that human consciousness must be present to *make* the world exist is a debatable one. Here, however, the human dilemma, not the logical one, is the point.)

The abuse of the child Jean serves to dramatize the failure of generative love in personal human relationships, a cruelty that Bill attributes to a failure of memory and extends to a universal level. Cruelty, Bill remarks, often results from acting on impulse, without recourse to memory: "Love and the moral sense are both rooted in memory. . . . The stronger your memory, the more you view each act in the context of your whole life and the less likely you are to yield to the sudden, base impulse." The same failure to think *contextually* can be seen on an international scale when nations neglect to act within a framework of the whole, to consider how each action will "disturb the universe."[18] Intellect separated from the context of history and the imaged future, thought freed from memory and irresponsible to posterity, is an abomination. The mind oblivious to global considerations, cut off from the anchor of the past and hence oblivous also to responsibility, makes monstrosities possible.

Dr. Joel, the resident physician on the island, puts events into historical and mythological context. In olden times, he observes, men justified killing (one might say justified their war mythologies) by rationalizing that they were making the world safe for women and children; women and children had a status outside nationality and their lives were preserved because "they belonged to life, not to death. They were the future made flesh, respected by both sides in a quarrel between men." Now, women wear uniforms, and children are the first to die. He raises hard questions: Is it possible that civilization actually erodes the natural love of a parent for the young? Is child abuse a by-product of civilization?

17. Ibid., p. 44.
18. Ibid., p. 102.

Agamemnon might sacrifice Iphigenia to a god for the sake of a victory, or Genghis Khan kill thousands of the children of an enemy, but never before, he believes, have people been prepared to sacrifice millions of children to weapons whose destructive power exceeds all comprehension. Making a mythological link, he calls nuclear bombs the Pied Piper of today, for they have seduced adults to endanger the lives of their children by bargaining for the "security" of nuclear arms. Today's adults in power are in his view more culpable than the citizens of Hamelin, however, for those who control nuclear weapons know that children are pawns in "our obscene bargain with death."[19]

Dr. Joel makes a further mythological link to the story of the Garden of Eden, seeing it as an image of "history, not prophecy." We were too blind, in short, to recognize paradise when we were in the midst of it. His summation of the five causes of nuclear war have been enumerated earlier: our "automatic amnesia for the unbearable," the trauma of rapid technological change that undermined belief in personal immortality, a paranoid fear of communism, boredom (the most lethal of all), and, finally, misguided patriotism: "In a nuclear world any man who calls himself a patriot should be clapped in an insane asylum before he has a chance to wreck the world."[20] Clarkson implies through Joel's statements the need for the kind of mythology Joseph Campbell has also called for, a mythology inclusive of all peoples.

Contextual thinking can also be seen in Lois. As Jean lies dying of radiation sickness (Frisky is already dead), Lois sings to her a ballad from Rudyard Kipling's "Toomai of the Elephants," a story in *The Jungle Book*:

> Shiv, who poured the harvest
>
> and made the winds to blow,
>
> Sitting at the doorways
>
> of a day of long ago,
>
> Gave to each his portion,
>
> Food and toil and fate,
>
> From the king upon the guddee

19. Ibid., pp. 118–19. It is true that the history of childhood shows many shameful instances of the exploitation, abuse, and socially sanctioned sacrifice of children's lives (cf. the Children's Crusade of the Middle Ages). The fictional Dr. Joel's point is not that such indifference or cruelty is new but that never before have so many children's futures and indeed lives been willfully placed in jeopardy in an absurd scenario of Mutually Assured Destruction.

20. Ibid., pp. 158, 161–67, passim.

> to the beggar at the gate.
>
> All things made he,
>
> Shiv the Preserver.
>
> Ma-ha-deo! Ma-ha-deo!
>
> He made all,
>
> Thorn for the camel,
>
> Fodder for the kine,
>
> And mother's heart for sleepy head,
>
> O little son of mine![21]

(She changes "son" to "child," as she had in years past for her own daughter.) This use of literary tradition puts Jean's death into the perspective of the creation and destruction of all life, but at the same time it rings hollow and ironic, for the reader recognizes it betokens the death of our world.

Terminal beach imagery permeates the novel's closing scene. Lois, now the sole survivor, takes shelter in a hollow spot on the beach where she and her husband had picnicked in better times. As she grieves her own loss of life and the death of the world, she is startled to hear the joyous song of a small brown bird. The bird must have been sheltered from the radioactive dust and remained in the hollow by instinct or chance. For the first time since the bombs fell, she weeps to hear "innocent joy. For I was not innocent. I shared the guilt of all my species." The lone bird, without nest or mate, singing to the lone human being, presents an unforgettable image of end-time and impending geocide. Lois lies down to sleep in the hollow, the only place in the world that is "windless and clean."[22]

Clarkson's novel, by its vivid depiction of the end of life on Earth, is an explicit as well as implied plea for an awakening of human wisdom to embrace a mythology of peace.

"Level 7": An Underworld Dystopia

Level 7 by Mordecai Roshwald employs techniques often used in speculative fiction of nuclear disaster to heighten irony: the "diary" approach, a narrator of limited perspective whose intensifying madness dawns upon the reader to create a growing horror, and "cognitive

21. Ibid., pp. 130–31.
22. Ibid., pp. 182–83.

alienation,'' or defamiliarization. The diary is that of Officer X-127, a missile launch push-button operator sequestered in an underground bomb shelter. (Although writing takes on a survival value to him early in his narrative, and gives him both a fleeting sense of "the *significance of being*" as distinct from "being *somebody*," and a temporary escape from the "half-being" of his underground existence,[23] it is not ultimately a creative means for survival, and hence this novel is not included in the later discussion of the novels featuring the creative artist or journalist.)

In one example of ironic inversion, X-127 at first passionately desires to return to the earth's surface, to see sunlight again, but light eventually becomes associated with hellish destruction above. Assigned to Level 7 for life (the bottommost level) and commissioned to help operate the "offensive" part of the military machine, he and his fellow push-button operators are told that they hold the destiny of the world "beneath the tips of your fingers."[24] Such power contrasts with their virtual prisoner status, for they had no choice in the job and were simply chosen as the most suited psychologically to endure a confined and limited existence. In his *Fictions of Nuclear Disaster*, David Dowling refers to the "inverted pyramid" of the underground shelter levels as an "enclosed, suffocating society," a "technological womb." (One might compare the "hole" perceived by William Cowling in Tim O'Brien's *The Nuclear Age*, discussed in chapter 1.) The inverted pyramid, Dowling adds, images a "perfect, Morlockian manifestation of the technological vision, a tunnel vision" that supposes that the greatest isolation grants people the greatest degree of safety.[25] The setting itself to some degree reflects what Harold L. Berger terms the narrator's "emotionally cool and socially indifferent personality." Berger points to these qualities as evidenced X-127's eventual passionless marriage to the similarly cold woman psychologist, P-867, known, like all the underground inhabitants, only by a code number. The rigidly controlled environment, where sex is nothing more than "therapeutic and procreative," depersonalizes him still further.[26] He retains nonetheless enough insight to realize he is a "monster" if he loses the emotional component of human nature.[27]

23. Mordecai Roshwald, *Level 7* (New York: McGraw-Hill, 1959), p. 16.

24. Ibid., p. 12.

25. David Dowling, *Fictions of Nuclear Disaster* (Iowa City: Univ. of Iowa Pr., 1987), pp. 64, 66.

26. Harold L. Berger, *Science Fiction and the New Dark Age* (Bowling Green, Ohio: Bowling Green Univ. Popular Press, 1976), p. 150.

27. Roshwald, *Level 7*, p. 56.

The dehumanizing effects of the sensory deprivation experienced in the underground womb/tomb manifest themselves when, hospitalized from the shock to his digestive system caused by eating a small piece of chocolate that he and P-867 consume to celebrate their marriage, the protagonist confesses enjoying the pain as a relief from the "deadening routine."[28] In so sterilized, contorted, and mechanistic a world, pain becomes a sign of life and individuality.

Level 7 is a minor masterpiece of the cautionary tale; its bitterly ironic dedication "To Dwight and Nikita" underscores its author's antiwar stance. The narrator's naiveté and his eventual drug- and shock therapy–induced passivity contribute to the reader's growing sense of the pity and terror of it all.

The protagonist undergoes a brief episode of spiritual conversion when he feels spontaneous compassion for the two "doves," a married couple from Level 3 who voluntarily leave their shelter to see what remains of the surface world after the accidentally triggered automated war. X-127 feels grateful to the doves for activating the "hidden button" of compassion in his soul and the consequent sense of unity with other human beings, banishing his existential aloneness. He speculates on why it is so hard for humans to find this button of compassion, yet so easy for them to "push the ones that launch deadly rockets." Here is his insight into the human capacity for evil, at heart a recognition identical to Trent's in Kopit's play. Yet X-127 cherishes no hope for achieving universal compassion: "At the bottom of this super-clever, super-stupid business there still remain some human beings in whose souls a button remains unpushed."[29]

The novel has much to say about the importance of myth in education and the forming of personality. X-127 becomes acquainted with R-747, a woman whose assignment is to prepare instructional material for children. She devotes her time to creating a "new mythology," one adapted to fit the facts of an underground existence. The "old" mythology will no longer "work" for obvious reasons; in just one example, hell can no longer be "downward" and heaven "upward": The directions must now be reversed since the deepest level within the earth has become the safest and best place to be. R-747 proposes that, in fact, "perhaps Level 7 itself will be the new heaven."[30]

28. Ibid., p. 89.
29. Ibid., p. 157.
30. Ibid., p. 70, pp. 71–73, passim.

R-747 shows X-127 a myth she has composed entitled "Gamma, Alpha and Little Ch-777," calculated to teach children the danger of the world above ground, now ruled by "Strontium 90," shortened in a clever conceit to "St," or "saint," because no one wants to pronounce his dread name. She gives it a didactic moral: "Be happy here. If you are curious to know what happens above Level 7, think of poor Ch-777 who paid for his curiosity with his life."

A more imaginative myth is composed by the narrator himself, entitled "The Story of the Mushroom" and designed for children to hear from "the Sacred Tape" by simply pushing a button. (There are no longer any books.) The wildly proliferating mushroom (representing the mushroom cloud and proliferating nuclear arms) grows and grows, emitting a noisome odor that finally becomes so hideous that people are forced underground to escape from it. Eventually the mushroom covers the entire earth with "shadow and stink," and one day it *bursts*, destroying everything on the earth's surface.[31] No moral is stated and none is needed.

The traditional symbolic associations of the mushroom and reasons why it triumphed over competing metaphors as the virtually universal image for destructive atomic power have been noted in Spencer R. Weart's discussion of "Mushroom and Mandala" in *Nuclear Fear: A History of Images*. In Western consciousness, mushrooms have been associated "with dank, dark places, rot and poison . . . death." Yet since some mushrooms are edible, they have life-sustaining connotations as well. As a folkloric symbol, the mushroom has the ability to spring up swiftly and mysteriously, giving it associations of uncontrolled, cancerous growth. Children's stories often portray the mushroom as having magical qualities and sometimes functioning as an umbrella to shelter small creatures. The mushroom is hence an apt metaphor for transmutation, that is, "life opposing death—perhaps even life arising from death," as well as a signifier of magical power.[32] Jean de Brunhoff's *The Story of Babar*, in which the young Babar replaces the old king after the latter dies of eating a red mushroom with white spots, illustrates an archetypal transformation from old to new: "The King is dead, long live the King!"[33] In

31. Ibid., pp. 75–76.
32. Spencer R. Weart, *Nuclear Fear: A History of Images* (Cambridge, Mass.: Harvard Univ. Pr., 1988), pp. 401–6. See also Robert G. Wasson, *Soma, Divine Mushroom of Immortality* (New York: Harcourt Brace Jovanovich, 1971).
33. Jean de Brunhoff, *The Story of Babar*, trans. Merle Haas (New York: Random House, 1933), p. 34.

Roshwald's mythic use of the mushroom, however, the mushroom clearly signifies death, with no hint of the possibility of transmutation. The annihilation is total.

In yet another irony, the war continues verbally even after the entire earth is in ruins, as the dying castigate each other with radio messages, using terms such as "war criminals," "inhuman beasts," "unprogressive," "reactionary," "child murderers'," and "arch-criminals of human history."[34] The exchange of insults becomes a media event to relieve the boredom.

H. Bruce Franklin has praised Roshwald's achievement in dramatizing "the unimaginable: the extinction by nuclear war of all human consciousness." He questions the motivations for letting *Level 7* go out of print in the United States in 1981 (despite good sales records), whereas since that time there have been new editions in Romanian, Danish, and Norwegian.[35] As a unique and bitter countervision to nuclearism, *Level 7* should be studied by all who care about the fate of the earth.

Other Visions of the End

Although *Canticle for Leibowitz* by Walter M. Miller, Jr., falls chronologically at this point and has certain elements in common with the visions of geocide discussed here, its use of Gaia imagery and its cyclic view of human history make it a candidate for a later discussion (see chapter 7).

"Fail-Safe"

Fail-Safe by Eugene Burdick and John Harvey Wheeler, Jr., merits mention here as a well-known thriller satirizing the automation of war as part of a suicidal war mythology leading to the annihilation of all life on Earth. Once more, the ultimate war begins by accident. A malfunction in a condenser in the laboratory of a military command post mistakenly shows missiles from the USSR bearing down on the United States. A retaliatory strike is launched and U.S. missiles destroy their target despite recall attempts. A remorseful U.S. president orders the

34. Roshwald, *Level 7*, p. 133.

35. H. Bruce Franklin, *Countdown to Midnight: Twelve Great Stories about Nuclear War* (New York: Daw Books, 1984), p. 24.

destruction of New York City as a proof of our nation's good faith and sincere regret for the error.[36]

Fail-Safe dramatizes the split between the specialist's devotion to brain and the consequent neglect of visceral truth. One woman is depicted as opposing this split—the wife of the general who takes on the assignment of dropping a nuclear bomb on New York City, knowing his family will be vaporized—whereas another woman character (not a sympathetic one) expresses to a key male character her envy of men who wield destructive power. The latter instance poses an intriguing exception to the usual feminine opposition to war mythology. The novel succeeds as a spellbinding satire of suicidal war mythology, depicting but rejecting the Superman and Lone Ranger mentalities so dominant in the military establishment.

"Dr. Strangelove" and the False Myth of Nuclearism

A film classic of 1964, Stanley Kubrick's *Dr. Strangelove, or How I Learned to Stop Worrying and Love the Bomb*, depicts a world devoid of any creative survival ethic, where the tormented protagonists are moved only by their infernal love of power and destruction, the antithesis of *biophilia*. [37]

The film was based on British novelist Peter George's *Two Hours to Doom* (published under the pseudonym Peter Bryant, with the U.S. edition bearing the title *Red Alert*). George's novel, an earnest cautionary tract against the dangers of accidental nuclear war, is a perfectly serious conventional future war novel trimmed with 1950s atomic technology and military jargon. The script of *Dr. Strangelove*, penned by director Stanley Kubrick and novelist Terry Southern, with George given co-credit, transforms the flat-footed and morally earnest narra-

36. Paul Brians, whose insights and bibliographical notes in *Nuclear Holocausts* are indispensable to any student of nuclear fiction, refers to Michael G. Wollscheidt's statement in *Nuclear War Films* (Carbondale: Southern Illinois Univ. Pr., 1978, p. 70), that Peter George, who wrote *Red Alert* (New York: Ace, 1958; published in England as *Two Hours to Doom*) under the pseudonym Peter Bryant, sued Burdick and Wheeler for plagiarizing his novel (Brians, p. 150). *Fail-Safe* was made into a Columbia Pictures film in 1963.

37. Kubrick's film is a comic adaptation of Peter George's *Two Hours to Doom* (see note 36). The film script by Terry Southern and Stanley Kubrick was novelized by George and published as *Dr. Stangelove, or How I Learned to Stop Worrying and Love the Bomb* (New York: Bantam, 1964; reprint, with an introduction by Richard Gid Powers, Boston: Gregg, 1979). Powers's introduction explores these complex interrelationships.

tive of the earlier book into a savage travesty of nuclearism through its verbal wit and comic pyrotechnics.

Red Alert portrays the insane situation of accidental nuclear war triggered by a SAC (Strategic Air Command) general who believes a preemptive strike to be the only way to secure peace on earth. The attack fails because of a lucky mistake: The one B-52 that eludes Soviet defenses drops its H-bomb on an uninhabited area, not its intended urban target. In *Red Alert* the automatically triggered Doomsday machine of *Dr. Strangelove* is absent. Whereas George's story at its close presents the strategy of automatic retaliation (Doomsday missiles in underground silos) as a deterrent to Soviet threat, *Dr. Strangelove* merges the concept of automatic retaliation into the Russian Doomsday Machine as the factor that makes it impossible to prevent an accidental launch of nuclear weapons from escalating into total war. As Powers notes, *Red Alert* "oozes with a syrupy sort of sentimentality and domesticity," whereas *Dr. Strangelove* sustains its black comedic attitude of "savage misanthropy."

Novelized under Peter George's name, the film brilliantly parodies the false myth of the Bomb as a kind of infernal deity. The novelization, a lost classic for a number of years, has been reprinted with a superbly incisive introductory essay by Richard Gid Powers. Since this scholarly text is not readily accessible to young readers and since it is the film version that they are more likely to know, this discussion will be limited to the movie.

In the mode of black comedy, *Dr. Strangelove* demolishes the military establishment, the government, and the "mad scientist" cliché of science fiction, and, most of all, travesties the mentality that makes nuclear war possible. The absurdist treatment underscores again the irony of a situation in which weapons can go out of human control, spelling disaster for the entire planet. Richard Gid Powers points to the grotesque effect of seeing "a preposterous race of human vermin absolutely devoid of principle or honor, enthusiastically obsessed by the twin goals of sex and power . . . armed with instruments of absolute destruction." Powers uses the phrase "grotesque predicament" in the sense the term is used by Shakespearean director Jan Kott to signify "entering into a contest against a machine that the victim himself has programmed to be unbeatable."[38] Superpowers locked into strategies of Mutually Assured Destruction epitomize this bizarre situation.

The satire of nuclear folly appeals to the human need to play out the fear of total destruction. The process of the escalation of nuclear ten-

38. Richard Gid Powers, introduction to *Dr. Strangelove*, pp. vi–vii, xi.

sions beautifully dramatizes the process of *schismogenesis*. *Schismogenesis* is anthropologist Gregory Bateson's term to describe the interchanges that accelerate the differences between people. He originally used the concept to apply to the way in which one person's boasting, for instance, spurs another's, and vice versa, until hostility mounts and the relationship breaks down.[39]

General Jack D. Ripper, who initiates the catastrophe, manifests a paranoid schizophrenic fear that his "bodily fluids" are being sapped and polluted by means of a Communist conspiracy that operates through fluoridation of the U.S. water supply. The Air Force base from which he issues orders to Strategic Air Command pilots is ironically emblazoned with billboards and posters proclaiming "Peace Is Our Profession." General Ripper, compelled by his insane fears, determines to destroy the USSR by a preemptive strike against Soviet targets.

Aware of the general's insanity, Captain Mandrake (Peter Sellers) vainly tries to forestall disaster by obtaining the recall code known only to Ripper, who refuses to supply it. As tension mounts, the U.S. president (also played by Sellers) convenes key staff in the War Room and, against the advice of Chief of Staff "Buck" Turgidson, deploys Army troops to storm General Ripper's post to force him to reveal the code that can stop the planes before they reach the point of no return.

There are flashes to *Leper Colony*, the SAC bomber piloted by Captain "King" Kong (Slim Pickens), a "sly, exuberant, sneaky-dumb comic cowboy" who is little different from the character Pickens played in countless Westerns, except that Kubrick gives him "an H-bomb to ride instead of a horse." The very grotesquery of the characters, comparable to those popularized by Sellers on the "Goon Show," operates to distance the viewer/reader from the self-destructive, abominable human race set on suicide or, more accurately, geocide.[40]

The dramatic tension is heightened through cuts to the *Leper Colony* as it progresses toward its target and loses radio contact with the base. At the Air Force base, General Ripper takes his own life rather than submit to questioning by the Army forces that break through his defenses. Captain Mandrake, though hindered by a dense Army officer bent on taking him captive, improbably succeeds in piecing together the recall code from clues among the general's papers. All but one of

39. See Gregory Bateson, *Steps to an Ecology of Mind: A Revolutionary Approach to Man's Understanding of Himself* (New York: Ballantine Books, 1972), pp. 68–72, 108–11, 126–27.
40. Powers, introduction to *Dr. Strangelove*, pp. xiv–xv.

the remaining SAC bombers are successfully recalled, the maverick being, of course, *Leper Colony*, which cannot receive the recall message because of damaged radio equipment.

Dr. Strangelove (Sellers in his third role), the wheelchair-bound and spastic mad scientist, comprehends the terrible truth: The Doomsday Machine will be set off when the bomber strikes its target. The frantic president, realizing there is no other way to forestall the destruction of the earth, pleads with the Soviet premier to shoot down the U.S. plane before it can carry out its mission.

The one possibility for survival of the race lies in flight to the underground mine shafts. Dr. Strangelove glows with perverted sexual passion as he describes how life could continue underground, where he imagines females might exceed males by a ratio of ten to one. These speculations vaporize, however, as the hands of the nuclear clock touch midnight, *Leper Colony* fulfills its purpose, and the Earth is obliterated under a burgeoning mushroom cloud.

The portrayal of Strangelove blatantly conveys a major theme of the film—the obsessive, quasi-religious, quasi-erotic love of the power of death wielded by the bomb. Spencer R. Weart in *Nuclear Fear* notes the film's portrayal of "perverse sexuality" in the warriors' erotic fantasies of destruction. At the close of the film Dr. Strangelove springs from his wheelchair as the Doomsday Machine explodes, seemingly rejuvenated by the energy emanating from massive slaughter. Since Strangelove is portrayed as a "sometime Nazi," Weart finds in him an explanation of "what underlay all nuclear weaponry—the '*strange love*' for doing harm."[41]

The film succeeds as superb satire, vividly representing what Merritt Abrash calls the "hidden logic" underneath the so-called deterrence policy, a logic that betokens an inevitable progression toward nuclear holocaust.[42] A difficulty with Kubrick's absurdist satire voiced by Paul Brians arises from the fact that viewers or readers may be left feeling *there is no choice*, that no human action can stem the tide sweeping the earth to doomsday. As Paul Brians notes, absurdist treatments of nuclear catastrophe become "a form of not thinking" if they lead people to conclude matters are beyond their control.[43]

An alternative to Brians's view can be drawn from exploring some comments on the drama made by psychiatrist Robert J. Lifton. On the one hand *Dr. Strangelove* portrays the impulse to press the button, to feel the "orgiastic excitement" of destroying everything, to nullify

41. Weart, *Nuclear Fear*, pp. 413–14.

42. Merritt Abrash, "Through Logic to Apocalypse: Science Fiction Scenarios of Nuclear Deterrence Breakdown," *Science Fiction Studies* 13, pt. 2 (July 1986): 129–38.

43. Brians, *Nuclear Holocausts*, p. 86.

anxiety by getting it all over with. This is the desire for the "Big Whoosh," Chernus's term mentioned earlier. However, the other dimension of the drama is the implicit "wisdom," says Lifton, of seeing "the radical absurdity or madness' of the world-destruction we are contemplating"—an opening of consciousness to what Teilhard de Chardin called the "noosphere," where we are privileged with a glimpse of "a form of human identity so inclusive that it embraces the entire species."[44] In short, the drama can leave us with a perception of the unity of all life. From such a vision, we may be able to derive what Robert Fuller has called "a better game than war" through which we can work out our hostilities.[45]

Powers makes a case for the film as Stanley Kubrick's triumph over his personal fears of nuclear annihilation. Kubrick's reaction to the "fatuousness" of George's book and his ability to transmute it into absurd comedy liberated him, as a creative artist, from the paralysis of nuclear fear. By transforming the banal book into a brilliant satire, the film-maker made himself believe that "the bomb and all that it implied was absurd," and that "caring about it was absurd." He was then freed to go on with "his true calling, the making of movies, and to give up trying to save the world."[46]

It is left to the individual to decide the degree to which Kubrick's exorcism of his fear of global annihilation may serve a similar need for the viewer/reader. In any event the drama makes an indelible statement about the power of human folly and destructiveness. The articulation of a possible way out of the labyrinth of perverse nuclearism must be found elsewhere.

"Cat's Cradle": Humanity as Short-Sighted Children

Cat's Cradle is typical Kurt Vonnegut in being playful, often flippant. The narrator, John ("Call me Jonah"), sets out to write a book,

44. Robert J. Lifton, "The Image of the End of the World: A Psychoanalytical View," in Facing Apocalypse, pp. 46, 48 n. 31. Note 31 is an acknowledgment of indebtedness to Erik Erikson's unpublished paper, "A Developmental Crisis of Mankind."

45. This phrase is from Robert Fuller's cassette recording, "A Better Game Than War," available from New Dimensions Radio, P.O. Box 410510, San Francisco, CA 94141–0510. Fuller, an educator formerly on the faculty of Oberlin College, advocates that the "better game" may be travel and face-to-face conversation with citizens from as many different cultures as possible. In this way, the supposed "alien" or "enemy" can become a friend.

46. Powers, introduction to Dr. Strangelove, p. xviii.

The Day the World Ended, about what a number of well-known people were doing on the day Hiroshima was struck with an A-bomb.

Throughout the story, author and protagonist draw on *The Books of Bokonon,* fictional writings attributed to one of Vonnegut's most ingenious characters. Bokonon is a cynical yet wise guru, a philosopher who is arrogant, indecorous, and self-deprecating all at once, an apparent alter ego for Vonnegut. Bokonon challenges both God and man with equal aplomb, confounding pomposity and stupidity wherever he finds them. Useful "fictions" are validated by the epigraph to the book, which advises us all to "live by the foma [harmless untruths] that make you brave and kind and healthy and happy," a piece of wisdom from the fabled *Books of Bokonon.*

Cat's Cradle satirizes war, with science's latest triumph, "ice-nine" (cf. "asinine"), a metaphor for technologies of destruction, especially the atomic bomb. Hoenikker, the brilliant scientist whom Vonnegut associates with J. Robert Oppenheimer, discovered ice-nine, which causes the atoms of mud (and anything else with water content it may chance to touch) to freeze into crystals at normal atmospheric temperatures. Intended to rescue the U.S. Marines from muddy situations, it has an unanticipated side effect—the power to destroy life. John's quest to find out all he can about Hoenikker, now deceased, leads him on an odyssey that turns out to be a race to keep ice-nine from turning the earth into a lifeless glacier (cf. the later concept of nuclear winter).

Certain iconic, mythic figures emerge in the novel. One is Vonnegut's figurative view of all humans as "children" in the face of war: As Ambassador Horlick Minton says in his address to the people of San Lorenzo, he can think of those who have been murdered in war only as "lost children." Partly because of the loss of his own son in warfare, he has no use for war mythologies; he says,

> Perhaps when we remember wars, we should take off our clothes and paint ourselves blue and go on all fours all day long and grunt like pigs. That would surely be more appropriate than noble oratory and shows of flags and well-oiled guns.[47]

Vonnegut also establishes a link between creativity and the playfulness natural to children. In accepting a Nobel Prize, Hoenikker explains his creativity as deriving from his persistent dawdling, "like an eight-year-old on a spring morning on his way to school. Anything can

47. Kurt Vonnegut, *Cat's Cradle* (New York: Holt, Rinehart and Winston, 1963; Dell, 1987), p. 170.

make me stop and look and wonder, and sometimes learn."[48] It is the title image, the cat's cradle of a string game used to amuse children, that crystallizes the connection between playfulness and the creative imagination. Bokonon makes a connection between divine creativity, spiritual growth, and play when he declares, "Peculiar travel suggestions are dancing lessons from God."[49]

There is, however, a negative, destructive aspect to play as well. Vonnegut sees the child's potential as a dangerous, careless player with the toy of massive destruction, in this case ice-nine but metaphorically nuclear weapons. The narrator questions, "What hope can there be for mankind . . . when there are such men as Felix Hoenikker to give such playthings as *ice-nine* to such short-sighted children as almost all men and women are?"[50] Vonnegut gives us the richly paradoxical image of the child as creator/destroyer, at once woefully ignorant of his power and innocent in a terrible, often catastrophic way of the possible consequences of his toying around with powers far beyond his control. Archetypally, this is the Magician in the negative guise.

Cat's Cradle implies what Vonnegut has articulated elsewhere, namely our need as human beings for leaders who are stern pessimists about human nature and realists about ecology and the natural environment (maybe incorporating some of Bokonon's qualities of the wise fool) but also "generative" thinkers, who value the well-being of future generations.[51] In his "A Letter to the Next Generation from Kurt Vonnegut, the Literary Wit of Our Time," Vonnegut points out how the flood of information (chiefly "bad news") from media cuts off our chance to "wax wise" and then expands upon nature's inherent lack of concern for life. In a bold imaginative leap he postulates that we have nuclear warheads aimed at each other to distract us from our expanded knowledge of nature's cruelty. His serious and sage advice is to avoid "abysmally ignorant optimists" as leaders; rather, choose leaders who present "Nature's stern but reasonable surrender terms" in no ambiguous language. Nature has, he says, six demands of humans if they are to survive: Reduce and stabilize the population; halt the poisoning of the environment; "stop preparing for war and start

48. Ibid., p. 17.
49. Ibid., p. 50.
50. Ibid., p. 164.
51. Erik Erikson, quoted by Daniel Goleman, "Erikson, in His Own Old Age, Expands His View of Life," *New York Times*, June 14, 1988, p. C14. Erikson and his wife, Joan, describe "generativity" as having two "faces": *caritas* (they define as "caring for others") and *agapé* (empathic love).

dealing with your real problems"; learn to "inhabit a small planet" (global thinking); "stop thinking science can fix anything, if you give it a trillion dollars"; and, most significantly for present purposes,

> Stop thinking your grandchildren will be OK no matter how wasteful or destructive you may be, since they can go to a nice new planet on a spaceship. That is *really* mean and stupid.[52]

The kind of thinking Vonnegut calls for is in Erikson's term "generative," global, and holistic. In his global mythology, the child is an icon of humanity's creative and destructive potentialities. These two powers are *dialectical*, not *dichotomous*, elements of human consciousness, and recognition of their systemic nature is one step toward bringing them into harmony. This is in turn a step toward healing and wholeness of the imagination and a prerequisite to the appreciation of a mythology of peace.

"Final Warning"

A more simplistic satire of nuclearism can be seen in Dudley Bromley's *Final Warning*, in which the bomb-obsessed protagonists in their zeal to prevent nuclear cataclysm bring about the event. Holly (transparently nicknamed "Pandora") and Roman, her cohort, bribe President Carlos Martinez, leader of a small South American state, to construct a laboratory where they can make atomic bombs. By showing how easy it is to do so, they hope to prove the need for mandatory strict safeguards on nuclear weapons materials.

The idealistic Holly wants to bring about a better world through her "final warning," but succeeds only in blowing up the world to teach it a lesson.[53] The lesson kills almost all the pupils. A former CIA (Central Intelligence Agency) man, one of the few to survive the blast, tells the story as an illustration of how well-intentioned people can be seduced by the "craziness" of nuclearism. A contemporary version of the Pandora myth, the story unhappily perpetuates the notion that a woman is responsible for the release of evils into the world. Though published by Children's Press, the book is poor fare for young readers; it may find an audience among those who can stomach heavy-handed sermonizing against the dangers of becoming like one's enemy, in this case the

52. "A Letter to the Next Generation from Kurt Vonnegut, the Literary Wit of Our Time," *Time* 131, no. 6 (February 8, 1985), Special Advertising Section, unp.
53. Dudley Bromley, *Final Warning* (Chicago: Children's Press, 1982), p. 73.

risk of peacenik becoming bombaholic (a well-established cliché in nuclear fiction) in yet another instance of enantiodromia.

Picture Book Views: A Contrast

"When the Wind Blows"

A picture book that appeared almost simultaneously with *Hiroshima no Pika*, Raymond Briggs's *When the Wind Blows* has occasioned similar controversy over its intended audience. Briggs created the book in reaction to the classified "Protect and Survive" pamphlet issued by the British government. The cover pictures a British couple of retirement age in a tender, family-album pose, oblivious to the mushroom cloud looming behind them. James Bloggs ("Ducks" to his wife, Hilda) has filled his head with the platitudes used to disguise the terror of mass destruction. Consequently his thinking is fuzzy and his speech is full of malapropisms (e.g., he says "ultimate *determent*" instead of "ultimate *deterrent*"). His wife, when she thinks of war at all, imagines a replay of World War II and cheerfully supposes they will muddle through as they did before.

James is not quite so naive, yet in his bumbling fashion he places trust in a leaflet from the Public Library entitled "The Householder's Guide to Survival." The Public Library, after all, would not distribute misinformation (!) and its very possession of the publication somehow seems to domesticize the terror of the subject matter. When a newscaster urges civilians to make fallout shelters, James blanches, chokes on his sausages, and goes into action with the comment, "This is really it." Dutifully following the pamphlet directions, he makes an indoor shelter improvised from doors, with cushions and books on top (an advance, he believes, over the old-fashioned hole in the ground). Ron, their son, whom James consults by telephone, reveals between fits of hysterical laughter that he will not participate in the ritual of making "an Inner Core or Refuge." He has attended the Polytechnic and presumably knows the futility of such structures as his father painstakingly constructs.

The instructions in Briggs's narrative resemble those in a booklet prepared by the U.S. Civil Defense Preparedness Agency and published in 1972. *Your Chance to Live* was designed for use with schoolchildren. Done under contract with the Far West Laboratory for Educational Research and Development—an agency that explains its mission as helping to "create new and better opportunities for children to learn"—the booklet gives these directions for making your own fallout shelter:

> If you are caught short, improvise. Pile protective materials around yourself: piles of newspapers, furniture, sacks of grain. Create your shelter area in an inner room or closet. You can also improvise protection by digging a trench in your yard and covering it with lumber (or a door) and earth.[54]

The utter absurdity of such "preparations" as protection from nuclear warheads could not be more obvious.

Throughout *When the Wind Blows*, the artwork combines with the text silently and subtly to build up the tension. The comic-strip format is broken by unframed and almost wordless two-page spreads, the first of which shows a single nuclear warhead with the caption, "Meanwhile, on a distant plain." At the turn of a page, James is seen relaxed in his armchair, puzzling over how the Russkies, who were "on our side in the war," could now be the enemy. The imaginative retreat to a simpler time is made ludicrous. Similarly ludicrous are Hilda's obsessive housewifely concerns—her fretting over finger marks on pillows that are used to line their lean-to shelter—and her insistent modesty: She refuses to give up the convenience of using the toilet, an act forbidden in the bureaucratic regulations, and braves atomic radiation to do so. Fastidiousness triumphs over government recommendations, but the latter are even more absurd than her false pride.

Dominant images are the mushroom cloud; the warheads standing on a distant plain, at first like insanely overgrown bullets, then like giant wasps approaching through the dark sky bearing death; a nuclear submarine pointing its deadly snout at the reader like some enormous and lethal black shark. The explosion of the warhead takes up a double-page spread in stark white, tinged with pink around the edges (no words—this is the *flash*), followed by another two-page spread depicting the white flash merging into rose, then red, outlining the lean-to shelter where the Bloggses cringe. The colors darken to sickly brown-green hues, with James's exclamation, "Blimey," marking the inadequacy of words to convey the enormity of the event. The contrast in scale between the small cartoon-sized frames depicting the Bloggses and the unframed two-page spreads picturing the weapons visually expresses human frailty poised against the gigantic, uncontrollable forces that shatter the boundaries of their simple lives.

54. U.S. Civil Defense Preparedness Agency, *Your Chance to Live* SM 3-12, 1972 (Washington: GPO, 1973), p. 82.

When their vision returns, the couple awaken to realize they are still alive. Hopes for help from Emergency Services go unanswered and their deterioration from radiation is rapid. Despite their forced cheeriness, they are clearly dying inch by inch. James tries to be sanguine and philosophical, thinking it might be all right, after all, to wipe the slate "clean," to start "afresh," a good instance of the New Eden fantasy.

The irony is shattering. The Bloggses lie down in their lean-to to die, reciting fragments of religious comfort (the 23rd Psalm) and jingoistic patriotism ("Into the Valley of the Shadow of Death . . . rode the six hundred"). A more scathing indictment of the misuse of religious and falsely patriotic emotions to lull us into complicity in our own deaths is hard to imagine. As readers detached by Briggs's ironic techniques from the fate of the Bloggses, we have the luxury of purging our pity, anger, and terror at the fate of these innocents; it is easy for us to feel intellectually superior to this couple even though their common-sensical natures and hopeful persistence are beyond reproach. Their very common sense dooms them, for it is not adequate to cope with the irrational forces in control of superweapons. We know, as never before, that our nuclear destiny must not be left to the government planners.

"The Bomb and the General"

An instructive contrast can be made between Briggs's satirical approach and the naive fantastical picture book from Italy entitled *The Bomb and the General* (text by Umberto Eco, illustrations by Eugenio Carmi).[55] The story tells of a bad, bombaholic general whose desire to start a nuclear war is foiled when the atoms within the weapons decide of their own accord to abandon the bombs, seeing in their wisdom that it is better to live in harmony than to explode. The best touch of irony comes when the general is reduced to the status of a doorman, a job that gives him a chance to parade his uniform with gold braid. The difficulty with the book is its encouragement of the notion that atoms will save us from ourselves. (No mythological connection is made to validate the atoms as intelligent fantasy beings; human participation in the transformation of consciousness is left out, a considerable omission that leads to irresponsible wishful thinking.)

---

55. Considering the excellence of Eco's *The Name of the Rose* (Italy, 1980; New York: Harcourt Brace Jovanovich, 1983; originally published as *Il nome della rosa*), this slight book is the more disappointing.

"The Last Children of Schevenborn"

Recently made available to English-reading youngsters in translation from the German, *The Last Children of Schevenborn* (*Die letzten
Kinder von Schewenborn*), Gudrun Pausewang's "Lord of the Flies"
about nuclear winter, deserves the wider audience it can now command. Because it is not yet found in most libraries and because of its
importance as a stark, truthful depiction of nuclear winter told in prose
of considerable quality, it is summarized here. The story is told from
the viewpoint of Roland, a twelve-going-on-thirteen boy of a family of
five, who observes the destruction of civilization by a nuclear catastrophe. The poem used as an epigraph, Jorg Zink's "Am Anfang Schaf
Gott Himmel und Erde" (In the Beginning God Created Heaven and
Earth), is a parody of the Biblical creation story; it tells a "decreation"
story about the last seven days of the Earth. These come about because
of humanity's prideful cleverness and arrogant decision to take the future into its own hands. Too proud to remain images of God and wishing instead to *be* God, human beings bring calamity upon themselves.
Apocalyptic scenes are vividly presented: pollution, drought, illness,
fire, the quenching of the light, endless quiet—all foreshadowing the
horrors of the book.

The poem closes on a chorus of cosmic laughter from the angels,
amused by the end of the drama of the paltry human race. This bitter
laughter does not, however, set the tone of the book, for Pausewang
stays strictly within the boy's human point of view, thereby eliciting
compassion as well as irony.

The limited perspective gives the narrative much of its emotional
punch. The voice of innocence, sustained through severe suffering,
merges into the embittered voice of experience too dire for most "children's" books. Pausewang truthfully depicts the effects of nuclear devastation, refusing to patronize young readers or to suppress the horrors
of the stench of disease; starvation; the plundering; the mistrust of nature that comes when water, source of life, turns deadly; the despair of
the hardening of hearts from too much grief; the deaths of many children; dehumanization; the "deadness" of time after the bomb; the
curses of elders by the young; the father's merciful killing of his infant
daughter (who is born with no eyes as a result of genetic damage).

This act of infanticide is related as part of an ironic parody of the story
of Christ's birth: Roland's parents, Klaus and Inge, are shut out of their
dwelling in Schevenborn (once the grandparents' home before the elder
couple, visiting in another city, were vaporized by the flash of detonation). The pregnant Inge, possessed by the need to see with her own

eyes that their former home is indeed gone forever (a good instance of denial) forces Klaus and Roland on a futile journey across the wasteland. Returning to Schevenborn they find their only remaining shelter taken over by others, who refuse to give up their squatters' rights.

With no room there or at the inn, Inge gives birth to the child in an abandoned park in the deadly midwinter chill. When she dies shortly after, leaving the eyeless child motherless, the father puts an end to its life, against Roland's pleas. There is a parallel here with the monstrous birth alluded to in the closing lines of William Butler Yeats's poem "The Second Coming" ("And what rough beast, its hour come at last,/Slouches towards Bethlehem to be born?"), as the sightless child signifies a world without vision, and its death betokens the end of civilization.

No more hair-raising yet moving tale of the dreadful wasteland of nuclear winter has been written (only *Wolf of Shadows*, following, comes close). Despite its negations, however, Pausewang's narrative does not stifle hope utterly. On the contrary, there are acts of compassion even in this near-Inferno, as when Roland takes care of Annette, a miserable dying child whom he brings to his home. Pausewang's last children of Schevenborn, the last generation of our race, are portrayed as still retaining the capacity for choice, the human difference. Just before the end, Roland affirms his decision to go on teaching the dwindling numbers of children to read, write, and reckon: "Our world will become a peaceable world, even though it will endure only for a short time."[56] The afterword explicitly states the author's hope that her story can enable us to forestall a destiny like that of Schevenborn. Her narrative stands as a lucid example of the cautionary nuclear tale; its translation into English is a landmark event for nuclear literature.

"Wolf of Shadows"

Another novel for youth, Whitley Strieber's *Wolf of Shadows*, was created in response to children's letters to Strieber and James W. Kunetka following their enormously successful *Warday, and the Journey Onward*, a journalistic depiction of the aftermath of a one-day nuclear war between the superpowers. Many children expressed concern about what happened to the animals. The tale is told from the perspective of Wolf of Shadows, an outsider (hence of the shadows) who heroically assumes leadership of the pack after a nuclear war because he is

---

56. Gudrun Pausewang, *The Last Children of Schevenborn*. Translated from the German by Norman Watt. (Saskatoon: Western Producer Prairie Books, 1988). Available from the

recognized as the strongest and best (hence the alpha male) by the alpha female. The Wolf is anthropomorphized in the sense that the reader is made privy to his thoughts, yet he remains credible, possibly because books such as *Julie of the Wolves*, by Jean Craighead George, and *Never Cry Wolf*, by Farley Mowat, have prepared the audience for empathic identification. Katherine Paterson observes that readers will "care more for him than for the human characters," adding that the weakest feature in the powerful story is the intrusive human conversation, though "the relationship between Wolf of Shadows and his human dependents rings true."[57]

Because the perspective is the wolf's, the reader is distanced from the human characters, a mother and two daughters who flee Minneapolis after a nuclear war (the father is dead). One child dies soon after from severe burns. The mother and her remaining child attach themselves to the wolf pack in order to survive. The courage and dogged determination of the mother as well as a vividly imagined, bleak scene of nuclear winter combine to create an effective cautionary tale. However, Strieber's call in the afterword for humanity as a species "to dismantle the [nuclear death] machine and use our great intelligence on behalf of the earth that bears us, instead of against her" seems more appropriate for politically active adults than for child readers. His plea is an important one, but children are hardly prepared to take on the task. We may hope nonetheless that young readers of this story may gain a vision of the interdependency of all life on Earth that in turn may help them create what their elders have intuited but failed to realize, namely a holistic and ecologically sound mythology as the basis for harmony among all living things.

It is tempting to suggest a Jungian interpretation of the Wolf as embodying the shadow within, with which each individual must come to terms, but Strieber's Wolf is presented as a positive, good emanation of nature. On some level, nonetheless, the story may imply our need to reconstitute the human family and human relationships through

---

publisher, 2310 Millar Avenue, P.O. Box 2500, Saskatoon, Saskatchewan S7K 2C4 Canada (ISBN 0-88833-236-X). Reprinted in England as *The Last Children* (Julia MacRae, 87 Vauxhall Walk, London SE11 5HJ; ISBN 0-86203-402-7). Published originally as *Die letzten Kinder von Schewenborn, oder sieht so unsere Zukunft aus?* (Ravensburg: Otto Maier, 1983). The passage quoted is my translation of the original German edition, page 125. Pausewang's prize-winning *Die Wolke* (1987), not yet translated, treats a nuclear power plant catastrophe.

57. Katherine Paterson, a review of *Wolf of Shadows*, by Whitley Strieber, *New York Times Book Review*, December 1, 1985, p. 39.

learning to live in harmony with the "wolf" within each individual psyche, to acknowledge it rather than try to deny it, and thereby to lay a new foundation for our survival as a species. The words of the human mother to the wolf define the contrast between the wolf's natural wisdom of unity with all and the human alienation from nature and others: "The difference between wolves and me? Each of you is all of you . . . [whereas] people [had] become so separated from one another."[58]

"Sentries"

Gary Paulsen's four featured teenage characters in *Sentries* are designed to represent all humanity. Their lives do not intersect; they are unaware of one another, but all die together, obliterated by "an enormous *CLICK*" of a thermonuclear bomb, followed by "a white glare of such intensity that it rivals the sun."[59]

Each youth is on a quest for self-realization. Sue Oldhorn is an Anglicized Ojibway Indian who has rejected her traditional roots until an intoxicated fellow Ojibway, Alan Deerfoot, brings her face-to-face with herself by asking, "Are you whole?" (a question that suggests a fruitful line of interpretation along the lines of "Psyche and Wholeness" by Rachel Blau DuPlessis[60]). Sue begins to change, finding the value of her grandfather's traditional songs and stories, and gaining a sense of family and continuity.

Pete Shackleton, a rock musician, is a maverick, an individual who resists the "party current" and the ubiquitous drug culture of the rock music scene. He seeks "the sound," a certain musical peak experience marked by mystical rapture, a feeling he sometimes experiences in performance when he is overcome by the conviction that "we are all the same family."[61]

Laura Hayes knows what she wants in life—to be a sheep rancher—but her parents want something "better" for her. They come to see that, for her, to raise sheep means to "follow her bliss." David Garcia, an illegal Mexican immigrant, seeks the American dream of an abundant life. Of the four, he is the only one whose dream seems destined to fail for reasons other than nuclear destruction, for the haven he desires to find in the South Dakota potato fields offers little more than

58. Whitley Strieber, *Wolf of Shadows* (New York: Sierra Club Books; distributed by Knopf, 1985), p. 91.

59. Gary Paulsen, *Sentries* (New York: Bradbury, 1986), p. 164.

60. Rachel Blau DuPlessis, "Psyche or Wholeness," *Massachusetts Review* 20 (Spring 1979): 77–96.

61. Paulsen, *Sentries*, pp. 20, 161.

backbreaking semi-slave labor, and the fruits of his long exodus from his native land are frustration and anger. Through Garcia's experience, Paulsen implies a link between economic violence and nuclear violence, for both rest upon the "thingification" of people and the treatment of lives and nature as commodities.

Interspersed between the episodes of the four teenagers' lives are four Battle Hymns, three of them stories of the losses endured by war veterans, each of whom returns with something missing, psychologically or physically or both. Thus Paulsen communicates the futility, senseless waste, and permanent scarring that are the bitter fruits of acting out a war mythology. Battle Hymn Number Four tells of the nuclear annihilation of the world in an enormous flash-boom. The promise the Sentries may have held for a better, more human community of Earthlings is negated in one moment. Paulsen depicts the death of the natural world as well, for the very last image is of a mother tiger and her cubs, full of the voracious energy of life, vaporized with all else. A fitting epitaph for the vanished life on Earth, killed by her short-sighted children, might be *sic transit gloria nuclear mundi*. Paulsen does not moralize, however; this dire cautionary scenario scarcely needs any exposition of its truth.

The Ambivalence of End-Time Myths

End-time myths may help us to work through our fears of nuclear devastation and turn our energies to seeking a peaceful future. We need, however, to guard against the possible self-deception that lurks beneath the fascination with what Warren Wagar deals with in *Terminal Visions: The Literature of Last Things*. As he astutely notes, a historical view of the pervasiveness of "end-times" reveals a certain insincerity or "chic bleak" often underlying the contemporary interest in "last things": He cites the example of the Virginia clergyman who founded End Time Foods, Inc., selling dehydrated victuals for "the dislocations sure to come." Literature is not immune to this deplorable exploitation of nuclear fear (or simple fear of change).[62]

Traditional cyclic views of time depict the end as the gateway to new life, whereas linear-time narratives show the end as the culmination of history, the end of time and the human story as we know it. Either con-

62. Warren Wagar, *Terminal Visions: The Literature of Last Things* (Bloomington: Indiana Univ. Pr., 1982), pp. 3–5.

cept can be exploited, and either can be self-defeating in giving rise to despair, since the cyclic view perpetuates the feeling that there is no escape from the wheel of time (the cycle being endlessly repeated) and the linear view perpetuates the similarly discouraging notion that all human endeavors are ultimately doomed, for all things will pass away in the twinkling of an eye. The alternative "hopeful" scenario would see temporal experience as spiraling upward, in the vein of Goethe's *Faust* (a perspective difficult to find in the twentieth century, much less in nuclear fiction). Despairing views may give rise to what James Blish calls "chiliastic panic" as humanity approaches the end of a century or millenium.[63] These "ax-time" scenarios have value to the degree they can help us as readers to envision an alternative, bombless world and inspire us with energy to seek it. Ultimately, only individual readers can decide which narratives evoke this response for them.

63. Quoted in Brian Stableford, "Man-Made Catastrophes," in *The End of the World*, ed. Eric S. Rabkin, Martin H. Greenberg, and Joseph D. Olander (Carbondale: Southern Illinois Univ. Pr., 1983), p. 125.

CHAPTER 6

Survivors in an Atomized Eden

Pseudomyth

Nuclear fiction displays a number of false mythical patterns, what might be called pseudomyths. Sometimes the pseudomyth is displayed in order that it may be unmasked. Two such instances can be found in Phyllis Naylor's *Dark of the Tunnel* and Raymond Briggs's *When the Wind Blows*, both of which expose the falsity of the myth of "civil defense." Another popular pseudomyth, as professor of religion Ira Chernus has noted, is the idea that people can survive by means of "relocation" (sometimes by flight to another planet, a contemporary version of the Biblical motif of the flight into the wilderness); and the myth of a new Adam and Eve who survive to rebuild civilization, the featured theme of the books in this chapter. The naive faith in the possibility of a new beginning from the nuclear wasteland has been expressed in its most blatant and chauvinistic form in the words of Senator Richard Russell, who, in advocating more nuclear weapons, affirmed, "If we have to start over with another Adam and Eve, I want them to be Americans." All of these false myths are charged with pseudoheroic notions of survival, and Chernus is correct in his assertion that they appeal seductively to our yearnings to be transformed, new beings born out of chaos, who with our sacred wisdom will rebuild a world from the ashes. The peculiarly American form of this myth emerges in the "Captain America Complex," depicting the common people, left helpless after a great catastrophe, saved by the appearance of an all-powerful stranger who sets things right, a stranger who will probably be characterized as a "technological genius."[1]

1. Ira Chernus, *Dr. Strangegod: On the Symbolic Meaning of Nuclear Weapons* (Columbia: Univ. of South Carolina Pr., 1986), pp. 88–89, 101, 103, 105. Sen. Russell is quoted by Chernus on page 105.

The inherent danger of these false myths is evident, for they can lull us into complacency. They persist, nonetheless, often with the validation of religious faith. A. G. Mojtaibai, author of *Blessed Assurance: At Home with the Bomb in Amarillo, Texas*, examines the connection between nuclearism and the apocalyptic religious scenario. Amarillo, where all the nuclear weapons built in this country are assembled, is also the home of a number of fundamentalist sects who, despite their differences, share a fascination with Armageddon. Mojtaibai demonstrates what J. Anthony Lukas calls the "spiritual and psychological fit" between their belief in "the Rapture—the divine rescue of true believers from the approaching holocaust"—and their acceptance of nuclear weapons. Their focus on the Second Coming fits neatly with the belief that nuclear holocaust is inevitable and allows them to come to grips with "a loss of control and runaway technology." The missing ingredient in the theology of the Rapture is identified by Lukas, who reviewed Mojtaibai's book for the *New York Times:* Adherents of belief in the Rapture lack a metaphorical vision of "community, a shared humanity in which all God's children must find their way haltingly, but together, toward peace and justice." Lukas believes the Book of Revelation and the Rapture metaphor today are being used in a self-aggrandizing, irresponsible way "to buttress the self-righteous" more than "to comfort the afflicted." Such a mythology encourages the believers to think they will be saved, others damned— a belief hinging on the simplistic dichotomization of the world's peoples into good and evil. Mojtaibai recognizes that in such a world, "accommodation or negotiation with the enemy becomes unthinkable . . . peace is humanly impossible, and war inevitable."[2] Such thinking, a good instance of what psychiatrist Jerome D. Frank calls the psychology of the Enemy, can only become self-fulfilling prophecy.

This chapter will examine nuclear fiction displaying the pervasive mythic pattern of the degenerated New Eden, a bomb-blighted wasteland where nature has been denatured and the new Adam and Eve, who have somehow escaped radiation, struggle to exist.[3] The discussion will be organized around certain key topics: (1) the conditions endured by the new Adam and Eve and their relative status as man and woman, as well as their relationships with children; (2) the accuracy of the picture of aftereffects of atomic devastation (the truth about conse-

2. J. Anthony Lukas, "The Rapture and the Bomb," a review of *Blessed Assurance: At Home with the Bomb in Amarillo, Texas* by A. G. Mojtaibai, *New York Times Book Review,* June 8, 1986, p. 7.

3. Paul Brians discusses this theme in *Nuclear Holocausts: Atomic War in Fiction, 1895–1984* (Kent, Ohio: Kent State Univ. Pr., 1986), p. 62.

quences);(3) the condition of the natural world and its receptiveness to life (friendly or antagonistic); (4) the attitudes toward technology (valued or feared); and(5) the emerging value system and its implicit or explicit survival ethic.

Because these narratives often incorporate a vision of cyclic time, a brief analysis of a text exemplifying the cyclic time structure will be presented first.

David Macaulay's "Baaa": The Model of Cyclic Time

Portrayals of time as cyclic harmonize well with the ancient "wheel of fortune" metaphor, which takes the view that whatever one's position in life, it will change: the lowly will rise and those of high estate will be humbled. The notion was extended from the individual to the societal level. The idea that kingdoms and civilizations rise and fall in an unending cycle is an ancient one, as can be seen in many mythologies, one example being that of the Greeks, in which one set of gods reigned for a time, only to be replaced by another.

An elementary instance of cyclic time underlying a narrative can be seen in David Macaulay's picture book *Baaa*, which is set in an indeterminate time and may or may not reflect the aftermath of a nuclear holocaust. The sheep who become the dominant species on earth in the wake of an unspecified catastrophe that destroys humankind easily become infected by human vices. Macaulay writes in the tradition of the animal fable, in which the animals are, as May Hill Arbuthnot, the children's literature expert, once said, "ourselves in fur." Their cannibalism serves as an effective metaphor for their cupidity and, like the animals in George Orwell's *1984*, they out-Herod Herod in their tyranny over those who are weaker. Macaulay effectively foreshadows their fate, which will be exactly like that of the humans they replaced. As the French would say, the more things change, the more they remain the same—a proverb that sums up the "law" of cyclic time. *Baaa* exemplifies the usually ironic mode of narratives with a cyclic time structure: what will be, will be, but it is bound to be more of the same—an attitude implicitly cynical.

"Ape and Essence"

One of the bitterest early portrayals of life after the bomb is Aldous Huxley's *Ape and Essence*. A fable about a future dystopia, structured as

a narrative within a narrative, the story depicts a totalitarian society re-
plete with macabre, disturbing elements, among them the treatment of
women as inferior beings, despised but tolerated because they are
needed to perpetuate the race. In this abhorrent state of affairs, men
are not happy either; all dwell in a loveless world where jailors are no
more to be envied than slaves. The love relationship that grows between Dr. Poole and Loola is the only hint of a way out of the infernal
society, and they survive only through flight.[4]

In the frame story, the narrator and his companion discover the
manuscript of a drama by the deceased playwright William Tallis
when it falls off a garbage truck. Tallis's work is set in the year 2108
and portrays the deteriorated West Coast society found by the New
Zealand Rediscovery Expedition, sent to the coast of California after a
nuclear conflict called the Third World War. New Zealand in nuclear
fiction is the darling of the gods, for it is one place on earth seemingly
immune to atomic cataclysm. The leader of the New Zealanders is Dr.
Poole, who finds a crudely distorted post-cataclysmic culture twisted
in body and soul by the effects of radiation, with the horrors of genetic devolution quite accurately portrayed. The society is controlled
by misogynistic men, chief among them the Arch-Vicar of Belial. Sex
is held in contempt, but its orgiastic power breaks out in bloodthirsty
rituals. Women are hated precisely because of their sexual and generative powers, now viewed as tainted because of the high incidence of
defective, mutated births. The subjection of women is religiously
sanctioned by the ''Shorter Catechism,'' which describes woman as
''the vessel of the Unholy Spirit, the source of all deformity, the enemy of the race.''[5]

This institutionalized loathing for women stems first from the fact
that men, having destroyed civilization through their misuse of technology, need a scapegoat for their guilt; and second, from women being illogically held responsible for bringing forth monstrous offspring.
The latter unfortunates are ritually destroyed at periodic satanic orgies.

The generative power of nature has become poisoned. Boys are
taught to despise girls and sexuality is termed ''Malicious Animal Mag-
netism.'' Minor abnormalities are tolerated, but anything over the pre-
scribed limit is cause enough to liquidate the unfortunate at the Purifi-

---

4. In *The Handmaid's Tale* (New York: Fawcett, 1986), Margaret Atwood portrays a
similarly rigid class structure imposed by men, and an environment in which women are
both subjugated and prized for their fertility. Though the cataclysm that brings about the
repressive regime is not a nuclear one, the parallels with Huxley's *Ape and Essence* are
nonetheless remarkable and worth study.

5. Aldous Huxley, *Ape and Essence* (New York: Harper, 1948), p. 52.

cation.[6] Mothers of mutants are publicly shamed and suffer the terror of seeing their irregular children destroyed in the name of Belial.

The story of this loathsome future world reads like message literature of the most blatant kind, yet its anger is understandable: Huxley was provoked by the assassination of Gandhi, the atrocities of the European Holocaust, and the destruction of Hiroshima and Nagasaki by what he perceived to be a diabolical misuse of technology. In Tallis's film script (the story within the story is meant to be made into a movie) the Arch-Vicar explains to Dr. Poole at one point how Belial, the ruling devil, came to power: He gradually gained the possession of great national leaders, fastening upon them "at the point where they ceased to be human beings and became specialists."[7]

Critic Keith M. May, in his fine essay on *Ape and Essence* in *Aldous Huxley*, observes that Huxley's aim in writing the novel was "to undermine the feeling of security of those who cannot take evil seriously." The pictured "imaginary nadir" of history reflects Huxley's concern over the "vanishing spirituality" of humankind. In this troubling narrative, Huxley looks into the abyss of evil within the human psyche and shows how evil is fed by fear. Fear alone, however, cannot explain the worship of Belial, who is not a being, but a nonentity—the mass, "general" will that corresponds to no individual's real will. Belial comes into power because people no longer believe in evil as real. Denial of our own "glassy essence" or spirit-nature results in subordination to the calculative intellect as arbiter of truth, and the consequences are deplorable.[8]

The scene depicting Faraday, Einstein, and Pasteur—exemplars of the creative intellect in pursuit of yet unrevealed truth—shows them degraded and enslaved by baboons, creatures of impulse and lust. Metaphorically this expresses Huxley's insight into how humans, who are both spiritual essence and clay, have become unbalanced, victims of their own least-exalted qualities.

Dr. Poole is Huxley's mouthpiece to expound his belief that "love, joy and peace . . . the fruits of the spirit" are the essence of humanity and the world, yet, as he also observes, "the fruits of the ape-mind, the fruits of the monkey's presumption and revolt . . . . hate and unceasing restlessness and a chronic misery," rule over human affairs. Through his love of poetry and philosophy, Poole shows a sympathy with Shelleyean idealism, and a persistent belief in "that Light whose

6. Ibid., pp. 63, 71.
7. Ibid., p. 97.
8. Keith M. May, "*Ape and Essence* (1948)," in *Aldous Huxley* (London: Paul Elek Books, 1972), pp. 177–179, 181.

smile kindles the Universe, / That Beauty in which all things work and move.'' The worship of technology has rent the ''web of being,'' dealt a blow to sustaining universal Love, and fear consequently rules the world. Technology, though it raises our standard of living, increases the probability of our violent deaths.[9]

Huxley manages, by stretching the limits of credibility, to wrench something positive out of his hellish scenario. Poole grows attached to Loola, a woman of this infernal world distinguished by her compassion for the victims of its cruelty. Together, Poole and Loola flee to take refuge with a group of mavericks called ''hots'' because their sexuality is not seasonal like that of most of the inhabitants of the Belialian culture. The hots are, in short, biologically like humans of our own time. The relationship between Poole and Loola expresses Huxley's easy-to-overlook, subordinate positive theme, that sensual love can be, in Keith M. May's words, ''the gateway to the divine.''[10] The bitter satire of humanity's destructive selfishness and willful lunacies epitomized in such atrocities as the use of atomic weapons holds center stage.

As the fictional creator of Poole and Loola's world, Tallis plays a joke on himself in the closing scene of the script, for he imagines the two lovers standing beside his (Tallis's) own headstone, where Poole, given a hardboiled egg by Loola, cracks it upon the headstone, peels it, and eats it, scattering fragments of shell over the grave. This self-mockery on the fictional screenwriter's part may also betoken the triumph of new life (the egg being an ancient symbol of life beginning again). If there is a survival ethic emanating from this narrative, it rests upon a rejection of materialistic, technological solutions to human problems, and embraces, instead, spiritually based values, including a respect for nature and her processes.

''That Only a Mother''

This study for the most part excludes short stories, but Judith Merril's ''That Only a Mother,'' besides being the first fictional treatment of atomic weapons by a woman, provides a needed contrast to Huxley's *Ape and Essence* in its rendering of a woman's tender acceptance of her mutant child; indeed, she cannot even *see* the infant daughter's variation from the norm and perceives instead only a beautiful, verbally precocious little girl. During her pregnancy Maggie has worried about the grotesquely mutated births caused by an extended, limited

9. Huxley, *Ape and Essence*, pp. 37, 142, 153.
10. May, *Aldous Huxley*, p. 188.

nuclear conflict. Her husband, Hank, is absent, working in an underground facility where he designs nuclear weapons. Hank is not present when the baby is born, and Maggie writes to assure him that despite the occurrence of other mutant births and consequent acts of infanticide by hysterical fathers, "*ours* is all right."

Hank returns on leave and is momentarily struck by his daughter's verbal ability, but to his horror he finds, when he tries to take the oddly wriggling infant in his arms, a "sinuous, limbless body. *Oh God, dear God* —his head shook and his muscles contracted in a bitter spasm of hysteria. His fingers tightened on his child—*Oh God, she didn't know.*"[11] The reader is left at the close of the story wondering what will become of the child. In her study of science fiction, Martha Bartter has speculated, will the "perfectionist father" kill the child? If so, his act "stands as evidence of the end of human reproduction in a damaged world."[12]

Critic H. Bruce Franklin observes that "even sympathetic critics have radically misinterpreted this complex tale about mutually exclusive male and female definitions of fantasy and sanity." He poses a series of probing questions:

> Did Maggie truly not know, or is her maternal blindness to her child's defects merely a better survival mechanism than the military blindness that had caused them? Will Hank, otherwise portrayed as a loving husband despite his job of impersonally designing instruments of mass killing, continue to tighten his fingers until he succeeds in carrying out on a domestic level what he does for a living? . . . Who is more sane and rational, the adoring mother of the story's title or the father gripped by "hysteria" (a word derived from *uterus*) when faced with the fruits of his labor?[13]

In Franklin's teaching experience, students' debates over the last question usually divide along predictable gender lines. One can only conjecture about the kind of "survival ethic" Merril's story implies. However, she assuredly is making a strong case for loving the "different" rather than rejecting them on the grounds of abnormality. This

11. Judith Merril, "That Only a Mother," in *Isaac Asimov's Science Fiction Treasury*, ed: Isaac Asimov, Martin Greenberg, and Joseph Olander (New York: Bonanza Books, 1980), pp. 434, 440. Originally published in *Astounding Science Fiction* (June 1948).

12. Martha A. Bartter, *The Way to Ground Zero: The Atomic Bomb in American Science Fiction* (New York: Greenwood Press, 1988), p. 228.

13. H. Bruce Franklin, "The Bomb in the Home: Stories by Japanese and American Women Experts on Nuclearism," paper presented at the Modern Language Association Conference, New Orleans, December 28, 1988.

short story rates high in its portrayal of the truth about consequences of our failure to value the power to create over the power to destroy.

"Shadow on the Hearth"

Whereas Huxley satirizes a degenerate world in which life that deviates from a "norm" must be destroyed, Merril's story portrays the opposed male and female parental views of a mutant child and leaves them to the reader to evaluate. Her novel *The Shadow on the Hearth*, [14] the first novel by a woman on the theme of atomic weapons, continues to explore the domestic perspective through its portrayal of the effects of nuclear war on a typical family of the 1950s. The speculative nature of the novel is clear from the dedication: "For Shmuel, the teacher, who kept asking 'Why?' " Merril's work, like Helen Clarkson's later novel, questions why the human race seems dead set on the destruction of civilization.

The story is told through the eyes of Gladys Mitchell, an ordinary Westchester housewife whose husband, Jon, commutes to work in New York City. Their son, Tom, is away at college in Texas. When the atomic disaster strikes, teenage daughter Barbara is at school, two-year-old Ginny at home, and Gladys is doing laundry. Veda, the housekeeper and nanny who commutes from the city, is improbably saved from fatal radiation exposure by staying in bed the day of the attack, having first made her boardinghouse room airtight against drafts. (For this idiosyncratic behavior, she is suspected by the authorities of sabotage.)

Paul Brians and Jane Winston-Dolan, in their essay "Nuclear War Fiction by Women Authors," discuss *Shadow on the Hearth* in the context of feminine perspectives on nuclear war and the theories of "eco-

---

14. *Shadow on the Hearth* was adapted for television and broadcast on the Motorola Television Hour in 1954 under the title "Atomic Attack." The movie preserved the main plot features and the characters, but H. Bruce Franklin has identified certain revealing differences: among others a change in the name of the antinuclear teacher from Garson Levy to Garson Lee, and a shift in his characterization from an admirable idealist to a "confused pacifist who learns the necessity of violence when Gladys' house is menaced by looters." The "squadman" neighbor becomes "transformed from a lecherous local Mussolini into a paragon of sympathetic efficiency," and the radio becomes "the voice of benevolent, patriarchal authority" whereas the novel pictures it as an "insidious presence." There are other changes, all contributing to the conversion of the "antimilitarist" novel into "defense" propaganda. As of 1989, the U.S. government was still distributing "Atomic Attack" as a civil defense training film. (Unpublished essay used with permission of the author.) The 1954 television version of "Atomic Attack" may be purchased for $45 plus postage from International Historic Films, Box 29035, Chicago, IL 60629.

feminist ideology." Life-affirming eco-feminist values, refined over centuries of masculine domination, must be brought to bear upon the problems (largely male-created) posed by the threat of atomic warfare.[15] In Brians and Winston-Dolan's discussion, *Shadow on the Hearth* contrasts to the "simple-minded adventure stories" that show how the "heroes," in the chaos following nuclear devastation, thrust women violently back into strictly limited housekeeping and "victim" roles, and impose the "masculine values of toughness, ruthlessness, and technical competence" in a world that has grown "too harsh for compassion, nurturance, and idealism." In a peculiar, paradoxical way, these atomic adventure novels "justify the very values which are likely to precipitate such a war."[16]

Merril's novel, on the other hand, challenges the social patterns that deny women access to scientific knowledge and make them, in an atomic crisis, dependent on men's technological expertise. Things are changing, however, for Merril contrasts generations when she shows daughter Barbara rejecting a passive role in the aftermath of the destruction. To a greater degree than her mother, Barbara displays competence and levelheadedness, as well as her admittedly stereotypical natural aptitude for nursing.

Before the bombs strike, Gladys has enjoyed being oblivious to politics and willfully ignorant of matters such as atomic bombs or radiation sickness. Under the stresses of anxiety for her husband Jon's fate and the symptoms of radiation sickness in her daughters, she takes an active, less stereotypical role. H. Bruce Franklin notes how the novel highlights the superficial abundance of American society in the late 1940s and 1950s through the Mitchell family's progress toward the American dream of a suburban home and material blessings, and exposes "the official and personal deceit underneath," the "fascist-militarist nightmare inherent in the dream." As an example, the "squadman" for the local area, the next-door neighbor, is unmasked in this emergency as the power-mad and sex-hungry instrument of a "fully-developed police state."[17]

15. Paul Brians and Jane Winston-Dolan, "Nuclear War Fiction by Women Authors," paper presented at Interface '84: Eighth Annual Humanities and Technology Conference, Marietta, Ga., October 25–26, 1984. For more on the atomic adventure novel, see Brians, *Nuclear Holocausts* pp. 88–92.

16. Specifically, Brians and Winston-Dolan mention Susan Griffin's *Woman and Nature: The Roaring Inside Her* (New York: Harper Colophon, 1978), and the pamphlet by Susan Koen, Nina Swaim, and friends, *Ain't No Where We Can Run: A Handbook for Women on the Nuclear Mentality* (Norwich, Vt.: WAND, Box 421, 05055, 1980).

17. Franklin, unpublished essay.

Gladys sees through him, thinking to herself, "Why, he's having fun!"[18]

Another blemish on the American complexion emerges through the presentation of Dr. Garson Levy, now a physics teacher, who seeks refuge with the Mitchells as a political fugitive, a "public enemy," because he has opposed preparations for nuclear war. In a similar fashion, Dr. Spinelli, who tries to deal with radiation sickness and the psychological fall out of the bomb, was barred from his first career choice in biochemistry because he had signed antinuclear petitions. He reminds Gladys, when she says she never believed any nation would *use* the atomic bomb, that *we* did: "We used it in 1945. In Japan. Why wouldn't somebody else use it on us?"[19]

Official lies on the part of the government—that no missiles can get through our defenses, that the United States has won the war—are juxtaposed to the ruins of the nation's cities, burgeoning radiation sickness, and Gladys's awakening awareness of her true plight. "No longer able to depend on men for security, she unleashes repressed strengths, and her selfless nurturing, now linked to a deepening consciousness, helps save her daughters from both radiation and the state."[20]

Merril's gifts as a storyteller are well used in this novel to portray with quiet realism the sufferings of ordinary people in the aftermath of a nuclear explosion. Her most remarkable achievement, however, is her powerful metaphorical presentation of the vulnerability of small children. The dead birds observed by Gladys on the ground outside the house (signifying her sensitivity to nature) arouse the two-year-old Ginny's fears, but the reader is unprepared for Ginny's sudden manifestation of radiation sickness. Late in the story we learn the source of her possibly fatal dose of radiation: her beloved, worn, blue toy horse, Pallo, which she had innocently left outside in the radiation-polluted rain and then taken inside to her bed. Barbara tells Gladys, "Doc found it with his little Geiger counter. Pallo's a Trojan horse, atomic style. He's hot—a one-man radioactive rodeo." Gladys reflects on the irony: "There was a clear picture in her mind—the worn blue horse and the pink and white girl safe on the pillow together, night after night. *Isn't anything safe? Not the rain or the house? Not even a little blue horse?*" When a child's beloved toy becomes a lethal instrument, the natural order it-

18. Judith Merril, *Shadow on the Hearth* (Garden City, N.Y.: Doubleday, 1950), p. 55.
19. Ibid., pp. 57, 77, 143.
20. Franklin, unpublished essay. See also the discussion of *Shadow on the Hearth* in Franklin's *War Stars: The Superweapon and the American Imagination* (New York: Oxford Univ. Pr., 1988), pp. 177-79.

self seems to be broken. As Gladys says out loud, "Would anything ever be safe again?"[21]

Gladys's growth toward wholeness in a fragmenting world represents a developing mythical pattern for the hera of nuclear fiction. A clear life-affirming survival ethic is implied: Become involved in political action before it is too late; take some responsibility for making the world safe and for promoting respect for the natural order.

"Re-Birth, or the Chrysalids"

John Wyndham's *Re-Birth, or the Chrysalids* tells the story of young people living in a post-"Tribulation" society ruled by a fear of deviation from "the true image of God" (cf. *Ape and Essence* in the attitude that mutants are "accursed"). David, the youthful protagonist, discovers he is one of an emerging mutant species possessing psychic powers, for he can send thought pictures, or "thought shapes," to other similarly endowed individuals over great distances. He and his little brother, Petra, are in mortal danger because their gift is considered "blasphemy" by those, like David's father, who believe "The Norm is the Image of God."[22]

David's friend, Sophie Wender, is exiled when she is discovered to have extra fingers and toes. Offspring who have obvious deviations from the norm are killed at birth or exiled to the Fringes. Questioning of "orthodox" authority is severely punished, as seen in the story of Marther, who, in his journal of travels into the Wild Country, the Badlands, and the Fringes, had speculated that "deviations, so far from being a curse, were performing, however slowly, a work of reclamation." This "heresy" landed him in court.[23] David's Aunt Harriet drowns herself and her mutant infant daughter after being berated for producing a "false image" and questioning the justice and morality of the law that demands she sacrifice her imperfect child.

David is befriended by his Uncle Axel, who sees the positive side of the boy's dangerous gift and the value in this "new quality of mind." Romance blossoms when David finds Rosalind, another telepath. Petra, with his exceptionally strong telepathic powers, begins to receive thought pictures from a woman in "Sealand" (New Zealand), where

21. Merril, *Shadow on the Hearth*, p. 275.

22. John Wyndham, *Re-Birth, or the Chrysalids* (New York: Ballantine, 1955), p. 32. Originally published as *The Chrysalids* (London: Michael Joseph, 1955).

23. Ibid., p. 72.

the more evolved "think-togethers" enjoy an advanced level of civilization.[24]

Guided by directions from the Sealanders, the young telepaths escape their repressive society and head for the Fringes. A philosophical Fringedweller puts their unusual powers into a fresh perspective, criticizing the narrow ethnocentricity of David's people, who, in their arrogance, want to be "a lot more civilized" than God and refuse to accept the change and growth of the species. This mentor-figure declares that "Tribulation was a shake-up to give us a new start."[25]

After many dangers, the protagonists are rescued by the Sealanders, whose key woman gives them an enlightened view of human differences. Responding to David's temptation to take revenge on his father, she tells him that his father's kind and their way of thinking will not long survive: "The living form defies evolution at its peril; if it does not adapt, it will be broken. The idea of completed man is the supreme vanity: the finished image is a sacreligious myth."[26] Only the fossilized form can remain unchanged. Intolerance, because it opposes the life force, is doomed to self-destruct.

Wyndham's novel is a parable of youth siding for tolerance against racism and bigotry in all their guises. Relativistic values are prized; absolutes are anathema. Survival hinges on flexibility and acceptance of the natural rhythms of life. The hero and hera are the avatars of evolving new life-forms. (It is interesting to note that the music group Jefferson Airplane based its song "Crown of Creation" on this book.[27]) Yet for all its positive aspects, the view of a nuclear "tribulation" as a "shake-up" designed to give the human race a "new start" perpetuates the pseudomyth that humankind will evolve *upward* after a nuclear holocaust. The unfortunate U.S. title *Re-Birth* reinforces this falsehood.

"Alas, Babylon": The Captain America Pseudomyth

Pat Frank's *Alas, Babylon* may be, for older Americans, their first fictional introduction to the idea of nuclear war set on native soil. Reflecting the Cold War fears of the fifties, it portrays Russia as springing a nuclear attack on the United States, and the narrative follows the ef-

24. Ibid., pp. 95–96, 160, 173.
25. Ibid., pp. 183–84.
26. Ibid., pp. 216–17.
27. This is noted by Brians, *Nuclear Holocausts*, pp. 347–48.

forts of a small group of survivors in Fort Repose, Florida, as they struggle to meet their food and shelter needs and reestablish some semblance of civilization.

Randy Bragg, whose name speaks for itself as an embodiment of chauvinistic attitudes, learns through a coded message sent by his Air Force brother, "Alas, Babylon," that nuclear war is imminent. The overtones of apocalyptic thought in "Babylon," suggesting nuclear catastrophe as God's vengeance on a sinful, prideful, and self-indulgent nation, are evident. The local telephone operator, who has listened in, spreads the message, but only the local librarian has the cultural literacy to decipher the portent of the biblical allusion.

The radio broadcasts after the catastrophe are typically inane and either misinformed or propagandistic (cf. the radio messages in *Shadow on the Hearth*). The public library (the information provider of choice in so many nuclear fictions) draws crowds of people seeking practical emergency survival information. The characters are distanced from massive devastation, able to enjoy the spectacle of exploding missiles, and most of the severe casualties are offstage. David Dowling has commented on the novel's mirroring of the patriotic fervor of its era: Randy "explains radiation as nature's way of protecting the race, sets up a vigilante group, quotes from Benjamin Franklin, and learns with relief that although now a 'second-class power' America has enough nuclear fuel left to rebuild a once-proud nation."[28] Traditional values hold sway: Randy helps victims of a car accident because he cannot "shuck his code, or sneak out of his era," and the people flock to church, seeking the comfort of faith, which bombs and missiles have not vanquished.[29]

The novel's closing line is self-reflexive in its articulation of the Captain America myth: "We won it. We really clobbered 'em . . . not that it matters." The reader who looks beyond the verbal jingoism will see the irony of supposing anything has been "won" and be struck by the vivid presentation of materialistic losses: the economy reverts from a consumeristic, money-based one (the bank president blows his brains out because he cannot face a world where dollars are useless) to a bartering system (an advertisement offers a Cadillac in exchange for food and infant necessities). Greed for luxuries is grotesquely punished (looted gold jewelry is hot with radiation and inflicts burns upon the wearers). The novel's survival ethic is a combination of traditional as-

28. David Dowling, *Fictions of Nuclear Disaster* (Iowa City: Univ. of Iowa Pr., 1987), p. 91.

29. Pat Frank, *Alas, Babylon* (Philadelphia: Lippincott, 1959; New York: Bantam, 1960), pp. 98, 258. Page references are to the Bantam edition.

ceticism, pastoral values (including a return to the "simple" life), and loyalty to one's nation—under God. Concern for the ecological impacts of the catastrophe is absent: The awareness of the global dimensions of nuclear disaster was yet to be manifested in fiction.

"A Boy and His Dog"

Harlan Ellison's novella, "A Boy and His Dog," provides an example of the male-oriented atomic adventure tale with a macabre twist. Because it is well known, useful for contrast, and a minor classic of its kind, it is included here. Set in the American Southwest in 2024 in the aftermath of a nuclear holocaust that has all but destroyed civilization, the story features the boy Vic, a "solo," surviving in a symbiotic relationship with his telepathic, ultra-intelligent dog, Blood. Blood has been genetically engineered to search out enemies but lacks the ability to find his own food and depends on a human to forage for him. As John Crow and Richard Erlich point out in their essay, "Mythic Patterns in Ellison's *A Boy and His Dog*," the traditional human-animal relationship has become inverted: Blood is intellectually and emotionally superior to the boy and other surviving humans. Blood seems at first to belong to the well-known tradition of the helping animal of folk and fairy tales, but soon "goes beyond this role to become Vic's link to the lost pre-war civilization, teaching him reading, arithmetic, recent history, and 'Edited English' grammar. He becomes the culture-bearer of the bombed-out wasteland, superior to Vic in everything but the necessary skills of animal survival."[30]

The story's structure follows the familiar pattern of hero myths of initiation, with Vic descending into the underworld, facing a test of courage and manhood, and emerging with a new-found strength to undertake heroic tasks. Crow and Erlich show a fondness for the clever way Ellison both builds upon and mocks this pattern, for in his fictional wasteland "masculine and feminine are alien and hostile to one another; rebirth in such a world is impossible."[31] Vic's world is the antithesis of Riane Eisler's gylanic society, in which the masculine and feminine principles are in balance.[32]

The feminine life force has gone underground and sexual relation-

30. John Crow and Richard Erlich, "Mythic Patterns in Ellison's *A Boy and His Dog*," *Extrapolation: Journal for the Scholarly Study of Science Fiction and Fantasy* 18 (1977): 162.

31. Harlan Ellison, "A Boy and His Dog," in *The Beast That Shouted Love at the Heart of the World* (New York: Signet, 1974), p. 163. First published in *New Worlds* (April 1969).

32. Riane Eisler, *The Chalice and the Blade: Our History, Our Future* (New York: Harper and Row, 1987), p. 105.

ships in this poisoned society have become brutal and violent. Quilla June Holmes has escaped from the Topekan underground state, a sterile, mechanized bourgeois-like world inhabited by people who have lost their ability to question the cultural forms that imprison them in their own orthodoxies.[33] In contrast to the traditional underground (where the hero found renewal), the Topekan state offers no more hope for rebirth than the wasteland on the surface. Topekan males have lost their fertility, and Quilla June's attempt to seduce Vic into her underground world to impregnate the female population does not succeed. Neither the upper nor the lower worlds can sustain generative love, needed to transform the wasteland into a flourishing garden. The sterility is the result of a failure to sustain masculine and feminine principles in a balanced harmony.

Like the traditional mythic hero, Vic is tested in a number of ways. First, he must choose whether to follow Quilla June underground after she provocatively bashes him over the head with a flashlight. Her motives are impure: She wants his help in a plot to grab power over the underground society. His motives for pursuing her are also tainted with lust and the urge for revenge. Blood reproaches him for being a *"putz,"* and the argument between them brings out "the baseness of Vic's *macho* motivation."[34] Ellison's human characters, like those in *Wolf of Shadows*, are less sympathetic than the animal. After a bloody conflict in the underworld, where Quilla June's attempt to seize control is aborted and she betrays her bloodthirsty nature by gloating over the slaughter of her parents, she and Vic escape to the surface, where Blood is nearly dead from hunger and wounds sustained in fighting a "roverpak," a band of pillagers.

Blood must have food immediately, and Vic must choose between Quilla June's life and that of his dog. He elects to save the dog. Quilla June's gruesome end as rations for the canine has a certain poetic justice because of her ugly nature, but many readers will see misogyny in the tale. Vic adheres to a "me-first" survival ethic and loyalty to Blood, justifying his slaughter of Quilla June by saying to himself, "A boy loves his dog." Though he is haunted by her question for a long time—*"Do you know what love is?"*— he probably will never experience generative love: The survival ethic of this chilling story barely transcends the cannibalistic. (Only Vic's love for his dog, and Blood's for him, go beyond the level of "love" for rations.) Within Ellison's ironic scenario, it is hard to see how the

33. Crow and Erlich, "Mythic Patterns in Ellison's *A Boy and His Dog*," pp. 164–65.
34. Ibid., p. 164.

blighted wasteland can ever be regenerated. Vic and Blood can find no exit from the hellish, labyrinthine, repetitive cycle of killing in which they are caught. Perhaps to compensate for the misogyny of this story, Ellison has written a comic-book sequel in which Vic pays in kind for his murder of Quilla June.[35]

"Heroes and Villains"

Angela Carter's *Heroes and Villains* is set in the ravaged landscape following an unspecified catastrophe, seemingly a nuclear one as the text contains references to animal mutations. Marianne, the heroine, has been brought up in the "ivory tower" of her professor father, protected from the barbarians outside. She is captured after her parents' deaths and raped by the barbarian Jewel. Her sensual attachment to him ensues, along with her struggle to lead a worthwhile life among people reduced to savagery. She finds herself trying to reinvent lost meanings for life.

One of the worst problems faced by humanity in Carter's novel is the loss of the primordial ability to assign names to the variety of natural forms, a task that is, mythologically, the first assignment given to Adam. When she beholds the sea for the first time, she vainly tries to find names for the abundant marine life-forms. The variety of nature, once scrupulously classified by scientists, can no longer be expressed verbally. The linguistic impoverishment mirrors the destructuring of nature: Having lost their names, natural things have undergone "uncreation," have "reverted to chaos," no longer acknowledged by humankind, the namers, and hence no longer rendered "authentic" in human experience through the exercise of the human "gift of naming."[36]

The novel depicts a world where people who have lost linguistic abilities can no longer participate in the process of co-creating the world by giving voice to its wonders. It has been proposed that the greatest delights of life belong to those who can name them; hence, the

---

35. Ellison has defended his original "A Boy and His Dog" against charges of sexism and misogyny by alluding to a sequel, "Run, Spot, Run," in which Vic meets his match in a "hardcase female rover" (personal communication from Richard Erlich, June 16, 1989). The paperback reprint of the comic book adaptation, with a new sequel, is Harlan Ellison and Richard Corben, *Vic and Blood* (New York: St. Martin's Press, 1989).

36. Angela Carter, *Heroes and Villains* (New York: Simon and Schuster, 1969; Penguin, 1981), pp. 193–94. See also the comments by Michael Dorris and Louise Erdrich, "Bangs and Whimpers: Novelists at Armageddon," *New York Times Book Review*, March 13, 1988, pp. 1, 24–25.

most blessed people are those with the largest vocabularies.[37] The unblessed of Carter's novel, in stark contrast, not only suffer diminishment of their wordhoards but have also lost a "thou" relationship with their world and with one another.

As Marianne's father tells her, before the "fire" came, "everyone alive was interlinked," though some "more loosely meshed into the pattern than others." Post-catastrophe humanity is divided into separate species, *Homo faber* (to which he and Marianne belong), *Homo praedatrix*, *Homo silvestris*, and others.[38] The fragmentation of the once-single species into many is a metaphorical parallel for the breaking of the atom, creating a sort of Tower of Babel on the genetic level.

Time has also been affected, seemingly frozen by the nuclear catastrophe. The clock belonging to Marianne's professor father was at first a symbol of immortality, for it does not die in the conflagration as does her pet rabbit! Its symbolism changes when it becomes an intolerable reminder of a past forever dead. When Marianne buries the clock in a swamp, it is as though time itself has expired. Time as the professors experienced it still had a structure, whereas to the Barbarians it is formless. Marianne, we are told, loses "the very idea of time," for the Barbarians among whom she eventually lives do not "segment" their existence but leave it "raw in original shapes of light and darkness so the day was a featureless block of action and night of oblivion."[39] David Dowling notes that, in this and many other nuclear fictions, "time dribbles on in that horrific wasteland" familiar to us in literature since Eliot and Beckett.[40]

Carter's bleak novel conveys through its emphasis on linguistic holocaust the need to cleanse our linguistic habits now, before the self-deceiving doublespeak of nuclear discourse leads to our doom, before it is too late to seek a remedy. Survival may indeed rest upon the restoration of the integrity of language.

"Children of Morrow"

The plot of *Children of Morrow* by H. M. Hoover parallels that of Wyndham's *Re-Birth*, though on a more simplistic level. After the apparently atomic-weapons-induced Great Destruction, accompanied

37. This idea, in fact, is incorporated into Stanley Elkin's novel, *The Living End*, in which the protagonist, Ellerbee, is granted a larger vocabulary in order to "heighten his experience of Heaven and Hell" (quoted in Dowling, *Fictions of Nuclear Disaster* p. 10).

38. Carter, *Heroes and Villains*, pp. 11–12.

39. Ibid., pp. 21, 57.

40. Dowling, *Fictions of Nuclear Disaster*, p. 102.

by an ecological catastrophe alluded to as the "Death of the Seas," survivors are split into two groups: the conservative, antitechnology, repressive society, and the liberal, pro-science, and pro-technology society of telepaths. The main characters are children: Tia, a telepathic twelve-year-old, thought to be a witch by her fascist neighbors, and Rabbit, her stuttering nine-year-old friend, also telepathic, who turns out to be her half brother in the final recognition scene. The genetic change responsible for their superior mental powers is attributed to the consumption of some contaminated torula yeast rather than to radiation.

In Tia's world, fertile men are at a premium, and those who succeed in fathering children lead a privileged life with private rooms and other luxuries. The rulers are the "Fathers," of whom the chief is the "Major," "reputed to have fathered more children than any other man on the Base." The Major enjoys the status conferred by his fertility even though most of the children he sired have died. A sadistic, ugly, bloated figure, and a misogynist to boot, he is an indelible villain.[41]

The mythology of this fear-dominated society centers around the worship of the Great Missile, which, unknown to its worshipers, has been rendered quite harmless by the passage of centuries. The Major uses the Missile to preach a lesson against trying to rebuild "Paradise," his people's mistaken idea of the self-indulgent technological society (of our own time) whose destruction, as he tells them, was its God-ordained punishment.[42]

Tia learns to conceal her telepathic abilities after an incident during her childhood when she assisted in the rescue of a missing child through her visionary powers. She begins to dream of "Morrow," a strange place inhabited by a woman called Ashira and a man named Varas. Ashira is one of the "Elite, the direct descendent of Morrow and chosen heir to the Gyrestone, the symbol sacred to the Balance of the One.'"[43] After a series of adventures, wherein in good Dickensian fashion the children are presented as potential victims who just barely manage to elude dangers, Tia and her brother are rescued by the Elite of Morrow.

Hoover emphasizes the literary and artistic superiority of the society of telepathic mutants. Architecture and the other arts rate very high in the Elite society; the Master Library of Morrow, stocked with old books, tapes, films, and personal records from the twenty-first cen-

41. H. M. Hoover, *Children of Morrow* (New York: Four Winds Press, 1973), pp. 9, 11. There is a sequel, *Treasures of Morrow* (1976).

42. Ibid., p. 12.

43. Ibid., pp. 24–25.

tury, is highly valued. The subterranean survival shelter endemic to nuclear fiction has scarcely ever been more meticulously thought out, but the politics of its designer, an ancestor of Ashira, are those of a benevolent monarch. The ruler must be the individual with the "best mind in each generation," and a strict eugenic code is enforced. Only outstanding mental and physical specimens are allowed to reproduce. It is difficult to see how such a static, utopian society can continue to cope with change. In contrast to Wyndham's novel, the mythic and iconic elements seem less organic, and there is a lesser sense of a realized consciousness transformation in the utopian society. The "Balance of the One" implies a survival ethic based on harmony of nature and intellect, but the idea is not convincingly dramatized in the narrative.

Z for Zachariah

A book for young readers notable for the stamina of its teenage heroine and for its ironic variation on the Edenic myth of Adam and Eve is Robert C. O'Brien's Z for Zachariah. Ann Burden (the name a too obvious indication of her role as one of the last bearers of civilization) finds herself alone after a nuclear war. She has been spared because her home is in an ecological enclave sheltered from nuclear radiation. Other members of her family left her behind when they went to search for other survivors, but they never returned. The book begins on a high pitch of suspense:

> I am afraid.
> Someone is coming.[44]

Ann has sighted a smoke column that moves closer each day, and she reasons that where there is deliberately created smoke there must be intelligent life. She prudently takes shelter in a cave in order to observe the unknown individual from a safe vantage point. The lone man in plastic, preserved by his "safe suit" from radiation, turns out to be a disappointing Adam. Before Ann can warn him, he swims in the radiation-tainted creek and consequently suffers radiation sickness. Despite misgivings (he seems psychologically unbalanced), Ann compassionately nurses him back to health. John Loomis is unmasked as exploitative and dangerous, and the scene is set for a suspenseful power struggle. Ann successfully outmaneuvers his attempt at rape,

44. Robert C. O'Brien, Z for Zachariah (New York: Atheneum, 1975), p. 9.

and for some time they live separately, seemingly in a state of truce. The situation goes from bad to worse, however, until Ann's existence (physical as well as emotional) is threatened intolerably. Ultimately, she assumes the traditional "quester" role, setting out on her own armed with the safe suit, which she appropriates in retaliation for his having sadistically destroyed a book she loved. She also knows he has obtained the radiation-proof clothing by murdering another man. She cherishes a dream of finding congenial people and realizing her ambition to become an English teacher. Her last words to Loomis are a reproach: "You didn't even thank me for taking care of you when you were sick," an outburst she later acknowledges "childish."[45] Despite having lost virtually all her earthly belongings to a crazed shell of a man, she improbably resists despair.

The title, Z for Zachariah, harks back to Ann's childish supposition that since "A" was for Adam, the first man, "Z" must stand for Zachariah, the last human on earth. O'Brien has created an exemplary, courageous young woman who does not passively accept her dire circumstances but, in the terms of Joseph Campbell's mythic model, follows her bliss. The ending of the book validates the survival power inherent in wishing vividly, dreaming persistently. The survival ethic implied in this narrative may be phrased as "I dream, therefore I shall continue to exist," even though, considered on a realistic level, chances of her survival and fulfillment are exceedingly slim. Ann is admirable, nonetheless, as a hera who, in a time of destruction, persists in thinking creatively.

"Jenny: My Diary"

A much different novel from England, Jenny: My Diary by Yorick Blumenfeld, uses the conventional journal format to tell how Jenny and her children survive nuclear attack by taking refuge in a shelter called Worldham, a concrete maze built into a hill. Jenny and her husband had bought the shelter as a precaution, despite Jenny's misgivings about reverting to "the caveman days." The shelter actually provides many amenities, such as a generator, oil tanks, water tanks, air filtration, and decontamination rooms.

Before the catastrophe, Jenny and her husband are emotionally distanced, and she is involved in a clandestine extramarital affair. Conveniently for plot purposes, only Jenny and the two sons make it to the shelter when the bombs come.

45. Ibid., p. 188.

Critic Paul Brians points out several weaknesses of *Jenny* as credible fiction. The novel points up a key problem with "shelter" stories: Characters who are privileged by their wealth to survive "in comfort while the rest of the world is being destroyed" become "distinctly unsympathetic." Jenny however broods about this inequality herself, thus somewhat exempting her from the guilt of riches. Also, Brians notes, Blumenfeld falls into the convention of depicting women as "resisting technology, men as domineering and destructive," and the stress on human sexuality may seem peculiar.[46]

Given the enormous stresses of surviving in a "buried alive" situation (Jenny's phrase), there is remarkably little violence. At one point two men try to bash each other with chairs in a contest over power, but this is balanced by an instance of peaceful resistance. After the emergence from underground, Jenny and her companions successfully deflect a gang of marauders by letting them see their weakness and lack of desirable food. Jenny has been impressed early on during the calamity by the extraordinary "kindness" of the shelter group, though she wonders whether it might be a mask for weakness. She attributes the promiscuous sex of the shelter's inhabitants to "bottomless despair— the haunting, screaming emptiness that follows prolonged, intense fear. How is one to react to being buried alive?" She is drawn to Eric, husband of Carol (who dies later from radiation effects), and as their relationship grows Jenny displays an unexpected intellectuality that jars somewhat with her soap-opera style of emotional expression.

Overlooking the incongruities in the depiction of Jenny as a character, however, the reader can find some depth of psychological reality in her existential ponderings on her sense of self. Her despair is convincing; to survive, it is necessary to focus on

> self, self, self. This is truly the ME shelter. And tomorrow? I know there will never be time for trivialities again, like pretty dresses, or hats, or parties . . . and yet everything seems so impossibly trivial and meaningless.[47]

The dilemma seems clear: Selfhood, to have any meaning, needs interrelationships, caring, and mutual nurturing, but the survival situation demands a me-first mentality at odds with full personhood. Late in the book there occurs a metaphor of a spider's web that relates to this existential dilemma: The spider tries repeatedly to spin a web, but the web always comes out "off-balance." Jenny questions, does the spider

46. Brians, *Nuclear Holocausts*, p. 139.
47. Yorick Blumenfeld, *Jenny, My Diary* (Boston: Little, Brown, 1982), unp.

suffer from the effects of radiation? Has her own "web" become irregular? Can human "webs" of relationship ever recover their balance?

The last question may imply the novel's survival ethic: a restoration of balance. Eric has told Jenny the etymology of the word "chaos"—"the vast, eternal darkness of Greek mythology," derived from the Greek root meaning "to gape." "Chaos was pure cosmic principle." Only later, because the term was confused with the word meaning "to pour," did it become identified with "confusion and the lack of organization of the elements in space." There may be a suggestion that the world, having reverted in so many respects to chaos, creates the opportunity offered by emptiness, that is, potential. But the chances of rebuilding life in this diminished Eden are meager, as seen in Jenny's fearful ambivalence over the thought that she is pregnant with Eric's child: She does not believe the child has a chance to be healthy. She moreover loses the desire to keep her journal; in the final passage, where she sees herself in a mirror for the first time in many months, she is frightened by her own aspect. She thinks, "I did not recognize HER: ME. Yes, that was *ME*. I don't want to face her again." She resolves to write no more, but rather to "live in the present. A minute, an hour, a day at a time." This attitude stands in contrast to the one expressed in so much nuclear fiction, where the keeping of a diary often signifies hope—for the hope that resides in writing down one's experiences as a survivor is like the hope the dying Hamlet places in the surviving Horatio, that he will be present after his death "to tell my story" (Hamlet V, ii, 360). Jenny's inability to believe in the significance of recording her story bodes ill for the continuance of life.

"God's Grace"

The importance of language and speech to survival (already emphasized in *Heroes and Villains*) surfaces again in Bernard Malamud's *God's Grace*, set, in the tradition of the Robinsonade, on a remote Pacific isle after a nuclear holocaust has destroyed civilization. Calvin Cohn, the lone survivor, finds companionship among the chimpanzees, allying himself with a female chimp named Mary Madelyn. There are other biblical echoes, most significantly a perverse parallel with the story of Abraham and Isaac. Cohn takes the chimp Buz as his adopted "son." Buz, once an experimental animal, has been endowed by a scientist named Walther Bunder with the power of speech. He speaks by means of wires implanted in his throat. In the climax of the story, after Buz betrays his "father," "stepmother," and baby half sister (Cohn's daughter by Mary Madelyn) for a chocolate bar to satisfy his sweet tooth, Cohn snips the wires of Buz's voice box with a wire clipper. In a terrible retaliation, the apes, led by Buz, mutiny, take Cohn captive, and cut his throat (in a role reversal, making Cohn the "Isaac," the sacrificial victim).[48]

Critic Peter Schwenger has described the symbolic import of this act: "The wound in the throat is a central image in this story about the power of speech, the power to make stories."[49] Without this power, *human* survival ceases. The idea that the "blowing up" of the world brings about a "blowing up" of language occurs again and again in speculative fiction and is a key theme in Russell Hoban's *Riddley Walker*, discussed in chapter 7. Historian Spencer R. Weart connects the metaphor of "blowing up," common parlance for going into a rage, with the interior emotional root of human destructiveness. He links explosions as a "traditional symbol of inner destructiveness" to both the nuclear bomb and Auschwitz, all stemming from a failure to "control" the "murderous hostility" deep within the human psyche.[50] Failure to cope with this murderous hostility, to hold it within limits, is obviously contrary to any survival ethic. Malamud's novel, as a cautionary tale of a degenerate New Eden, where human relationships and human speech have been demolished, implies that reasoned, truthful, responsible discourse is a necessary component of the survival of a specifically human society.

"Emergence"

The heroine of David Palmer's atomic adventure novel, *Emergence*, is Candy Smith-Foster, an eleven-year-old super-intelligent mutant, avatar of a new radiation-immune species, who holds the promise of a new stage in human evolution. She has survived thermonuclear war in an underground shelter built by her father. One of the troublesome aspects of the book is the "unpleasantly telegraphic" style and the characterization of the heroine as "a typically insufferable Heinlein omnicompetent optimistic superhuman."[51]

The book will appeal to some readers, however, if only for its unu-

48. Bernard Malamud, *God's Grace* (New York: Farrar, Straus, and Giroux, 1982), pp. 215, 223.

49. Peter Schwenger, "Writing the Unthinkable," *Critical Inquiry* 13, no. 1 (Autumn 1986): 33–48. Quotation is from page 41.

50. Spencer R. Weart, *Nuclear Fear: A History of Images* (Cambridge, Mass.: Harvard Univ. Pr., 1988), p. 411.

51. Brians, *Nuclear Holocausts*, p. 277. The style may reflect the author's court reporter background. Brians's style cleverly echoes the inflated style of the character.

sual characterization of an adventuresome, supremely self-assured young woman. It is also notable as an atomic adventure story featuring a female protagonist, but it does not lend itself to serious discussion in terms of a survival ethic: Candy survives because she has been genetically programmed to flourish in the atomic wasteland. Mere humans, who lack fathers who have the foresight and knowledge to make their offspring impervious to the effects of radiation, must take their chances against the odds, and it is clear that the odds are abysmal.

"Doomsday Plus Twelve"

James Forman's *Doomsday Plus Twelve* depicts a small community in western Oregon twelve years after a nuclear Doomsday, which occurred in 1988. The featured character is the adopted daughter of an otherwise childless professional couple, rescued at the time of the cataclysm from the wreckage of a plane. A flash-forward finds her an attractive young lady, a cheerleader for the local athletic team.

The narrative is notable for its emphasis on the politics of the devastated world. Led by the plucky protagonist, a peace group from Oregon tries to convince a militant organization in California to desist from attacking Japan, now a major nuclear power, having successfully and peacefully occupied the United States after its destruction by another superpower. The "antiwar activism" is portrayed as "both rational and hopeful," yet Paul Brians has rightly criticized it as a hardly useful model, since it occurs *after* the war and is aimed at "a loosely organized group of vigilantes."[52] Its practical survival ethic, hinging on political action, comes much too late but is otherwise praiseworthy.

"Danger Quotient"

Annabel and Edgar Johnson's *Danger Quotient* has for its protagonist yet another genetic hybrid super-genius, eighteen-year-old K/C-4 (SCI), "Casey" for short, who, unlike Candy Smith-Foster, is likeable as well as brilliant. The setting is an underground colony of survivors of a twentieth-century nuclear war. The year is 2136, 130 years after War Three in 1996. Key Colorado, the world's greatest scientific complex, lies under what was once Denver. The Colorado complex specializes in technological problems (there is a Massachusetts complex that

52. Paul Brians, "Nuclear Fiction for Children," *Bulletin of the Atomic Scientists* 44, no. 6 (July/August 1988): p. 25.

has concentrated on the humanities!). Casey's assigned technological problem is to find a way to restructure the earth's ozone layer.

Casey, though artificially bred by a scientist named Eddinger in a test tube and then implanted in a surrogate mother whose name he does not know, displays regular human feelings. For instance, he misses having a father (he tries to think of Eddinger as such, without success) and "blood ties."[53] He is also human enough to wish to live a long life, but "Pinocchio," the computer that can predict life expectancies with great accuracy, has told K/C-5 (SCI) (a seven-year-old redhead with ambitions) that Casey's ELS (Estimated Life Span) will run just eight months and fourteen days. Naturally wishing to extend his life span, Casey puts his research into the dwindling ozone layer on the back burner and concentrates on his "danger quotient" theory:

> Our species evolved in a dangerous environment. The body was meant to function hard—if it doesn't, the vital organs atrophy. In this secure, controlled world of ours, there's nothing unexpected, no hazards that require life-or-death decisions, no risks to send the juices pumping. In the old days there must have been fierce struggles with the forces of nature. Here, we don't know the meaning of the word—there's no danger quotient in our lives.[54]

To research his theory, Casey travels back in time to three points in the twentieth century—first 1981, then 1918, and finally 1945. The police records of a Denver suburb for June 10, 1981, found in the archives (note a repeated theme: libraries are essential to finding a means of survival), tell of an amnesia victim answering to K/C-4's description (including the mismatched eyes and a certain tattoo on his buttock) who was brought into the police station in Lakewood, Colorado.[55] Police records give Casey the means to document his existence and his individual identity.

53. Annabel and Edgar Johnson, *Danger Quotient* (New York: Harper and Row, 1984), pp. 10–11.

54. Ibid., p. 14. The idea that a certain amount of danger causes a species to thrive can be seen in the musings of Neaera H., a character in Russell Hoban's *Turtle Diary*, who wonders whether the caged birds in the zoo may be "going decadent." She refers to a film in which Dr. (Konrad) Lorenz "pointed out the differences between two colonies of cattle egrets, one free and one caged. The free ones, who had to provide for themselves, were monogamous and energetic and kept their numbers within ecologically reasonable limits. The captive egrets were promiscuous, idle, overbreeding and presumably going to hell fast" (Russell Hoban, *Turtle Diary* [New York: Random House, 1975], p. 29).

55. Ibid., p. 16. The importance attached to police records brings to mind Milan Kundera's comment attached to his famous observation that "love is a constant interrogation." Kundera adds parenthetically, "Which means that no one loves us better than the

Casey's quest for his identity parallels his quest to save himself from an early death. The byzantine plot involves him in romantic and other human feelings, exemplified when he finds the "warm maternal breast" of Mrs. Hessler possibly "addictive" or when he is later attracted to Betsy.[56] He succeeds in establishing who he is—a mysterious figure who appeared at the moment in history when a desperate populace needed his guidance "to face devastation and live through it," and he learns his purpose:

> To learn the strengths of a defiant people who are left to pick up the pieces after the generals have popped their smoke. To recognize the qualities we would need to build our sanctuary and staff our systems in those last frantic days of exodus.[57]

It would be difficult to imagine a more seductive presentation of the Captain America Complex, featuring an all-American juvenile protagonist. Youngsters reading this novel will be enchanted by Casey as the embodiment of the "save-the-world" fantasies we all may indulge in at times; they should, however, be helped to recognize how this story perpetuates the false myth that when America needs a superhero, one will miraculously appear. Youngsters need a trenchant presentation of the truth about the consequences of nuclear catastrophe.

The narrative is enlivened with humor, but its convoluted plot and strained jokes will be better tolerated by teenagers than by more mature readers. *Danger Quotient* is a lively tour de force, a fantastic romp through time featuring an irrepressible, resourceful young man, an icon of strength and leadership. As futuristic fantasy, it succeeds in a way impossible to more earthbound semirealistic fiction, for disbelief must be suspended to enter Casey's world at all. There are touches of poetic insight, as in the moment when Casey first sees the mountains and looks in awe at their "pastel of fragile lavenders and greens, laced with sunlight like the scenery of some fairy-tale neverland." He feels compelled "to make a short speech about magnificent beauty and careening time and carelessness. About devastation and that

---

police . . . Absolutely. Since every apex has its nadir, love has the prying eye of the police. Sometimes people confuse the apex with the nadir, and I wouldn't be surprised if lonely people secretly yearn to be taken in for cross-examination from time to time to give them somebody to talk to about their lives." See *The Book of Laughter and Forgetting,* translated from the Czech by Michael Henry Heim (New York: Penguin, 1981), p. 163.

56. Johnson, *Danger Quotient,* pp. 93, 97.
57. Ibid., pp. 212–13.

marvelous sun turned malignant.''[58] The ''marvelous sun turned malignant'' consummately expresses the idea of nature becoming hostile, a recurrent image in literature of nuclear peril, but the narrative abandons Casey's assigned concern, the diminishing ozone layer, and thus misses the chance to make a serious comment on the ecological theme.

''After the Bomb''

After the Bomb by Gloria Miklowitz presents a positive portrait of youthful self-reliance in a more realistic and contemporary setting. The narrator is Phil, a teenager who successfully struggles to survive after the Russians accidentally set off a nuclear missile that devastates Los Angeles. By fortunate happenstance, he is in the family fallout shelter with his self-assured older brother Matt and Cara, the girl they mutually admire, when the blast occurs. In the tradition of the fairy-tale younger son, Philip outshines his older ''jock'' sibling, who panics, as well as a considerable number of incompetent adults who later in the narrative have to be forced by Philip's brandished gun to help bring water from a swimming pool to the overburdened hospital.

As in many post–nuclear-holocaust narratives, the survivors develop an ethic of ''me and mine first,'' a kind of self-reliance that is not exactly what Ralph Waldo Emerson had in mind. As Philip reflects, in a nuclear war ''God would be too busy elsewhere to look in on him,'' and he must therefore take matters into his own hands, living out the time-worn philosophy that the Lord helps those who help themselves. He does this in several ways: For example, when the wounded are triaged (sorted out and prioritized on the basis of who has the best chances of survival and therefore should be helped first), Philip switches his mother's designation tag to get her on a helicopter to be taken for treatment in another state.[59] This incident dramatizes the urgency of more adequate preparations for hospital care in a nuclear crisis, and this cautionary element is one of the strongest features of Miklowitz's narrative.

Philip's adoption of the ''me and mine first'' survival ethic is presented as admirable in the novel and all readers will rejoice that his mother has an edge in obtaining treatment. If one tries to translate this ethic from the personal realm and make of it a universal principle, however, hard questions are raised. On reflection, one can recognize

58. Ibid., p. 67.
59. Gloria Miklowitz, *After the Bomb* (New York: Scholastic, 1984), p. 141ff.

how it incorporates the myth of the chosen tribe (one's own) and falls dismally short of the ethic needed by a global, nuclear community.

This simplistic example may serve to illustrate the difficulty of reconciling one's *family* loyalties with an "all-embracing," all-inclusive mythology: This may indeed be the crux of the contemporary problem—that however appealing the idea may be, we find it virtually impossible in a crisis to see all our neighbors as equally valuable "family" members. Under pressure, ties of blood and affection move us more than theories.

After the Bomb: Week One tells of Phil's reunion with his father, who was in Pasadena when Los Angeles was devastated, dramatizes the impossibility of evacuating a large metropolis in an atomic emergency (countering the myth of civil defense), and contrasts two kinds of people—those who respond to the danger and deprivation with "grace under pressure" and those who resort to looting and violence. The effects of radioactive fallout are not dealt with, presumably because they would not surface until later, but this is questionable, given the knowledge we have of actual *hibakusha* experience, and suggests authorial (or editorial?) timidity. *The Last Children of Schevenborn* by Gudrun Pausewang (see chapter 5) is a far superior and more truthful narrative and, if it could be set side-by-side with this, would demonstrate the gulf between the wishful soft-pedaling of the consequences of nuclear destruction and the preferred fantasy mode of narration so characteristic of the American approach. The somber, frank honesty of Pausewang's story ultimately has much more survival value, for it serves as a trenchant warning of the need to change from a war to a peace mythology before the chance to do so is forever lost.

"Warday, and the Journey Onward"

Warday, and the Journey Onward by James Kunetka and Whitley Strieber depicts in documentary style a tour of America four years after Warday, October 28, 1989. The authors cast themselves in the roles of the journalists who, through interviews, census data, public documents, and their personal insights, chronicle the effects of a 36-minute war during which nuclear missiles from the USSR rain down on the United States. Seven million Americans die immediately and millions more succumb to the slow death of radiation disease. A powerful electromagnetic pulse (EMP) destroys electronic equipment, extinguishing almost instantly the heavily electricity-dependent American way of life.

Longer term effects are the splitting of the United States into semiautonomous units, some under occupation by the British or the Japanese; California, as befits a fantasyland, escapes most of the damage. A Chicano nation emerges in the Southwest, named "Aztlan," and "destructuralists" near Los Alamos echo radical Vietnam-era types. The radiation illness, plagues, famine, shortage of adequate medical treatment, and resurgence of superstition that follow the breakdown of the social order are depicted in detail, and the poignant passages on the fate of children are especially effective: A group of essays by children, revealing their fear of contamination from the spring rains, dramatizes the damage to the natural world and the tragic vulnerability of the young to sickness and violence.

The novel merits praise on several points. Paul Brians calls it, "despite its unremarkable style, its rudimentary plot, its political improbabilities and its shallow characters," the "most thoroughly researched of all the attempts to depict nuclear war realistically."[60] The book is valuable also for its cautionary aspect; one reviewer called it a "must read for the human race; it is so powerful that the ruin it depicts may ultimately be our salvation."[61] If so short a war can inflict so much damage, how dare anyone speak of "limited" nuclear strikes?

The authors, themselves the central figures in this future quest for an answer to the "What if?" of nuclear catastrophe, return from their odyssey with a question for all of us: Simply, how can we let this happen?

"Children of the Dust"

Louise Lawrence's *Children of the Dust* follows an English family through three generations, tracing the fortunes and misfortunes of survivors of a nuclear holocaust. The novel has three parts, "Sarah," "Ophelia," and "Simon," each named for the character whose story capsulizes the experiences of one generation. Sarah Harnden, a fifteen-year-old, has a last glimpse of a butterfly just before she closes the door on the "old" world a few moments before the nuclear blast hits her home.

Lawrence describes with stark realism the sufferings of a stepmother and three children (the father is absent but enters the story in the second narrative) trapped in their home by radioactive fallout. The stepmother cracks under the emotional strain of trying to survive in the

---

60. Brians, *Nuclear Holocausts*, p. 317.
61. Susan H. Williamson, review of *Warday, and the Journey Onward*, by James Kunetka and Whitley Strieber, *VOYA*, 7 (February 1985): 340.

cold and the dark, and it is teenaged Sarah who shows incredible strength. The stepmother's death leaves Sarah with a conscious mission in life, to survive long enough to deliver her younger sister Catherine, who alone has escaped contamination from radioactive water and dust, to a "sheltering amphitheater" in the hills, where a man named Johnson takes her in. Catherine fits into Johnson's view of his own sacred mission, to begin a "brave new world" with Catherine as his wife. Sarah, having fulfilled her purpose, gives her little brother William fatal pills to end his suffering and then swallows them herself in a spirit of religious abnegation.

"Ophelia" relates the story of those who survive in an underground bunker housing military personnel and scientists; among them is Bill Harnden, Sarah's father. For twenty years, he serves as a teacher to the children born in the bunker, including his daughter Ophelia. Ophelia and Dwight, her sweetheart, rebel against the fascist underground state whose hierarchical power structure perpetuates the prenuclear militaristic values. Critic Hamida Bosmajian has noted how Lawrence presents two alternative future societies: one the agrarian-based society operating in the still habitable areas of the radiation-scourged planet, the other this rigid (underground) militaristic state.[62]

Half sisters Catherine and Ophelia meet when Harnden, Dwight, and Ophelia escape to the surface and flee to the farm to warn Johnson of the militarists' plans to seize the agrarian commune's cattle. The values of the two societies clash when Ophelia learns that radiation-damaged mutant babies of the agrarian community as well as adults near death are administered mercy killing. Lilith, Catherine's daughter and a mutant, is praised by Dwight for her strength because she took the life of Catherine's last-born, genetically damaged child (cf. the dilemma posed by Merril in "That Only a Mother). Ophelia, who still operates from the tradition-bound values of the bunker, calls Lilith's act murder. A further struggle of values ensues; the "dinosaurs in a bunker" are pitched against the morally relativistic and innovative mutants outside. Dwight believes the mutants, who have learned to cope with change, have the better chance at survival, and he tells Ophelia, "It's the Liliths of this world who are going to survive in the long run . . . Not us."[63]

Simon, namesake of section three and Ophelia's son, emerges from the bunker to the outside, as all of the bunker society finally must. The

62. Hamida Bosmajian, "Writing for Children about the Unthinkable," *Children's Literature* 17 (1989), pp. 209–10.

63. Louise Lawrence, *Children of the Dust* (New York: Harper, 1985), pp. 116–17.

conflict of values is played out in his inner struggle to bridge his cultural difference with the "ape girl," Laura, actually his cousin, a daughter of Catherine. He feels revulsion for her skin covering of "snow-white fur" and her "primate features," but he owes her a debt of gratitude for saving his life. Laura explains that she is psychic and her geiger counter is "mind powered." Mutants such as she have adapted to the radioactive environment, are able to see ultraviolet light, can tell "where things will grow and where they will never grow," and can read people's auras, "white and gold and glowing [or] dark and depressing."[64]

Simon's aura is predictably dark and depressing; he is not only biologically inferior to his mutant cousin but he comes to feel morally inferior as well. The peace-loving mutant informs him that "violence is incompatible with intelligence" and that all life, everything, is "sacred." To help him try to see with her eyes, she takes him to Timberley, a reconstruction of a medieval cathedral, an architectural expression of the mutants' values.

Simon has one great asset: his "technological understanding," needed to supplement the visionary powers of the mutants. The book concludes with Simon's vision of the future, meant to merge the best of both the technological and the visionary: "Grandfather Harnden's seed had flowered, not into Simon, but into her. . . . They were better than he was . . . *homo superior*, the children of the dust."[65]

Radiation in this fantasy results not in a "genetic throwback" but in an upward evolution of the species and a world peopled by attractive beings with evolved psychic, intuitive powers and communal values, plus an aesthetic mode of life.[66] The dustcover of the book visually expresses this theme, with the Timberley castle/cathedral arising from a mushroom cloud of dust above the terra firma of the mundane Earth. The premise of the book—that a nuclear war is not only survivable but could engender a superior human species—helps, as reviewer Hannah B. Zeiger says, to "make the unthinkable an iota more possible." The novel thus raises an "ethical problem for our age,"—a problem posed by all books that use radiation "as a sort of magic wand" to transform humans into something more attractive than the present specimens.[67] There is not the slightest likelihood that radiation will validate "pseudo-Darwinian optimism": the known effects of fallout are "leukemia, persistent sores, excruciating

64. Ibid., p. 151.

65. Ibid., pp. 151, 164–65, 176–77, 183.

66. Bosmajian, "Writing for Children," p. 210.

67. Hannah B. Zeiger, review of *Children of the Dust*, by Louise Lawrence, *Horn Book Magazine*, 62, no. 1 (January/February 1986): 63.

pain, sterility, deformity, and stillbirths.''[68] What has become of the artistic obligation to portray the truth about consequences?

To present magic upward transformations as long-term results of radiation-induced genetic mutation, even in a fantasy setting, is artistically irresponsible. In the *Horn Book Magazine* reviewer's words, ''This vision of an El Dorado rising from the ruins of a blasted world is intensely disturbing.''[69]

''Winter of Magic's Return''

Pamela Service sets the fantasy of *Winter of Magic's Return* five hundred years in the future in Wales, where a new civilization modeled on Arthurian ideals is emerging. This young adult novel tells of a resurrected Merlin, Earl Bedwas, who wishes to usher in a new age of magic and sets out to Avalon with a boy, Welly, and a girl, Heather, to bring back King Arthur.

Nature is hostile, with the climate bitterly cold and many forms of plant and animal life extinct. Morgan le Fay has survived and, true to form, she opposes Merlin's desire to unite the divided and hostile factions of the world. The young protagonists resist her tempting offer of a share in her power and status as ''this world's elite'' if they will bow to her will.[70]

The fantasy can be enjoyed as a kind of ''Dungeons and Dragons'' episode, and the literary quality of Service's writing is commendable, but viewed from the perspective of an ethic of survival, the assumptions of the text are questionable. Paul Brians puts the book into this ethical perspective:

> Anyone old enough to read the book knows that an atomic bomb is not really going to blast the top off a mountain in which Merlin has been trapped for centuries and loose magic—complete with unicorns—on the world. Do we really want to encourage children to think of nuclear war as a gateway to a more exciting, adventuresome future?[71]

The Firebrats Series

Just as the survivalist adventure tale enjoys enormous popularity with adult readers, young people are drawn irresistibly to the nuclear

68. Brians, ''Nuclear Fiction for Children,'' p. 26.
69. Zeiger, review of *Children of the Dust*, p. 63.
70. Pamela Service, *Winter of Magic's Return* (New York: Atheneum, 1985), p. 146.
71. Brians, ''Nuclear Fiction for Children,'' p. 25.

thrillers offered by Barbara and Scott Siegel in their *Firebrats* series. In *The Burning Land*, Matt and Danielle, two sixteen-year-olds, meet fortuitously when a massive nuclear attack wipes out the United States. Spared by chance (they happen to be in the basement of a theater, conveniently supplied with the food that was to be catered for a reception), they are trapped for a month below. On their emergence they face a horrible spectacle of death, radiation disease, and danger from roaming bands of outlaws and wild animals. They begin a cross-country quest, heading for California, where Matt's parents were traveling when the East was devastated. Rarely, in nuclear adventure stories, does the quest head eastward; the west is still the horizon of promise.

The Robinsonade and love-romance elements of the plot, situating the two attractive, emotionally vulnerable young adults in a desperate survival situation, work their imaginative sorcery. The characters are depicted as wholesome, all-American types or, more accurately, stereotypes: Danielle is as lovely as a fairy-tale princess, Matt as handsome and brave as any Prince Charming. By dint of the American virtues of common sense, courage, and inventiveness, they escape from the pillagers and rapists (though narrowly, to add spice) and overcome immense natural obstacles to pursue their quest.

A theme of the wisdom of knowing nature's ways and techniques of wilderness survival emerges in the second book, *Survivors*. The young couple learns hunting, tracking, and self-defense from Payne Ordway, a backwoodsman. They soon discover that the skills they bring from their past, knowing how to play computer games, program VCRs, and run a microwave oven, are useless in the new world. Ingenuity, however, is still of value, as they demonstrate when they help Ordway outwit some scavengers, blowing them up with some old, almost-forgotten dynamite. An ecological theme is briefly explored in the third book of the series, *Thunder Mountain*, in which Matt and Dani and the three children they have found hiding in a mountain cave meet a veterinarian couple, the Fultons, latter-day Noahs who consider it their mission in life to gather as many animals as they can, male and female, to save them from extinction. As Mr. Fulton says, "For all we know, life on this planet is spiraling down toward extinction. The higher forms—the human—will be the first to go. But if man doesn't live on, maybe we can save the great animals of the world." The animals, after all, had no part in destroying the world, and they should be spared partaking in its death.[72] The logic of

---

72. Barbara Siegel and Scott Siegel, *Thunder Mountain* (New York: Pocket Books, 1987), pp. 89–90.

this seems irrefutable. There is, however, no model provided for humanity/nature relationships.

In book four, *Shockwave,* in which the protagonists elude the Phantom of the Truckstop, escape from a bloodthirsty gang of slavers who travel on motorcycles, and find refuge with six hundred other survivors in a ruined Denver, two other themes can be seen: one, the attempt to define the qualities that make survival possible, and two, Dani's picture of her relationship with Matt. Dr. Stoddard, called on to treat Matt after he incurs an injury, expresses her idea of the source of Matt's strength, reflecting to herself that perhaps *"what makes him a survivor is that he sees himself as an equal to every person that comes his way.* [73] This endows egalitarianism with remarkable survival power and brings out the strong democratic emphasis of the narrative. This ideal of equality also informs Dani's thought; she rejects the Denver resident, Brian, Matt's romantic rival, at least partly because he patronizingly seeks to "protect" her. She resents his solicitous attitude and angrily retorts that she will protect herself. "At least when I was with Matt," she reflects, "we protected each other. We were a team." One of the few positive mythic models presented in this story is provided by the partnership, or gylanic, model of the relationship between Matt and Dani. [74]

Considered in its entirety, the *Firebrats* series (which will undoubtedly grow longer, judging by its economic success) reflects a milder form, targeted at a younger audience, of the sex- and violence-drenched atomic adventure novels, exemplified by the *Survivalist* series of Jerry Ahern. Such fantasizing about surviving in a post-holocaust wasteland by virtue of one's wits and skills may encourage young readers to suppose the worst event might not be so bad after all. The net result of such thinking, as Paul Brians notes, is to encourage them "to accept their own annihilation." He continues, "Nuclear war is not a problem to be adjusted to, like blindness or divorce. Thinking about the unthinkable is crucial; becoming comfortable with it is suicidal." [75]

"Duende Meadow"

An odd mixture of elements of the atomic adventure novel and an evolving mythology of peace may be found in a novel that predated

73. Barbara Siegel and Scott Siegel, *Shockwave* (New York: Pocket Books, 1988), p. 97.

74. Ibid., pp. 135–36. The partnership model and the meaning of "gylanic" are found in Eisler's *The Chalice and the Blade.*

75. Brians, "Nuclear Fiction for Children," p. 27. A recent survey of other books and films in the atomic adventure mode may be found in Paul Brian's article, "Rambo's Relatives." *American Book Review,* March/April 1986, pp. 19–20.

the *Firebrats* series by a few years, Paul Cook's *Duende Meadow*. Six centuries after the so-called Last War (the Third World War), several hundred Americans live in a dark underground bunker beneath what was once the Kansas wheatfields. Their "ark" is a buried former shopping mall converted by farsighted technicians for the purpose of keeping a remnant alive in the event of a nuclear war, which occurred, as feared, in the twenty-first century. Duende Meadow, as the settlement is named, takes its name from the Spanish *duende*, meaning "ghostlike beings." Cook bases their transformation into ghosts, a process that made their survival possible, on a free interpretation of botanist Rupert Sheldrake's theories and speculations on the existence of morphogenetic fields. A morphogenetic field, or "m-field," as Cook calls it, is in Cook's words "the energy structure which gave an individual accretion of matter—living or otherwise—its particular form."[76] In their underground womb-tomb, the duendes wait for the Earth to heal.

Cook establishes dramatic tension between two modes of consciousness. First there is the combative, obsolete "twenty-first century consciousness" of certain Americans of the military Hive complex, notably one Sebastian Monaco, the antagonist and rival in love of the main character, Preston Kittredge. Kittredge exemplifies the mind of peace, representative of the Appleseeds who inhabit a separate but connected complex. When Kittredge, in a test of bravery and fitness, climbs a ladder to the Earth's crust and peers out, he is astounded to find the sunlight illuminating fertile wheatfields cultivated by English-speaking Russians. The militarists below, still at war in their minds with the USSR, are then posed against the peace-prizing Appleseeds, led by Preston Kittredge and his mysterious brother Jay, an intellectual and spiritual maverick. There is a slight romantic subplot making Preston and Sebastian Monaco rivals for the affections of a stunning and nubile seventeen-year-old, Holly Ressler.

In addition to trying to outwit and outmaneuver Monaco and others of warlike mind, Preston faces a mystery: the Russians appear to be peaceful, not like their ancestors, the "belligerent people" that

---

76. Paul Cook, *Duende Meadow* (New York: Bantam Books, 1985), p. 9. See Rupert Sheldrake's *A New Science of Life: The Hypothesis of Formative Causation* (Los Angeles: J. P. Tarcher, 1981) for Sheldrake's actual theories. A lucid explanation of Sheldrake's thought, suitable for upper middle grade and high school readers, may be found in "The Source of Concern," in Lyall Watson's *The Dreams of Dragons: Riddles of Natural History* (New York: William Morrow and Company, 1987), Chap. 5. Watson elucidates Sheldrake's theory of "formative causation" and describes a number of scientifically verified instances of "morphic resonance."

history claims once threatened the security of the United States, yet they speak of a Great War in Africa and ship strategic materials to support the cause. They follow a charismatic leader, the Awakener, for whom they exhibit reverential awe. The Awakener, it turns out, is a great spiritual leader, and the Great War is a battle against hunger and disease.[77]

The author succeeds in making his "bad guys" the exemplars of a war mythology. His militaristic characters, who might have stepped out of the pages of the atomic adventure novels of Jerry Ahern, are overcome (stretching the limits of credibility at times) by his "good guy" champions of peace, the exemplars of a new consciousness far different from that of the twenty-first century, which successfully destroyed civilization as we know it. Though the novel's survival ethic is ultimately one that affirms life-giving energies over a death-dealing psychology based on fear, readers will probably find the latter more impressively dramatized. The novel is important as a theater for playing out the two contesting mythologies vying for precedence in twentieth-century minds in terms bright high-school-age readers can digest.

Duende Meadows also shows Cook's keen awareness of the responsibility borne by writers of speculative fiction to be soothsayers, truthtellers, in picturing the certain consequences of nuclear war: At one point Jay Kittredge meditates on history, observing how no "kingdoms" were spared by the bombs. He then abjures a

> certain kind of literature from the old world [which] had survived with them down in the Meadow that suggested—in book after book—that not only would man survive, but also [pictured] a kind of fantasyland where the rules of science would be held in abeyance. The true horrors of nuclear war were almost ignored, and history had shown, tragically, that those writers had been fools to believe that anything but the worst could happen.[78]

Perhaps the greatest virtue of *Duende Meadows* is this insistence on the "true horrors" instead of the "fantasyland," although the idea of underground survival through the manipulation of morphogenetic fields is itself open to the charge of being, at the least, an unlikely event.

77. Cook, *Duende Meadow*, pp.206, 227.
78. Ibid., p. 161.

Touchstones for Recognizing Truth about Consequences in Narratives of Nuclear Catastrophe

The number of post–atomic holocaust narratives for young readers is growing, and the range in quality is remarkable—from accurate, careful depiction of probable events and effects to wild and misleading wishful thinking. This type of fiction requires special criteria, and while critics are still wrestling to define them, certain points can be set forth. For books that present images of life after the bomb, I have synthesized the following criteria, based on a blend of my readings, reflection, and the thoughts of other critics, in the hope they may be helpful in the discussion of nuclear literature.

First, look for accuracy in the depiction of probable effects of radiation. Factually based information is essential, and can be conveyed through fiction as well as nonfiction. Accuracy entails critiquing the pseudomyth that radiation can somehow improve the species. A variety of nonfiction sources presenting the facts in clear terms is needed to keep the imaginary accounts in perspective.

Second, total despair and absolute nihilism should be questioned: Even the direst (which are also probably the most accurate) depictions of the effects of nuclear explosions can also convey the idea that *this does not have to happen.*[79]

Third, give preference to narratives that treat nuclear conflict as avoidable. Question the assumptions of stories that portray nuclear devastation as caused by unknown or unbeatable forces against which there is no human defense; such stories evoke despair.

Fourth, seek out those narratives that suggest that nuclear conflict can be avoided by ethical, political, and psychological means—that is, by the adoption of different values, by action toward disarmament, and by a "new way of thinking," made vivid in a mythology of peace. Books that suggest scientific or technological solutions to the nuclear predicament (i.e., bigger and better bombs or arms systems such as "Star Wars") should be questioned.

Fifth, remember that a harsh view of the consequences of nuclear catastrophe has more survival value than mindless optimism, for it

79. See the remarks of Natalie Babbitt and Katherine Paterson, quoted in my article, "Hope Amidst the Ruins: Notes Toward a Nuclear Criticism of Young Adult Literature," *JOYS: Journal of Youth Services in Libraries* 1, no. 3 (Spring 1988): 321–28.

may bring us to our senses by making us realize that where nuclear catastrophe is concerned, a second chance does not exist.

Sixth, be wary of narratives that seem to use the nuclear destruction of civilization as a means of promoting the false myth of a successful New Adam and Eve or some version of the Captain America complex.

Finally, remember that ''fiction that depicts the death of the vast majority of humankind as anything other than an unmitigated disaster is antihuman.''[80] If it also neglects the consequences for animals and plants, such fiction is ''antibiophilic.'' In both cases, the life-affirming ethic is obviously lacking.

Reflecting on the books discussed in this chapter, one can only be struck by how poorly most of them measure up to these criteria. There is a missed opportunity for writers of sensitivity, intellectual honesty, and emotive power to give us stories, more adequate new myths for a nuclear world, that betray neither our need for truth nor our need for hope.

80. Brians, ''Nuclear Fiction for Children,'' pp. 26–27.

CHAPTER 7

The Quest for Wholeness in a Broken World

Symbolic Immortality and a Pattern That Connects

In post–nuclear holocaust narratives, activities involving symbolization—the keeping of a journal, the creation of art, or the perpetuation of some other symbolic structure (sometimes in the form of a library)—provide modes of survival. The video series "Tomes and Talismans" provides an example of the library as a preserver of the symbolic life of culture and art in the wake of a nuclear catastrophe. The series uses a futuristic after-war setting as a device to demonstrate the importance of libraries and library skills to the survival of a human way of life.[1]

Psychiatrist Robert J.Lifton speaks of the universal human desire for "symbolic immortality."[2] Faced with a knowledge of our mortality, we find consolation and hope of symbolic survival through the creation of literary works or artifacts. The narratives surveyed in this chapter share the theme of a quest for symbolic means of survival in a world swept bare of art and beauty, the landscape pockmarked by the craters left by nuclear explosions. The stories vary greatly in length, importance, and depth, but all depict the survival value to be found in the symbolizing power of creative imagination. Some present the storyteller as essential to rebuilding myth in the aftermath of the fragmentation of civilization; if a new society is to arise out of the ashes of the old, it is essential that that world be restoried. All of the books discussed, with one exception, have after-the-bomb settings, and all show nuclear holocaust as an irremediable catastro-

---

1. "Tomes and Talismans," Mississippi Educational Television, videotape.
2. Robert J. Lifton, *The Broken Connection: On Death and the Continuity of Life* (New York: Simon and Schuster, 1979), p. 18, especially the "creative" mode of immortality.

phe for humankind. At the same time, all are extrapolations from imaginative realities of the *present;* the states of consciousness they portray are with us already as psychological realities, our visions of what-may-be.

These narratives thus foreshadow a possible catastrophic future, yet it is a future we still have a chance to forestall. For sensitive readers, these tales can provide fragments to shore against our ruin, myths that symbolically express both the consciousness of the tremendous loss all forms of life will suffer if the worst is allowed to happen, and a counter-vision of some new ways of thinking (symbolizing, dreaming, perceiving) that could, if realized in time, transform and renew our world without the necessity of first annihilating it.

In short, these narratives present the idea that it may be possible to annihilate the pseudomyths of nuclearism, to triumph over its destructive mindset and "malignant ignorance" by substituting a powerful creative and integrative vision.[3]

This idea of transformation through the imagination, a process basic to archetypal psychology, is expressed in an essay by Norman O. Brown, who notes that a "new" civilization need not demand any "new refinement in higher culture" but comes about through a change in the imagination of "the folk who shape and are shaped by folklore and folktales." The "eschatological imagination of the lowly and oppressed," the "dream life of the masses," holds the key to cultural transformation.[4] The alternate worlds pictured in nuclear fiction offer a kind of dream life also, a dream life with the power to shape the future, for good or ill. The narratives presented here dramatize the tension between destructive and creative imaginative modes.

Symbolic Structuring of Experience: "Black Rain"

Robert J. Lifton's remarks from his perspective as a psychiatrist on Masuji Ibuse's *Black Rain* (see chapter 3) illuminate the importance of

3. Gregory Bateson saw humanity as destroying the planet out of malignant ignorance of its true nature (R. Morgan, "Epoch B," *New York Times Sunday Magazine,* February 29, 1976, p. 33). For Bateson, recognition of "the biological nature of the world we live in" is the missing link to "the sacred moment of perceptual change." See G. B. Brown and E. G. Brown, Jr., "Prayer Breakfast," *CoEvolution Quarterly* (Spring 1976), p. 84; and David Lipset, *Gregory Bateson: The Legacy of a Scientist* (Boston: Beacon Press, 1982), pp. 289–90, for an explanation of Bateson's view that politicians need to learn "to treat the world from a basis in biology" (Lipset, p. 290).

4. Norman O. Brown, "The Apocalypse of Islam," in *Facing Apocalypse,* ed. Valerie Andrews, Robert Bosnak, and Karen Walter Goodwin (Dallas: Spring Publications, 1987), p. 160.

journal-keeping in the context of the *hibakusha* experience. Lifton notes, "Only records, we seem to be told, can enable man to cope with the bomb." After Shigemutsu's initial "numbing" as a result of the disaster, he moves through a "mastery" of his trauma toward a "determination to stand fast and record everything." He spiritually transcends his suffering by his incessant recording and meticulous fulfillment of family obligations, together with insight into "the timelessness of everyday rituals and of nature's perpetual re-creation of life and beauty."[5]

There are three elements in Shigemutsu's "survival ethic": (1) his *symbolic* structuring of experience, (2) his active compassion on behalf of others, and (3) his recognition of the wholeness and beauty of life's natural cycles—a kind of merging of biological-aesthetical-spiritual sensibilities into an energy to move into the future. Shigemutsu thus provides a model of the survivor that combines elements of the traditional mythic hero (a knowledge gained through descent into the inferno of despair, plus a boon for the community to which he returns). There is a special emphasis, however, on the importance of his *symbolizing* of his experience. When he symbolizes his suffering through shaping it into a story, it becomes an artistic gift to the "common" good. Shigemutsu's tripartite survival ethic, based on history, can provide reference points for analyzing the experience of other fictional characters.

"The Burning Book": Seeking Symbolic Wholeness

The nuclear narratives embodying the quest to achieve reintegration and renewed wholeness by means of art, journal-keeping, or storytelling will be approached chronologically, with one exception. Maggie Gee's *The Burning Book*, a novel for adults from the perspective of the fictionalized *hibakusha*-at-a-distance, will be considered first for its conscious articulation of the idea that people can, through words and chronicles, ward off the mindless forces of mass destruction, winning a victory for life. The biophile may prevail through the symbolic power of language.

The Burning Book, set in contemporary England, chronicles three generations in the life of a family from the working classes. A book for mature readers, it emphasizes ecofeminist concerns; it has appeal for precocious teenagers, those who might also read Margaret Atwood's

5. Robert J. Lifton, *Death in Life: The Survivors of Hiroshima* (New York: Random House, 1967), p. 544. The appendix gives an appreciation of Ibuse's novel.

The Handmaid's Tale. In the last generation depicted in the book, the imaginations of Angela and her mother, Lorna, have become fixated on and morbidly obsessed with images of brokenness, epitomized in pictures of the *hibakusha*, "something broken, pleading for life."[6] The novel abounds in vividly drawn images of mutations (mutant children of Hiroshima victims, for example), burning (especially of books, representing the destruction of the collective wisdom of humanity), and imperiled birds and babies (both images of life's vulnerability).

For Lorna, images of people broken by nuclear war merge with images of the carnivorousness of all animal life. At a tender age she was haunted by the awareness that meat was once alive. As a young child she had been initiated into life's voraciousness when Maisie, her knowing little friend, enlightened her about lambs: "They lock up the animals out of the light and later kill them . . . *they tear off their fur and they hack them to pieces.*" After her first child is born Lorna becomes excruciatingly conscious that both birth and death are bloody processes. Her distorted imagination associates the biological realities of birth with the violent realities of war, resulting in a nausea bordering on madness. *"What if soldiers are butchers and babies are just raw meat?"* Lorna feels torn by opposed images of love and death, eros and thanatos, which she cannot reconcile. She has seen "through the back of the mirror" to realities most people ignore (in order to keep their sanity), and

> what she had seen was fear. She saw things without their clothes: She saw people were meat, and other people were killers. She saw there was love, as well, but the two sides didn't balance out. What they did was pull you in two; you didn't know what to believe. . . . Bodies weren't perfectly sealed: they could split and bleed like hers had.[7]

The imagery in this demented vision is comparable to that of the *Walpurgisnacht*, or witches' sabbath, of literary tradition. Whereas in classical literature that descent into a hellish imaginary realm traditionally precedes a vision of salvation, in Lorna's world the worst event—the nuclear annihilation of England—is yet to come.

Besides these tormenting images of existence perceived (or misperceived) as carnivorous and gross, Lorna feels oppressed and overwhelmed by the social expectations of women: "(Women were meant to look after people. Not just *one* person, but four. She'd never quite felt she was up to it . . . someone should look after *her*.)"[8]

6. Maggie Gee, *The Burning Book* (New York: St. Martin's Press, 1983), p. 21.
7. Ibid., pp. 46, 75.
8. Ibid., p. 273.

Daughter Angela resembles Lorna in her hypersensitivity. In this respect she may remind a reader of Sylvia Plath's Esther Greenwood, the protagonist of *The Bell Jar.* In her adolescence, Angela longs to become a writer, but she morbidly broods on catastrophe and finds that books in the library about the atomic bomb exaggerate her sickness. Facts "usually helped with fear," but factual knowledge about nuclear devastation shocks her deeply inside, soiling the world irreparably. She imagines the miracle of life "crushed to blind ash in a second. Ashes of writers inside their readers, turned to dead information." She dreams of "rewriting" the future.[9]

A peripheral character, Mrs. Perkins, the wife of a flag-waving, racially bigoted butcher, gives voice to the ancient complaint of women against men's obsessions with war. When she overhears her husband pontificating on the glories and heroism of war,

> a tide of pure resentment filled her: that they always had the power. They were just like babies, men. Inventing battles and fighting. It was pigs like him started wars. Then everything came to a halt. How dared they take them away, her secretive peaceful pleasures.[10]

She resents the loss of such simple pleasures as shopping for fruit, having coffee with a friend, playing with a little girl. The women in Gee's remarkable novel resemble the child in Hans Christian Andersen's "The Emperor's New Clothes" in their ability to see into the naked and nightmarish realities of war and indeed of existence itself. But they seem impotent to convert their despair and anger at human destructiveness into action on behalf of social and political transformation. Rather than placing hope in political or social action, Gee at the close of the book looks finally to words as holding hope of transcending the nuclear peril.

Gee's book is unique in its use of a technique that leads the reader to visualize the burning of the text being read. The final pages of the book are represented as charred. Her sustained use of the metaphor of burning, particularly the burnt book image, makes the book remarkably visual in its effect.

Libraries do not escape this imagined fiery holocaust. Angela finds no consolation when she searches through shelves of books for the facts on nuclear peril, for what she finds "seemed to say they were all dying." As poet T. S. Eliot has written, "After such knowledge, what forgiveness?" Angela imagines libraries burnt:

9. Ibid., pp. 242–43.
10. Ibid., p. 172.

> Why were the books all burning, where have the names all gone/
> dreams where everyone dies at once and the dead die over again.

The irony here is razor-edged. Libraries and books, traditionally the repositories of the human memory and hence the prime resource for hope of a meaningful future, are incinerated along with their human creators, so that Gee's earlier statement, "Nothing was lost which was written down . . . until the Chapter of Burning," resonates loudly.[11] The climax of the book comes with a nuclear blast that destroys all, including the book Gee is writing:

> Miracles of form became crackling bacon, miracles of feeling flashed
> to hot fat. Bleeding and terrified things pushed blindly against the pain
> which put out the light. . . . Books in their charred skins feel less pain.
> . . . All was as if it had never *tell me why is it dark already what happened why
> did we let our house burn down?* All was as if it had never been. Blackening
> paper, the last leaves burning.[12]

This literal holocaust of meaning itself is followed by four pages of blackened paper.

Yet this is not the end of the story, for Gee's final section, "Against Ending," implicitly values the power of words and spirit to "beat on against death . . . our bright lives beat against ending." The very last image is of soaring birds, in the manner of a concrete poem, whose visual pattern on the page lifts upward as if in groundless hope.

Critic Peter Schwenger in "Writing the Unthinkable" finds Gee's creation of a detached response in the reader comparable to Raymond Briggs's achievement in *When the Wind Blows*. The books are also alike in giving attention to "small" people, innocents caught up in "the looming threat of the end of time—or at least of chronicles." Voices from the past and future interrupt the narrative throughout the book, like "cracks" in time and in what Gee calls "the paper home" of her novel.[13] Schwenger comments:

> Yet these cracks, these intrusions into the conventional narrative of
> people's lives, are the real subject of the novel. They foreshadow nuclear
> war's ultimate and final intrusion into the world. For the "book" of the
> title is a microcosm, a fictive model of the world. Gee's book, as physical
> object, is its own most powerful metaphor: the effect of nuclear holocaust

11. Ibid., p. 223.
12. Ibid., p. 298.
13. Ibid., p. 52.

is as unthinkable as the coming of real fire to the pages of a fictive world consumed by it.[14]

Gee reminds the reader, through the burned pages of the book, of the actual threat of fire. Her metaphor of words "beating" against death offers hope that language—I like to think perhaps the words embody a new peace mythology, a biophilic survival ethic—may be the source of a victory for life over forces of mass destruction. This hope goes beyond the narrative itself, however, which shows breakdown, not breakthrough to a holistic consciousness, and thus it serves as an example of an aborted attempt at a creative synthesis of symbolic structuring, active compassion, and the recognition of the wholeness and beauty of life.

"Pattern for Survival"

A similar frustration of the creative impulse occurs in Richard Matheson's short story, "Pattern for Survival." The protagonist, Richard Allan Shaggley, in his isolation following a nuclear catastrophe, develops a daily pattern, or ritual, in an attempt to give his life meaning. Each morning he writes a lyrical science fiction love story, mails it (playing the mailman's part himself) to his "editor," Rick, who sends it to the publisher, R. A., who expresses appreciation, orders Shaggley to be paid by check and sends the manuscript to the linotypist, Dick Allen, who publishes it and has it ready for Shaggley to buy on his way home and read before he goes to bed to dream, awake, and write a new story—the cycle goes on endlessly. Such irrational behavior provides his only means of staying sane. In a world where he has lost the possibility to relate to others, he must split himself into compartmentalized personalities in order to experience any communication at all.

"A Canticle for Leibowitz"

A Canticle for Leibowitz by Walter M. Miller, Jr., has the well-deserved status of a classic among contemporary works of speculative fiction. It provides a rich source for studying the impact of the idea of atomic fission— and all that idea entails—on language, symbol, and myth, as well as supplying superb examples of the verbal strategies of a consummate writer stretching language to express the seemingly inexpressible.

14. Peter Schwenger, "Writing the Unthinkable," *Critical Inquiry*, 13, no. 1 (Autumn 1986): p. 47.

Canticle originally appeared as three stories—"A Canticle for Leibowitz" ("Fiat Homo", "And the Light Is Risen" ("Fiat Lux"), and "The Last Canticle" ("Fiat Voluntas Tua")—in *Fantasy and Science Fiction*. The action takes place after a massive worldwide nuclear war known as the "Flame Deluge." Time is viewed cyclically: history repeats itself. The nuclear holocaust of World War III is followed by the rebuilding of civilization, only to meet annihilation in World War IV. Throughout, the Order of Leibowitz stands for knowledge and tradition posed against ignorance and chaos.

"Fiat Homo" is set in a future dark age resembling the Dark Age of medieval Europe and closes in the year 3174; "Fiat Lux," six centuries later, depicts a neo-Renaissance; and "Fiat Voluntas Tua" pictures a technologically advanced civilization (much like our own) that essentially destroys the Earth in 3781. In a futuristic parallel to the Exodus from Egypt, a small remnant of the faithful escape on a starship to begin life on a distant star, carrying with them the apostolic succession as well as the Memorabilia, cherished fragmentary records of our own era, to Centaurus Colony. The ending holds little basis for objective hope, however, for as the starship thrusts heavenward with its precious cargo including a good number of children, the "visage of Lucifer mushroomed into hideousness above the cloudbank." The very last images are of hungry sharks seeking shrimp and whiting in an ocean polluted by fallout.[15]

The personage of the title, Isaac Edward Leibowitz, canonized centuries after his death, was a Jewish scientist before the conflagration. A survivor, he feels the need to do penance for the "sin" of science—the invention of nuclear weapons—by converting to the postwar Catholic church and becoming a monk. He founds the order of Albertus Magnus, devoted to preserving the Memorabilia, and is eventually martyred in the violent uprisings of the Simplification, when the illiterate mob of "simpletons" decimate the detested intelligentsia. His death is of the particularly gruesome sort reserved for saints and martyrs: He is betrayed, then half-strangled and roasted alive at once.

In contrast to much speculative fiction, Miller's novel implicitly views institutionalized religion quite positively and draws on religion

---

15. Walter M. Miller, Jr., *A Canticle for Leibowitz* (Philadelphia: Lippincott, 1959; New York: Bantam, 1961), pp. 277–78. Page references are to the Bantam edition. The cyclic structure and Miller's adherence to a "cyclic mythology" are noted by Martha J. Bartter as a refusal of "apocalypse," and the chance for life on another planet as not more than "the opportunity to repeat the same mistakes." See Martha J. Bartter, *The Way to Ground Zero: The Atomic Bomb in American Science Fiction* (New York: Greenwood Press, 1988), p. 231.

for mythological dimensions. It is these mythic elements that enable him to provide a final holistic vision.

The title, with its associations of song, sets the mood for Miller's incantatory style, intermixed with fragments of Latin, many untranslated; the uninitiated may find these a barrier or, on the other hand, may be challenged to decipher what novelist Walker Percy calls "a coded message, a book in a strange language."[16] Miller's prose melds this cabalistic quality with a metaphorical expression of the confusion of tongues after the holocaust, brought about by the intermingling of refugees as they flee from place to place. Critic Thomas J. Morrissey sees the novel's language as "an imperfect medium used by imperfect beings in their efforts either to reveal or obfuscate the truth. For the characters, linguistic precision is an elusive art."[17] The linguistic confusion, like that of Carter's *Heroes and Villains* (see chapter 6), is a metaphor for loss of meaning and coherence.

Brother Francis of Book I is the simple and humble saint. He functions as a foil for the Wandering Jew, a mysterious figure who appears in each section of the novel and represents the continuity of the messianic hope and Talmudic scholarship. Benjamin, as he is called, is woven into the narrative like a leitmotif. The Hebrew letters he inscribes on the "Fallout" shelter are thought by the almost illiterate Brother Francis to have the magical qualities of runes. When Benjamin reappears in Part II, searching for the Messiah, the last of Israel, he is in turn a foil for Thon Taddeo, the neo-Renaissance pedantic scientist, servant to an illiterate and savage liege lord. (Benjamin's attitude is biased against speculative inquiry per se, for he remarks later to the abbott, Dom Paulo, "Probing the womb of the future is bad for the child."[18])

The conflict between secular and sacred claims to authority is brought to a head by the New Literacy, as seen in the struggle between the reactionary librarian, Brother Armbruster, and the man of the new secular learning, the Thon. Both believe they have exclusive claims to have custody of the Memorabilia, and indeed of all knowledge. It is the Memorabilia, as the written symbolization of culture, the collective "journal" of civilization, one might say, that will be the chief concern of this discussion. The novel is richly complex, thus not lending itself to summary, and the details drawn on here are of necessity highly selective.

16. Walker Percy, "Walter M. Miller, Jr.'s *A Canticle for Leibowitz*: A Rediscovery," *Southern Review*, 7, no. 2 (1971): 572–73.

17. Thomas J. Morrissey, "Armageddon from Huxley to Hoban," *Extrapolation*, 25 (Fall 1984): p. 207.

18. Miller, *Canticle for Leibowitz*, pp. 37, 142.

Many of the basic images, motifs, and myths are established in Book I through the story of Brother Francis's accidental discovery of fragments once belonging to the not-yet-canonized Leibowitz in a "Fallout Survival Shelter." "Fallout" is misconstrued as a legendary monster. Francis unwittingly plays an important role in Leibowitz's canonization, as the documents he unearths are later added to the Memorabilia. In a delightful irony obvious to the reader, the documents are actually mundane, consisting of Leibowitz's last shopping list (including a "pound pastrami . . . can kraut, six bagels," for Em), and a memo to pick up "Form 1040, Uncle Revenue," plus a diagram of a transistorized radio circuit design. Commonplace fragments of language and an ordinary sketch, no longer comprehended, become mythologized and revered because of their very association with the now-awesome technological age of the past and a sainted former scientist.

For the most part it is the clerics of Abbey Leibowitz, and in Part II the one-eyed poet, who attempt to attain and preserve linguistic precision, to use language to reveal truth. Opposed to their efforts is the political cant of secular leaders, such as Thon Taddeo's illiterate liege lord who signs his decrees with an X, and the Thon himself, addicted to serpentine, prevaricating language. In his attempt to win possession of the Memorabilia for secular scholars like himself, the Thon declares that the new "prince" of Truth will rule when "men of science" ascend to power and master the earth. He makes these claims in his debate with Brother Armbruster, the old, querulous, pedantic librarian who wishes to keep the rare books chained, to banish the newly rediscovered electrical "witch-light" from his sanctuary, and to retain the crucifixes. Dom Paulo concedes to the secularization of knowledge by ordering the crucifixes removed from the library, saying "This is *not* a church."[19]

The Defense Minister of Part II, akin to Thon Taddeo in his service to mammon, uses words in the same serpentine way for the same distorted purposes. The Thon betrays his consternation at a reporter's reference to his government as "the War Ministry," and icily replies, "Madam, as you very well know, we do not have a *War* Ministry here; we have a *Defense* Ministry." This nuclearese is reinforced when he speaks of "the nuclear annihilation of an Asian city as the 'so-called Itu war disaster'."[20]

Those characters in the novel who faithfully attempt to reveal the

19. Ibid., pp. 175, 123–24.

20. These insights are from Morrissey, "Armageddon from Huxley to Hoban," p. 207, quoting *Canticle,* pp. 215–16.

truth through their words, the defenders of linguistic precision, fall into two categories. First are the clerics and prophets, with their passion for preserving the Memorabilia as pure knowledge against the attempts of secular scholars who would put all knowledge to the service of political power, without regard to the consequences. The Wandering Jew, who keeps alive the rigorous intellectual questing of Talmudic scholarship as well as the hope of the Messiah, is among these truth seekers. Second are the creative artists, represented by the Poet of Part II whose glass eye symbolizes his "perception of 'true meanings.'" Dom Zerchi of Part III, the last earthly abbot of the Order of Leibowitz, ranks among the clerical soothsayers. When he becomes aware that physicians are prescribing euthanasia to victims of radiation sickness on humanistic grounds, Dom Zerchi sarcastically attacks the prevailing euphemisms: "Due process, they call it. Due process of mass, state-sponsored suicide with all of society's blessings." He personally tries to intervene to prevent a radiated woman and child from being sent to "Eucrem" (a contraction of "euthanasia-crematorium").[21] Prevarications and euphemisms aptly convey the abuse of language that has become the rule rather than the exception in the self-deluding, self-destructive society of Part III.

Though "good" and "bad" characters can be sorted out to a large measure on the basis of their regard for linguistic precision, Miller does not fall into the simplistic trap of saying merely that bad people lie and good speak truth. Even those who abjure speaking with forked tongue find language itself presents barriers to clear communication. In Part III, Dom Zerchi struggles with his "dragon," the Abominable Autoscribe, a computer designed to write letters through a process of automated translation in languages he cannot speak. The technical marvel perversely breaks down, however, and produces nothing more than a word salad. The comic relief of this episode masks a deep truth, the post-Babel linguistic fragmentation that hampers the pursuit of understanding and peace. All humans, good or bad, wrestle with the inherent semantic and linguistic barriers to communication. Morrissey has pithily summed up the situation: In Miller's world, "the diplomats all speak different languages, [yet] they all speak the same tongue—doublespeak." Without exception, all "must wrestle with the many impediments inherent in human communication. . . . Not all those with tongues speak the truth and not all those with ears want to hear it."[22]

21. Miller, *Canticle for Leibowitz*, pp. 182, 241, 253.
22. Morrissey, "Armageddon from Huxley to Hoban," p. 208.

Miller's literary genius manifests itself vividly in his ability to create fresh new myths, or transmutations of "old" myths into new forms. A full explication of the mythological or legendary elements in *Canticle* would fill many pages, so here I shall simply list a number of them without elaboration: the myth of the Memorabilia, associated with the images of the Bookleggers and Memorizers who try to preserve intellectual riches against the assaults of war, pillage, and ignorance; the *false* myth of anti-intellectualism that brought about the Simplification, aimed at liquidating the learned and created to serve political ends; the myth of the Tower of Babel, newly interpreted to explain the confusion of tongues after the Flame Deluge; the myth of the Wandering Jew, given a new vitality and a new pathos; the myth of Saint Poet of the Miraculous Eyeball, whose glass eye sees wonders and truths invisible to the ordinary eye; the myth of Rachel, the mutant Mrs. Grales' "second" head, which awakens to prophesy toward the close of the novel; and, in small glimmers, a whole-Earth myth, a fragmentary Gaia vision. It is the rudimentary Gaia vision that will be explored here as an illustration of Miller's unifying artistic vision.

Miller's narrative in the last book hints at the Gaia vision in at least two ways: the implied perspective of the starship and the space colonies to which the ship and its occupants are destined, and, in an absurdist version, Brother Joshua's meditation as he spins a globe on his desk. By spinning the globe he hopes to gain a perspective on all of human history, to see the Earth whole. Joshua knows that "Lucifer has fallen" (i.e., fire is descending to consume the Earth) and the end is at hand. The apocalyptic moment concentrates his vision, and he questions *where* the destruction has struck and *why* the Lord has allowed it. Vainly, he spins the globe in reverse, as if by doing so he could reverse time:

> If Mother Gaia pirouetted in the same sense, the sun and other passing scenery would rise in the west and set in the east. Reversing time thereby? . . . He kept spinning the globe in reverse, as if hoping the simulacrum of Earth possessed the Chronos for unwinding time. A third of a million turns might unwind enough days to carry it back to the Diluvium Ignis (Flame Deluge). Better to use a motor and spin it back to the beginning of Man.[23]

The idea that there is a second chance for humanity is treated ironically, and yet, by allowing the starship to escape and thrust heavenward, Miller allows a bare possibility of a new beginning in another

23. Miller, *Canticle for Leibowitz*, p. 214.

place. Miller is unambiguous about the enormity of the odds against success. However weak the practical worth or likelihood of migration to another planet, it has value as myth, *so long as its strictly mythological nature is realized*. The only starship that can actually launch our race into a new era of life and peace is the starship that might discover a "new" planet within our own psyches, a new, transformed consciousness. Such a planet may lie sleeping unaware on our shoulders, ready to awaken like Rachel and save us from our own destructiveness. If the Gaia vision is to have any other value than as a basis for irony, it must be implemented before the catastrophe; after the event, it is only another ironic image for a paradise forever lost.

Of the three paradigmatic elements of Shigemutsu's survival ethic, the one that seems most applicable to *Canticle* is the first: the symbolic structuring of human experience, accomplished in this novel through the Memorabilia. Compassion for others is also evident when the bicephalous head of Mrs. Grales, the awakened Rachel, administers the sacrament to the dying Dom Zerchi with one word, "Live." This is confirmed by his vision of "primal innocence" and the "promise of resurrection" in her eyes. Rachel has ambiguous symbolic connotations, but on one level she may be interpreted as a Martyr figure, whose sacrificial act of suffering leads Dom Zerchi to realize that the "evil" in the world is not suffering "but the unreasoning fear of suffering." He voices his recognition that "the trouble with the world is *me*. Try that on yourself."[24] Such insight into one's own shadow side seems the necessary preliminary to creating a new "head" (as Mrs. Grales literally has)—an awakened state of consciousness—and to being able to move toward a meaningful personal and planetary mythology based on interrelatedness and compassion.

"Where Late the Sweet Birds Sang"

Kate Wilhelm's *Where Late the Sweet Birds Sang* alludes in its title to Shakespeare's sonnet number seventy-three, the well-known lament for the loss of youth, heralding the approach of old age and death, with the speaker likened to the leafless tree, its branches now bare of melodious birds. The last lines of the sonnet emphasize, however, the preciousness of life as weighed against the "black night" that swallows it up, and the listener is admonished to "love that well which thou must leave ere long." In short, awareness of transience and the inevitability of loss makes the loved one all the more precious.

24. Ibid., pp. 271, 274–77, passim.

This elegaic mood is sustained in the novel, which relates the story of a world polluted by radiation to the point of ecological collapse, suffering from plagues, famine, worldwide blight—in short, global catastrophe. A few farsighted people of the Sumner family have established a scientific research center for the purpose of cloning humans, most of whom have lost their fertility. Problems develop when the clones, with their think-alike and look-alike group consciousness, prove unable to perpetuate humanity. Humans become pariahs, yet they hold the only hope for a future.

Wilhelm develops a strong theme of the identification between women and nature, and the importance of feminine perspectives to a survival ethic, anticipating in this 1976 work much of the current eco-feminist ideology. A second theme, however, is of equal or greater importance: the value of the diversity and individuality of human beings, which cloning eliminates. Only sexual reproduction makes the maverick or nonconforming individual possible; cloning removes the creative presence of the different person from the human story, effectively dehumanizing the world.

The Myth of the Woji, invented by Mark (who is not a clone), illustrates the point. The Woji lived deep in the woods, Mark tells the clones, and nearly froze in the bitter winter. A leafeater, he had no sustenance after the leaves fell off the trees. The winds increased, and he was buffeted by ice and wind. An inspiration came to him: He convinced a spruce tree to let him make its leaves into needles. "Then he climbed to the very top of the spruce tree and yelled at the ice wind, and laughed at it and said it couldn't hurt him now, because he had a home and food to eat all winter."[25] Woji successfully challenges the ice wind's best efforts to freeze him out of the spruce tree, and soon the other trees want their leaves turned into needles as well. The maple tree, which had laughed at the ice wind's efforts to overcome the Woji, is punished by continuing to shed its leaves, making it "naked" in the freezing cold. The clones predictably dislike the story, sensing its challenge to their valuing of conformity.

The story expresses the kernel truth of the book—the importance of defying the norm in order to be creative and adaptable (two qualities the clones lack). The Woji is the Trickster Hero who embodies the "comic" survival ethic: His ability to laugh and to evoke laughter is life-enhancing. Mark is a human embodiment of the Woji spirit. He finds a book in the cloned Barry's office with a passage that reads, "What is

25. Kate Wilhelm, *Where Late the Sweet Birds Sang* (New York: Harper and Row, 1976), p. 160.

right for the community is right even unto death for the individual. There is no one, there is only the whole." Angered, he declares the book "a lie . . . . I'm an individual! *I am one!*" And when Barry asks if he has seen what happens to a strange ant when it falls into another colony of ants, Mark says simply, "But I'm not an ant."[26] The hive or bureaucratic mentality has no survival value in his eyes, and events of the novel bear out his assertion that ant behavior is counterproductive for humans.

The woman/nature link can be seen especially in Molly, Mark's mother, who is a clone with a difference, a talent for original art. (She prepares him for his link to nature by telling him the trees will talk to him when he needs them, before she drowns herself in despair, dreaming of Mark's father, Ben.) As a young woman, she had distanced herself "from the male-defined reality in which she had grown up," and she discovers that she can understand the voices of trees and the river. The other clones, in contrast, are "alienated from their organic ties with the earth," fear the forest, and want its "hostile environment" cleared to make way for habitation.[27]

The symbolic structuring of experience shows itself in this novel both in Molly's art (which has some survival value for her, though temporary) and in Mark's myth-making capacity. His ability to see himself in the Woji's role makes his frustration of the clones' plot to kill him more credible. Further, as a storyteller, he will be able to pass on a symbolized tradition to the children of the settlement he establishes, which outlives the colony of the clones. It is apparent that Mark recognizes and respects the integrity of the natural world, and he shows compassion for those he rescues to begin a new community. Though hardly a full-blown biophile, in his act of bearing a "boon" to his green, living valley, he has affinities with the traditional mythic hero.

"Dreamsnake"

Vonda McIntyre's *Dreamsnake* depicts the hera as a person of holistic and biophilic vision, a healer, exemplar of Pearson's Magician archetype (see the Introduction to this text). The novel is exceptional in featuring a female as the quester-adventurer in contrast to the usual male-dominated atomic adventure novel. In the devastated post–nuclear-holocaust world, the courageous heroine, Snake, follows her quest vision. She is a healer who practices her art with the assistance of her

26. Ibid., p. 181.
27. Paul Brians and Jane Winston-Dolan, "Nuclear War Fiction by Women Authors," paper presented at Interface '84, Eighth Annual Humanities and Technology Conference, Marietta, Ga., October 25–26, 1984.

highly trained, highly valued snakes. Early in the narrative she heals a young boy, Stavin, with Grass, her beloved dreamsnake, but the boy's people kill the rare animal out of fright over its threatening aspect. Heartsick, Snake sets out to seek a replacement. Her best hope, she believes, lies with the technologically more advanced people who live in the City and have dealings with mysterious off-worlders. The quest theme is interwoven with the story of the romance between Snake and Arevin but, contrary to the format of the traditional romance, it is he who plays the role of the rescued heroine figure of conventional literature.

Although Snake has no success with the City-dwellers, she manages to save a young girl named Melissa from slavery and sexual abuse. Melissa is a mutant, considered ugly by her enslaver, a hard-to-believe wretch named Ras. Snake recognizes the inner beauty and intelligence of the child and eventually adopts her, planning to give her the chance to become a healer like herself.

A digression is necessary to explain McIntyre's depiction of a highly evolved system of psychic control over fertility and reproduction. The people of Snake's and Arevin's clans conceive only at will; they are trained in a process of "biocontrol," by which the man renders himself infertile by raising his genital temperature through concentration. A man who fails to learn this technique suffers social ostracism. A dramatic instance of such ostracism is seen in the story of Gabriel, with whom Snake has a brief liaison. She equips him to regain respect and status in his society by giving him her more advanced knowledge of the biocontrol technique. Healers like Snake never have children; they adopt them and bring them up collectively.

The culminating adventure of the book traces Snake's quest to the broken dome, a remnant of an ancient nuclear war, where dreamsnakes are in plentiful supply. She is accompanied by Melissa and the "crazy" who has been harassing Snake throughout her travels, a man obsessed with an insane desire for the dreamsnake she no longer has. He agrees to guide her to the ruler of the dome dwellers, a man called North, who turns out to be a sadistic, deranged, and pitiful mountebank who keeps his followers in bondage with the help of the dreamsnakes' venom.

After extended torturous treatment, Snake learns the secret of breeding dreamsnakes: Because they are triploid, not diploid, they require a trio rather than a pair to reproduce. Moreover, they need extreme cold at a certain stage of their gestation. Having made this discovery, she escapes, rescuing Melissa from North, and is joined at just the right moment (*deus ex desert*) by Arevin. The romantic thread of the story is happily resolved, and the villainous North is left among his dreamsnakes, seeking the forgetfulness of death.

The power of the story lies largely in the strength and nobility of Snake's character and in the sometimes luminous and mythic quality as well as inventiveness of the language, as in the description of the broken dome as lying "across the hillside like a quiescent amoeba."[28]

McIntyre's story presents a valiant woman of mythic dimensions who exemplifies the wholeness sought by Psyche in Rachel Blau Du-Plessis's reinterpretation of the myth (see the Introduction). Snake's symbolic name signifies the "positive," good serpent or dragon of Eastern iconography in contrast to the commonly deprecated serpent of the Western world's Garden of Eden. McIntyre implies that the serpent power, sexuality in its creative aspect, holds the key to the engendering of love and compassion. In this novel McIntyre succeeds in incorporating a strongly feminist mythology that draws on the tradition of *caritas* (the medieval thinkers' name for self-forgetting love) and *agapé* (the ancient Greek word for the same phenomenon). Snake relies on this creative power of consciousness to overcome hatred and fear.

One troublesome aspect of the novel is the implication that Snake's superior powers have been induced by radiation. It is contradictory to all evidence to suppose that radiation gives people paranormal powers or makes them more loving and magnanimous. Since McIntyre gives no causal explanation for Snake's psychic abilities, however, it might be hypothesized that the highly developed perception and sensitivity shown by Snake have evolved through the process of natural selection because these qualities create a survival advantage.

Snake's gift is not for symbolic structuring of experience but for the art of making people whole. Her artistry belongs to the healing arts. Her healing powers rest upon her intuition of the wholeness of nature, a kind of mystical apprehension of unity. As for the third component of the *Black Rain* survival ethic, she clearly incorporates compassion on behalf of others. Like the traditional mythic hero, she contributes a rare and much-needed boon to her community.

"Riddley Walker"

Many believe Russell Hoban's *Riddley Walker* to be the most artful narrative example of nuclear fiction yet invented. In its metaphorical use of

28. Vonda McIntyre, *Dreamsnake* (Boston: Houghton Mifflin, 1978), p. 248. The first portion was originally published in *Analog* (October 1973), under the title "Of Mist, Grass, and Sand."

broken, fragmented language to image the bomb's destructiveness, it has no peer. Set in England about twenty-four hundred years after a nuclear holocaust that seems to have occurred in 1997, and covering a period of only a few weeks, the novel features twelve-year-old Riddley as first-person narrator. Riddley's postcatastrophic civilization resembles that of the early Saxons: Bows and spears are the only weapons (the rediscovery of gunpowder is a major event of the novel), literacy has vanished, and it is only through a seriously fractured oral tradition that people know anything about the past. The preholocaust tradition survives, however, distorted and mythologized, and people exhibit an almost religious awe for the ancient scientific era (our own), the era of the "1 Big 1," their name for the atomic bomb. Ironically, they suppose that the rediscovery of nuclear power could usher in a new golden age.

Several key myths have currency in Riddley's world. There is, first and foremost, the "Eusa" story, based on a misreading of the Legend of St. Eustace. The legend is known from a document that has survived the devastation, preserved in the English of the twentieth century. (Note the parallel to the legend woven around Leibowitz's shopping list and the veneration of his circuit design as a religious relic in A Canticle for Leibowitz.)

The language of Riddley's era is a combination of "slang, street argot, and debased terminology from a dead computer culture."[29] Readers puzzled by the phonetic spelling will find that pronouncing the text aloud helps to comprehend it. The orality demanded by reading aloud helps to transport us into the consciousness of a preliterate culture. Linguistic fragmentation symbolizes the fragmentation of meaning wrought by the atomization of the material world.[30] Riddley, sensitive to language and open to a dawning awareness of the devolution the bomb has inflicted on the world, seeks to understand the meaning of the Eusa story, the central myth of his culture.

Not everyone in Riddley's culture agrees with the enshrinement of high technology, however. As David J. Lake has pointed out, there is a public debate over Progress, with those stressing its advantages ranged against those who advocate that it is wiser to be content with "a more primitive life at one with Nature and instinctive wisdom."[31]

29. Schwenger, "Writing the Unthinkable," p. 45.

30. James Joyce, in Finnegan's Wake (1939; London: Faber and Faber, 1975), uses the phrase "the abnihilisation of the etym" and, in an earlier passage concerning old age, writes "We are once amore as babes awondering in a wold made fresh where with the hen in the storyaboot we start from scratch" (pp. 353, 336). The latter could serve as an apt description of the situation of Riddley and his fellows.

31. David J. Lake, "Making the Two One; Language and Mysticism in Riddley Walker," Extrapolation, 25 (1984): 158. For a linguistic approach, see also, John W. Schwetman,

Like so many post–nuclear-holocaust narratives, *Riddley Walker* portrays mutants with telepathic gifts caused by the effects of radiation; in
addition, there are telepathic, mystically gifted dogs (canine relations,
perhaps, of Blood in Ellison's "A Boy and His Dog"; see chapter 6).[32]
The novel is Riddley's mythic quest, and its central conflict is his temptation to embrace the lure of external power (control over others) versus the pursuit of his creative gifts as a mythmaker and puppeteer.
Riddley has inherited from his father the job of "connexion man," a
wonderfully fitting name for the person who synthesizes the fragments of human experience into a story, an integral whole. The connexion man interprets the "Eusa show," a Punch-and-Judy-type puppet
show that serves as the only surviving religious institution as well as a
dispenser of cultural propaganda for the hashish-addicted populace.

The Eusa story tells of Eusa (a linguistic confusion of U.S.A. and St.
Eustace) and Mr. Clevver (clever), who represent the "Puter Leat,"
the powerful computer elite of politicians and scientists who split the
atom (called the "Little Shynin Man") and caused the burning of the
world. According to the received tradition, Mr. Clevver took from Eusa
the secret of the 1 Big 1 (the bomb) and, after the thermonuclear holocaust that resulted, Eusa was punished with torture and mutilation,
then finally beheaded (compare the torture and murder of the intelligentsia during the Simplification described in *Canticle*). As an archetype of the sacrificial victim, Eusa has become a cultural savior figure or
spiritual guide.

At twelve-year intervals, a secret reenactment of the Eusa show is
held at Cambry (once Canterbury), where the "Ardship" (once Arch-
bishop) and the remnants of the "Eusa folk" (a small tribe of mutants
believed to have psychic powers) are herded into the basement of the
once-magnificent cathedral and interrogated about "radiant lite" and
other "linguistic fragments of the past" in a futile attempt to make
them reveal the secrets of the makers of the 1 Big 1.[33]

Like the tyrants of any age, the power-hungry of Riddley's time

---

"Russell Hoban's *Riddley Walker* and the Language of the Future," *Extrapolation* 26
(1985): 212–19. Schwetman argues that the cyclical time Hoban uses as a basis for *Riddley
Walker* parallels the cycles of time seen in Walter J. Miller Jr.'s *A Canticle for Leibowitz*.
Further, though the language of Hoban's book is "a return to medieval language," it is
nonetheless "a logical extrapolation of twentieth-century English" (p. 219).

32. Hoban also uses the dog in the context of metaphysical symbolism in his highly
philosophical novel for young readers, *The Mouse and His Child* (New York: Harper,
1976).

33. Morrissey, "Armageddon from Huxley to Hoban," p. 210.

crave the godlike sensations that come from wielding death-dealing weapons. The attraction of the power of technology is so awesome that even the artistically oriented Riddley can hardly resist it as he stands with his psychic dogs on the edge of the Power Ring Ditch (the site of an enormous nuclear blast), where he experiences its erotic-mystical allure. The Power Ring is symbolic of destructive technology, yet it hints also at the Unknown and Unknowable, and arouses emotions akin to the "egotistical sublime" mentioned in the discussion of Kopit's *The End of the World* (chapter 5). On its brink Riddley feels emptied, yearns for the explosion of the 1 Big 1, and simultaneously experiences sexual arousal.

His triumph over the seductive allure of external Power comes somewhat later, in Cambry (Canterbury), when in a mystical vision he comes to realize that

> I dint want no Power at all. . . . I cud feal some thing growing in me it wer like a grean sea surging in me it wer saying, LOSE IT. Saying, LET GO. Saying, THE ONLYES POWER IS NO POWER.[34]

Riddley's victory over his inner attraction to external Power is the turning point of his character growth and signifies a radical change in his consciousness. In Joseph Campbell's terms, he decides to follow his bliss, meaning to "go where your body and soul want to go," not live in the realm of "occasional concerns."[35] Riddley's rejection of external Power climaxes a process of growth that progresses through three "knowings."

It is Lorna Elswint, a wise, mystically gifted woman, who reveals to Riddley the myth that has become the oral history of the world, the story of "Why the Dog Won't Show Its Eyes." The tale is an "allegorical explanation of how humans advanced from fear of nature to control over it and of what happened when they used their power irresponsibly."[36] It tells of a time "befor peopl got clevver" when instead of cleverness they had "the 1st knowing," an intuitive, feminine, and earthy knowledge of their oneness with nature, a knowledge the dog has never lost. Thus, the first knowing was an experience of the unity of all life and beings.

But this primordial couple (cf. Adam and Eve) are not content with this "good time"; they covet a 2nd and even a 3rd knowing. The 2nd

34. Russell Hoban, *Riddley Walker* (New York: Summit Books, 1980), pp. 166–67.
35. Joseph Campbell, *The Power of Myth*, with Bill Moyers, ed. Betty Sue Flowers (New York: Doubleday, 1988), pp. 118–19.
36. Morrissey, "Armageddon from Huxley to Hoban," p. 210.

knowing is their knowledge of how to dominate the animals; they turn from hunting and gathering to domesticating other species. With ownership comes anxiety for their property; they make the dog into a guard dog, and become calculating, always "counting." Now materialists, they reduce everything to numbers.

What they lack is rest. Night, the source of the first wisdom, loses all significance to them, and they desire endless day. In search of uninterrupted light, they proceed to the 3rd knowing—the self-destructive knowledge of atomic power, which led to a terrific explosion and "nite for years on end"—the Dark Ages from which Riddley's civilization has emerged.[37] Power over the environment, the myth tells us, becomes dangerous at the point where it tries to deny the "night" side of the consciousness—the dark, intuitive, and feminine source of life itself.

Riddley's 1st knowing comes when he establishes a telepathic rapport with the wild dogs. His 2nd knowing occurs when he experiences wonder at the "shyning" of some broken machines that he and the blind Lissener chance to come upon in a "Power place." He is moved to exclaim,

> O what we ben! And what we come to! . . . How cud any 1 not want to get that shyning Power back from time back way back? How cud any 1 not want to be like them what had boats in the air and picters on the wind? How cud any 1 not want to see them shyning weals terning?"[38]

Here is the ancient *ubi sunt* theme (Where are the snows of yesteryear?), now immeasurably more poignant, considering the extent of the loss. There is never any doubt, in Hoban's tale, that nuclear holocaust is an unmitigated disaster for humanity.

The coming of Riddley's 3rd knowing occurs when he renounces the temptation of external Power in favor of creative power. There is, however, a culminating insight that comes to Riddley at the close of the novel. It occurs after he takes to the road with a new show—the Punch and Pooty performances that will replace the Eusa shows made obsolete by the reinvention of gunpowder. He sums up his relationship to a creative power when he says, "Its the not sturgling for Power thats where the Power is. Its in jus letting your self be where it is. Its tuning in to the worl [world] its leaving your self behynt."[39] Creative energies manifest themselves when the "self" is left behind, forgotten.

37. Hoban, *Riddley Walker*, pp. 18–19.
38. Ibid., p. 100.
39. Ibid., p. 197.

Writing is important in Riddley's scheme of things; he wishes to discover what he calls "the idear of us"—the idea of how to be human. Goodparley, the "pry Mincer" of Inland, tells him how words give form to our actions, create myths, and shape the future:

> What ben makes tracks for what wil be. Words in the air pirnt footsteps on the groun for us to put our feet in to. May be a nother 100 years and kids wil sing a rime of Riddley Walker and Abel Goodparley with ther circel game.[40]

Words are sadly inadequate, however, to convey truth without distortion, and Riddley realizes this: "Some times theres mor in the emty paper nor there is when you get the writing down on it."[41]

Peter Schwenger's critical comments show how Riddley's attempt to express himself with clarity and unity is frustrated by the truth expressed in the old Eusa story: "Lukin for the 1 yu wil aul ways fyn thay 2." Thus, "throughout the book the old mythic symbols are continually dividing into new meanings as they emerge in new contexts." The primary symbol of this quest and its endless elusiveness is the circle—the "Fools Circel 9wys" that represents all the "Chaynjis" (transitions) one must go through in seeking the mystery that lies at what Schwenger in a marvelous phrase calls "the ground zero of our existence."[42] The sense in which Riddley can be seen as a "tribal shaman" with an intuitive sense of the ultimate unity of the "multiplicity of things" (the central concept of all mysticism) has been most cogently explored by critic David J. Lake, who explains the novel's embodiment of the concept of the Fall (in the myth called "Why the Dog Wont Show Its Eyes") as coming about through " 'clevverness' and a constant desire for possessions and for power." The narrative shows how those who seek these ends are "divided from Nature/Tao/Unity, and are therefore self-divided also." The Eusa story incorporates this same theme of the Fall through the metaphor of the fission of the atom as "an emblem of the great fission within humanity, and between humanity and God/Nature." The dogs are emblematic of "those beings who never separate themselves from the Unity and its instinctive, intuitive wisdom."[43]

The decision Riddley makes to follow his bliss—his vocation as a dramatist and puppeteer—shines forth as the novel's most important

40. Ibid., p. 121.
41. Ibid., p. 161.
42. Schwenger, "Writing the Unthinkable," pp. 46–47.
43. Lake, "Making the Two One," pp. 164–68, passim. See his excellent analysis of the mysticism of the novel for a more detailed explanation.

message for our own time: "among small or big explosions and violent scrambling for power, the wise, intuitive, creative person can only stand aside and preach wisdom in symbolic form."[44] The novel goes beyond the cautionary tale, for it presents an alternative vision, showing a way of seeing the world and life as whole, a positive transformation of consciousness away from "control" and into creativity. In Riddley's case, the vision will manifest itself through dramatic art.

"The Green Book"

The Green Book of Jill Paton Walsh, the distinguished author of *Unleaving* and a number of other fine novels, is a slim volume for youngsters of middle-school age. About the only things it has in common with *Riddley Walker* are its futuristic setting and the theme of survival through creative symbolization of experience. Because it uses an "off-world" setting, it would be excluded from this study except for its nearly unique treatment of the theme of the destruction of the Earth in a narrative for readers of so tender an age.

The story tells of a motherless family forced to flee the "Disaster" on Earth by voyaging to the planet Shine. Each person is allowed to take one book. The protagonist, Pattie, chooses to take a blank book that becomes her diary (and, we later learn, the text of *The Green Book*): She is a budding creative writer. Books and writing symbolize the continuity of tradition, serving as the "memorabilia" of Earth for the inhabitants of the new space colony; they are lifeboats of the symbolic systems that make us human.

The new planet is named for its glittery, sparkling surface, which ironically is hostile to life—the plants are crystalline and at first seem inedible. Sarah, the middle child, saves the lives of the colonists when she secretly grinds the crystalline wheat grains into flour, cooks the meal, and eats it, taking a chance that it might prove nourishing. It does. On a very basic, simplistic level, both Pattie and Sarah contribute to survival: Pattie's gift is her talent for creating stories, carrying on the mythic tradition, whereas Sarah's is the "maverick" action, motivated by a mixture of self-interest and compassion for others, of risking her life to sustain life.

Young readers will find the novel thought-provoking, raising such questions as "Can people survive on another planet?" and "What might extraterrestrial life be like?"[45] The brief narrative does not allow for char-

---

44. Ibid., p. 159.
45. Nancy C. Hammond, review of *The Green Book,* by Jill Paton Walsh, *Horn Book Magazine,* 58, no. 6 (December 1982): 652–53.

acter development, and there is little of Paton Walsh's usual richness of imagery and literary allusion. Some would find the book undesirable in view of the credence it lends to the notion that flight to other planets might offer humanity a viable escape from nuclear annihilation; to her credit, Paton Walsh does not present life on Shine as surpassing life on Earth. On the contrary, this new locale is anything but a paradise to be gained. The mood is somber, and its effect might be compared to that of an eloquent little verse entitled "A Hundred Planets":

> If I had a hundred planets to choose from,
> the one I'd pick is the Earth.
> Some may have more light and less shadow,
> but lacking the colors of ocean and meadow,
> What is a planet worth?[46]

Anyone reading *The Green Book* will come away with an appreciation of the value of Earth.

"Brother in the Land"

Robert Swindells's novel for young readers, *Brother in the Land*, tells of the events that follow a devastating nuclear attack on England. Danny Lodge, the narrator, must fight for his own life and for that of his little brother Ben in a harsh survivalist environment. The epigraph for the book is from the Papyrus Ipuwer: "He who places his brother in the land is everywhere." The import of the quotation becomes clear only near the close of the book.

At the moment of the blast, Danny has taken shelter from a heavy rain in a "pillbox" (a concrete bunker) left over from World War II. With his ear pressed to the ground, he hears a "rumbling way down, like dragons in a cave; receding, growing more faint as the dragons went deeper, till you couldn't hear them at all."[47] The dragon metaphor can be read as an ironic allusion to heroic myth, for Danny as the potential hero is a near-child, whose quest becomes one for mere survival and whose wasteland is surely beyond reclamation.

As is typical in narratives of nuclear devastation, a new ethic

46. This poem by poet Aaron Kramer appears in his discussion of his own slowness in responding to the knowledge of Hiroshima, "Hiroshima: A 37-Year Failure to Respond," in *Writing in a Nuclear Age*, ed. Jim Schley (Hanover, N.H.: University of New England Press, 1984). Reprint of *NER/BLQ: New England Review and Bread Loaf Quarterly*, 5, no. 4 (Summer 1983).

47. Robert Swindells, *Brother in the Land* (New York: Holiday House, 1984), p. 7.

emerges quickly. Danny recalls a book a teacher had shown them about nuclear war, which had predicted such things as radiation burns but had entirely neglected what people would feel—an overwhelming sense of *futility* —and how their emotions would affect the way they would relate to each other. People are quickly sorted into two classes: those who are "shadows who pass you by" (compare the "ghost" people of the bombed-out Hiroshima landscape) and "enemies after your stuff." When Kim, a girl Danny likes, is about to kill a man to save herself, Danny prevents her, for he still operates by the old morality, but he thinks, "We were in a new game. The old rules no longer applied. There were no rules in this game; only the ones we made up as we went along. Maybe Kim was better suited to the new game than I was. Maybe I'd had no right to stop her."[48]

Nature, no longer nurturing, turns hostile, with the "black rain" deadly to all living things. People lose feeling for their own relatives, sending them off to die as callously as some gentiles in World War II betrayed the Jews, thinking "sooner them than us." The "authorities," whose task it presumably should be to organize resources to relieve suffering and help as many as possible to survive, become corrupt and exploitative enemies—worse hoarders than any of the others. A further example of treachery occurs when Rhodes, the former coach at Danny's school, turns to extreme survivalist tactics and knowingly blows up the truck carrying Danny's father, in order to rob it.

Language becomes deadly and polluted as well. The use of animal and mechanical metaphors for people (what Robert Frost called "downward comparisons") indicates the loss of sensitivity. People in shelters are called "badgers"; the deranged, who wander aimlessly about, babbling, are called "spacers"; those dying of sickness are called "terminals." Two other depersonalizing terms become current—"Goth," for a plunderer from the outside (i.e., anyone not local), and "Purple," for those who have turned to cannibalism to survive (from the song, "Purple People Eater"). Swindells shows through this devolution of language how inherently dangerous are the habitual metaphors people use to dehumanize one another, how perversion of language leads to the perversion of human relationships and ultimately escalates to genocide, ecocide, even geocide. Social historian E. P. Thompson points to the language of nuclearism, whereby, to give just one example, the deaths of millions of our fellow citizens are called "disagreeable consequences," a linguistic distortion that prepares our minds to be "launching platforms for exterminating thoughts." We

48. Ibid., pp. 9, 34.

think others to death as we define them as the Other: the enemy: Asians: Marxists: non-people. The deformed human mind is the ultimate doomsday weapon—it is out of the human mind that missiles and the neutron warheads come.[49]

Language becomes a means of "thingafying" people, or, in Campbellian terms, of turning "thous" into "its." Addressing something (even an inanimate thing) or some being as a "thou" places you into an entirely different relationship than if you address the same entity as an "it." Joseph Campbell has spoken eloquently of how much we might learn from native Americans, who addressed "all of life as a thou."[50] A leap of perspective to the I–thou way of speaking to other living things would be a quantum leap toward the valuing of life. Swindells shows novelistically how what we wish to destroy, we destroy first through linguistic devaluation.

The ultimate "it"-ifying of others, cannibalization, is pictured as beginning long before the nuclear blast when the minds of people became saturated with

> death and destruction on T. V. newsreels till it meant nothing to us— till it didn't shock us any more. If we'd realized in time what was happening to us, if we'd clung on to our reverence for life, then we'd never have launched those missiles.[51]

These are the words of Branwell, who temporarily becomes a mentor for Danny, but the idealistic hopes vested in him are shattered. Branwell believes people are reverting to "preneanderthalism," when there were no human feelings for the sick and no honor for the corpses of the dead. Despair threatens to discourage the conception of new life, as shown when Danny, in response to the news that Maureen is going to have a child, says that it is not much of a world to bring a child into. Kim's reply illustrates the usual gender-based attitudinal contrast: "It won't be easy. But it's what people will have to do, isn't it, if the human race isn't to die out." Later on, however, when Danny wants to marry her, she fears their offspring might be monstrous, thinking of the babies born after Hiroshima. Matters are not helped when Ben finds a deformed butterfly with seven misshapen wings, unable to do anything but flutter ineffec-

49. E. P. Thompson, "Overthrowing the Satanic Kingdom," in *Protest and Survive*, ed. E. P. Thompson and Dan Smith (New York: Monthly Review Press, 1981); reprinted in *The Nuclear Predicament: A Sourcebook*, ed. Donna Gregory (New York: St. Martin's Press, 1986), p. 323.
50. Campbell, *The Power of Myth*, pp. 78–79.
51. Swindells, *Brother in the Land*, p. 76.

tually. Not long after, a "hiroshima turnip"—all gnarled and misshapen and inedible—is discovered in the garden.[52] Basic trust in the goodness of generative nature has been shattered.

As in Carter's *Heroes and Villains* (chapter 6), time in this wasteland becomes shapeless. Like marooned and isolated castaways, with no radio or television to give structure to their days, they ignore clocks and calendars. Unlike Robinson Crusoe, who was constrained by his puritanical work ethic to keep a careful record of his time, people take to estimating it "by the sun's position, the pains in our bellies, and the quality of the light."[53] Time is shaped, if at all, by biological necessities.

Hope is briefly sought in the attempt to revive religion. Someone finds a carved stone in a shattered church; Branwell identifies it as an image of the "green man, . . . a pagan god with trees sprouting out of its mouth and leaves all round its head: a symbol of spring, when life comes out of death." There is a brief period when it seems a humanly decent world might emerge, but this hope evaporates. When Kim and Danny and Ben (now sickened from radiation) find Rhodes is plotting to rob them of their few hidden provisions, they experience the nadir of disillusionment. Ben dies soon after and is buried in the snow. The allusion of the title becomes clear.

The despair of Swindells's narrative is relieved by two factors: One, Danny never betrays Ben, his little brother, but steadfastly protects him and loves him even beyond death; and two, Danny finds a way to turn language to a preservative, even restorative, purpose by faithfully recording in his diary all that takes place, believing that if he writes down what has happened after the nuclear horror, "maybe it would stop them from doing it again." He plans to hide the document, when he and Kim move on, where future archaeologists might find it. This symbolic legacy to an unknown future is the last thing he can give to "little Ben, my brother. In the land."[54]

"Fiskadoro"

Denis Johnson's *Fiskadoro* is set in a not-too-distant future in what remains of the United States, "Twicetown," located in the southernmost Florida Keys. Twicetown is so-called because it was twice spared annihilation when "dud" nuclear weapons failed to detonate. Twice has the further thematic meaning of a repetitive pattern of destruc-

52. Ibid., pp. 75, 126–27.
53. Ibid., p. 54.
54. Ibid., p. 151.

tion/reconstruction/destruction, doomed to recur in an eternal cycle: Johnson's vision of time is cyclical. The narrative is notable for featuring minority characters as survivors. Many are fisherpeople, and Fiskadoro's mythically rich name derives from *pescador* (fisherman) and *fisgador* (harpooner).

Fiskadoro is a bright and restless adolescent who treasures his inherited clarinet. The story traces his painful initiation into the realities of death and sexuality; he endures his father's drowning at sea, then the prospect of his mother's death from radiation-induced cancer, and, atop this sorrow, undergoes a painful, traumatic ritual of sexual initiation at the hands of a strange tribe of pseudo-Islamic swamp dwellers whose males practice subincision.

Fiskadoro early in the story approaches A. T. Cheung, a musician and erstwhile businessman, leader of a ragtag performing group that calls itself, in a ludicrous misnomer, the Miami Symphony Orchestra. Cheung's consciousness is an artistic one. He endeavors to give coherence to his splintered world by two means: One, through nurturing a moribund musical tradition and two, through exploring the riddle of the past, the reason for the decline and destruction of the world that had existed before the Quarantine. He is subject to epileptic seizures, during which he sees a Tiny White Dot associated with "the Ultimate White of the Nucleus, the Atomic Bomb."[55]

Cheung's main link to the riddled past is his ancient Vietnamese grandmother, Marie Wright, whose life spans The End of the World, which began in her estimation in Saigon in 1974, when her English father committed suicide, her mother went mad, the city fell, and she narrowly escaped death to come as a refugee to the United States.

The novel's theme is the mystery of survival. It gives no credence to heroic survival myths, at least not in any traditional sense of the heroic. To survive is, in Marie Wright's case, to be *saved*, not for any reason or deserving, but simply because she was saved, because a sailor impulsively jumped off the boat and dragged her, a drowning refugee, to safety. The fact that she had no part or choice in her own rescue brings out the absurdity of existence, the role of mere chance in human destiny.

This existential absurdity relates to the "cosmic laughter" that surfaces in the story as a response to Mr. Cheung's recognition of the humanness he shares with a bizarre figure called "Mr. Flying Man," an

---

55. Denis Johnson, *Fiskadoro* (New York: Knopf, 1985), p. 82. This echoes Herman Melville's symbolic use of white in *Moby Dick*. See especially the chapter on the Whiteness of the Whale.

"Israelite" (one of a tribe of seafarers of mixed blood) who visits him to supply him with marijuana, smokes with him, and enjoys his music. The two in a flash of recognition see themselves as "fellow entities in the same universe," and "they begin to laugh."[56] Their ability to laugh identifies them as "comic" figures in Joseph Meeker's sense of the word (*The Comedy of Survival*) and further suggests the value of humor as a survival mechanism.

The symbolizing, mythmaking function can be seen in Cassius Clay Sugar Ray, Cheung's half brother and another bizarre figure, who has woven a legend around the "Trading Alliance," a creative fiction he spins in a successful effort to save his life, for it placates a hostile group from the North into allowing him to try out the idea. As a larger-than-life figure, he inspires others to belief, helping to create a future in a world robbed of a past. This is true in spite of his Trickster nature, for he takes part in profiting from the sale of contraband, radiation-tainted goods.

There is little comfort in the novel's ultimate view of life, and the nuclear fragmentation of the world is seen as an unmitigated loss. Johnson's vision is the detached stoic one; like the persona of the Old Testament Ecclesiastes, he finds life's meaning to manifest itself through Being, not through a teleological process of Becoming. Fiskadoro's loss of memory, and hence of any historical identity, makes him the ideal person to survive in a world whose history is a nightmare of destruction: Unlike Cheung, who is tormented by the inability to know more than fragments of the past, and who agonizes over the reasons why humankind has suffered so terrible a devolution, Fiskadoro, who seems to gain psychic powers as a result of his traumatic initiation, is "ready" when the mysterious invaders come. Cheung accepts, finally, the lack of control humans wield over their destinies; he ruminates over the fact that the Cubans will come, as rumored, the world will end again, and

> everything we have, all we are, will meet its end, will be overcome, taken up, washed away. But everything came to an end before. Now it will happen again. Many times. Again and again. Something is coming and something is going—but that isn't the issue. The issue is that I failed to recognize myself in these seagulls.[57]

The seagulls Cheung refers to have just been described by the prescient Fiskadoro as arrogant, like little professors. Thus Johnson ex-

56. Johnson, *Fiskadoro*, p. 54.
57. Ibid., p. 219.

presses through Cheung the human need for humility, for seeing one's comic aspect, and for apprehending the Oneness of life. Answers are denied us, but we can nonetheless enjoy moments of mystical epiphany, of wonder at the shining forth of Being. This, Johnson seems to say, is enough.

Fiskadoro implicitly embodies the tripartite survival ethic of the symbolic structuring of experience (the mythmaking capacities of Fiskadoro, who must create an identity for himself), compassion for others (Cheung for Fiskadoro), and spiritual-aesthetic recognition of life's unity (Cheung's moment of vision).

"The Postman"

The Postman by David Brin is richly endowed with elements of myth-in-the-making. The story conveys the anguish suffered by the inhabitants of the now-mythical United States, who have lost their unity and community in the aftermath of a nuclear disaster. The protagonist, Gordon Krantz, is an itinerant minstrel who, despite the brokenness and harshness of his world, radiates a "persistent optimism." The various myths in the novel all relate to the theme of responsibility for the common good, and it is their differing perspectives on this theme that will be highlighted here.

The story takes place in the dismal days sixteen years after a nuclear war and an ensuing nuclear winter. A handful of survivors in what was once the Pacific Northwest battle disease, starvation, fear, and dehumanization in an effort to reinvent a human mode of life. Krantz ekes out his living by performing, from memory, scenes from the classic dramas (cf. Riddley Walker and his puppet shows). One night a band of pillagers strips him of his few belongings and leaves him naked to freeze to death.

Fortuitously, seeking refuge in a rusted postal truck, he stumbles on the remains of a long-dead postman. He clothes himself in the postal uniform and, appropriating the mailbag (which contains undelivered letters), assumes the role of letter carrier. To his amazement, people believe in his assumed identity, and gradually he grows into a self-conceived mythic postman who carries the hope for a "Restored United States." He embodies a new myth of possibility for reconstituting the splintered society. In a way somewhat analogous to the king of Renaissance times, his person is a microcosm of the state, except that now the state must be reinvented.

There are advantages to his revered postman role; he finds himself feted and regarded as a "demigod," but he also feels "trapped in his own lie," creative fiction though it is. He sees himself as a "dark-age con artist doing his best to survive in a deadly and suspicious world," yet there is a dimension of compassion for others within his role as well: The people want to believe in him, for they "hunger for wonder and something of the world beyond their narrow valley." Letters, even from the dead, give them this link to the outside and a promise of transcending the limits of their own space and time. They remember certain mailmen as heroic figures, for instance, one who used to sing as he delivered messages, "through sleet, through mud, through war, through blight, through bandits, and through darkest night." The generative-imaginative aspect of Krantz's role becomes biological as well when he magnanimously, at the couple's request, fathers a child for a woman named Abby and her sterile husband.

Late in the novel Krantz tells the myth of the United States, the country of once-upon-a-time, to George Powhatan and his people. Powhatan is the "squire" of the agrarian Sugarloaf Mountain community whose values are in harmony with the peace mythology of the Order of Cincinnatus (see below). Krantz wishes to persuade Powhatan and his followers to take responsibility for defending the egalitarian ideals of this wonderful, lost United States against the militaristic survivalists who threaten to seize control of all those who are weaker than they. The Postman weaves a romantic tale of "a nation of a quarter of a billion people who filled the sky and even the spaces between the planets with their voices . . . a *strong* people" who wore their strength lightly, "wonderfully crazy" in their laughter, their creativity, their self-accusation of terrible crimes. The latter practice made them compassionate; they settled most of their differences peaceably, and took "a clean, healthy life" for granted, "a life far gentler, far sweeter than any that had gone before" and perhaps any that would ever come again.

Krantz does not totally idealize these mythical Americans, acknowledging that they were "arrogant, argumentative, often shortsighted," yet he insists "they did not deserve what happened to them!"[58] Doomtime, or the Collapse as it is alternately called, came about not through the Americans' pride in their godlike powers—their invention of thinking machines and engineering of life—but "we were punished for dreaming, for reaching out." The climax of Krantz's appeal is the American ideal of being at one's best in a crisis, and of "helping one another when it counted most."[59] The immediate result of his eloquent

58. David Brin, *The Postman* (New York: Bantam Books, 1985), pp. 202–3.

59. Ibid., *Postman*, pp. 204–5. The rationale for the punishment is not further explained, but there may be a parallel with Dom Zerchi's ponderings on the "riddle of evil" as residing, paradoxically, in the desire to rid life of the "evil" of suffering: The

plea is disappointing, but in the long view, as shall be seen, Krantz's mythic vision works its magic, and its egalitarian ideal of responsibility is vindicated in action.

A second myth in *Postman* is the myth of Cyclops, "a gentle, wise machine," a supercomputer that had actually "died" many years before, but whose benevolently despotic governance continued through the Wizard-of-Oz-like intrigues of the "Servants of Cyclops," devoted to bringing about a rebirth of life-enhancing technology. The mythical Cyclops rules in what remains of Corvallis, Oregon. The voice of Cyclops is Joseph Lazarensky, a thin, gentle old scientist who loved Cyclops as a son, a machine "more *human*," as he says, "than I had been." Before he expired, Cyclops had conceived the Millenium Plan to rebuild civilization. Lazarensky is explicitly compared to Oz when Krantz sees through him and thinks, "Dorothy herself could not have felt more betrayed." But Lazarensky justifies his use of the Cyclops myth, for it was the kind of deception that worked "at Delphi and Ephesus," and it did no harm. After all, those who sought Cyclops's pronouncements believed in the "impartiality" of the computer, though they "would never trust a living man." When Cyclops is unmasked, Krantz regrets the loss, and he reiterates a question that runs throughout the book like the lament of a Greek chorus: "*Who will take responsibility now, for these foolish children?*"[60]

One who aspires to that responsibility but for the wrong reasons is Nathan Holn, the archetypal survivalist, the "high priest of violent anarchy," now dead but perpetuated by his book, *Lost Empire*. The philosophy of the Holnists is pro-feudalistic, hierarchical, based on Holn's basic law of life, "Some command, others obey," a pattern he believes to be "honorable and natural." Thus he justifies his dream of empire.

The militaristic war mythology embraced by the Holnists, led by General Macklin, is posed against the peace mythology represented historically by the Order of Cincinnatus. While Krantz and a young ally, Johnny Stevens, are prisoners of the Holnists, Krantz explains the Order to the young man. Founded by George Washington, the Order of Cincinnatus required its members to "remain farmers and citizens first" and be soldiers only in their country's need. Johnny, innocent of

---

"dreaming" and "reaching out" seem much like the efforts to "minimize suffering and maximize security" that, if sought as ends in themselves, result in their opposites, "maximum suffering and minimum security." See Miller, *Canticle for Leibowitz*, pp. 271ff.

60. Brin, *Postman*, pp. 151–52, 150, 152, 154, 209.

history, learns that Cincinnatus was a Roman general of the ancient days of the Republic. Weary of fighting, he retired from the army and returned to the land, where he hoped to farm in peace. Emissaries from Rome sought him out to rally his countrymen against invaders, and his success in doing this led to an offer of the crown. He declined, returning to his agrarian life.

Holn hated the Order of Cincinnatus, whose values were so obviously averse to his dream of empire. He also had contempt for Alexander Hamilton, Thomas Jefferson, and "that evil genius, Benjamin Franklin," who upheld the Order and its ideals against the likes of Aaron Burr.[61]

The events of the novel validate the truth of the peaceful, agrarian mythology of the Order of Cincinnatus, reflected in George Powhatan and his followers, but with a difference. The hand-to-hand battle between General Macklin and Powhatan, presented as a struggle between two epic figures (reminiscent of Hector and Achilles) defines the difference. Macklin represents, in addition to Holnist values, the "augments" of a physical kind, bred and trained as fighting machines, genetically and environmentally programmed for battle. Powhatan, in contrast, is revealed to be an "augment" of the mind and will, a student of psychic arts, with an aversion to the power of the sword. His primary "control" is over his own consciousness; he fights only in self-defense. In this struggle, witnessed by Krantz, Powhatan is victorious.

An individual's responsibility, in the framework of Powhatan's mythology, is first to cultivate his or her own spiritual enlightenment. As in yogic traditions, however, the mind/body connection is honored. As one who finds his power in a spiritual vision of life's unity, Powhatan also represents the responsibility for compassionate action.

Brin does not neglect to represent the link between women and nature and to dramatize feminine sympathies for a peace mythology. Powhatan is urged by the women of his community into the "public" arena; they, having been moved by the idealism of Krantz's myth of the United States as well as the Legend of the Women of Willmette, convince him to render service in the cause of peace.

The women of Willmette espouse the values of Dena, whose views of women's responsibility are outlined in a letter she writes to Krantz, which Powhatan reads, as it is delivered, or misdelivered, to him. Dena and her band of followers have come to two conclusions about men: At one extreme there are those who are "wonderful beyond belief" (here she would include Krantz), and at the other, there are those

61. Ibid., pp. 257, 234, 232.

who are "bloody lunatics." The former have given us "power and light, science and reason, medicine and philosophy," but the latter have invented "unimaginable hells." Most men fall between these extremes, but these middle-ground, gray-area males are ineffectual in shaping the world and hence may be discounted.

Women, Dena argues, are at fault for leaving the control of the world in the hands of men, and she and her women's army of Willmette determine to seize their chance—their last chance—to compensate for the failures of their foremothers. They will accomplish their goal of establishing peace by "culling out" the "bastards" (the power-mad men). She calls on women "to CHOOSE among men, and cull out the mad dogs."[62]

Dena's plan becomes history. A band of forty women, determined to end a terrible war, lead a rebellion against the Holnists. Despite their valor, they are defeated (some of them are guilty of collusion with the Enemy).

The irony of Brin's presentation of the collapse of the efforts of these women is plain. They are doomed to fail because they adopt the strategies of the men they oppose, becoming like the warlike enemy in their effort on behalf of peace. The dynamics of these events, a playing out of the principle of enantiodromia, are convincingly portrayed.

Though Brin paints these women with some sympathy and leaves to the reader the merits of their plan to sit in judgment on men (executing those they deem unfit), he leaves their relationship to responsibility in question and, ultimately, since they are shown as failing in action, they are relegated at best to the supporting roles of mentors or gadflys. "Even the best men—the heroes," we are told, "will sometimes neglect to do their jobs. *Women, you must remind them, from time to time.*"[63]

The openendedness of Brin's narrative rings true: Krantz will continue with his postman mission, Powhatan will stand against the Holnists. The Women of Willmette will live on in legend and perhaps inspire other women to bring their life-centered values into dialogue in the public arena, to take a responsibility they have disastrously hitherto shunned and left almost exclusively to men. As in life, however, no single myth can be said to triumph. This avoidance of any doctrinaire message, this delicate ambivalence, is part of the novel's art. The different, contesting myths of responsibility portrayed must succeed or fail on their merits, as the human story in all its complexity goes on.

Brin achieves a nice balance among the claims of myriad mythologies of war and peace, and it is clear that his sympathies lie with peace,

62. Ibid., pp. 207ff.
63. Ibid., p. 286.

respect for life, respect for the integrity of the land, and a certain humility. He avoids the Captain America complex (neither Krantz nor Powhatan has illusions of saving the world). The Postman stands, however, as a symbol of relatedness, links among human beings, and the acceptance of the responsibilities relatedness entails. The Postman's myth is life-serving and may hold promise for re-storying, re-mythologizing, his world.

Art as the Inclination to Order Pitted against Dread

The life-affirming survival ethic emerging from this survey of the journalist, the creative artist, and other characters devoted to the symbolization of human experience in nuclear fiction can be expressed in terms of the power of language and the restorative value of words. When woven into story and myth, language can restructure human experience, give it a renewed coherence and meaning. In traditional societies, the seer, who goes beyond ordinary knowledge to apprehend the unity and wholeness of life, and the poet, who symbolically integrates the holistic vision in an artistic form that can be communicated to others, perform these functions. The fictional seers, artists, or "maker" figures, who stand out as carriers of hope for their fictional communities, may simply raise the awareness of readers, render them more thoughtful, more alert to realities of relationship. The poet Seamus Heaney has said that words, though sometimes only weightless chimeras,

> remain our truest means of sifting the chances of earth and pledging ourselves to a possible life in a threatening future. The best art continues to find occasions to contemplate, without being overwhelmed, man pitted against dread.[64]

Art, at its best, transcends dread, sometimes paradoxically by giving it a local habitation and a name, a shape through which it may be confronted and hopefully vanquished. By its essentially aesthetic "inclination to order," in poet John Haines's phrase,[65] art nourishes courage and lays the foundation for the kind of inner peace that can make a worldwide vision of peace one step closer to realization.

64. Seamus Heaney, note to "The Birthplace,"in *Writing in a Nuclear Age*, p. 150.
65. John Haines, "Death Is a Meadowlark: Memorials and Consolations from a Work in Progress," in *Writing in a Nuclear Age*, p. 127.

CHAPTER 8

Gaia as Cosmic Myth

"Perhaps if we named it we'd treat it better,
stop gouging it out and mucking up its veins,
plaster no more concrete on its skin.
Name it for a goddess, we might honor it, even."
—Evelyn Ames, "Naming the Earth"

Seeing through the Eyes of Our "Splendid Moon Men"

In Robert Heinlein's *The Green Hills of Earth*, Rhysling, the blind balladeer on the Venus Shuttle, writes from his perspective in space a lyric celebrating Earth:

We pray for one more landing
on the globe that gave us birth.
May we rest our eyes on the fleecy skies
and the cool green hills of Earth.[1]

Astronaut Rusty Schweickart remembered Rhysling's ballad when, from his observation point on the moon, he saw the fair face of Mother Earth. In a letter to a friend, Schweickart spoke of his awe at the sight of "this incredibly beautiful blue planet, our home, our mother," floating in the silence of space.[2]

1. Robert Heinlein, *The Green Hills of Earth* (Chicago: Shasta Publishers, 1951), p. 194.
2. Russell L. Schweickart, letter to Paul Winter, January 25, 1982. Reprinted in "What Is Gaia?," brochure accompanying "Missa Gaia: Earth Mass" by Paul Winter (Living Music Records, Box 68, Litchfield, CT 06579; 1982), unp.

This image of our fragile globe suspended in the void of space has changed for all time the way we see our planetary home.[3] What had seemed so vast is now perceived as a "small spot, that little blue and white thing." Even so, it is the unique home of everything preciously "human"—"all of history and music and poetry and art and death and birth and love, tears, joy, games." As a consequence of his off-world experience, Schweickart underwent an inner change that altered his relationship to Earth. He writes in "No Frames, No Boundaries": "And you realize from that perspective that you've changed, that there's something new there, that the relationship is no longer what it was." Perceptions of time, space, and value would never be the same again, for "when you go around the Earth in an hour and a half, you begin to recognize that your identity is with that whole thing. And that makes a change."[4]

This privileged insight transformed Schweickart's consciousness. Where previously he had seen frames and boundaries—boundaries of state and nation and limited loyalties—he now saw one fragile planet, and the cherished Earth evoked awe, respect, and love. As Joseph Campbell would say, it became clear that the "monad," or unit of society, was no longer the nation but the globe, encompassing all humankind.[5]

Schweickart was not the only one of the astronauts to experience a consciousness-expanding effect. "The Other Side of the Moon" documented how a number of astronauts changed as a consequence of their moon flights. Schweickart and a Russian cosmonaut spoke of their mutual feelings of "a responsibility to preserve life on Earth" and a "gut feeling" about the "interlocked system," the "ecosphere," as unique and infinitely precious, appreciated as peerless when poised against the dark unknown of space.[6]

Edgar Mitchell, a veteran of the *Apollo 14* flight, found his mystical peak experience in space a gateway to the exploration of other psychic experiences. While in orbit, he was struck by an irrefutable feeling of a palpable, intelligent system shaping the cosmos, and, not wanting the

3. These photographs are reproduced in *The Home Planet*, conceived and edited by Kevin W. Kelley for the Association of Space Explorers, with original design concept by Carol Denison (Reading, Mass.: Addison-Wesley, 1988).

4. Quoted in *Earth's Answer: Explorations of Planetary Culture at the Lindisfarne Conferences*, ed. Michael Katz, William P. Marsh, and Gail Gordon Thompson (New York: Harper and Row, 1977), pp. 12 and 11.

5. Joseph Campbell, *The Inner Reaches of Outer Space* (New York: Alfred Van Der Marck Editions, 1985), p. 19.

6. "The Other Side of the Moon," produced by Lemle Pictures, Inc., 1989, for the South Carolina ETV Network. Broadcast on PBS in July 1989.

moon voyage to be the apogee of his life, he has gone on to dedicate his energies to exploring inner space, the nature of consciousness, founding the Institute of Noetic Sciences.[7] Jim Irwin of the *Apollo 15* mission similarly speaks of the spiritually transforming power of the ascent to a lifeless world (cf. the mythic heroic journey to the underworld and its similar consciousness-transforming effect). Irwin stresses his consequent search to "serve God" in his research on Mt. Ararat, where he participates in archeological exploration seeking historical evidence of Noah's Ark.

Al Bean, now an artist (something he had not known he wanted to be until after his moon trip), preserves memories of the moonwalks through his paintings. He believes he and his fellow astronauts "became more like they really were deep inside" as a result of their off-world voyage.

Those who found no dream or aspiration to replace the realized, euphoric one of space travel experienced "coming down to Earth" as a void, an emotional depression. Stewart Roosa of *Apollo 14* phrased it succinctly: "Now that I've been to the top of the mountain, where do I go from here?" In some cases, the rise in expectations, the desire to "optimize" all areas of their lives, had devastating consequences for their personal relationships, including a number of broken marriages.

Such divine discontent is the downside of the heroic adventure. Daedalus in his aspiring toward the sun risks the disintegration of his wings and a plummeting into the sea. For the most part, the net result of space flight in these men's lives seems to be an increased reflectiveness, a turning inward for some value more enduring than ephemeral celebrity. For those who opened themselves to the sense of wonder, existential questions became uppermost.

The Dark Side of the Moon Experience

Not every thoughtful person involved in the thrust into space, as participant or witness, found the experience an expansive or euphoric one. Twenty years after the astronauts of *Apollo 11* —Neal Armstrong, Edwin E. (Buzz) Aldrin, and Michael Collins—touched down on the moon in July of 1969 in a ship named *Columbia*, the literary reflections of the venture were reviewed by Thomas Mallon in "One Small Shelf

7. The Institute of Noetic Sciences, 475 Gate Five Road, Suite 300, P.O. Box 909, Sausalito, CA 94966-9922.

for Literature."[8] Mallon notes the "paucity of fiction and poetry" on the topic and calls it "one of the most underwritten of historic events." His article surveys the notable exceptions—John Updike's Rabbit's apathetic ponderings on the event (in *Rabbit Run*, while it is occurring, he doesn't "feel anything yet" about it), Norman Mailer's incorporation of this "witnessing man's first departure from the planet" into his picaresque hero's preoccupations with such "personal earthly problems as his weight and his wives" in *Of a Fire on the Moon*, and, more recently, Paul Auster's use of the event in his novel *Moon Palace*. [9]

Mallon notes how, eleven years after Donald A. Wollheim published his anthology of lunar stories, he reprinted it with an appendix giving the responses of science fiction writers to both the plaque left by the astronauts, emblazoned "We Came in Peace for All Mankind," and an alternative one proposed by I. F. Stone, reading in part, "Their Destructive Ingenuity Knows No Limits and Their Wanton Pollution No Restraint. Let the Rest of the Universe Beware." Isaac Asimov was among those who "wanted to feel the nobility of the mission but acknowledged that 'every word [Stone] says has a strong element of truth in it." The challenge is to balance the hope and promise inherent in space exploration with the "arrogance" of the act and the feeling on the part of some that humankind is not yet ready to "deal with all that emptiness."[10]

Some have felt that the net effect of space ventures has been to *contract* rather than to expand our imaginations. In 1969 C. P. Snow predicted that the act of human beings walking on the moon would limit our horizons, lead to "cosmic claustrophobia," and drive writers of science fiction inward to explore the inner space of human biology and psychology.[11] His prognostication seems validated by the astronauts' own experiences. Inner space, to some, is an even greater challenge to the imagination. Snow's views were echoed by Kurt Vonnegut: "We are permanent prisoners on this planet. It's the only planet we'll ever

8. Mallon is the author of *Arts and Sciences* (New York: Ticknor and Fields, 1988) and *A Book of One's Own: People and Their Diaries* (London: Picador, 1985).

9. Mallon calls Mailer's an "oddball book" but "the only one worthy of the occasion" ("One Small Shelf for Literature," *New York Times Book Review Section*, July 16, 1989, pp. 1, 26–28).

10. Mallon, "One Small Shelf for Literature," p. 28, quoting from Carter Scholz's 1976 story, "The Eve of the Last Apollo." Mallon also refers to *Seeing Earth: Literary Responses to Space Exploration*, ed. Ronald Weber (Athens: Univ. of Ohio Pr., 1980); and Tom Wolfe's *The Right Stuff* (New York: Farrar, Straus, and Giroux, 1979).

11. C. P. Snow, "The Moon Landing," *Look*, August 26, 1969, quoted in Thomas Edward Sanders, ed., *Speculations: An Introduction to Literature through Fantasy and Science Fiction* (New York: Glencoe, 1973), p. 3.

have." The "extraordinary trips," Vonnegut believes, must now be made in our own minds. "Man's principal enterprise is going to be to endure, as long as he can, under worsening conditions."[12] If Vonnegut is right, the best conclusion we can draw from the Gaia image is that we had better treat our fragile Earth with tender care and reverence. Personalizing it by addressing it with Gaia's name is one step toward that goal and could do much to encourage the adoption of the biophile's perspective.

A Brief History of Gaia as Goddess

In ancient times science and theology were one. Inhabitants of the area now known as Greece regarded Mother Earth as a divinity, the first among the gods; Hesiod in the *Theogony* speaks of Gaia as Creatrix. Merlin Stone relates in *Ancient Mirrors of Womanhood: A Treasury of Goddess and Heroine Lore from Around the World* how, long before Zeus was "born," Gaia was worshipped at the site of the holy mountain Olympia, before the name was changed to the masculine "Olympus." At the foot of Mount Parnassus, site of ancient Pytho, later known as Delphi, Gaia's words were heard through the Pythian priestess, before Dorian priests claimed Pytho for Apollo. Deep within Parnassus, nonetheless, Gaia was preserved in the form of the divine lioness sitting on a throne. Mycenaean artifacts found at the Delphi shrine, Stone suggests, point to a link between the Gaia image and goddess reverence on Crete.[13]

The primeval goddess Earth, or Gaia, was celebrated by Homer, who sang of "Gaia, Universal Mother, firmly founded, Oldest of all the Holy Ones." This was centuries after her best-known shrine at Delphi, associated with the sacred serpent child, variously called Delphyna, Python, or Typhon, was usurped by intruders from the north who installed Zeus, their own god, in Gaia's stead. Memory of the Earth goddess persisted. Homer tells how Apollo used his torches and arrows to overtake Pytho, dealing Gaia's priestess, the pythoness Delphyna, a fiery death. Aeschylus vindicates Apollo through telling a different tale, centuries later, wherein Phoebe, a daughter of Gaia, be-

12. Kurt Vonnegut, interview in *TV Guide*, March 11, 1972; quoted in Sanders, *Speculations*, pp. 3–4.

13. Merlin Stone, *Ancient Mirrors of Womanhood: A Treasury of Goddess and Heroine Lore from Around the World*, illus. by Cynthia Stone (New Sibylline Books, 1979; Boston: Beacon Press, 1984), p. 362. Riane Eisler discusses goddess reverence on Crete in detail in *The Chalice and the Blade: Our History, Our Future* (San Francisco: Harper and Row, 1989).

stows the shrine upon Apollo as a gift. Euripides gives yet another version of the story, saying that Apollo killed Gaia's serpent child, guardian of the cave of the oracle, and thereafter had to endure Gaia's punishment, being haunted by nightmares.[14] The whereabouts of the written records and the Delphic laws, called the Sibylline, remain a mystery—perhaps destroyed, perhaps secreted on the dusty shelves in the labyrinthine libraries of the Vatican. Diodorus claimed the Sibylline records were the source of Homer's epics.[15] Certainly their reemergence, if indeed they still exist, would be a momentous historical and literary event.

From Goddess to Scientific Theory: The Gaia Hypothesis

In *The Chalice and the Blade: Our History, Our Future*, Riane Eisler has noted the link between the "lost, ancient spirituality" of the prehistoric partnership societies, most notably in Crete, and the Gaia hypothesis of chemist James Lovelock and microbiologist Lynn Margulis, which sees the Earth as "one complex and interconnected life system."[16] The intuited truth undergirding the ancients' reverence for Gaia, whom they experienced as something more than a spherical rock coated with a layer of ocean, air, plants, and animals, has resurfaced in recent times in the scientific theory called the Gaia hypothesis. Gaia's name, shortened to Ge, has persisted in the scientific context in the prefixes of *geology* and *geography*. Today, the holistic perspective of antiquity, revitalized by a "space-eye" view of Earth, is reemerging, and the realization that the Earth, though made of much the same raw materials as the sibling planets of Mars and Venus, is a beautiful anomaly, alone in having just the right combination of air, water, and temperature to favor life, has the valorization of science.

At the same time that ordinary people were simply awed by the marvel of the sight of Earth from space, scientists were using their measur-

14. Stone, *Ancient Mirrors of Womanhood*, pp. 364–65. Stone notes that the myths of Daphne, Gaia's priestess, and Creusa, both harassed by Apollo, may reflect memories of the male deity's usurpation of Gaia's shrine. Stone also tells of Delphi's checkered later history. The shrine was sacked by the treasure-seeking Celts, claimed by the Romans in the days of the empire, looted by the Emperor Constantine to enrich Byzantium, and closed by Emperor Theodosius, who regarded it as a threat to Christianity. It was laid to ruins by Arcadius, an early ruler of Christendom.
15. Ibid., p. 366.
16. Eisler, *The Chalice and the Blade*, p. 75.

ing instruments to reinforce the finding that the other planets are, as James Lovelock puts it, "bare and barren and as different from the Earth as a robin from a rock." Lovelock's Gaia hypothesis views Earth as a unique ecosystem, one biosphere, "a single giant living system and one with the capacity to keep the Earth always at a state most favorable for the life upon it." Lovelock credits novelist William Golding with coining (unearthing would be more exact) the name Gaia to express the unified being of Earth.[17] Besides recognizing the "personhood" of the Earth, the personal name expresses an I–thou relationship between humans and their planet home, a relationship basic to the perspective of the biophile.

The Gaia hypothesis proposes that Earth has the capacity to regulate her climate and composition to keep them close to optimal for all the "creatures great and small" who inhabit her. ("It" is no longer a suitable pronoun, given this personal context.) Scientific theory thus reinforces the intuited, mystical sense of humanity's kinship with all other species. Since all life is a part of Gaia, destroying any of our sibling species means destroying a part of ourselves. Though the importance of the human species might seem to be diminished in this view, "our membership in this great commonwealth of living things," as Lovelock notes, holds "possibilities for comfort" as well as dismay:

> It may be that the role we play is as the senses and nervous system for Gaia. Through our eyes she has for the first time seen her very fair face and in our minds become aware of herself. We do indeed belong here. The Earth is more than just a home, it is a living system and we are part of it.[18]

Paradoxically, the status of humankind is both humbled in this view (we are but a part of a living system) and simultaneously exalted (we are the conscious "mind" of the system). Biologist Lewis Thomas, speaking of how the photographs of Gaia from space stirred his imagination, called upon human beings as "the brightest and brainiest of the Earth's working parts" to realize their potential to become "a sort of collective mind for the Earth, the *thought* of the Earth."[19] This Gaia

17. "What Is Gaia?" See also James Lovelock, *Gaia: A New Look at Life on Earth* (New York: Oxford Univ. Pr., 1979); and Stephen H. Schneider, "Gaia: A Goddess of the Earth?" *1988: Yearbook of Science and the Future* (Chicago: Encyclopaedia Britannica, Inc., 1987), pp. 28–43.

18. Lovelock, quoted in "What Is Gaia?"

19. Lewis Thomas, foreword to Paul R. Ehrlich, Carl Sagan, Donald Kennedy, and Walter Orr Roberts, *The Cold and the Dark: The World after Nuclear War* (New York: W. W. Norton, 1984), p. xxiv.

perspective and its recognition of responsibility for nurturing the life of the planet—essentially the biophile's vision—holds hope of countering the forces that would sweep us toward global catastrophe.

The Gaia hypothesis has been controversial since it was introduced by Lovelock in the seventies. Ironically, he had secretly hoped his theory that "The Earth is alive!" would be condemned by theologians; instead it was his fellow biologists who were scandalized, and Lovelock was invited to preach at the cathedral of St. John the Divine in New York City. The long mythic tradition regarding Gaia as alive has been surveyed, but even as scientific theory the living Earth was not new. To cite just one instance, the Scottish geologist James Hutton wrote in 1785, "I think the Earth is a superorganism."[20] As the statements published in 1988 reporting on the Gaia conference sponsored by the American Geophysical Union in San Diego witness, many scientists can accept the "weak" as opposed to the "strong" version of the hypothesis. The strong hypothesis is the poetic one, the metaphor of Earth-as-"superorganism" as biologist Paul Ehrlich scornfully called it; it sees Gaia as purposefully, willfully, working to make the environment of Earth hospitable—as a nurturing "Mother" to the planet's beings. Similar concepts, under various names, have been embraced by some notable scientists: T. H. Huxley's "physiography," Herbert Spencer's "progressive development," and Alfred Lotka's assertion in 1925 that the "entire system" of species and environment evolve inseparably.[21]

The weak hypothesis, in contrast, simply maintains that "the non-living and living represent a self-regulating system that keeps itself in a constant state or at least within a limited range of conditions"— Lovelock's more recent statement of his theory.[22] Some felt this is no more than an elaboration of the concept of homeostasis, hardly controversial. Some claimed the "purposive" theory was untestable, but others identified a way to test the Gaia hypothesis through a "feedback loop" linking microscopic phytoplankton, reflectivity of stratus clouds, and climate.[23] A further problem with the strong hypothesis and its willful Gaia, as some pointed out, is that what is optimal for one

20. John P. Wiley, Jr., "[Gaia] Phenomena, Comment and Notes," *Smithsonian* 19, no. 2 (May 1988): 30.

21. Ibid., quoting Ehrlich and summarizing the scientific history.

22. Lovelock, quoted in Richard A. Kerr, "No Longer Willful, Gaia Becomes Respectable," *Science*, 240, no. 4851 (April 22, 1985): 393.

23. This test was proposed by Robert Charlson of the University of Washington and his colleagues. See Kerr, "No Longer Willful," p. 395. Lovelock has suggested a "Daisyworld" model to test his theory. See Wiley, "[Gaia] Phenomena," p. 32.

species may be disastrous for another: "What is optimal at one and the same time for a pig, a penguin, and a porpoise?"[24] Lovelock, having considerably modified the "poetic" elements in his statement of the hypothesis, thus placating his hard-headed colleagues, seems to have abandoned the attempt at scientific heresy. He is not, if he ever was, sentimental about Gaia, saying recently that she is "merciless" to "species that screw up," eliminating them "with all the feeling of a microbrain in an ICBM."[25] In the present context, this statement could be construed as a warning to all humans, but it must be pointed out that our species has itself invented the "microbrain," thus considerably complicating the metaphor. Lovelock's adoption of a war metaphor is revealing (showing how easily we fall back on mechanical or "Enemy" images), but it also expresses a paradox, namely that the nurturing Mother Goddess has another face, a dark, terrible aspect, reflecting the "voracity" of life, its feeding upon death. Mother Nature, our life source, is also the source of our universal fear of death that spares no creature.[26]

Gaia and Space-age Myth

Moving into space was a quantum leap for the human imagination, an event that has been compared in its evolutionary significance to the emergence of sea creatures onto land. Myth, as Joseph Campbell notes, has not yet caught up with the heliocentric universe, and yet we are now in need of integrating into our consciousness the space-age perspective on Earth. Myth needs to make a quantum leap of the imagination, and Gaia as logo has a part to play in this process.

In contrast to the metaphors and motifs associated with the "nucleated" imagination—the Wasteland, Nuclear Winter, the Bombaholic, the Thanatos Syndrome—there stands Gaia in her Mother aspect, with the associated images—the Peaceable Kingdom, the vision of peace (the literal meaning of *Jerusalem*). Chrystos is not exaggerating when she says, "We have lost touch with the sacred. To survive we must begin to know sacredness." Referring to the likelihood of nuclear or environmental disaster, she asserts that *"nothing short of completely altering*

---

24. Wiley, "[Gaia] Phenomena," p. 32.
25. Lovelock, quoted in Wiley, "[Gaia] Phenomena," p. 31.
26. Ernest Becker's *The Denial of Death* (New York: Free Press, 1973) is a brilliant exploration of the idea that the denial of death is "the mainspring of human activity" (p. ix).

the whole culture will stop it.''[27] (The parallel with Einstein's assertion of the need for a radically new way of thinking is clear.) Myth can bring about the transformation. A functioning mythological symbol, Joseph Campbell observes, is ''an energy-evoking and -directing sign,'' which releases the ''culturally imprinted IRMs [innate releasing mechanisms] of the human nervous system.''[28] Our culture now has such a symbol, thanks to the Moon Walk of our astronauts.

Campbell maintains the moon landings have made us conscious of Earth as a Blessed Place, a sanctuary, an ''oasis in the desert of infinite space, . . . an extraordinary kind of sacred grove,'' which has been ''set apart for the ritual of life.'' Our ''splendid moon-men,'' as he calls them, can serve as heroes for our time, for they have helped us to see humanity as reflecting the universe and the universe as ''a reflection magnified of our own most inward nature: so that, we are indeed its ears, its eyes, its thinking, and its speech, or, in theological terms, God's ears, God's eyes, God's thinking, and God's Word.'' Seeing ourselves in this light, as participants in a continuous act of creation, is indeed a heroic picture of human destiny—to be ''the mind . . . of space.''[29]

Campbell soars to poetic heights in explaining the need for a ''now'' mythology:

> On our planet . . . all dividing horizons have been shattered. We can no longer hold our loves at home and project our aggressions elsewhere; for on this spaceship Earth there is no ''elsewhere'' any more. And no mythology that continues to speak or to teach of ''elsewheres'' and ''outsiders'' meets the requirement of this hour.[30]

The mythology of this moment calls for nothing less than a radical paradigm change. Campbell's idea of each individual being conscious of himself or herself as not simply a single ego competing for space on this planet but ''equally as centers of Mind at Large—each in his own way at one with all and with no horizons''—was expressed again more recently in his *The Inner Reaches of Outer Space.* There he says (without mentioning the term Gaia) that the sight of the Earth from the moon as seen by the astronauts, showing the planet free of ''sociopolitical division'' and recognizing its ''interdependencies,'' affirms its ''one life.'' This holistic vision is neither new nor unnatural, but simply rediscov-

27. Chrystos, ''No Rock Scorns Me as a Whore,'' in *Writing in a Nuclear Age,* ed. Jim Schley (Hanover, N.H.: University Press of New England, 1984), p. 172.

28. Joseph Campbell, *Myths to Live By* (New York: Bantam, 1973), p. 219.

29. Ibid., pp. 245, 257, 272.

30. Ibid., p. 275.

ered. It has been present in the visions of mystics of all eras of history and can be found in traditional Native American lore. Campbell chooses the specific example of Black Elk, who saw his mountaintop as "the central mountain of the world"—the Center which is Everywhere, whose circumference is nowhere.[31]

A related concept of transformation of human consciousness is found in Teilhard de Chardin's "Omega point," the point where "human beings become conscious of their own evolution and, hence, of themselves." De Chardin called for a vision of "unity and connectedness," with the intelligent life

> born on this planet and spread over its entire surface, coming gradually to form around its earthly matrix a single, major organic unity, enclosed upon itself; a single, hypercomplex, hyperconcentrated, hyperconscious arch-molecule, coextensive with the heavenly body on which it is born.[32]

The truth of the "fabric of living things," as Gregory Bateson said, cannot be ultimately expressed through the logical mode of scientific expression: "The cybernetic equivalent of logic is oscillation" (oscillation, that is, between "yes/no", "on/off"). Only metaphor and its extension, story, can hold "the whole fabric of mental interconnections . . . together. Metaphor," he remarked, "is right at the bottom of being alive." In this realization lies the strength of Gaia as image: And its use in the scientific context reflects the "central aspect of the emerging new paradigm . . . the shift [in science] from objects to relationships." Stories, he added, are "the royal road to the study of relationships."[33]

Gaia and the Needs of Literary Imagination in a Nuclear Age

The significance of Gaia as an image of the interrelatedness of all things (Gregory Bateson's "the pattern which connects") can be best

31. Campbell, *The Inner Reaches of Outer Space*, pp. 124ff. Campbell locates this transcendent vision in its eighteenth-century Deist version on something we carry with us every day—the U. S. dollar bill.

32. Teilhard de Chardin, *The Phenomenon of Man* (New York: Harper and Row, 1965), quoted in David P. Barash and Judith Eve Lipton, *The Caveman and the Bomb* (New York: Mc Graw-Hill), p. 261.

33. Gregory Bateson, quoted in Fritjof Capra, *Uncommon Wisdom: Conversations with Remarkable People* (New York: Bantam Books, 1988), pp. 76–78.

appreciated in contrast to the image of the loss of a connection with nature. A remarkable essay by Terrence Des Pres provides an illuminating discussion of the human consequences of the contemporary loss of a harmonious connection with the natural world. Des Pres writes in "Self/Landscape/Grid" about how the nuclear peril has changed our experience of nature, both our own human nature and the natural external landscape. Whereas once we experienced nature as a source of myths of permanence, the unchanging reality underlying life cycles of renewal and rebirth, it is no longer possible to feel secure in the thought that "generations come and go, but . . . *the earth abideth forever.*" Instead, "with the advent of the nuclear age there is no assurance that anything will remain for the phoenix to rise from."[34]

Moreover, our experience of ourselves as beings within nature has been irremediably changed, for as Des Pres points out, the terror of "nuclear wipeout"

> drastically alters how we receive and value our experience. Birth, for example, or one's own death; surely having children troubles us in ways not known before, and we need to feel that each of us shall have a death of his or her own, simply in order to feel fully possessed of our lives.[35]

Thus, the consciousness of nuclear arms has altered perceptions of both birth and death. Death is no longer personal and individual when it is mass death on a scale hitherto unprecedented and dealt by an anonymous enemy. Des Pres calls for more writing "informed by nuclear knowing," a kind of knowing he feels many contemporary writers demonstrably avoid. With few exceptions, writers today adhere to traditional literary models of a prenuclear era when nature presented a much different face than it does now. Nature for writers of the past was a source of "the myth of renewal and rebirth": Emerson, for instance, can say, "In the woods, we return to reason and faith. There I feel that nothing can befall me in life—no disgrace, no calamity (leaving me my eyes), which nature cannot repair." Des Pres rightly observes, "His notion of calamity isn't ours."

In contrast to the self of Emerson's time, the self today is "invaded by forces wholly alien to personal being" and its place in a "concrete landscape . . . is also a site on the nuclear grid." We live in the awareness, subliminal but real, that nuclear warheads are trained on us; we

34. Terrence Des Pres, "Self/Landscape/Grid," in *Writing in a Nuclear Age*, ed. Jim Schley (Hanover, N.H.: University Press of New England, 1984), p. 8.
35. Ibid.

are targets of faceless "enemies" who are similarly targeted by "our" warheads. "Self and world, nature and landscape, everything exists in itself *and* as acceptable loss on the nuclear grid."[36] We are counted as data in some computer's estimate of the "tolerable level of destruction."

Des Pres finds hope in the power of language, and particularly of poetry, to enable our imaginations to find some measure of wholeness. For poetry, as he says, can "wed" the opposites, keep them in a bearable tension. To keep the "grimness" and the "glory" in balance is "poetry's job. And now that the big salvations have failed us, the one clear thing is that we live by words."[37] And, I would add, by seeking for viable myth.

Holistic Gaia Vision and the Gylanic Partnership Ideal

A holistic Gaia perspective can also illuminate the difficulties caused by the cultural compartmentalizing of masculine and feminine, the kind of divisive thinking that stands in the way of realizing what Riane Eisler calls the "gylanic," or partnership, model of society. Science fiction's long tradition of compartmentalizing feminine and masculine has been noted by many scholars, among them Albert I. Berger in his "Love, Death, and the Atomic Bomb: Sexuality and Community in Science Fiction, 1935–55." Berger explores the reason why early science fiction stereotyped women in such rigidly compartmentalized roles. Associations between women, sex, stagnation, and death became standard assumptions. One reason for this pervasive sexism of early science fiction was the largely adolescent male readership of early science fiction magazines, who wanted their intellects, not their gonads, stimulated. There was furthermore the larger tradition of mythology within which the adolescent male was required to be celibate (cf. Parsifal) in order to succeed in his quest for the Grail, the "sacred talisman" that could cure the ills of the wasteland. Only the knight pure in heart and body could bring healing to the wasteland alienated from nature, from the divine, and from its true spiritual roots. American literature draws upon this tradition of the heroic loner but eliminates the link between celibacy and spiritual, social or moral values. Henry Nash Smith characterized the outcome of this heroic myth of the American West in these terms: "By the end of the

36. Ibid., pp. 9–10.
37. Ibid., p. 12.

[nineteenth] century, the hero had become a morally ambivalent figure whose only constant characteristic is violence."[38] Thus viewed, the quest of the Western hero becomes a kind of Lone Ranger flight of the alone to the Alone, requiring that middle-class "respectability" be shunned. Integration into the community, which would include an alliance with the feminine, becomes a form of oppression the Western hero must avoid at all costs. In this aborted form of myth, the traditional mythic hero's return to the community and contribution to its good have been lost. And, some might say, an ethos of masculine maturity is discarded as well.

In this climate of distrust for the feminine, science fiction by the 1950s had evolved, with the dawn of tranquilizers and the lobotomy, into a genre in which the "perfect woman" was sometimes depicted as a machine, like the robot in Lester del Rey's "Helen O'Loy." The greatest fulfillment for this robot woman was housewifery. During the fifties and earlier, science fiction neglected the complexities of interpersonal relationships, to the detriment of women characters. Ursula LeGuin, herself a science fiction and fantasy writer par excellence, asserted that "once science fiction began to talk about real people, as opposed to stereotypes, it would of necessity begin to talk about women."[39] Science fiction and its cousin, nuclear fiction, have far to go, however, to free themselves from what Eve Ottenberg calls "the cult of quantitative intelligence."[40] Attention to the quality of relationships among fictional human beings has increased with the entry of more women writers into the ranks of the creators of this genre.

When speculative fiction attempted to portray nuclear catastrophe after World War II, it had not only to include women but to heed (if the writer was sensitive) the experiences of actual people who lived through the A-bomb devastation of Hiroshima and Nagasaki. It is noteworthy that actual survivors' stories bear no resemblance to the adventurous "loner" myth, but instead (whether by men or women) center upon concerns conventionally assigned to women: caring for others and trying to revive compassion, hope, and a reconnection to nature. The "new manner of thinking" Einstein believed necessary for human survival may be imaged in the compassionate action of these *hibakusha* and also seen, to a degree, in the "feminine" mode in nuclear fiction. There is, however, no neat division along gender lines, for both male and female authors have created exceptional characters of

38. Alfred I. Berger, "Love, Death and the Atomic Bomb: Sexuality and Community in Science Fiction, 1935–1955," *Science Fiction Studies* 8 (1981): 283.

39. Ibid., quoting LeGuin from *Vertex* 2 (December 1974).

40. Eve Ottenberg, "Big Brain, No Nerve," *The Village Voice* 25, no. 9 (March 3, 1980): 34.

both genders who exhibit a Whole Earth, holistic way of perceiving reality. This is the view I term the Gaia perspective.

As we approach the end of a century and the end of a millenium imperiled by threats of both nuclear disaster and ecological collapse, stories that can offer a "pattern which connects" and a concept of peaceable human relationships, mythic ways to shape a global future, are at a premium. The global perspective that radiates from the Gaia image has a key role to play in re-storying the world with a mythology of peace. We may hope that the increasing recognition of holistic perspectives will draw us away from nuclearism, which is based on a "dominator" model of human relationships, and toward a gylanic, partnership model of society.[41] Cosmic myth, awakened by space voyaging, has the power to evoke compassion for all life. Colin Berg in his essay on "The Art of Return" asks why the photographs of earth from space move human beings so profoundly. His answer is that they give us a glimpse "of the perspective of the mystic and bring us an overwhelming and tangible sense of being part of a whole more vast than concepts can define." The experience of perceiving wholeness and connectedness is inseparable from the experience of compassion: "To walk as round beings on a round planet, cognizant of being interwoven in a circular web of connection with all beings, is to understand forgiveness."[42]

A Global View of Children's Literature

Richard Bamberger, writing from his international perspective on youth literature, has expressed a number of insights helpful in seeking a global approach to Whole Earth themes in children's books. In his lecture "Trends in Modern Literature for Children and Young People," he notes five contemporary phenomena:

1. The trend toward a world literature
2. The trend toward world orientation and international understanding
3. The fantastic story or the breakthrough of the irrational
4. The attempt to overcome the "cultural lag" in form and content

41. See Eisler, *The Chalice and the Blade*, pp. 105–6, for an explanation of her distinction between the partnership and dominator models of organization, as well as the terms *androcratic* and *gylanic*.

42. Colin Berg, "The Art of Return," *Parabola*, 12, no. 3 (August 1987): 67.

5. The movement away from formulas and toward freedom of form and content.[43]

The trends toward world literature, world orientation, and international understanding, and the "breakthrough of the irrational" are pertinent here. In respect to a world literature for children, Bamberger notes how after World War II the idea that disastrous wars stem from "narrow-minded national attitudes" spurred a "one world" theme. Some writers of youth literature made a conscious attempt to advance ideals of "cooperation between the peoples, peaceful coexistence, and also at last an unequivocal *renunciation of all war.*"[44] He cites as an example of the theme of the renunciation of war Erich Kastner's *Die Konferenz der Tiere* (The Animals Conference), based on an idea of Jella Lepman, and notes the influence of Lepman's *Die Kinderbuchbrucke* (The Bridge of Children's Books) toward the founding of the International Youth Library in Munich and the International Board on Books for Young People.[45] Not surprisingly, picture books, as universally understood graphic expressions, are the most globally successful format, as the Biennale exhibition in Bratislava attests.[46] World orientation can be seen in the "multitude of translations"; translation from one language into another implies a certain respect for the other's cultural achievement. Bamberger admits the existence in the past of a "shameful" tendency to promote "national egotism and disparagement of other nations" and cultures, and points to such posturing as the beginning of "political catastrophe." Today, as always, nationalistic-chauvinistic elements are hallmarks of inferior publications.[47]

Bamberger's remarks raise a classical critical challenge: Can the artistic quality of a book (for children or adults) be separated from its *ideological* content? The argument between the purely aesthetic, apolitical view of literature and the view that literature has an obligation to be *morally* and politically responsible is an ancient and on-going one. Children's literature, some would argue, is by its very nature didactic, seeking whether

43. Richard Bamberger, "Trends in Modern Literature for Children and Young People" C. C. Williamson Memorial Lecture No. 7 (Nashville, Tenn.: George Peabody College for Teachers, School of Library Science, 1973, c1974), p. 1.

44. Ibid., p. 3.

45. Bamberger lists some titles related to nuclear fiction: Karl Bruckner's *Sadako will leben* (The Day of the Bomb) from Austria; M. Druon's *Tistou les pouces verts* (Tistou with the Green Thumbs) from France; and, on the theme of the atom bomb, Gianni Rodari's fantasy, *La torta in cielo* (The Cake in the Sky), from Italy.

46. Bamberger, "Trends in Modern Literature for Children and Young People," p. 6.

47. Ibid., p. 7.

overtly or covertly to inculcate certain cultural values in the young, and unfortunately this zeal too often results in heavy didacticism.

In his discussion of the breakthrough of the irrational, Bamberger does not deal specifically with the effects of the space age on youth literature worldwide. The breakthrough of the irrational could well be expanded to include the peril of "irrational" weapons and a war beyond human control, alien invasion, and so on, but these themes are not mentioned. In fairness, such themes have been popularized around the globe primarily in film: Movies such as *Star Wars* and *2001: A Space Odyssey* have added immeasurably to the consciousness of Earth as one organic being. The examples of an explicit Gaia awareness in children's literature remain rare, and it is hoped that an increasing number of writers will treat the theme.

The question of adult motives in presenting didactic literature to youth brings to mind a passage in Russell Hoban's *Turtle Diary*, in which the protagonist, an author of children's stories, asks herself in an odd moment what her calling is all about, and concludes that those who write books "for children" as well as those who write about the books written for children

> are really worrying about themselves, about keeping their world together and getting children to help them do it, getting the children to agree that it is indeed a world. Each new generation of children has to be told: "This is a world, this is what one does, one lives like this."

In existential terms, this is a somewhat sardonic rationale for the pedagogical function of myth and story, used by adults to counter their own fear that "a generation of children will come along and say: 'This is not a world, this is nothing, there's no way to live at all'."[48] In imagining these incorrigible youngsters, Hoban might almost be describing what Ernest Becker has called the contemporary "crisis of heroism" among youth, which is also the crisis of our culture. Becker observes

> that youth no longer feel heroic in the plan for action their culture has set up. . . . youth have sensed—for better or for worse—a great social-historical truth: that just as there are useless self-sacrifices in unjust wars, so too is there an ignoble heroics of whole societies.[49]

Admittedly, the ignoble heroic mythology of entire cultures cannot be set aside by space-age images and holistic consciousness alone. Nor

48. Russell Hoban, *Turtle Diary* (New York: Random House, 1975), p. 113.
49. Becker, *The Denial of Death,* pp. 6–7.

can a new heroic mythology be invented simply by taking thought. The best we might hope for is that the current crisis of heroism (or the lack of any viable heroic model) might be partially met by an emergent humility and respect for the fragility and sacredness of the cosmic order. The Gaia image can help bring an expanded, more compassionate consciousness to all peoples on our shared "Spaceship Earth."

Related Images of Wholeness in Myth and Contemporary Religious Thought

Just as the myth of Psyche as interpreted by DuPlessis provides a model of wholeness for the individual, and the ancient image of King Arthur's Roundtable provides what Andrew Bard Schmookler calls a vision of "a cosmic order in which all are accepted" (all knights, he might have said, to be more exact), I propose the image of Gaia as a contemporary symbol for the "bio-civisphere," defined by Schmookler as "a biosphere governed by consciousness." Schmookler, like Joseph Campbell, sees "group narcissism" (e.g., an exclusive myth such as the idea of a Chosen People) as corrosive to human relationships: "The world cloven into the chosen and the rejected is a violent one, as each defends an image of self that he inwardly senses is a lie."[50] What the myth of Psyche expresses on the level of the individual's search for wholeness, Gaia images on a cosmic level. However, a literary expression of the Gaia myth for contemporary times that can speak to masses of people has yet to appear. Brian Aldiss's Helliconia trilogy (see the section "Gaia Images in Literature" in this chapter) is a move in the right direction, but its appeal may be primarily to science fiction aficionados. A Gaia parable accessible to ordinary readers worldwide, penned by a writer of quality, would fill an urgent need.

Ancient Mythic Visions of Human Destiny

Annie Gottlieb, in her upbeat book *Do You Believe in Magic? The Second Coming of the Sixties Generation*, discusses the genre of "apocalyptic

---

50. Andrew Bard Schmookler, *Out of Weakness: Healing the Wounds That Drive Us to War* (New York: Bantam, 1988), pp. 19l and 111.

fantasy,'' including several books of nuclear fiction (*Warday, or the Journey Onward, Wolf of Shadows,* and *The Nuclear Age*) plus such assorted titles as *The Stand* by Stephen King and the movie *Ghostbusters,* a comic treatment of ''save-the-world'' fantasies. Two contemporary social groups allied only by their obsession with apocalypse are identified: first, the right-wing fundamentalists (with their belief in the Rapture) and second, survivors of the sixties generation. She believes the first group would rather see the world end than change, whereas the sixties survivors believe the old world has *already* ended and the transformation to New Age thinking has already occurred. Only a few people, however, have acknowledged the transformation.

Gottlieb contrasts two kinds of apocalypse, the dominant ''Western'' one of the Second Coming as described in the biblical book of Revelation, and the lesser-known end-time vision of the Hopi Indians. Greater hope for the Earth lies in the Hopi perspective, for their myth describes alternate endings for the world, with the outcome depending on human choice. They visualize the path of human destiny as having two branches, one going up and onward, the other breaking apart and fading. The Hopi end-time myth stresses the human capacity to select the desired ''end.'' ''The [end] you believe in is the one you go with.''[51] Belief creates its own reality. The excellence of the Hopi myth lies in its awareness that human beings bear a responsibility of choice in shaping the future for all beings on the planet.

Ira Chernus, in *Dr. Strangegod: On the Symbolic Meaning of Nuclear Weapons,* similarly points to alternate visions of the end. Biblical myth has given us both the Peaceable Kingdom and Armageddon. We can choose the bloodbath of Armageddon or the new Kingdom of Peace. Chernus proposes that humanity embrace the image of a ''bombless,'' nuclear-free world as a new metaphor for heaven. With the human gift of mythmaking, the vision of boundless peace in a nuclear-free world can counter the pseudomyth of the children of today as ''the last generation.'' The essential heroic myth of today must express wholeness on a global as well as an individual level. As Chernus observes, ''only a synthesis of dark and light, unconscious and conscious, symbolic and literal, mythic and political, can offer the power of true wholeness.'' Both visions are necessary—that of a Bomb*ed* and that of a Bomb*less* world—if we are to ''imagine the real,'' in theologian Paul Tillich's phrase.[52] Despite this need for a balance between light and dark vi-

51. Annie Gottlieb, *Do You Believe in Magic? The Second Coming of the Sixties Generation* (New York: Time Books, 1987), pp. 386ff.

52. Ira Chernus, *Dr. Strangegod: On the Symbolic Meaning of Nuclear Weapons* (Columbia: Univ. of South Carolina Pr., 1986), pp. 167–68.

sions, it is obvious by now that literary representations of the bombed world far outnumber those of a bombless paradise.

The latter, of course, is much harder to create in a credible fiction. Speculative fiction lags behind speculative religious thought in proposing a vivid mythology of peace. The controversial fusion of creation theology (not to be confused with the "creationist" point of view, which is quite different) and theoretical physics expressed in *Manifesto for a Global Civilization* by Matthew Fox and Brian Swimme (theologian and physicist, respectively) serves as a case in point. Fox and Swimme propose the metaphor of a musical symphony to represent the universe, hardly a new idea (cf. the ancient concept of the "music of the spheres") but one that can now claim the validation of theoretical physics. The mechanistic view of the universe, with its "billiard ball" metaphor for the interaction of energies, no longer corresponds to the world understood as an organic, living whole.[53] Physicists like Swimme find themselves aligned with views traditionally assigned to visionaries and religious mystics.

Throughout the *Manifesto* the two authors use the graphic of the ringed atom as a logo. The implication seems to be that atomic energies underlie the organicism of the universe. Paradoxically, the atom is both the energy that drives all existence and the source that can spell its doom. In another work, Fox adopts metaphors drawn from dance to express his insights into the nature of human relationships. A dance figure he calls "Dancing Sarah's Circle" is posed against another termed "Climbing Jacob's Ladder" to visualize two divergent approaches to relationships. Sarah's Circle, being spiral-like and communal, contrasts to Jacob's Ladder, hierarchical and competitive in structure. Each image epitomizes its own sort of spirituality. Fox believes the Jacob's Ladder model of reality— restrictive, elitist, based on survival of the fittest—no longer serves the needs of a "global village." Sarah's Circle, nonelitist and oriented to the survival of all, answers much better to humanity's needs at this point in our development.[54] Seeing our connections to the Circle (the pattern that connects once again) can help us make the psychological and spiritual links that make creativity and compassion possible, for both depend on *seeing* and making connections among diverse components.

In another work Fox deals with the essential difference between the

53. Matthew Fox and Brian Swimme, *Manifesto for a Global Civilization* (Santa Fe, N.Mex.: Bear Books, 1982), pp. 11–12.

54. Matthew Fox, *A Spirituality Named Compassion and the Healing of the Global Village, Humpty Dumpty and Us* (San Francisco: Harper and Row, 1979), pp. 44ff.

human dilemma of today and of earlier times: the "new" element in our contemporary situation is

> the global demand on our consciousness. The global pain, the global interconnections of beauty and pain. The invitation to create a global civilization of love/justice and ecological harmony is a new invitation. And so too are the global means to carry out this New Creation.[55]

As Chernus, Fox, Swimme, and many other thoughtful people realize, the nuclear crisis needs a spiritual answer. Fox finds the answer in the choice to let go of war, just as societies have elected to let go of slavery.[56] His insight is identical to one expressed by Michael in Julian Thompson's *Band of Angels* (see chapter 4).

Gaia Images in Literature: "Canticle," "Helliconia Winter," and "Pennterra"

Many current developments in the world, such as the upsurge in terrorism and religious fanaticism, the depletion of the ozone layer, and the burgeoning problems of pollution, considered in themselves, signal impending planetary doom. It may seem that the idea of a Peaceable Peopledom on Spaceship Earth has little hope of prevailing, that the hopeful, unifying movements such as ecumenism in religion and *glasnost* in politics are frail in comparison with the threats. On the level of symbol, however, there is considerable evidence that the Gaia image has permeated consciousness and is working in subliminal ways to exert its effect. A local public television broadcasting station uses the turning globe as its logo, as do many news programs, but its positive effects on consciousness have been questioned by no less a writer than Doris Lessing. Lessing has commented on the onmipresence of the Gaia symbol, which she views as having an ambiguous impact on a child's consciousness:

> For a while in England practically every [television] program was introduced with a world turning. Contrast the child brought up on that . . . with my grandfather. He didn't have a concept of the world as a small turning thing. He was thinking of his village. He never thought about

55. Matthew Fox, *Original Blessing: A Primer in Creation Spirituality* (Santa Fe, N.Mex.: Bear and Co., 1983), pp. 255–56.

56. Ibid., p. 13.

planets and Mars and space probes and the influence of the cosmos on people—he was concerned with whether the church organ was in tune.[57]

The sense of the Earth as a small turning thing feeds a conviction of the precariousness of life, of "how easily things can vanish"—what novelist Henry James called the imagination of disaster. In this context the influence of the televised Gaia image seems baleful, dwarfing the child in the overwhelming hugeness of a cosmic perspective. Lessing's grandfather's world of the church organ is more human in scale. On the other hand, it must be pointed out that the world of two generations ago, with its more limited and localized perspective, was also prone to militaristic chauvinism. Think for instance of Rudyard Kipling's 1899 poem, "The White Man's Burden," written in response to the American assumption of control over the Philippines at the close of the Spanish-American War. Kipling urged a paternalistic stance toward the Filipinos, whom he called "new-caught, sullen peoples."[58]

Lessing is making a point in favor of small-scale as opposed to global-scale thinking. Her views harmonize with those of farmer and ecologist Wendell Berry, who notes that the use of the adjective *planetary* by environmentalists who wish to urge us to "heal" the planet actually "describes a problem in such a way that it cannot be solved." Against the "heroes of abstraction" he sets his modest view that "our understandable wish to preserve the planet must somehow be reduced to the scale of our competence." That is, we must begin to love and preserve our "humble houses and neighborhoods." "Love," he points out, "is not, by its own desire, heroic. It is heroic only when compelled to be. It exists by its willingness to be anonymous, humble, and unrewarded."[59] Aspects of Berry's thinking are reminiscent of the anonymous saying, "It isn't the mountains ahead that wear you out; it's the grain of sand in your shoe." Attention to the grain of sand may equip us to scale the mountain later.

Lessing's comment does not explore the possible good—especially in ecological awareness—stemming from the sight of Earth as small, fragile, and in need of human care. The fragility and interconnectedness of life are overriding facts of the contemporary world, and all, including children, need to assimilate this truth.

57. Quoted in Mervin Rothstein, "The Painful Nurturing of Doris Lessing's Fifth Child," *New York Times,* June 14, 1988, p. C21.

58. Kipling's poem is quoted with commentary under the title entry in *Benet's Reader's Encyclopedia,* 3d ed. (New York: Harper and Row, 1987), p. 1061.

59. Wendell Berry, "The Futility of Global Thinking," *Harper's Magazine,* September 1989, pp. 16, 18.

A full study of the Gaia image in literature is beyond the scope of this discussion. Just a few striking examples will be highlighted here, to illustrate how Gaia functions symbolically in close linkage with themes of survival and ecology.

An ironic use of the Gaia image as a basis for religious-philosophical speculation on human destiny has been pointed out previously in discussing Walter J. Miller, Jr.'s *A Canticle for Leibowitz* (see chapter 7) in which Dom Zerchi seeks insight into the meaning of the seemingly endless cycles of creation and destruction in human history. He wishes he might spin time backward to Eden, so humans, having botched the fate of Earth so badly, could have another chance. A much more extensive elaboration of Gaia as the tutelary spirit of planet Earth can be found in Brian Aldiss's *Helliconia* books, especially in *Helliconia Winter.* The preceding volumes, *Helliconia Spring* and *Helliconia Summer,* introduce and develop the theme of nuclear winter. As Paul Brians points out, Helliconia's winter is natural, not brought about by nuclear war, but Aldiss makes an effective parallel with the hazards of nuclear winter on Earth and also manages to satirize the arms race "by depicting the political leaders who insist on ruthless extermination of the enemy as fools who fail to realize the essential interdependence of all Helliconian life."[60]

Though the off-world settings of the Helliconia books would, strictly speaking, exclude them from this study, *Helliconia Winter*'s incorporation of the Gaia concept is so exceptional and vivid that it requires comment here. No attempt will be made to summarize the complex plot, describe the extensive cast of characters, or do justice to the overriding theme; the purpose is simply to note Aldiss's interpretation of Gaia. Gaia is seen as the tutelary spirit of Earth, who keeps the planet in a "balance of vitality" through "cybernetic controls." Gaia is a "sister" to the Original Beholder. The Original Beholder is the spirit that holds all living forces in balance, and its nature is "azoiaxic," meaning "something beyond life round which all life revolves, which was itself unloving and the Life." Akin to Gaia, the Original Beholder is a "vast cooperative entity" that creates "well-being."[61] After a nuclear war devastates Gaia, she regenerates herself, perhaps helped by communication with the Original Beholder. Those humans who somehow survive are of a slightly different genetic stock from their predecessors; they are

60. Paul Brians, *Nuclear Holocausts: Atomic War in Fiction 1895–1984* (Kent, Ohio: Kent State Univ. Pr., 1987), p. 87.

61. Brian Aldiss, *Helliconia Winter* (New York: Atheneum, 1985), pp. 182, 218, 220.

strong on empathy . . . that gift of entering into the personality of another, of experiencing sympathetically his or her state of mind, [a gift
which] had never been rare. But the elite had despised it—or exploited it.
. . . Now empathy was widely dispersed among the race. It became a
dominant feature, with survival characteristics.[62]

This empathy, or "thinkfeel," a union of head and heart, is a
"quantum leap in consciousness" that endows people with a survival
advantage. It alters the relations between humans, rendering them
peaceful, and humanity's relationship to the land is transformed as
well. People no longer asked "What can we get out of this land?" but
"What best experience can we have on this land?" The "new sport" is
"rethinking" assumptions about everything.[63]

Aldiss's trilogy contains much that cannot be briefly conveyed; it
can be appreciated fully only by mature readers who are motivated to
read it in its entirety. It incorporates a unique treatment of the intimate
connection between the good of the biosphere and the good of the human race, for human beings, as the most complex form of life on Earth,
are the most vulnerable to changes in biospheric conditions. "However they might rebel against the idea, their corporate lives were never
more than part of the equipoise of the planet to which they belonged."[64] Sadly, only those who came later and shared in Gaia's re-
birth were able to recognize the connection. It would be equally true to
say that only those who recognized the connection could partake in the
rebirth. The fate of the Earth dwellers is peripheral to that of the Helli-
conians, but the parallels are worth scrutiny.

Another adult novel with an off-world setting is Judith Moffet's
Pennterra. Pennterra is also a planet with a tutelary spirit, Tanka Wakan
(whose name is an inversion of the Dakota Indians' name for their collective gods, Wakan Tanka[65]). One of the characters remarks that
Earth, which has been rendered uninhabitable by a global catastrophe,
might have enjoyed a different destiny "if Earth had had the power
and wisdom to say to your parents' parents: *You may not do this. If you
do this, you will die.*"[66]

It must be observed that since Gaia lacks a voice, our writers must
speak for her. The idea of storytellers as the "voice" of Gaia is explic-

62. Ibid., p. 138.
63. Ibid., p. 177.
64. Ibid., p. 125.
65. Manfred Lurker, *Dictionary of Gods and Goddesses, Devils and Demons* (New York:
Routledge and Kegan Paul, 1984), p. 377.
66. Judith Moffet, *Pennterra* (New York: Congdon and Weed, 1987), p.382.

itly stated in Aldiss's *Helliconia Winter* at the point when words are said to "give tongue to the planet," and the following equation is set forth:

> Story was to words as Gaia was to Earth and the Original Beholder to Helliconia. Neither planet had a story until mankind came chattering onto the scene and invented it—to fit what each generation saw as the facts.[67]

Just as story expresses relationship (as Bateson said, is the "royal road to relationships"), it can express the relatedness of human and planetary destiny.

Gaia Images in Children's Literature

Instances of an explicit Gaia image in children's literature (excluding books with off-world settings) are rare. Compared to novels with settings on *terra firma*, those with an off-world vantage point, such as Jill Paton Walsh's *The Green Book* (see chapter 7), can more easily create the dramatic illusion of "seeing Gaia whole." An exhaustive search would be required—beyond the limits of this study—to find many instances of the Gaia symbol within narratives with realistic Earth settings. Only a few instances can be cited here. Stephanie Tolan uses a negative version of the Gaia image in *The Pride of the Peacock*, describing Whitney's imagination of a ruined Earth after nuclear catastrophe, a skeletal wreck, "a little blue ball floating through the silent, cold darkness of space, with no eyes to see it happening, no mind to feel sorry, no heart to mourn all the birds and animals and plants and stupid humans."[68] This is the image of the "bombed" world, a picture of the type Ira Chernus has called essential to evoking our energies to make the "bombless" planet a reality.

The interconnectedness and relatedness of Earth's beings may be expressed through other images, sometimes through the metaphor of the web, as in Pamela Service's post-nuclear-holocaust novel for young adults, *Winter of Magic's Return*. It appears in the guise of Master Foxworthy's teaching that "the fate of all the earth was interconnected" and in Earl's vision of renewal:

> The pulse of warmth rose to the crumbling surface, to the rich soil. Roots sank into it and drained out warmth and life. Plants raised their

67. Aldiss, *Helliconia Winter*, p. 220.
68. Stephanie S. Tolan, *The Pride of the Peacock* (New York: Charles Scribner's Sons, 1986), p. 45.

heads to the sky, giving nourishment and shelter to life that huddled among them or bounded over them.

The web closed, the patterns settled into place.

All nature, says Earl, who is Merlin resurrected, is "tied in glowing traceries, in interlocking spheres. The web of force and power and rightness was part of all creation and part of him. Part of his cells and consciousness and joy."[69]

A Filmic Model of Cosmic Interconnectedness: "E. T."

Film can also provide a mythic model of interconnectedness, in this instance extending beyond Earth to space. *E. T.: The Extra-Terrestrial in His Adventure on Earth* might be considered a cosmic myth for children of the space age.[70] In elementary form, *E. T.* presents certain timeless mythic patterns, giving youngsters an introduction to a view of humanity's place in the cosmos. Stephen Spielberg, the film's creator, has called *E. T.* "the humanistic answer to the technical revolution," though he insists he does not intend to disparage technology. In fact, as he emphasizes, the lovable personality of E. T. helps make outer space more accessible to the imagination.[71]

The Extra-Terrestrial's heart-light and healing finger seem to signify a nurturing universe, a kind of cosmic father/mother, seemingly ancient yet paradoxically childlike. This ambiguity implies a resolution of the conflict between the "adult" world (seen as vaguely corrupt and destructive, yet in control of technology) and the "child" world, imaginative, open to experience, receptive, and loving.

With his serpentine eyes and fetuslike appearance, E. T. represents a new birth, symbolic of the new life of extraterrestrial space. The telepathic sympathy that develops between him and Elliott (the major child character) suggests a "new consciousness" taking shape, *beginning with children*. It is as though the *anima mundi* (or perhaps one might say "Gaia") is in the process of becoming self-aware, awakening to the Earth spirit's power to love and be loved. The relationship of *E. T.* to nuclear fiction is tenuous, but by the very fact of its space-age setting it

69. Pamela Service, *Winter of Magic's Return* (New York: Atheneum, 1985), pp. 7, 151.

70. See my "*E. T.*: A Cosmic Myth for Space-Age Children," *Children's Literature Quarterly*, 8, no. 2 (Summer 1983): 3–5.

71. Quoted in Ed Naha, "Inside *E. T.*," *Starlog*, 63 (October 1982): 65.

presents a picture of resurrection and ascent from death against an implicit background of the fear of the unknown. It opens up to a youthful audience the concept of a friendly universe, a place where it is always possible to "phone home." Thus, in skeletal form, *E. T.* provides a mythos for interplanetary vision and points toward a new cosmic consciousness.

Conclusion

Based on this survey of experiences of the astronauts, the theories of some notable philosophers, and selected examples of literary and film images, I believe the cosmic image of Gaia, in the process of being assimilated into the consciousness of people worldwide, can bring us into touch with the timeless realm of the Great Story, with what T. S. Eliot called "the still point of the turning world."[72] In the literary realm, the potential of the Gaia image as a mandala and as an inspiration for stories that express a Whole-Earth mythology is only beginning to be realized. It is my conviction that Gaia visualized has the power to make us newly aware of the preciousness of all creation, to reinvoke a sense of the sacredness of being. The "heroic" role in this context becomes that of generating a global vision, opening the eyes of all to see the unity of life, to experience its beauty and value, and to embrace a life-affirming ethic of survival. The hero/hera with this kind of perspective leads us into the realm of the mythic "larger self," helping us to transcend the limits of our individual space and time. Empathy with this larger self can help us find the key to a living mythology of peace.

72. T. S. Eliot, "Burnt Norton," II, l.16, in *The Complete Poems and Plays, 1909–1950* (New York: Harcourt, Brace, 1952), p. 119.

CHAPTER 9

A Life-affirming Ethic

"It is impossible to remake the country." Quite so, but it is not impossible to remake the country in the *imagination*. . . . I want to place a value on everything I touch.

—William Carlos Williams[1]

Mythology-Deprivation = Life Without Adventure

Of the Titans, the Elder Gods of the ancient Greeks, Chronos was the chief. He ruled with his sister-queen, Rhea. Fearful that one of his children was destined to dethrone him, Chronos swallowed them as soon as they were born. Zeus, the sixth child, escaped being consumed when Rhea had him secreted away in Crete, giving her husband a great stone wrapped in swaddling clothes to devour in the child's place. Eventually the grown Zeus challenged Chronos, forced him to regurgitate the stone and the engorged children (who marvelously were restored to life), and, after a fierce and bloody ten-year battle, established himself as undisputed ruler among the gods.

It has been maintained that Chronos, as "ultimate consumer and ultimate waster" ("to waste" in the sense of "to kill," the sense the verb acquired during the Vietnam War) is the unacknowledged god of contemporary Western civilization. His cannibalism of his own children is an apt metaphor of our society's endemic "adultism," as theologian Matthew Fox has observed. Fox is only one of many who have

1. William Carlos Williams, quoted in *Writing in a Nuclear Age*, ed. Jim Schley (Hanover, N.H.: University Press of New England, 1984), p. 145.

marshaled an array of shocking statistics to document the fact that young people worldwide are being consumed and devoured by burgeoning violence, drug abuse, stress, physical and sexual abuse, ineffective education, unemployment, starvation, crime, poverty, and, as if that were not enough, the inherited burden of a staggering national debt that means each child born in the U.S. already owes $65,000.[2]

"Adultism" is defined as the opposite of respect for youth, a loss of reverence for their well-being, resulting from intense self-interest. Senator Daniel Patrick Moynihan expressed his belief that "the United States in the 1980s may be the first society in which children are distinctly worse off than adults."[3] The worst deprivation of all is of a kind difficult to represent statistically, and that is the lack of "a vision or an adventure" whereby talents and energies can be creatively channeled, which only a "living cosmology" can provide. It is probable that most youngsters today associate "adventure" with video or computer games or possibly with the "Choose Your Own Adventure" series of books, not with their own lives.[4] This prospect of "life without adventure" is the newest form of abuse.[5] It means youth live with a void that needs to be filled with a live, functioning mythology.

Without a living cosmology, a mythology that lends meaning, life's *humanness* is sacrificed. Socrates spoke of the unexamined life as not worth living, and the same can be said for a life totally centered on survival concerns. Humanistic psychologist Jean Houston, codirector of the Foundation for Mind Research of New York, has much to say on the loss of humanness experienced in our culture and the urgent need of people in our highly technological, materialistic society to acquire inner powers equal to our outer powers, an idea with which Riddley Walker would be sympathetic. We are, Houston says, the "people of the parentheses," the era in between the old, limited consciousness and the not-yet-quite born era of Second Genesis. In *The Possible Human: A Course in Extending Your Physical, Mental, and Creative Abilities*, she notes how Western consciousness has been dominated since the eighteenth century by the mechanistic world view, what Blake called "single vision and Newton's sleep," a view that exalts materialistic values, the industrial standardization of society, and the single-

2. Matthew Fox, *The Coming of the Cosmic Christ: The Healing of Mother Earth and the Birth of a Global Renaissance* (San Francisco: Harper and Row, 1988), pp. 181ff.

3. Ibid., p. 184. Fox credits the Moynihan quotation to Fred M. Hechinger, "America Lacks Agenda on Needs of Its Children," *Oakland Tribune*, May 11, 1986, sec. C-7.

4. The "Choose Your Own Adventure" series is published by Bantam. A sample title is *Pinocchio's Adventures*, by James Razzi (Toronto: Bantam, 1985).

5. Fox, *Coming of the Cosmic Christ*, p. 183. ·

minded devotion to cause-and-effect relationships to explain events. The results have been disastrous to the human spirit: "In the interests of an extraordinarily narrow notion of 'progress,' culture is disintegrating, computers are replacing consciousness, and the erosion of human reality is being enacted and mirrored on the stage of nature in the erosion of the planetary ecosystem."[6] We all benefit from technological marvels resulting from the applications of Newtonian science, but the *effects* of such changes are also with us, and some of them are deadly (pollution from toxic industrial or nuclear waste being an obvious example). For every new technology there will be effects the discoverers did not foresee, and some of them are certain to be ill effects (an idea skillfully elaborated in Robert C. O'Brien's *Mrs. Frisby and the Rats of NIMH*). It is significant in this connection that the expression "side effects" has a universally bad connotation. No one speaks of *salutary* side effects. The notion of "progress" through technology is at best a questionable one.

In our "parentheses," in-between world, where a living mythology/cosmology is still in the making, the human predicament remains, as Ernest Becker has said, to meet and vanquish the problem of "meaninglessness," in short, "the overcoming of that which would negate life."[7] On this score, it is obvious that our culture is not doing well by its youth. If we cannot remake the world, as William Carlos Williams tells us, we can perhaps remake our imaginations, which in turn will shape our future.

Shaping the Direction of Change: The Quandary of Technology

Recently Isaac Asimov, the closest humanity can come to a contemporary Renaissance man, was asked his perception of the alternatives open to our society today in respect to technological change. He outlined three choices:

1. We can retreat, abandoning the technological changes. This, he noted, is almost never done, and is extremely unlikely.
2. We can find other technologies to counter or compensate for the dangers of the technology that is creating the problem.

6. Jean Houston, *The Possible Human: A Course in Extending Your Physical, Mental, and Creative Abilities* (Los Angeles: J. P. Tarcher, 1982), pp. xiv, 213.
7. Ernest Becker, *The Denial of Death* (New York: Free Press, 1975), p. 279.

3.   We can evade the problems (the most commonly chosen action), establishing endless committees that file reports but never apply their findings.[8]

Placing Asimov's remarks into the context of the problems created by nuclear peril, alternative one would require the complete elimination of nuclear arms—an ideal solution, but, like all utopian solutions, one not likely to materialize. Alternative two underlies the attempt to implement the Strategic Defense Initiative (SDI, or "Star Wars"), increasingly admitted to be a probably unworkable proposal. And alternative three is, obviously, nothing short of suicidal. What then remains? There was one other dimension to Asimov's remarks, which emerged in answer to the question, "What is the greatest risk to human life on Earth in the next fifty years?" His answer implies a fourth alternative, reminiscent of Einstein's call for a new way of thinking. Significantly, Asimov did not name nuclear cataclysm as our greatest risk. Recognizing that our world is so interconnected as to make the isolation of one risk factor virtually impossible, Asimov replied (possibly overreacting to the exceptionally hot and humid summer of 1988), "the Greenhouse Effect." He concluded that maybe our best hope lies in *globalization* of our thinking. We need, moreover, to "put the energy we now put into war and weapons into solving the problems" that imperil human survival. Here, in my view, he opens up a *fourth* and viable alternative—as "people of the parentheses," we can adopt a new holistic perspective, thus shaping the direction of change through a change within our consciousness.

Planetary Consciousness as a Systems View of Life

A systems approach to problem solving can be found in many contemporary disciplines, expounded by various thinkers. Fritjof Capra, for example, drawing on Gregory Bateson, has elaborated his concept of "a systems view of life" in *The Turning Point: Science, Society and the Rising Culture*. Capra points to the Earth as Gaia, "a living planetary being," a unified "living system," continually evolving, to reinforce his idea of a "new paradigm," which includes "a profound ecological

8. Isaac Asimov, address at Rensselaerville Institute, Rensselaerville, N.Y., July 23, 1988.

awareness that is ultimately spiritual."[9] Insights of science are impelling us to a spiritual view of the unity of life and to the realization that the very universe is sustained by intelligent awareness and a value-creating consciousness.

Jean Houston, who refuses to be disheartened by the proliferation of a "failure of nerve" on our planet, uses an analogy drawn from gardening (again, the wisdom of the Earth) to urge us to remember that "breakdown is always the signal for breakthrough."[10] The paradigm change required for survival needs an expanded consciousness:

> We find ourselves in a time when extremely limited consciousness has the powers once accorded to the gods. Extremely limited consciousness can launch a nuclear holocaust with the single push of a button. Extremely limited consciousness can and does intervene directly in the genetic code, interferes with the complex patterns of life in the sea, and pours its wastes into the protective ozone layers that encircle the earth. . . . Extremely limited consciousness is accruing to itself the powers of Second Genesis. And this with an ethic that is more Faustian than god-like.[11]

Roshwald's *Level 7* provides a beautiful metaphor for the peril of "limited consciousness," expressed, as we have seen, through the steady deterioration of the mind of the narrator as the underground haven, constructed through technology, becomes less and less habitable. Houston urges us, as people of the parentheses, to throw off the manacles of limited consciousness, to become the *people of the breakthrough*, aware of the pattern that connects, knowing that the present planetary anguish portends the "coming of wisdom" that will enable us to "partner the planet" toward the new era.[12]

Houston adds force to her vision of planetary consciousness with her concept of the "planetary person." The planetary person differs from the "regional or cosmopolitan" person:

> To be planetary means to be part of a wholly different modality of knowing and being, which involves a profound consciousness of the earth, a potentiating recovery of one's historical self, and an actual learn-

9. Fritjof Capra, *The Turning Point: Science, Society and the Rising Culture* (New York: Simon and Schuster, 1982; Bantam, 1988), p.285.
10. Houston, *The Possible Human*, p. 213.
11. Ibid.
12. Ibid., pp. 213–14.

ing from the genius of other cultures. This person is both the consumma-
tion of where we have been and the next stage of the spiral.[13]

The spiral is Houston's metaphor for temporal change and growth,
and is rich in symbolic associations, of cosmic forms in motion,
growth, dance (especially dances of healing and incantation), breath
and spirit, and mandalic patterns.[14]

The planetary person does not belong exclusively to science fiction,
and traditional literature lends an example in the native American
Chief Seattle, who was gifted with insight into the interconnectedness
of all things:

> The earth does not belong to man, man belongs to the earth. All
> things are connected like the blood that unites us all. Man did not weave
> the web of life, he is merely a strand in it. Whatever he does to the web,
> he does to himself.[15]

The web metaphor is a richly symbolic one, to be explored later in this
discussion.

The need for a new consciousness has also been expressed in the
"hundredth monkey" thesis of Ken Keyes, Jr. His *The Hundredth Monkey* explains how the thesis originated in the story of a group of Japanese monkeys of the *Macaca fuscata* species, observed in the wild for
over thirty years. After the monkeys were given sweet potatoes
dropped in the sand, an 18-month-old female discovered spontaneously that the potato was more pleasant to eat if she washed it. Her
playmates learned the trick of washing the potatoes and taught their
mothers. Significantly, "only the adults who imitated their children
learned this social improvement." When it comes to *new* learning,
adults, it seems, must take lessons from their juniors. Before long, the
one hundredth monkey had learned to wash the potatoes; by evening,
almost *all* were doing so. "The added energy of this hundredth monkey somehow created an ideological breakthrough!" Furthermore, the
new practice inexplicably jumped over the sea, where other monkeys
began washing their sweet potatoes.[16]

13. Jean Houston, *Lifeforce: The Psycho-Historical Recovery of the Self* (New York: Delacorte, 1980), p. 191.

14. J. E. Cirlot, *A Dictionary of Symbols*, 2d ed., translated from the Spanish by Jack
Sage, foreword by Herbert Read (New York: Philosophical Library, 1971), pp. 305–6.

15. Chief Seattle, quoted by Joseph Campbell in *The Power of Myth*, with Bill Moyers,
ed. Betty Sue Flowers (New York: Doubleday, 1988), p. 34.

16. Ken Keyes, Jr., *The Hundredth Monkey* (Coos Bay, Oreg.: Vision Books, 1982), pp.
11–17, passim.

When a certain critical number of minds achieve a new awareness, goes the thesis, it may be communicated from mind to mind by extra-sensory means. Rupert Sheldrake, the English theoretical physicist, would speak of the creation of a "morphogenetic field" of thought. A morphogenetic field is literally a form-making field, created when a critical number of independent minds concentrating on the same thought bring about a change of consciousness. Each one of us, Keyes believes, has the potential to be the one hundredth monkey who pro-vides the psychic energy to "change the consciousness of the entire planet," to provide the added energy of consciousness to achieve a nuclear-free world. Keyes's thesis, in tune with Houston's thought, is that "we are the bearers of a new vision. We can dispel the old destruc-tive myths and replace them with the life-enriching truths that are es-sential to continued life on our planet."[17] At a time when we are almost thirty years beyond the point where it was discovered that children growing up in the United States had six to eight times more strontium-90 in their bones than did their parents, the urgency of a need for change seems inarguable.[18]

Metaphors of Nature in Transformation

In a previous chapter Terrence Des Pres's exploration of the loss of a harmonious connection with the natural world as a result of nuclear anxiety illuminated the role of poetry in maintaining a balance between the "glory" of life and the consciousness that we exist as targets on a nuclear "grid." Des Pres's expression of the truth that nature before-the-bomb served as a source of comfort and of ideas of permanence ("Earth abideth forever") is complemented in a meaningful way by the equally true insight of a Jungian analyst, Wolfgang Giegerich, in his essay on "Saving the Nuclear Bomb." Giegerich, concentrating on na-ture in the wild, traces the shift in the meaning of "nature" from threatening "wilderness" to its diminution into "zoo." Whereas once wilderness surrounded the civilized community, and frail human be-ings sought sanctuary from its terrors (this is shown through passages from seventeenth-century evening prayers), we must now protect and conserve what remains of natural wilderness, fencing it in as a sanctu-ary, zoo, or national park, surrounded by civilization. Mother Nature,

17. Ibid., pp. 6, 151.
18. *Bulletin of the Atomic Scientists,* 17, no. 3 (March 1962): 44.

the goddess who reigned over life and death, has been reduced to a "problem child." Nature has become denatured, as though "senile and helpless," dependent on her now-grown children.[19] Evidence of this paternalistic stance toward nature is the landmark document from the United Nations General Assembly, the "World Charter for Nature." Called by Thomas Berry "one of the most impressive documents of the twentieth century," it has inexplicably received scant attention.[20]

The psychological consequences of this deep reversal in humankind's relationship to nature are subtle and terrible. Now that we have "fenced in" the once-chaotic wilderness, captured and caged it, it becomes "useful" in small doses, to stimulate us through "tourist excitement" or "entertainment" in our spare time.[21] It becomes, in short, a commodity. But it also becomes, as Giegerich sees, something much more sinister.

It may be true as Giegerich believes that as humans we need to feel in some irrational depth of our being that our existence is "embedded in terror" to feel at home on earth (this seems an aspect of inner truth in acknowledging our mortality and vulnerability—in a word, our "creatureliness").[22] We find in the nuclear bomb the "last wilderness—the wild in its modern guise, our twentieth-century version of all-encompassing wilderness, its last remnant." Thus encapsulated, it is no longer "out there" but "in here." It has become the only place where we can "deposit our anxiety . . . our last *genuine* and *real* connection to something bigger and more powerful than we."[23]

This idea of the bomb as surrogate deity has of course been put forward before. Giegerich's linking of it to his metaphorical expression of the "zooifying" of nature is his strikingly original point. It dramatizes the fact that the roots of nuclear peril are in our loss of nature as an object of awe and reverence. We can compare the idea of the film *Koyaanisqatsi*, a wordless documentary set to the music of Philip Glass, and composed of unforgettable images of nature "out of balance"—the meaning of the title.[24] In Giegerich's apt metaphor, we no longer feel

19. Wolfgang Giegerich, "Saving the Nuclear Bomb," in *Facing Apocalypse*, ed. Valerie Andrews, Robert Bosnak, and Karen Walter Goodwin (Dallas: Spring Publications: 1987), p. 100.

20. Thomas Berry, *The Dream of the Earth* (San Francisco: Sierra Club Books, 1988), p. 240.

21. Giegerich, "Saving the Nuclear Bomb," p. 104.

22. Ibid., p. 106.

23. Compare Ernest Becker's thesis in *The Denial of Death* that terror is the basic fact of human existence.

24. *Koyaanisqatsi* is the Hopi Indian word meaning "life out of balance."

ourselves to be children of Mother Nature but rather her anxious parents. We recognize, as we look about us, that our "child" Nature is mortally threatened, and we seek a cure for an illness. Yet paradoxically, the only physician for Nature would seem to be Nature herself.

A "Space-Station" World or an "Atopia"?

Recently a related view has been advanced by Bill McKibben in his disturbing essay, "Reflections: The End of Nature." McKibben traces the so-called greenhouse effect hypothesis back to 1884, when it was proposed under a different name by Svante Arrhenius in his doctoral thesis; several other scientists have indulged in similar speculations.[25] McKibben's own hypothesis concerns what he views as human hubris intervening in the processes of the natural world to the extent that we have ended its "separation from human society." The once "sweet and wild garden" of Nature has been turned into a subset of human activity, a "greenhouse," and this means a disruption of the once deep, constant natural rhythms. Genetic engineering is the most flagrant example of human intervention in nature's processes: One biologist has called it "the second big bang," recognizing its cosmic significance as equal to that of the "Big Bang" from which our universe theoretically evolved. In 1988, the first patent for a genetically engineered animal, a mouse genetically designed to develop cancer, was licensed to DuPont. As a further example of human tampering with Nature, McKibben draws on Brian Stableford's prediction in *Future Man* of genetically engineered "battery chickens," hunks of flesh "without unnecessary heads, wings, and tails," grown in laboratories where they could be pumped with nutrients and fitted with tubes to eliminate wastes.[26] Those familiar with today's agribusiness and its mass-production poultry farming will recognize this monstrosity as a mere extrapolation from the already denatured chicken. The blurring of the line between the animal and the inanimate has already occurred: witness also the Bionic Man of popular mythology.

For those distressed by this vision of an artificial "space-station"

25. Arrhenius's doctoral thesis dates from 1884 and was done at the University of Uppsala.

26. Bill McKibben, "Reflections: The End of Nature," *New Yorker*, September 11, 1989, pp. 76, 81, 83, 98–99. Brian Stableford is described as taking a "celebratory" view of such things as these bionic nonchickens. See *Future Man* (New York: Crown, 1984).

world capable of supporting both "our numbers and our habits" (of overconsumption), McKibben proposes an alternative future based on a "biocentric vision" (the view taken by "deep ecology") mindful of the "integrity of the planet," where human reason counters blind adherence to "biological imperatives toward endless growth in numbers and territory." This alternate future world, termed an "atopia," is possible only through restraint, through choosing "to remain God's creatures instead of making ourselves gods."[27] The real challenge, as McKibben argues, is to control our own voracious desires for more and ever more, and to accept our creaturely status. The medieval philosophers called it the virtue of humility.

Thomas Berry: "The Dream of the Earth"

More and more voices strike a similar note. Scientist and ethicist Roger Sperry in *Science and Moral Priority: Merging Mind, Brain, and Human Values* calls for a "new ethic, ideology, or theology that will make it sacrilegious to deplete natural resources, to pollute the environment, to overpopulate, to erase or degrade other species, or to otherwise destroy, demean, or defile the evolving quality of the biosphere."[28] Another of the most convincing exponents of respect for Earth's integrity, philosopher Thomas Berry, admonishes us in his meditative *The Dream of the Earth* to listen to the Earth's own voice, to heed the entire "community of Earth, including its geological as well as biological entities," who can "direct us in our efforts to bring about a 'biocracy." Earth herself is the "ultimate custodian" of Earth. We need "a mystique of the land" to counter our civilizational addiction to the mystique of industrialism.[29] Some of the archetypal symbols and images to help bring about the necessary cultural transformation, in Berry's view, are the archetype of the Great Mother, the metaphor of Life as a Great Journey of creative evolution, the mandalic image of an "omnicentered universe," the Cosmic Tree, and the Tree of Life. Such metaphors and symbols can revivify our sense of what it means to be human and help us to enter once again into "the larger community of living species." No amount of tinkering with our educational, political, or economic systems can meet the challenge

---

27. McKibben, "Reflections," pp. 100–102, 105.
28. Roger Sperry, *Science and Moral Priority: Merging Mind, Brain, and Human Values* (New York: Columbia Univ. Pr. 1983), p. 115.
29. Berry, *Dream of the Earth*, pp. xiii, 23, 33, 35.

we face today, which is to achieve a radical change in the mode of consciousness through which we perceive reality.[30]

Berry believes we can be helped by understanding the three functional principles of the Universe—differentiation, subjectivity, and communion.[31] Differentiation is the primordial principle that manifests itself in the amazing variety of things (I would compare what the poet Gerard Manley Hopkins calls "all things counter, original, spare strange" in his poem "Pied Beauty" or what the medieval thinkers termed "God's plenitude"). The second principle, subjectivity, shows itself in the increased "interiority that goes hand-in-hand with increased complexification of being"; and the third, communion, is seen in the knowledge of the universe as a single though multiform *"energy event."*[32] Berry urges that we look to the "nature mysticism" of the Native Americans so we may emulate their reverence for the natural world. He recommends particularly Jamake Highwater's *The Primal Mind: Vision and Reality in Indian America* for a fuller appreciation of the native American tradition, and he relates, as anecdotal evidence, the honor given to the Earth Mother archetype (the Corn Mother): When a child is born, an ear of corn is placed beside it to betoken "the role of a mothering principle with powers beyond that of the human mother."[33]

An important part of Thomas Berry's message is his insistence on the need for a "New Story" capable of evoking an "entrancement" with life in children, so they may "have the psychic energies needed to sustain the sorrows of the human condition." The New Story can provide a living cosmology only if it can combine "personal meaning together with the grandeur and meaning of the universe."[34] Unhappily neither the secular society nor the religious tradition now supplies this sort of vision. Unless we can invent, or reinvent, such a Story, our movement toward what Berry calls "a sustainable human culture" is bound to falter. He believes, like McKibben, that we are our own worst enemies: Far from being "the splendor of creation," we must now admit our "pernicious" effect on the Earth, for we threaten to bring about "the termination, not the fulfillment of the earth process. If there were a parliament of creatures [cf. *Die Konferenz der Tiere,* chapter 8], its first decision might well be to vote the humans out of the community, [as] too deadly a presence to tolerate any further."[35]

30. Ibid., p. 42.
31. Ibid., p. 45.
32. Ibid., pp. 45–46.
33. Ibid., pp. 184, 186–87.
34. Ibid., pp. 123, 131.
35. Ibid., pp. 206, 209. The parallel with the thought of Joseph Meeker is apparent.

The Search for Healing Metaphors

From Giegerich's metaphor expressing one source of our troubled relationship with our world, and his insistence that we need to "listen" to what the bomb has to teach us; from Bill McKibben's insights on the end of nature as we have known it and his proposed "atopia"; and from Thomas Berry's dream of a biocracy, we turn to a survey of similar metaphors that have been proposed as possibly "healing" or restorative ones—not just for our relationship to the wilderness specifically, but to the whole universe of human interactions with our fellows, with our environment, with the wilderness within—our own private terrors. A basic contemporary metaphor of transformation, that of Gaia, has been treated already. Several more specific metaphors will be enumerated here.

The World as Symphony

The Earth as Gaia is intimately related to the metaphor of the world as a symphony, the concept expounded by Matthew Fox and Brian Swimme in *Manifesto for a Global Civilization*. Its relevance to other metaphors needs brief elaboration. Fox is a theologian whose ideas are in keeping with "process" theology, which views God as an evolving being and humans as events rather than finished entities. Fox and physicist Swimme are convinced that the task of our era is "the creative transformation of the whole world into a single community out of the diverse peoples of the planet." Drawing on their respective disciplines (theology and quantum physics), the authors propose a paradigm shift from the classical, mechanistic view of the world as "a billiard table with the billiard balls glancing off one another" to a view more consonant with contemporary theoretical physics—the world as a symphony: "To begin with the assumption that the world is music is to enter the way of re-creating the meaning of the human being and thereby the world."[36] In a world seen as symphony, listening becomes the sense possibly most vital to survival. (Note the similar centrality of listening in Giegerich's thought.) Only by listening can we hope to blend with the pitch and accommodate the tempo of the other players in the ensemble.

Fox and Swimme critique the metaphor of world as machine, most familiar today in its contemporary version, the world as giant super-

36. Matthew Fox and Brian Swimme, *Manifesto for a Global Civilization* (Santa Fe, N.Mex.: Bear Books, 1982), pp. 6, 12–13.

computer. Any such mechanistic view ignores the mathematical proof of "the incompleteness of the theoretical system for arriving at the full truth," and "the impossibility of reducing human creativity to the logical process of the machine." The mind, whatever mathematical or logical system it employs, arrives at "notions that are beyond the power of proof within the system itself." The flowing well provides a better metaphor for mind, with the springing forth of water an image of creativity. Creativity, above all other aspects of mind, is the specifically human quality.[37]

The World as Arena for Creativity and Play: LeGuin's "Always Coming Home"

Creativity being the most specifically human quality, some propose cultivating it as an alternative channel for aggressive energies. A brief example must serve present purposes. In Ursula LeGuin's *The Word for World Is Forest*, ritualized singing contests are both an art form and a means to release aggression: "the better artist wins."[38] This idea summons up the delightful notion of the world's armies transformed into choral societies that stage artistic competitions. Stewart Brand, of *Whole Earth Catalog* fame, recognizing that humankind loves war, has in a similar vein proposed redesigning "current war forms" into "softwar." Softwar is "conflict which is *regionalized* (to prevent injury to the uninterested), *refereed* (to permit fairness and the certainty of a win-lose outcome), and *cushioned* (weaponry regulated for maximum contact and minimum personal disability)." The image that comes to mind is, obviously, sports, precisely Brand's intention.[39]

The redesign of war into a semi-artistic, semi-sporting event has been thought of before, as Brand points out, in T. H. White's version of King Arthur, where the wealthy, richly appareled knights were enticed to stop harassing the poor people by the formation of "a high tone clobbering club, with chivalry, girls, and pennants."[40] Is it conceivable that the Society for Creative Anachronism might, after all, hold the key to a peaceful world through softwar?

Robert Fuller has suggested finding a "Better Game Than War" through travel to those parts of the world considered to be in the en-

37. Ibid., pp. 6, 14–15.
38. Ursula LeGuin, *The Word for World Is Forest* (New York: Berkley/Putnam, 1972), p. 71.
39. Stewart Brand, *II Cybernetic Frontiers* (New York: Random House/Bookworks, 1974), p. 92.
40. Ibid., p. 93.

emy camp in order to talk to the people face-to-face and form friend-ships. From his own experience, he concludes these personal connec-tions are the key to reducing hostilities.

The world as an arena for creativity is one theme in Ursula LeGuin's *Always Coming Home*, in which it interweaves with metaphors of wholeness on many levels. In its very form, this novel embodies a new way of thinking. It combines narrative with archeological documents on the customs and beliefs of the people (their language, stories, hous-ing, clothing, food, musical instruments, art, etc.) in a form LeGuin calls "future archaeology." The book is accompanied by a cassette con-taining music of the Kesh, a people whose lives are attuned to the rhythms of the world (cf. the world as symphony, above).

The character whose life story provides the chief narrative thread has a father who comes from the tribe of war-thirsty Condors and a mother who is of the gentle Kesh. The daughter's life is lived in tension between the opposed values. In her later years, she has won the name "Stone Telling" for her myth-making abilities. She reflects on the trag-edy of her parents' lives: Each of them could see with "only one eye" and were thereby limited in their consciousness.[41] (Compare poet Wil-liam Blake's notion of "single vision," which he relates to "Newton's sleep," the mesmerization with measurement to the detriment of spir-itual realities.) Stone Telling knows that since all of us have limitations, we must remember "what we do not know" to transcend the "one-eyed" condition.

Her own wisdom is hard-won. As a girl and young woman, she en-dures the loss of fully human status while she lives with the Condors, her father's tribe, a rigid, hierarchically structured, and fear-dominated people. Concerned lest the "sacred" word be defiled, the Condors forbid women and farmers, the classes at the bottom of the power structure, to write.

The stages of Stone Telling's life are epitomized in her names. First she is "North Owl" to her mother. As a girl she is enchanted by a vi-sion of Condor power and insists her name is "Condor's daughter." To her father's tribe she is "Ayatyu," or high-born woman, a name indicative of their rigid elitist consciousness. When she escapes back to her own people and enjoys restoration of her full humanness, she names herself "Woman Coming Home." As a venerated creator of mythic narratives, she becomes "Stone Telling."

Her greatest reward in life has been in the "work of handmind." As

---

41. Ursula LeGuin, *Always Coming Home*, composer, Todd Barton; artist, Margaret Chodos; geomancer, George Hersh (New York: Harper and Row, 1985), p. 29.

she remarks, ''The hand that shapes the mind into clay or written word slows thought to the gait of things and lets it be subject to accident and time.''[42] The merging of handwork and mindwork into handmind reflects the psychological wholeness prized by the Kesh. Their way of thought eliminates the dichotomizing, problematizing approach to life, and values interconnectedness as well as an androgynous consciousness.

LeGuin's chart of ''Generative Metaphors'' is especially valuable for its graphic presentation of the way metaphors shape our self-concepts, our relationships, and the world we inhabit.[43] Some metaphorical means of picturing the universe are counterproductive because they generate hostile or exploitative relationships. Life viewed as War, for example, generates struggle, with the ''subjection of the weak to the strong'' and encouragement of enmity (cf. Riane Eisler's concept of the ''dominator'' society). Language in the context of life as War becomes a vehicle of control. Similarly, the metaphor of Lord generates a hierarchical power structure, with desire for relationships of superiority. Language becomes a medium for gaining and maintaining power. Perhaps most telling is the metaphor of the universe as a machine, resulting in exploitative human relationships and language reduced to utilitarian communication.

Other metaphors generate relationships more attuned to a mythology of peace. The metaphor of the universe as Animal (an organic whole—compare the image of Gaia), for example, generates life, interdependent relationships, and a context where language fosters kinship.

The universe as Dance (cf. Matthew Fox and Brian Swimme's universe as symphony) generates music, ''horizontal linkings'' among people, and a context for language as a medium of ''connection.'' The universe as House generates ''stability,'' relating to others as ''inside/outside,'' and fosters language as ''self-domestication.'' Finally, the metaphor of ''the Way'' generates change, a view of the universe as a ''mystery; balance in movement,'' and relationships of ''unity'' with other wayfarers ''on the way.'' Language in this context becomes ''inadequate'' to express the totality of life.

On the principle of ''complementarity'' developed by Danish physicist Niels Bohr—who recognized that ''reality is too rich to be adequately represented by any one model or even one paradigm''—I suggest that the metaphorical models of the Animal, the Dance, the

42. Ibid., p. 175.
43. Ibid., pp. 83–88.

House, and the Way, woven into the fabric of LeGuin's book, are especially valuable for analyzing how a given narrative structures relationships.[44] Throughout *Always Coming Home* LeGuin implicitly affirms a peace mythology and a survival ethic of wholeness. Occasionally the affirmation is made explicit, as in this passage from "Person and Self," in which Old Jackrabbit speculates on the possibility that the universe may be a person:

> Maybe in all things there is one person, one spirit whom we greet in the rock and the sun and trust in all things to bless and help. Maybe the oneness of the universe manifests that one spirit and the oneness of each being of the many kinds is a sign or symbol of that person. . . . Thinking human people and other animals, the plants, the rocks and stars, all the beings that think or are thought, that are seen or see, that hold or are held, all of us are beings of the Nine Houses of Being dancing the same dance.[45]

In contrast to Old Jackrabbit's view of Being, the "Backward-Head" people, to whom the Kesh attribute the "poisoned lands" and the "polluted waters" of earth, held distorted values. Since the Kesh believe people are responsible for their acts, they see the Backward-Heads as responsible for "the permanent desolation of vast regions through the release of radioactive or poisonous substances [and] permanent genetic impairment."[46] They conclude that the Backward-Head people were willfully evil; they had their heads on "wrong."

In their appreciation of multiplicity, their closeness to the earth, their sense of organic unity and valuing of handmind work, the Kesh are a vivid fictional paradigm for a society in harmony with peace mythology. The world of the Kesh is not utopian (on the contrary, LeGuin warns against utopian fallacies), but it supplies what Condor society lacks. Condors perpetuate the values of the Backward-Head people, who bear an uncomfortable resemblance to the people of contemporary America. The Condors also take themselves far too seriously. They could learn from Carol Pearson's idea that the "fool, or trickster," the character that has superseded the antihero in much contem-

44. Willis Harman and Howard Rheingold, in *Higher Creativity: Liberating the Unconscious for Breakthrough Insights* (Los Angeles: J. P. Tarcher, 1984), p. 12, referring to Niels Bohr, *Atomic Physics and the Description of Nature* (Cambridge Univ. Pr., 1934).

45. LeGuin, *Always Coming Home*, p. 307. For the Houses of Being, see pp. 43–49, "The Serpentine Codex."

46. Ibid., p. 159.

porary fiction, opens up comic and optimistic "possibilities for fullness of life even in the modern world."[47]

The World as Dialogue

The metaphor of the world as dialogue relates well to the world as symphony, for both exalt the importance of listening. The dialogue metaphor brings out the value of both listening and speaking—the give-and-take of word and idea. Three subcategories of metaphorical dialogue will be considered here: dialogue with the spectral voices of Hiroshima and Nagasaki, dialogue with women's voices, and dialogue with nature.

Listening to Hiroshima and Nagasaki

Denise Levertov in her poem "On the 32nd Anniversary of the Bombing of Hiroshima and Nagasaki" provides a vivid statement of the need to *listen* to the voice of the "shadowgraph" of a human form burnt into stone at Hiroshima by "unearthly fire." She imagines the stone, given voice, saying from its long sleep:

> something can yet
> be salvaged upon the earth:
> try, try to survive,
> try to redeem
> the human vision
> from cesspits where human hands
> have thrown it, as I was thrown
> from life into shadow.[48]

Historical reimagining of this voice from the past can awaken what Mary Watkins calls the "moral imagination."[49] Watkins's work in developing imaginal dialogues around the topic of nuclear war provides a source for raising awareness of the importance of the imagination in preventing nuclear holocaust.[50] A lively imaginal dialogue with voices

47. Carol S. Pearson, *The Hero Within: Six Archetypes We Live By* (San Francisco: Harper and Row, 1989), p. xv.

48. Denise Levertov, "On the 32nd Anniversary of the Bombing of Hiroshima and Nagasaki," in *Facing Apocalypse*, pp. 56–58.

49. Mary Watkins, " 'In Dreams Begin Responsibilities': Moral Imagination and Peace Action," in *Facing Apocalypse*, pp. 70–95.

50. See Mary Watkins, *Invisible Guests: The Development of Imaginal Dialogues* (Hillsdale, N.J.: Analytic Press, 1985).

from the ruins of the past may help us keep to the path called by the Hopis the "upward" one, deflecting us away from disaster.

Listening to Women's Voices

It may be that the movement toward listening to women's voices dates from the publication of *The Woman's Bible* by Elizabeth Cady Stanton and her colleagues in 1898, though many in our society still suffer from selective, gender-biased hearing loss. The achievement of Stanton and her colleagues, however, merits recognition, and it is lamentable that so few young people know of it. As for the current scene, Ursula LeGuin has commented that the voices of women are "a new thing in our time"; it is as though a sleeping giant has awakened and become articulate. In an address to poet Gary Snyder's class in Wilderness at the University of California–Davis, LeGuin remarked,

> The women are speaking. Those who were identified as having nothing to say, as sweet silence or monkey-chatterers, those who were identified with Nature, which listens, as against Man, who speaks—those people are speaking. They speak for themselves and for the other people, the animals, the trees, the rivers, the rocks. And what they say is: We are sacred.[51]

LeGuin identifies the experience of women with "true wildness," for it is outside the Dominant (male) culture's experience; yet, she points out, this "wild country" excluded from mainstream cultural consciousness is also "where all children live" (of both genders) and it is therefore puzzling that adult men are afraid of it.[52] Men in our culture, awakening in adolescence to the devaluing of the feminine, learn to fear and suppress it in themselves.

As one more representative of women's voices (there are too many to do more than sample here), Merlin Stone stands out for her monumental gathering of goddess-lore from many cultures in *Ancient Mirrors of Womanhood: A Treasury of Goddess and Heroine Lore from Around the World*. The preface makes her point that this treasure of women's heritage is "generally unfamiliar," yet the "continuity of spiritual wisdom" that belongs to all of us, though almost totally ignored in education and popular literature, has much to say to our time, if we would listen to it. Her interpretation of "yin," the female principle

---

51. Ursula LeGuin, "Woman/Wilderness (1986)," in *Dancing at the Edge of the World: Thoughts on Words, Women, Places* (New York: Grove Press, 1989), pp. 161–63.
52. Ibid., p. 163.

(the complement of "yang," the male principle in Taoist thought) is of special interest: Though yin is sometimes presented as totally passive, waiting to be acted upon by yang (cf. the Sleeping Beauty myth), ancient texts suggest that yin is not so much passivity as "a specific form of activity." Stone finds an analogue for this yin activity in the wisdom of water that flows around a great boulder rather than crashing against it. In short, yin wisdom follows the organic processes of Mother Nature, a path "more likely to assure a reaching of the destination" than opposing it.[53] A major source for this interpretation of yin is the well-known *Tao Teh Ching*, or *I Ching*, written about 600 B.C.E. by Lao Tzu.

A goddess story particularly rich in its significance for young girls is the tale of Gum Lin and Loy Yi Lung. Gum Lin, the mortal heroine, cooperates with the daughter of the dragon, Loy Yi Lung, to learn the "natural patterns of the dragon" so they can succeed in retrieving the golden key from the dragon's treasure hoard. Only the golden key can open the stone gate, releasing the life-giving waters of a mountain reservoir to save the drought-stricken people of Gum Lin's village.[54] The tale is worth a more detailed analysis than is appropriate here, but the cooperative nature of the heroic venture and its valorization of gentle but consistent and determined action to overcome obstacles are of much relevance for female gender-identity formation.

Stone makes an eloquent plea on behalf of reclaiming the links between goddess reverence and the "sanctity of nature":

> Faced with the all too real threats of the continually escalating accumulation of nuclear weapons, poisonous pollution of land, sea, and air, and the complete extinction of many species of life on earth, perhaps even our own, we might do well to examine the rituals, parables, and symbolism of spiritual beliefs that included regarding various aspects of nature as sacred—thus inviolable.[55]

Listening to the goddess myths is one way to recapture the wonder and respect for nature so central to survival. As ecologist Roy Rappaport once remarked, "Knowledge will never be able to replace respect in man's dealings with ecological systems."[56]

53. Merlin Stone, *Ancient Mirrors of Womanhood: A Treasury of Goddess Lore from Around the World*, illus. by Cynthia Stone (Boston: Beacon Press, 1979), pp. 3, 26.

54. Ibid., pp. 35–40.

55. Ibid., p. 18.

56. Roy Rappaport, quoted in Brand, *II Cybernetic Frontiers*, epigraph.

Listening to Images: "The Nuclear Horror and the Hounding of Nature"

There was a mythical time when all things in nature could speak to us: The streams, trees, and animals spoke in a language meaningful to the human ear. Although this mythical time is preserved for us in fairy tales, most people, in the era since nature has been "denatured" and caged, have grown deaf to it.[57] In his remarkable essay on "The Nuclear Horror and the Hounding of Nature: Listening to Images," Daniel C. Noel makes a connection between our "hounding" of nature and the destructive use of the intellect through a brilliant analysis of Russell Hoban's *Riddley Walker*. Readers must turn to Noel's essay to mine its riches, for my commentary will be limited to its implications for the metaphor of the world as dialogue.

Drawing on archetypal psychology—particularly the Jungian idea of the power of artistic images to speak to our psyches on a deep, nonverbal level—Noel relates a number of personal experiences, synchronically linked to *Riddley Walker* and to Pisanello's painting of "The Vision of St. Eustace," a key source of imagery for Hoban's story. Noel expresses the *ecological* necessity of listening to images, drawing his examples from images of the "degenerate future" of Riddley's world and the details of Pisanello's painting. The painting depicts the enrapt St. Eustace, mounted on a horse and surrounded by hunting hounds, beholding a stag between whose antlers is a miniature Christ on the cross.

The imagery of hunting as a "hounding" of nature, and the identification of Christ with the hunted stag (and with all of nature as humankind's prey) relates to ecological themes in Riddley's world and our own. The implication is that we have impoverished our relationship to the natural world through reducing it to an arena for hunting and killing. A symbolic parallel is drawn between the cornering and killing of the stag in the painting and the "hounding" intellect that, through grasping the secrets of nature hidden in the atom, brought calamity on the world. "The Eusa Story," the key mythic narrative in the novel, translates the hounding of nature theme into "a mythic version of nuclear physics."[58]

---

57. At least in fiction we can still find those who "hear" the language of nature. Two good examples are Neaera H. and William G., characters in Russell Hoban's *Turtle Diary* (New York: Random House, 1975).

58. Daniel C. Noel, "The Nuclear Horror and the Hounding of Nature: Listening to Images," *Soundings: An Interdisciplinary Journal*, 70 (Fall/Winter 1987): 292. See *Riddley Walker*, pp. 30–36, for the Eusa Story.

A further contrast is drawn by Noel between the disastrous consequences of the "hounding" intellect—ultimately, in Hoban's terms, splitting the "Addom/Adam/Atom"—and the native American respect for nature's bounty as "sacred game."[59] Noel refers to Marilou Awiakta's story of her Cherokee Indian mother's answer to her childhood question, "What is the atom, Mother? Will it hurt us?" Her mother refrained from calling the atom inherently evil or proclaiming we should cease to inquire into its nature, instead saying simply, "We have to have reverence for nature . . . and learn to live in harmony with it." The atom, too, is nature. Years later, Awiakta found insight through her memory of the "sacred white deer of the Cherokee, leaping in the heart of the atom": she thought of her ancestor's belief that "if a hunter took the life of a deer without asking its spirit for pardon, the immortal Little Deer would track the hunter to his home and cripple him. The reverent hunter evoked the white deer's blessing and guidance." Awiakta urges humans to relinquish their anger and create a "listening space" in order that they may "attain harmony with the atom in time."[60] The time grows short for this attainment! It is remarkable that Awiakta uses the musical analogy—harmony—and, like Giegerich, urges us to an attitude of reverence in dealing with the atom, rather than simple opposition. Noel observes the similarity between Awiakta's imagery of the Little Deer and Hoban's "Hart uv the Wud" and "Littl Shynin Man, the Addom," and concludes, "All these figures spoke of a choice placed before us: If human beings must hunt, we can hunt with a spirit of sacred reverence, respecting nature as an independent reality of infinite worth."[61]

Only "heartfelt reimagining" can help us hear the messages the images carry. Ultimately, as Noel points out, images are "the essence of human nature," for like people they harbor "creativity and unpredictability that both enrich and threaten us." Unless we open our inner ear to what Hoban calls "the idear uv me"—the necessary self-confrontation and self-understanding that can come only from "openness to our own inner images"—we shall never know ourselves. And "if our literalizing objectivity has destroyed what is most essential about us, how can we avoid destroying ourselves? If we are deaf to the violence of the past recorded in the human imagination, how can we

59. This idea is elaborated in Paul Shepard, *The Tender Carnivore and the Sacred Game* (New York: Charles Scribner's Sons, 1973).

60. Marilou Awiakta, "What Is the Atom, Mother? Will It Hurt Us?" *Ms.* (July 1983): 48.

61. Noel, "The Nuclear Horror," p. 299.

hear the violence coming in the all-too-pressing future?"[62] Deafness, like muteness, must prove self-destructive.

There is a basis for hope, perhaps, in Penelope Mesic's answer to the question, "Why do nuclear arms continue to be made and nuclear power plants continue to be built?" She finds the answer in a "failure of imagination, which is remediable," not in "our moral nature," which cannot be altered.[63] The failure of imagination can be remedied to some extent through listening; and the anger Awiakta calls for us to banish can be defused by dealing with what Spencer R. Weart has called the "inner bomb," the inner "imaginary explosiveness that creates the objective 'real' weapon."[64] Riddley Walker's channeling of energies into artistic powers and simultaneous rejection of the temptation to external, technologically based power provides a model of choice.

The Role of Story in Developing Wholeness of Vision

Story, as well as poetry and other arts, has a key role to play in the development of the kind of planetary vision essential to the biophile survival ethic. John Gardner in his marvelous mock epic *Grendel* named his bard the Shaper. Poets and imaginative writers of all kinds shape human imagination in subtle but important ways—remember the Zebra Storyteller. Science fiction has a special role to play, for it has become, as Noel Perrin says, "the chief refuge for metaphysics. It's where you go in literature if you want to hear people openly and seriously talking about meaning, and especially meaning in a world increasingly made and controlled by ourselves."[65] We look to science fiction for new paradigms of being.

If it is true, as Houston and others believe, that the planetary vision, the *Zeitgeist* stemming from our venture into space, is a more powerful mandala for our era than any vision of war, then it follows that what Houston calls "visionary" science fiction can serve as a psychological

62. Ibid., pp. 304–5, 306.

63. Penelope Mesic, review of *Riddley Walker*, by Russell Hoban, *The Bulletin of the Atomic Scientists* (June/July 1982), pp. 49–50.

64. Spencer R. Weart, *Nuclear Fear: A History of Images* (Cambridge, Mass.: Harvard Univ. Pr., 1988), p. 411.

65. Noel Perrin, "Science Fiction: Imaginary Worlds and Real-Life Questions," *New York Times Book Review*, April 9, 1989, p. 37.

power source. She distinguishes three features of the visionary mode of science fiction:

1. It deals with new ways of being, new modes of consciousness, new "patterns" for "the weave of life."
2. It may provide an image of the trans-human, "mystic" vision of the whole, with the individual a part of the pattern.
3. It links, at its best, the ancient or traditional wisdoms (the old myths) to new techniques or provides new perspectives that combine the humanistic/technological.[66]

Houston does not mention specific titles, but Susan Weston's *Children of the Light* might qualify as an example. Weston shows people in a postcatastrophe setting called "Idamore" establishing a nurturing, nonhierarchical society, based on maximizing of individual abilities, cooperation, and respect for the natural cycles, in contrast to "Freehold," a society that imposes rigid social controls, and a third group, led by religious fanatics who have lost touch with reality. *Children of the Light* could fruitfully be critiqued against Houston's criteria.

Many of the novels discussed in this text use nuclear catastrophe as a metaphor for the transformation of consciousness, the end of an old "mind" and the opening of a new. A considerable number of novels for young readers incorporate this idea of consciousness transformation: Hoover's *Children of Morrow*, MacIntyre's *Dreamsnake*, Service's *Winter of Magic's Return*, and Wyndham's *Re-Birth, or the Chrysalids*. The difficulty with this depiction of an expanded consciousness as a by-product of nuclear radiation, as observed before, is its possible implication that the chaotic social change wrought by nuclear cataclysm leads to positive personal transformation. Spencer R. Weart has noted that although the individual may need to experience chaos before rebirth, it is a dangerous fallacy to suppose the chaos of war can redeem an entire civilization. Readers must be alert to the fact that the transfer of the idea of breakdown leading to growth from the personal to the societal level is fraught with difficulties. "Wars leave most people not more trusting and reasonable but less so."[67] In using these novels with young readers, it is vital to make this point. *Riddley Walker*, in contrast, never allows the reader to forget the debilitating long-range societal

66. Jean Houston, "Spiral Into Life," an interview with Michael Toms (New Dimensions Radio, WRPI, Troy, N.Y., June 3, 1988), cassette.
67. Weart, *Nuclear Fear*, p. 224.

and psychological effects of nuclear cataclysm. Because of this, it is the more successful in implying the need for planetary vision *now,* not later.

Criteria for Evaluating Fiction of Planetary Vision

Still in its infancy, the evolving genre of planetary fiction presents a critical challenge. Criteria for evaluating its worth have been articulated by Jean Houston. Her criteria are summarized here with my own elaborations. The best works of science fiction do one or more of the following:

1. Show a planetary vision of unity and wholeness, the interconnectedness of all beings, to be a more powerful and seductive idea than any vision of war or fragmentation.
2. Show the "weave of life" as sacralized (Joseph Campbell would say "transparent to transcendence").
3. Transcend dualistic thinking (the "problem" approach or either/or, we/they, or similar dichotomies).
4. Show the protagonist as embodying a new way of being, thus exemplifying the new mode of consciousness.
5. Incorporate both male and female stories or perspectives.
6. Provide examples for channeling energies into creativity and compassion, rather than destruction or war.
7. Envision celebratory communities in which a balance and harmony of inner-outer life may be achieved.
8. Provide a mythic element.[68]

I would add one more criterion:

9. Exhibit a sense of humility about the position of human beings vis-á-vis other species: Move toward what Thomas Berry calls "biocracy."

Few books can score high against such demanding specifications. Certain books may meet specific criteria; *Riddley Walker,* for example, provides a good instance of energies turned toward creativity and away from war. The application of these criteria to works of science fiction could be a challenging exercise for young adults with a penchant for speculative thought.

68. Houston, "Spiral into Life." See also Stone, *Ancient Mirrors of Womanhood.*

The Primacy of Choice

Skeptics will maintain that little if anything can be done to reverse the trend toward disaster—ecological, biological, political, or military. Scientists have of late given considerable attention to an apparent cyclical pattern in the history of catastrophic extinctions. The latest findings on at least five worldwide catastrophes are reported in Rick Gore's article, "Extinctions"; some scientists believe our era exceeds all others in the immensity of mass extinctions of species. The difference today, Gore points out, is that we are *conscious* of what is happening and can therefore do something to halt it: "Perhaps . . . for the first time a living creature can gaze out across the species of the earth and say: This is beautiful. I care. I will not let it go."[69]

Cynics will say we have passed a critical point of no return in our march toward the abyss. Voices of hope are all the more important in a time of doubt and darkness. It is crucial to keep fresh the awareness of the human power to respond to threatening situations with intelligent choice. Rene Dubos, the distinguished professor of environmental biomedicine who concerned himself with questions of the quality of the human environment, observed late in his life that

> human beings are rarely passive witnesses of threatening situations. Their responses to threats may be unwise, but they inevitably alter the course of events and make mockery of any attempt to predict the future from extrapolation of existing trends. In human affairs, the *logical* future, determined by past and present conditions, is less important than the *willed* future, which is largely brought about by deliberate choices—made by human beings.[70]

Or, as Albert Einstein is reputed to have said, "imagination is more important than knowledge," for it is the imagination that can project the desired, willed future.

69. Rick Gore, "Extinctions," photographs by Jonathan Blair, *National Geographic* 175, no. 6 (June 1989): 698. Other articles of similar theme are James Trefil's "Stop to Consider the Stones That Fall from the Sky," *Smithsonian* 20, no. 60 (September 1989): 81–93, on asteroids as precipitants of mass extinctions; and Jon Van's "Study Links Ice Ages, Greenhouse Effect," *Chicago Tribune*, Friday, August 1, 1989, sec. 1, p. 3, a report of the study by Douglas MacAyeal, University of Chicago geophysicist, and Dean Lindstrom, of the University of Illinois at Chicago, demonstrating through computer simulation a causal link between carbon dioxide levels and ice age cycles.

70. Rene Dubos, "Education for the Celebration of Life: Optimism in Spite of It All," in *Education for Peace and Disarmament: Toward a Living World*, Douglas Sloan, ed. (New York: Teachers College Press, 1983), p. 270.

A moving example of the failure to exercise human choice can be found in the film *The Mission,* a dramatization of a historical attempt by two Jesuit priests to preserve the native Guarini Indians of a South American jungle mission in the eighteenth century. The Indians were considered expendable by both sides in a power struggle between the Portuguese and the Spanish. A Jesuit emissary from Rome, Altamirano, who for reasons of political expediency allows the mission and the Indians to be destroyed, is shocked by news of the extent of the massacre and asks the Portuguese military chiefs, "Have you the effrontery to call this slaughter 'necessary'?" "Yes," says the one. "This is how the world is," says the other. As the papal representative, Altamirano finally comprehends the irreversible horror of what he has allowed to happen. He pauses painfully, and then says, "No, this is how we have *made* the world."[71] In short, the choice is ours, to go along with the "hounding of nature" and the destruction of the weak, or to resist the exploitation of nature and those who live close to nature, in short, to affect human destiny in a more positive direction.

To do so requires a certain perspective, a view of the world as an arena for witness and action. We can respond to the nuclear threat, as Robert Musil resolved to do after the Cuban Missile Crisis, by seeking to *do* something. In the words of the Greenpeace Philosophy, we can "personally bear witness to atrocities against life" and "take direct, nonviolent action to prevent them." The commitment is to life and the protection of life.[72] Examples of activism in both fictional and nonfictional settings have been discussed in chapter 4, "The Peace Pilgrim."

As real-life pilgrims of space and time, we can only speculate on what the future may bring. To neglect to speculate, however, would be to forfeit the opportunity to choose among alternatives. It is indubitably true, as literary critic De Kerckhove said in 1984, that the "psychic end" of the nuclear bomb "will be reached when the whole culture is so completely transformed that it is structured for integration rather than for its present trend of disintegration."[73]

Such a cultural transformation will be precipitated at least partly through integrative symbols provided by the literary imagination. One who expresses hope despite the cynics is poet Seamus Heaney. In his poem "Alphabets," Heaney uses two images, called "exemplary" by

71. *The Mission,* Warner Brothers, 1986. Based on the play *The Mission,* by Robert Bolt (New York: Penguin, 1986).

72. From the pamphlet "Confrontation," available from Greenpeace USA, 1611 Connecticut Avenue NW, Washington, DC, 20070.

73. De Kerckhove, "On Nuclear Communication," *Diacritics,* 14 (Summer 1984): p. 80.

critic Helen Vendler, to serve as metaphors of the planetary perspective. The first is the Renaissance humanist and necromancer who adorned his abode with "a figure of the world with colours in it" so he could be always mindful of our spherical planet in relationship to the universe; the second is the scientist-astronaut, who also tries to keep a global vision before his eyes. However inadequate our "infant" alphabet may be for symbolizing the truths of our world and universe, we may take courage from the realization that, as Vendler says, "Ours is the first generation to have a perceptual (rather than conceptual) grasp of the world as a single orbiting sphere," or, in Heaney's image, as "the risen, aqueous, singular, lucent Ooh."[74] What we do with this perceptual change depends at least in part on the imaginative vision imparted by writers of speculative fiction.

A Sampling of Educational Choices

Given the centrality of concern over the nuclear threat among both adults and children, it is remarkable to say the least that so little educational time is devoted to discussing and brainstorming on the topic. A full survey of educational resources would require another volume (and a substantial one, to be sure), but a few suggestions for educational applications closely linked to this discussion will be given here.

1. *Imagining alternative futures.* James Robertson's *The Sane Alternative: A Choice of Futures* provides a particularly good framework for reading and open-ended discussion about possible futures. He provides a thematic structure consisting of five suggested scenarios: (1) Business-as-Usual, the view that the future will very much resemble the past and the present; (2) Disaster, the view that catastrophic breakdown is beginning in many areas of life; (3) the Totalitarian Conservationist (TC) Future, which sees disaster as likely unless we avert it through the acceptance of authoritarian rule; (4) the Hyperexpansionist (HE) Future, the view that the answer to our problems lies in "accelerating the super-industrialist drives in Western society" (development of space colonies, nuclear power, and genetic engineering, for instance, are all favored by those who hold this view); and (5) the Sane, Humane, Ecological (SHE) Future, which holds that, far from accelerating, we need to change direction: "the key to the future

74. Helen Vendler, *New York Times Book Review*, 35, no. 7 (April 28, 1988): 41–45, passim, with quotations from Seamus Heaney, *The Haw Lantern* (Farrar, Straus, and Giroux, 1988).

is not continuing expansion but balance—balance within ourselves, balance between ourselves and other people, balance between people and nature." Growth beyond our present capacities will be psychological and social—these are the new frontiers.[75]

Robertson endorses the SHE future, further characterized as egalitarian, decentralist, optimistic, conservationist, and open to "breakthrough," a term that suggests an affinity with Jean Houston's thought.[76] Young people could fruitfully be involved in reading and dialogue with Robertson's scenarios as stimuli. His work also provides a basis for role-playing the fourteen different kinds of people whose interactions could help to shape the future as a Sane, Humane, Ecological one. Readers are referred to his book for a complete description of the cast of characters, but role number 9 is of particular interest to the concept of the biophile: people who are "paradigm shifters, the ideological revolutionaries," whose function is *"metaphysical reconstruction"* and who are involved in the exploration and communication of "new concepts of power, wealth, work, growth, learning, healing," and so on, as appropriate to the future SHE society.[77]

2. *Exercising skills of creative problem solving.* A technique for creative problem solving has been devised by E. Paul Torrance and reported by Charles E. Martin, Bonnie Crammond, and Tammy Safter, who also describe their techniques for creative questioning as applied to "Little Red Riding Hood."[78] The five steps in the creative problem solving process are (1) finding the facts through reading (some topics, of course, do not lend themselves to a strictly "factual" approach); (2) identifying the real problem, which is not always obvious; (3) brainstorming for solutions, with wildly original and novel ideas encouraged; (4) evaluating alternatives and settling on the solution that seems best; and (5) finding acceptance for the solution by convincing others of its value.[79]

3. *Using imaginal dialogues.* The "numb" and "aware" characters identified by Mary Watkins in her dialogue work (discussed in chapter 4) are reiterated here as a possible basis for role-playing to heighten

75. James Robertson, *The Sane Alternative: A Choice of Futures,* foreword by Hazel Henderson (St. Paul, Minn.: River Basin Publishing Company, 1978), pp. 16–18, passim.

76. Ibid., p. 19.

77. Ibid., pp. 120–22.

78. E. Paul Torrance, "Creative Problem Solving," (thesis, University of Georgia, Athens, 1979), describes the steps in the Creative Problem Solving (CPS) process. See Charles E. Martin, Bonnie Crammond, and Tammy Safter, "Developing Creativity through the Reading Program," *The Reading Teacher* 35 (February 1982): 568–72.

79. These steps are also summarized in Joanne E. Bernstein and Masha Kabakow Rudman, *Books to Help Children Cope with Separation and Loss: An Annotated Bibliography,* 3 (New York: Bowker, 1989), pp. 63–64.

self-awareness and clarify one means of dealing with fears of disaster. The six "numbed" character types are (1) the child, who excuses himself or herself from the task of dealing with nuclear issues and leaves it to those who are older (this dialoguing assumes even young children can transcend the "child" role in some measure, as the children do in Vigna's *Nobody Wants a Nuclear War*); (2) the worker or specialist, who narrows concerns to the job at hand, leaving nuclear issues to others; (3) the "naturalist," or one who takes to the woods, real or figurative, out of escapist motives; (4) the suburbanite, whose horizon is limited to a circumscribed concern with a secure job, pleasant home, family, and friends; (5) the "hedonist," who seizes the moment to "bliss out" on whatever form of pleasure seems most likely to anesthetize him or her from nuclear fear; and (6) the "gray lifers," who find it is all they can do to manage their own day-to-day existence.

Watkins's "aware" characters fall into three broad categories: (1) immobilized "victims" so overwhelmed by awareness as to be petrified with despair; (2) "activists" comprising two subtypes—either young, energetic, and confident that social issues can be solved with enough effort, or burnt out, angry, and bitter, full of disillusionment and feelings of inadequacy; and (3) those who love and value life, whose concern and dedication are "renewable" because their actions flow naturally from their emotions.[80] The biophile clearly belongs here.

4. *Exercise in imagining a world without weapons thirty years hence.* Participants are first asked to imagine what life would be like in a nuclear-arms-free world thirty years from the present. Second, they are "asked to work backward from this utopic image and describe (as a historian might) events at each five-year period from the future image to the present reality," identifying the events that are necessary to the actualization of the ideal future image. The second step is critical, for "utopic imagining alone," without the definition of steps toward the desired outcome, can "lead to the breakdown of the very vision it promulgates."[81]

5. *Exercise in archetypal thinking.* The six archetypal characters identified by Carol S. Pearson in *The Hero Within: Six Archetypes We Live By* have been outlined previously: the Innocent, who lives in paradise, oblivious to the world's ills; the Orphan, centered on safety, fearful of abandonment, who denies the "dragon" and waits to be rescued by another; the Martyr, who appeases the dragon through self-sacrifice;

80. Watkins, "In Dreams Begin Responsibilities," pp. 80–88, passim.

81. Ibid., pp. 93–94. Note 1, page 94, credits Elise Boulding and Warren Ziegler with extending Fred Polak's theory of "the image of the future" to "our present planetary crisis."

the Wanderer, who aims for autonomy, fears conformity (cf. the Lone Ranger) and, quite unlike the Lone Ranger, tends to flee conflict with the dragon; the Warrior, whose chief fear is to be thought weak and who makes bold to slay the dragon; and the Magician, who values authenticity above all, fears superficiality and alienation from self and others, and directs his or her energies to wholeness and balance. These archetypal characters offer a framework for stimulating sessions in role-playing and writing. The Magician comes closest to harmonizing with the biophile, but people might be asked to imagine the consequences for the biocivisphere stemming from each of the archetypes.[82] Pearson's thought is multilayered and her book should be read in full by those who undertake to apply her ideas.

6. *Using writing to elicit new ways of thinking about change.* Becky R. McLaughlin, drawing on concepts of "social-epistemic rhetoric" as found in the thought of James Berlin and Raymond Williams, and recognizing like them that rhetoric *always* serves ideological claims, acknowledged or not, has urged the adoption of a frankly political, dialectical linguistic writing process in the classroom.[83] This "social-epistemic rhetoric is described by Berlin as a rhetoric self-consciously used as "a political act involving a dialectical interaction" among the material and social worlds and the individual writer, with "language as the agency of mediation."[84]

McLaughlin defines to the students her own stance as a pacifist, "a stance that embraces non-violent methods for achieving and/or maintaining peace" and "does not condone war whether it be conventional or nuclear." She then identifies "root" or systemic causes of war, such as a system based on a logic of binary oppositions (United States against the USSR, right against left, capitalism against communism, etc.). The effects of patriarchal authority and the endorsement of "competition rather than cooperation" are also brought into question.[85]

To illuminate the destructive effects of the nuclear arms race on rela-

82. Pearson, *The Hero Within*, pp. 20–21.
83. Becky R. McLaughlin, "In the Classroom: How to Combat Nuclear War Using Female Gender Identity Formation, the Idea as Gift, Pop Music, and Brecht's 'Alienation Effect,' " paper presented at the Midwest Modern Language Association Conference, St. Louis, Mo., November 3–5, 1988, and used in this chapter with permission. McLaughlin credits James Berlin, "Rhetoric and Ideology in the Writing Class," *College English* 50 (1988), pp. 477–94; and Raymond Williams, "Alignment and Commitment," *Contemporary Literary Criticism*, ed. Robert Con Davis (London: Longman, 1986), pp. 124–29.
84. Berlin, "Rhetoric and Ideology in the Writing Class," p. 488.
85. McLaughlin, "In the Classroom," p. 2.

tionships of all kinds, from personal to international, McLaughlin draws on the differences between male and female gender-identity formation and those between a "commodity" and a gift. Carol Gilligan's *In a Different Voice* employs a literary illustration of the difference in the way men and women define themselves during the crucial stage of adolescence by referring to James Joyce's *Portrait of the Artist as a Young Man* and Mary McCarthy's *Memories of a Catholic Girlhood*. For young Stephen Daedalus, leaving childhood meant "renouncing relationships in order to protect his freedom of self-expression," whereas for Mary McCarthy, the end of childhood meant "relinquishing the freedom of self-expression in order to protect others and preserve relationships."[86] Students can be asked to consider how this valuing of "the self defined through separation rather than connection, the self concerned with abstract principles, such as freedom, rather than nurture," relates to our social problems of discord and war.[87]

Lewis Hyde's *The Gift: Imagination and the Erotic Life of Property* is drawn on to illuminate the difference between a gift, which "establishes a feeling-bond between two people," and the sale of a commodity, which "leaves no necessary connection."[88] As McLaughlin observes, it is not surprising that "a society that values the self defined through separation and individuation is also a society that values the sale of commodities rather than the exchange of gifts."[89] Students could be asked to describe how an act familiar to all of them, such as the use of sources in a research paper, would be viewed in a society where one's status hinged not on the amassing of commodities but on the giving of gifts, and where ideas were viewed not as possessions to be hoarded but as treasures to be bestowed.

McLaughlin challenges her writing students to create essays that question the ideological status quo, that are directed at making their audience

> think about change, about a world free of nuclear weapons, a world that perceives itself as a global community rather than separate, individuated nation-states, a world of people related and connected rather than a world of islands both isolated and insulated.[90]

86. Carol Gilligan, *In a Different Voice: Psychological Theory and Women's Development* (Cambridge, Mass.: Harvard Univ. Pr. 1982), p. 157.
87. McLaughlin, "In the Classroom," p. 4.
88. Lewis Hyde, *The Gift: Imagination and the Erotic Life of Property* (New York: Random House, 1983), p. 56.
89. McLaughlin, "In the Classroom," p. 6.
90. Ibid., p.14.

She also exhorts them to think critically about spoken and written language they see or hear every day in all settings, for, "as the famous Russian linguist Mikhail Bakhtin believed, it is expression that organizes experience and not the other way around." The ideal classroom for promoting relationships and connection would be modeled on the female paradigm of gender-identity formation and prefer cooperation to competition; it would encourage collaborative writing, for instance, instead of "isolated 'self-expression'."[91]

7. *Using rock music to stimulate critical thinking about war.* The war themes of rock music, as McLaughlin points out, offer a basis for eliciting critical thinking. The fact that many students may already know these lyrics and will be startled to find them in the classroom only enhances the opportunity to maximize the "cognitive alienation" effect, as vital to teaching as to science fiction. Specific references include "My Future's So Bright I've Got to Wear Shades," by Timbuk 3, with a lyric about an atomic blast; "Russians," by Sting, an attempt to humanize the "enemy" by showing them as loving their children; Bob Marley's "War" from the album *Rastaman Vibration;* U2's "Like a Song" and "Seconds"; Joe Jackson's "Right and Wrong" from the album *It's a Big World;* and the Police's "Bombs Away" from *Zenyatta Mondatta,* on the theme of government hypocrisy. There is much to be said for opening up the classroom to the so-called nonliterary (by traditional lights), for much is missed by limiting our attention to what is labeled "literature." As McLaughlin says, those who are writing about their concern over the nuclear threat are not necessarily published by mainstream publishers; rather, "their medium is music; their message is peace; and we're hearing it on the radio, not studying it in the classroom."[92] The kind of critical thinking McLaughlin's approach exemplifies, including media other than the printed word, is essential in today's highly manipulative culture, in which no one escapes being besieged by an overload of information, all of it inevitably overlaid with ideological bias, and very little of it, in all likelihood, oriented to a biophilic survival ethic.

8. *Exercise in the application of Houston's criteria for visionary science fiction.* Jean Houston's criteria, discussed earlier in this chapter, are an excellent starting point for challenging students to think critically about visions of the future set forth by writers of all kinds. It would be illuminating to apply them, for instance, to the *Firebrats* series.

91. Ibid., p. 9. See Williams, "Alignment and Commitment," p. 127, for comment on collaborative writing.
92. McLaughlin, "In the Classroom," p. 10.

The International Outlook:
U.S.–USSR Exchange of Visions
of the Future

Along with the recent heartening development of an atmosphere of reasoned discourse between the United States and the USSR, scholarly attention is beginning to be paid to how Soviet authors and filmmakers have imagined a nuclear holocaust. Two recent sources need mention: "Nuclear War Themes in Soviet Science Fiction: An Annotated Bibliography'," by Vladimir Gakov and Paul Brians; and "And That Was the Future: The World Will End Tomorrow," by Paul Brians. The latter article gives a bird's-eye view of the past forty years of stories about "the last great war on planet Earth." Brians also identifies some highlights from recent Soviet nuclear fiction and the post-holocaust film, *Letters from a Dead Man*—"a powerful portrait of the collapse of civilization as the few remaining humans prepare to take refuge underground from the nuclear winter which has followed an accidentally caused nuclear holocaust."[93] Vladimir Gakov plans to bring out an anthology of Soviet nuclear war fiction to make available for the first time a major sampling of Soviet writers on the topic.

Brians raises provocative questions about the "future of the nuclear future": Will the progress of disarmament mean that interest in the subject will decline? Will the vogue for "macho nuclear adventure fiction" wear itself out? Will more women contribute their distinctive perspective? Will writers from Third World countries, as nuclear proliferation continues, add to their almost nonexistent contributions to nuclear fiction?[94] All of these questions are well worth scrutiny and suggest directions for further research.

The annotated bibliography by Gakov and Brians, "Nuclear-War Themes in Soviet Science Fiction," is a unique resource containing sixty entries, with a number available in English translation. Besides the Gakov anthology, *Prisoners of Power* by Arkady and Boris Strugatsky, a tale of the consequences of a limited nuclear war on a distant planet, is singled out for special praise. It is hoped that works such as Vladimir Mikhailov's *Togda pridite i rassudim* (Come Then and Let Us Reason Together) will also soon be available in English; this particular novel is called a "brilliant combination of two major themes: the nuclear arms

93. Paul Brians, "And That Was the Future: The World Will End Tomorrow," *Futures* (August 1988), p. 433.
    94. Ibid.

race and ecological damage," starting from the premise that "the danger of humankind's atomic self-destruction is merely Nature's defensive reaction against humanity's brutal attack on her" (a thesis certain to be appreciated by Noel and Giegerich, among others).[95]

Full Circle: The Biophile's Ethic

This quest for a life-affirming survival ethic in literature of nuclear holocaust has come full circle. It began with reasons for searching out a functional mythic paradigm to lead us, as myth is meant to do, into the future. Whether we are still like LeGuin's Backward-Head people, caught in self-destructive, dichotomous, "machine" modes of thinking, or more like Jean Houston's "people of the parentheses," seeking individual and social transformation through a change in consciousness, one thing seems quite certain: A paradigm shift toward a perspective of reality as relationship holds our best hope for survival. The biophile proposed as the hero or hera for this time of fragmentation, adultism, and the unprecedented stresses of a global demand on our consciousness is the standard bearer of a new, relational way of thinking, holistic, personal and transpersonal, egalitarian and inclusive rather than exclusive, spurred by love of the Earth and all creation.

An earlier chapter suggested Gaia as a logo for the biophile. It has become a symbol so pervasive, so commonplace in various media that its power as a poetic image is at risk of being trivialized. We need constantly to see Gaia with new awareness of her wonders. The January 2 1989, issue of *Time* magazine, in place of the Man or Woman of the Year, featured on its cover the Planet of the Year, showing a fettered, embattled Earth.[96] Certainly it is admirable to give this attention to our long-suffering planet, but honoring Earth for only one year will do little to solve our problems. Will such celebrity spoil Gaia? I think not. Like Cleopatra, nothing will spoil her infinite variety, except perhaps

---

95. Vladimir Gakov and Paul Brians, "Nuclear-War Themes in Soviet Science Fiction: An Annotated Bibliography," *Science Fiction Studies* 16, pt. 1 (March 1989), pp. 77–78.

96. *U.S. News and World Report* had earlier featured "Planet Earth" on its October 31, 1988, cover with the caption, "How It Works: How to Fix It" (revealing the hubristic assumptions that first, we *know* how it works, and second, we can "fix" it—rather than, as Thomas Berry and other adherents of deep ecology believe, that we must respect Earth's own rhythms and look to Earth herself for the wisdom to find a balance between our demands on her and what she can sustain). The cover of *National Geographic* 174, no. 6 (December 1988) featured a holographic image of the "Endangered Earth" with the question, "Can Man Save This Fragile Earth?" (Why not consult women?)

her wayward, thoughtless children, we Earthlings. If we fail at the modest heroism of affirming the value of life, will the Original Beholder revive Gaia, as in Aldiss's fiction?

This we cannot know, but one thing is within our certain grasp: We can take responsibility for our choices. Ursula LeGuin in her essay on "Heroes" reassesses two great English explorers of Antarctica—Robert Falcon Scott (1868–1912) and Ernest Henry Shackleton (1874–1922). She notes Shackleton's "pernicious" identification of Nature as an enemy "arrayed against us" (a phrase from his journal): After all, LeGuin reasons, it distorts reality to suppose we can challenge Nature or that Nature sets herself in opposition to us petty humans. Readers interested in sorting out LeGuin's complex evaluations of the two men—her admiration for Scott as "that unheroic creature, a writer . . . who saved what could be saved from defeat, suffering and death" (through the artistry of his journal record), and her rejection of Shackleton's attitude of "playing hero" and "posturing" in blaming Nature for his "defeat" (though she loves him for saving his men and believes he acted rightly)—should read her fine essay. Scott displayed "real heroism" in her estimation because he took responsibility for his failure, "witnessed truly," and "kept on telling the story."[97] Scott seems to have operated by certain assumptions of what I would deem the "old" heroic mythology, for the overriding image is that of a lone, stoic figure, vainglorious, heedless of the lives of others. In contrast, Shackleton helped his men to survive against remarkable odds, through mutual nurturance and cooperation.[98] He comes closer to the biophilic ideal, for all his lack of distinction as an artist. It is not surprising that LeGuin should hold Scott in higher esteem, being the writer she is.

There are no easy certainties about what constitutes heroism in our time, and it is well to remember Marcello Mastroianni's remark, quoting the film director Antonioni: "Who's a hero under the atomic bomb? Or who isn't one?"[99] The most expressive image for the need to

97. Ursula LeGuin, "Heroes (1986)," in *Dancing at the Edge of the World*, pp. 172–75, passim.

98. Robert Falcon Scott's diary was published as *Scott's Last Expedition*, ed. Leonard Huxley, with a preface by Clements R. Markham (London: Macmillan, 1913; Dodd, Mead, 1964). Ernest Henry Shackleton wrote *The Heart of Antarctica: Being the Story of the British Antarctic Expedition, 1907–1909* (Philadelphia: Lippincott, 1909). Shackleton also wrote *South* (New York: Macmillan, 1926). The reader may consult *Shackleton, His Antarctic Writings (Selections)* (New York: P. Bedrick Books, 1983). The most enthralling account of Shackleton's adventures, however, may be Alfred Lansing's *Endurance: Shackleton's Incredible Voyage* (New York: McGraw-Hill, 1959; Carroll and Graf, 1986).

99. Quoted in Robert Jay Lifton, *The Broken Connection: On Death and the Continuity of Life* (New York: Basic Books, 1979), p. 342n.

find a balance between our human connectedness on one hand and our separateness and individuality on the other may be the net or web. As images of connectedness, the net and web relate to Gaia, as all symbolize interrelatedness. However, the ambiguous and paradoxical qualities of human relationships may be more adequately visualized in the net/web metaphor.

Transpersonal psychoanalyst Ralph Metzner, in his article "Knots, Ties, Nets, and Bonds in Relationship," explores the net as an image in the classical Greek myth of the liaison between the goddess of love, Aphrodite, and the god of war, Ares. Aphrodite's official husband, Hephaistos, the lame blacksmith of the gods, secretly fashions a net of strong, gossamer-fine golden threads that he uses to capture the adulterous and clandestine lovers. He then summons the other Olympians to behold the spectacle of the illicit lovers caught in his web. Surprised and immobilized, they become figures of ridicule. In this example the net represents what Metzner calls the "tender trap" of love, humorously rendered.

The etymologies of *net* and *noose* can be traced to the Latin *nectere*, meaning to bind, fasten, or tie, but *nectere* is also the root of *node*, *nexus*, and *connection*.[100] The human predicament is to be bound by the same ties that link us to others. The net can be negative (restricting) or positive (connecting; cf. E. M. Forster's "only connect"). The net or tie is transformed from negative to positive if *consciously*, intentionally chosen:

> A net, or tie, or bind is experienced as limiting or immobilizing if we are caught or trapped involuntarily—then we are the victims. If on the other hand we use it consciously and intentionally, then the tie, or network, or connection provides the channels by means of which communication and the exchange of energy can take place.

If the intention is free, "captivity" is transformed to "liberation."[101]

Metzner draws a parallel between the "captivity/liberation" paradox and the similarly interwoven concepts of fate and destiny. In Indian thought, Fate or Karma is decreed, fixed, unavoidable—an outgrowth of past actions. Destiny, on the other hand, corresponds loosely with the Indian *dharma*, for it is "future-oriented, free and flexible: it is our purpose or destination, what we choose to be and do, our prime intention in life." We live out our destinies through exercising

---

100. Ralph Metzner, "Knots, Ties, Nets, and Bonds in Relationship," *Journal of Transpersonal Psychology* 17, no. 1 (1985):43.

101. Ibid., p. 44.

choice, in cooperative relationships with others. If we succeed in liberating our wills from the consequences of "past, karmic actions and tendencies," we are freed to experience ourselves not as "victims of fate" but as responsible for our destinies—free to choose our freedom.[102] In Pearson's scheme of archetypes, we can transcend the Martyr to become the Magician.

What can all of this tell us in the context of our nuclear-imperiled plight? I suggest that the hero/hera for our nuclear era is that person, whether a real, breathing human being or a fictional construct of one, who gives us the boon of freedom from the false myths of karmic, fated destruction, and engenders in their stead a clear vision of the *dharma* or destiny we may freely choose—intend and freely choose—to be life-honoring, Earth-valuing cocreators of our universe. We can become meaning-makers, dedicated to the overcoming of that which would negate life.

Wendell Berry offers wise guidance when he exhorts us to cease our "robbery" of nature, stop indulging in "fantasies" of the "infinite availability of finite resources" (perhaps our most flagrant self-deception), to "prefer small-scale elegance and generosity to large-scale greed, crudity, and glamor," to center our attentions on making communities, loving our actual neighbors (not those we would pick out), and to "find work, if you can, that does no damage. Enjoy your work. Work well." His is a call to an unsung, quiet acceptance of "the innate limits of human intelligence and responsibility."[103] This is a heroism that seeks no reward but the intrinsic satisfaction of beholding life in the process of fulfilling itself. It epitomizes a biophilic value system.

The literature of nuclear catastrophe can contribute significantly to embodying the biophile's vision of alternative *willed* futures. Much of it vividly depicts *unacceptable* futures and thereby delineates avenues to avoid. At their best, nuclear-catastrophe narratives have the emotive power to fill readers with the conviction that the irreplaceable, beloved planet Earth and every cherished thing upon it must be spared destruction—not only spared destruction, but nurtured and reverenced.

In concentrating attention on fiction of the possible future, it should not be forgotten that traditional literature also has much to say of the ideas and ideals that create the shape of things to come. Love for life

---

102. Ibid., p. 45.
103. Wendell Berry, "The Futility of Global Thinking," *Harper's Magazine*, September 1989, pp. 19, 22.

and Earth-wisdom are not new, only in need of translation into a space-age context. The wisdom of the past speaks even more eloquently today, as concerned thinkers seek responses to ever more difficult and challenging human dilemmas. In his introduction to Kevin Crossley-Holland's translation of *Beowulf*, Bruce Mitchell notes this connection across the ages:

> Today, in this nuclear age, with man's inhumanity to man daily more apparent on all levels and the powers of darkness in seeming ascendancy throughout the world, we may see *Beowulf* as a triumphant affirmation of the value of a good life: as the poet says, *Bruc ealles well*. [1.2163] Make good use of everything.[104]

"Good use" does not, in the context of the poem's heroic ethic, mean utilitarian exploitation, but something closer to "enjoyment," celebration of the inherent goodness of all things. Instead of being like Chronos, the ultimate consumer, or his children, the consumed, we can choose the way of the meaning-maker, a way of true humanness. We can make optimal "use" of the imagination's power to find connections, to see the well-being of all living things as linked both fearfully and wonderfully. We can look to our best writers for models of the "good use" of the gift of life. Life-cherishing is the basis of the biophile's survival ethic. Given such a life-prizing orientation, we may perhaps, like William Carlos Williams, be moved to value "everything we touch."

104. Bruce Mitchell, introduction to *Beowulf: A New Translation*, by Kevin Crossley-Holland, (New York: Farrar, Straus, and Giroux, 1968), p. 29.

Cumulative Bibliographies

Introduction

Primary Sources

Barker, Rodney. *The Hiroshima Maidens*. New York: Viking, 1985.

Briggs, Raymond. *When the Wind Blows*. New York: Schocken Books, 1982.

Bruckner, Karl D. *The Day of the Bomb*. New York: Van Nostrand, 1962.

Childress, Alice. *A Hero Ain't Nothin But a Sandwich*. New York: Coward-McCann, 1973.

Haugaard, Erik. *The Little Fishes*. Illustrated by Milton Johnson. Boston: Houghton Mifflin, 1971.

Hersey, John. *Hiroshima*. New York: Knopf; 1946, expanded ed. 1985.

Lawrence, Louise. *Children of the Dust*. New York: Harper and Row, 1985.

Lifton, Betty Jean. *A Place Called Hiroshima*. Photographs by Eikoh Hosoe. New York: Kodansha, 1985; distributed by Harper.

Maruki, Toshi. *Hiroshima no Pika*. New York: Knopf, 1985.

McIntyre, Vonda. *Dreamsnake*. Boston: Houghton Mifflin, 1978.

Miller, Walter M., Jr., *A Canticle for Leibowitz*. Philadelphia: Lippincott, 1959; New York: Bantam, 1961.

Nolan, Christopher. *Under the Eye of the Clock*. New York: St. Martin's Press, 1988.

O'Brien, Robert C. *Z for Zachariah*. New York: Atheneum, 1974.

O'Brien, Tim. *The Nuclear Age*. New York: Knopf, 1985.

Pausewang, Gudrun. *The Last Children of Schevenborn*. Translated by Norman Watt. Saskatoon, Saskatchewan: Western Producer Prairie Books, 1988. Reprinted in England as *The Last Children*. London: Julia MacRae, 1989. Originally published as *Die letzten Kinder von Schevenborn*. Ravensburg, Germany: Otto Maier, 1983.

Plath, Sylvia. *The Bell Jar*. London: Heineman, 1963 (Victoria Lucas, pseud.); New York: Bantam, 1971.

Shelley, Mary. *Frankenstein, or the Modern Prometheus*. 1818; Washington, D.C.: Orchises, 1988.

Strieber, Whitley. *Wolf of Shadows*. New York: Knopf, 1985.

Secondary Sources

ANTHROPOLOGY

Bateson, Gregory. "The Pattern Which Connects: Gregory Bateson," in *Uncommon Wisdom: Conversations with Remarkable People*. Edited by Fritjof Capra. New York: Bantam, 1988.

Gimbutas, Marija. "The First Wave of Eurasian Steppe Pastoralists into Copper Age Europe." *Journal of Indo-European Studies* 5 (Winter 1977): 277–338.

Levi-Strauss, Claude. *Structural Anthropology*. Translated by Claire Jacobsen and Brooke Grundfest Schoepf. New York: Basic Books, 1963.

CHILDREN'S LITERATURE

Cullinan, Berneice. *Literature and the Child*. 2d ed. New York: Harcourt Brace Jovanovich, 1989.

Hunter, Molly. "A Need for Heroes." *Horn Book Magazine* 59 (April 1983): 146–54.

Kaminski, Winifred. "War and Peace in Recent Children's Literature." Translated and adapted by J. D. Stahl. *Children's Literature: Annual of the Modern Language Division on Children's Literature and the Children's Literature Association*, 15 (1987): 55–66.

Kingston, Carolyn T. *The Tragic Mode in Children's Literature*. New York: Teachers College Press of Columbia University, 1974.

Literature for Today's Young Adults. Edited by Kenneth L. Donelson and Alleen Pace Nilsen. 3d ed. Glenview, Ill.: Scott, Foresman, 1989.

Sadker, Myra Pollack, and David Miller Sadker. *Now Upon a Time: A Contemporary View of Children's Literature*. New York: Harper and Row, 1977.

Twentieth Century Children's Writers. Edited by D. L. Kirkpatrick with a preface by Naomi Lewis. 2d ed. New York: St. Martin's Press, 1983.

HISTORY

Boyer, Paul. *By the Bomb's Early Light: American Thought and Culture at the Dawn of the Atomic Age*. New York: Pantheon, 1985.

Eisler, Riane. *The Chalice and the Blade: Our History, Our Future*. San Francisco: Harper and Row, 1987.

Weart, Spencer R. *Nuclear Fear: A History of Images*. Cambridge, Mass.: Harvard Univ. Pr., 1988.

LITERARY CRITICISM

Barr, Marleen S. *Alien to Femininity: Speculative Fiction and Feminist Theory*. New York: Greenwood Press, 1987.

Bartter, Martha. *The Way to Ground Zero: The Atomic Bomb in American Science Fiction*. New York: Greenwood Press, 1988.

Suvin, Darko. *Metamorphoses of Science Fiction.* New Haven, Conn.: Yale Univ. Pr., 1979.

MYTH

Campbell, Joseph. *The Hero with a Thousand Faces.* 1949; Princeton, N.J.: Princeton Univ. Pr., 1972.

_____. *The Inner Reaches of Outer Space.* New York: Van Der Marck Editions, 1985.

_____. *Myths to Live By.* Foreword by Johnson E. Fairchild. New York: Bantam, 1973.

DuPlessis, Rachel Blau. "Psyche, or Wholeness." *Massachusetts Review* 20 (Spring 1979): 76–96.

Edwards, Lee R. *Psyche as Hero: Female Heroism and Fictional Form.* Middleton, Conn.: Wesleyan Univ. Pr., 1984.

Hopcke, Robert. *A Guided Tour of the Collected Works of C. G. Jung.* Foreword by Aryeh Maidenbaum. Boston: Shambhala Publications, 1989.

Kung-Sun, Yang. *Book of the Lord Shang.* Translated by J. J. L. Duyvendak, with an introduction and notes. San Francisco: Chinese Materials Center, 1974.

LeGuin, Ursula. "Heroes." In *Dancing at the Edge of the World: Thoughts on Words, Women, Places.* New York: Grove Press, 1989.

Neumann, Erich. *Amor and Psyche: The Psychic Development of the Feminine, a Commentary on the Tale by Apuleius.* Translated from the German by Ralph Mannheim. Princeton, N.J.: Princeton Univ. Pr., 1956.

Pearson, Carol S. *The Hero Within: Six Archetypes We Live By.* San Francisco: Harper and Row, 1989.

Stone, Merlin. *Ancient Mirrors of Womanhood: A Treasury of Goddess and Heroine Lore from Around the World.* Boston: Beacon Press, 1979.

_____. *When God Was a Woman.* San Diego: Harcourt Brace Jovanovich, 1976. Published in England as *The Paradise Papers* by Virago, Ltd.

Sun-Tzu. *The Art of War.* Translated by Samuel B. Griffith. Foreword by B. H. Liddell Hart. New York: Oxford Univ. Pr., 1963.

Walker, Alice. *In Search of Our Mother's Gardens.* New York: Harcourt Brace Jovanovich, 1983.

Weart, Spencer R. *Nuclear Fear: A History of Images.* Cambridge, Mass.: Harvard Univ. Pr., 1988.

Wilmer, Harry A. "Archetypes." In *Practical Jung: Nuts and Bolts of Jungian Psychotherapy.* Wilmette, Ill.: Chiron Publications, 1987.

PHILOSOPHY AND RELIGION

Berry, Thomas. *The Dream of the Earth.* San Francisco: Sierra Club Books, 1988.

Brand, Stewart. *II Cybernetic Frontiers.* New York: Random House/Bookworks, 1974.

Eliade, Mircea. *Cosmos and History*. Translated by Willard R. Trask. New York: Harper, 1959.

Facing Apocalypse. Edited by Valerie Andrews, Robert Bosnak, and Karen Walter Goodwin. Dallas: Spring Publications, 1987.

Fox, Matthew. *A Spirituality Named Compassion and the Healing of the Global Village, Humpty-Dumpty, and Us*. San Francisco: Harper and Row, 1979.

———, and Brian Swimme, *Manifesto for a Global Civilization*. Santa Fe, N. Mex.: Bear Books, 1982.

Keen, Sam. ''Original Blessing, Not Original Sin: A Conversation with Matthew Fox.'' *Psychology Today* (June 1989), pp. 54-58.

Meeker, Joseph. *The Comedy of Survival: In Search of an Environmental Ethic*. Foreword by Konrad Lorenz. Introduction by Paul Shepard. Illustrated by William Berry. Los Angeles: Guild of Tutors Press, 1980.

Miller, Arthur. ''Tragedy and the Common Man.'' *New York Times*, February 27, 1949, sec. 2, pp. 1, 3. Reprinted in *The Theater Essays of Arthur Miller*. Edited with an introduction by Robert Martin. Foreword by Arthur Miller. New York: Viking, 1978.

The Promise of World Peace. Haifa: Baha'i World Center, 1985.

Rose, Hilary. ''Hand, Brain, and Heart; A Feminist Epistemology for the Natural Sciences.'' *Signs* 9 (Autumn 1983): 73–90.

Stanton, Elizabeth Cady. *The Woman's Bible*. 1895–98; New York: Arno Press, 1972.

Thompson, William Irwin. *Darkness and Scattered Light: Four Talks on the Future*. Garden City, N.Y.: Doubleday, 1978.

Turner, Victor. *The Ritual Process: Structure and Antistructure*. Hammondsworth, England: Penguin/Pelican, 1974.

PSYCHOLOGY

Gilligan, Carol. *In a Different Voice: Psychological Theory and Women's Development*. Boston: Beacon Press, 1976.

Miller, Jean Baker. *Toward a New Psychology of Women*. Cambridge, Mass.: Harvard Univ. Pr., 1982.

Chapter 1. The Role of a New Heroic Model

Primary Sources

Burdick, Eugene, and Harvey Wheeler, Jr. *Fail-Safe*. New York: McGraw-Hill, 1962; Dell, 1969.

Childress, Alice. *A Hero Ain't Nothin' But a Sandwich*. New York: Avon, 1974.

Dennis, Nigel. *House in Order*. New York: Vanguard Press, 1966.

Des Pres, Terrence. "Self/Landscape/Grid." In *Writing in a Nuclear Age.* Edited by Jim Schley. Hanover, N.H.: University Press of New England, 1984.

Elder, John. "Seeing Through the Fire." In *Writing in a Nuclear Age.* Edited by Jim Schley. Hanover, N.H.: University Press of New England, 1984.

Frank, Pat. *Alas! Babylon.* Philadelphia: Lippincott, 1959.

Grosholz, Emily. "Arms and the Muse: Four Poets." In *Writing in a Nuclear Age.* Edited by Jim Schley. Hanover, N.H.: University Press of New England, 1984.

Holst, Spencer. "The Zebra Storyteller." In *Fantastic Worlds: Myths, Tales and Stories.* Edited with commentaries by Eric S. Rabkin. New York: Oxford Univ. Pr., 1979.

Kaplan, Milton. "Atomic Bomb" [poem]. In *Commentary,* March 1948, p. 262.

O'Brien, Tim. *The Nuclear Age.* New York: Alfred A. Knopf, 1985.

Percy, Walker. *The Thanatos Syndrome.* New York: Farrar, Straus, and Giroux, 1987.

Roshwald, Mordecai. *Level 7.* New York: McGraw-Hill, 1959.

Vonnegut, Kurt. "War Preparer's Anonymous" [speech]. *Harper's* 268, no. 1606 (March 1984): 41.

Writing in a Nuclear Age. Edited by Jim Schley. *NER/BLQ: New England Review and Bread Loaf Quarterly* 5, no. 4 (Summer 1983); Hanover, N.H.: University of New England Press, 1984.

Secondary Sources

EDUCATION AND PSYCHOLOGY

Bachman, Jerald G. and Lloyd Johnston. *Monitoring the Future.* Ann Arbor: Univ. of Michigan, Institute for Social Research, 1975– . Annual.

Barth, Joseph. *The Art of Staying Sane.* Boston: Beacon Press, 1948.

Beardslee, William, and John Mack. *Psychosocial Aspects of Nuclear Developments: A Report of the Task Force on Psychosocial Aspects of Nuclear Developments of the American Psychiatric Association.* Washington, D.C.: The Association, 1982.

Buergenthal, T., and J. Torney. *International Human Rights and International Education.* Washington, D.C.: UNESCO, 1976.

Coles, Robert. "Children and the Bomb." Adapted from *The Moral Life of Children* (Atlantic Monthly Press, 1986). In *New York Times Magazine Section,* December 8, 1985.

"Education and the Threat of Nuclear War." *Harvard Educational Review* 54 (August 1984).

Education for Peace and Disarmament: Toward a Living World. Edited by Douglas Sloan. New York: Teachers College Press, 1983.

Escalona, Sibylle. "Children and the Threat of Nuclear War." In *Behavioral Science and Human Survival.* Edited by Milton Schwebel. Palo Alto, Calif.: Science and Behavior Books, 1965.

"The Face of the Enemy." *Psychology Today* 2 (1968): 24–29.

Frank, Jerome D. "Psychological Determinants of the Nuclear Arms Race." *Directions in Psychiatry*, Lesson 28. New York: Hatherleigh Company, 1981.
_____. *Sanity and Survival: Psychological Aspects of War and Peace*. New York: Random House, 1967.
_____. "Sociopsychological Aspects of the Nuclear Arms Race." In *Psychosocial Aspects of Nuclear Developments: A Report of the Task Force on Psychosocial Aspects of Nuclear Developments of the American Psychiatric Association*. Washington, D.C.: The Association, 1982.
LaFarge, Phyllis. *The Strangelove Legacy: Children, Parents and Teachers in the Nuclear Age*. New York: Harper and Row, 1987.
Law, N. *Children and War*. Washington, D.C.: Association for Childhood Education International, February 2, 1973.
Lifton, Robert J. *The Broken Connection: On Death and the Continuity of Life*. New York: Random House, 1967; New York: Basic Books, 1979.
_____. *Death in Life: Survivors of Hiroshima*. New York: Random House, 1967; New York: Touchstone Books, 1976.
_____. "The Psychologic Impact of the Threat of Extinction." *Directions in Psychiatry*, Lesson 27. New York: Hatherleigh Company, 1981.
Schwebel, Milton. "Nuclear Cold War: Student Opinions and Professional Responsibility." In *Behavioral Science and Human Survival*. Edited by Milton Schwebel. Palo Alto, Calif.: Science and Behavior Books, 1965.
_____. "What Do They Think about War?" In *Children and the Threat of Nuclear War*. Edited by the Child Study Association of America. New York: Duell, Sloan and Pearce, 1964.

FURTHER READING

Brians, Paul. "Nuclear Fiction for Children." *Bulletin of the Atomic Scientists*, 44, no. 6 (July/August 1988): 24–27.
Carlsson-Page, Nancy, and Diane E. Levin. *Helping Young Children Understand Peace, War, and the Nuclear Threat*. NAEYC Series, #321. Washington, D.C.: National Association for the Education of Young Children, 1985.
Children and War: Proceedings of Symposium at Siuntio Baths, Finland, March 24–27, 1983. Edited by Marianne Kahnert, David Pitt, and Ilkka Taipale. Geneva, Switzerland: GIPRI, 1983.
Gerzon, Mark. "Watching the World End: How Hollywood Faced Up to Nuclear War." *New Age Journal* (November 1983), p. 85.
Goldberg, Susan, comp. *Facing the Nuclear Age: Parents and Children Together*. Illustrated by Molly Barker. Toronto, Canada: Arrick Press, 1985.
Guenther, Nancy Anderman. *Children and the Threat of Nuclear War: An Annotated Bibliography*. CompuBibs #7. Brooklyn, N.Y.: CompuBibs, 1985.
U. S. Congress. House. Select Committee on Children, Youth, and Families. *Children's Fears of War: Hearing Before the Select Committee on Children, Youth, and Families, September 1983*. Washington, D.C.: 1984.

Van Ornum, William, and Mary Wicker Van Ornum. *Talking to Children about Nuclear War.* New York: Continuum, 1984.

Yudkin, Marcia. "When Kids Think the Unthinkable." *Psychology Today,* 18 (April 1984): 18–25.

LITERARY CRITICISM

Darko, Suvin. *Metamorphoses of Science Fiction: On the Poetics and History of a Literary Genre.* New Haven, Conn.: Yale Univ. Pr., 1979.

Marranca, Bonnie. "Nuclear Theatre." *Village Voice* (June 29, 1982), p. 103.

Wagar, Warren. *Terminal Visions: The Literature of Last Things.* Bloomington: Indiana Univ. Pr., 1982.

MYTH

Campbell, Joseph. *The Power of Myth,* with Bill Moyers. Edited by Betty Sue Flowers. New York: Doubleday, 1988.

Goleman, Daniel. "Personal Myths Bring Cohesion to the Chaos of Each Life." *New York Times Science Times,* May 24, 1988, pp. C1, C11–12.

PHILOSOPHY AND RELIGION

Anders, Gunther. "Reflections on the H-Bomb." In *Man Alone.* Edited by Eric and Mary Josephson. New York: Dell, 1962.

Camus, Albert. *Neither Victims nor Executioners.* Translated by Dwight Macdonald. With an introduction by R. Scott Kennedy and Peter Klotz-Chamberlain. Philadelphia: New Society Publishers, 1986.

Chernus, Ira. *Dr. Strangegod: On the Symbolic Meaning of Nuclear Weapons.* Columbia: Univ. of South Carolina Pr., 1986.

Education for Peace and Disarmament: Toward a Living World. Edited by Douglas Sloan. New York: Teachers College Press of Columbia University, 1983.

Eliade, Mircea. *Cosmos and History.* Translated by Willard R. Trask. New York: Harper, 1959.

Elliott, Gil. *Twentieth Century Book of the Dead.* New York: Charles Scribner's Sons, 1972.

Frank, Jerome D. *Sanity and Survival: Psychological Aspects of War and Peace.* New York: Random House, 1967.

Houston, Jean. *The Search for the Beloved: Journeys in Sacred Psychology.* Los Angeles: Jeremy P. Tarcher, 1987.

Schell, Jonathan. *The Fate of the Earth.* New York: Alfred A. Knopf, 1982.

Schneidman, Edwin S. "Megadeath: Children of the Nuclear Family." In *Deaths of Man.* Foreword by Arnold Toynbee. Baltimore, M.D.: Penguin Books, 1974.

Wilmer, Harry A. *Practical Jung: Nuts and Bolts of Jungian Psychotherapy.* Wilmette, Ill.: Chiron Publications, 1987.

SCIENCE

Conference on the Long-term Worldwide Biological Consequences of Nuclear War. Sheraton Washington Hotel, Washington, D.C., 1983, with Paul Ehrlich, Carl Sagan, Donald Kennedy, Walter Orr Roberts. *The Cold and the Dark: The World After Nuclear War.* Foreword by Lewis Thomas. New York: Norton, 1984.

Lovins, Amory B. and L. Hunter Lovins. *Energy/War: Breaking the Nuclear Link.* New York: Harper and Row, 1981, c. 1980.

Turco, R. P., O. B. Toon, T. P. Ackerman, J. B. Pollack, and Carl Sagan. "The Climatic Effects of Nuclear War." *Scientific American* 251, no. 2 (August 1984): 33–43.

_____. "Nuclear Winter: Global Consequences of Multiple Nuclear Explosions." *Science* 222 (December 23, 1983): 1283–92. The "TTAPS" paper.

SOCIOLOGY

Barash, David P., and Judith Eve Lipton. *The Caveman and the Bomb.* New York: McGraw-Hill, 1985.

Keniston, Kenneth. *Young Radicals.* New York: Harcourt Brace and World, 1968.

Chapter 2. Narratives of Life Lived in the Nuclear Shadow

Primary Sources

PICTURE BOOKS

Seuss, Dr. [Theodore S. Geisel]. *The Butter Battle Book.* New York: Random House, 1984.

Vigna, Judith. *Nobody Wants a Nuclear War.* Pictures by Judith Vigna. Niles, Ill.: Albert Whitman, 1986.

YOUNG ADULT AND POPULAR ADULT NOVELS

George, Peter. *Red Alert.* New York: Ace, 1958. Published in England as *Two Hours to Doom* (Boardman, 1958).

Hall, Lynn. *If Winter Comes.* New York: Charles Scribner's Sons, 1986.

O'Brien, Tim. *The Nuclear Age.* New York: Alfred A. Knopf, 1985.

Tolan, Stephanie. *The Pride of the Peacock.* New York: Charles Scribner's Sons, 1986.

Vonnegut, Kurt. *Cat's Cradle.* New York: Dell, 1970.

Wilhelm, Kate. "Countdown," in *The Downstairs Room and Other Speculative Fiction.* New York: Doubleday, 1968.

FILM SCRIPT

Southern, Terry, and Stanley Kubrick. *Dr. Strangelove, or How I Learned to Stop Worrying and Love the Bomb*. 93 min. Color RCA, 1964. Film script based on Peter George's novel, *Red Alert*.

FURTHER READING

Countdown to Midnight: Twelve Great Stories about Nuclear War. Edited with a historical introduction by H. Bruce Franklin. New York: Daw Books (Wollheim), 1984.

Oe, Kenzaburo, ed. *The Crazy Iris and Other Stories of the Atomic Aftermath*. New York: Grove Press, 1985.

Secondary Sources

EDUCATION AND PSYCHOLOGY

Bloom, Allan. *The Closing of the American Mind: How Higher Education Has Failed Democracy and Impoverished the Souls of Today's Students*. New York: Simon and Schuster, 1987.

Eiss, Harry. "Materials for Children about Nuclear War." A paper presented at the 18th Annual Meeting of the Popular Culture Association, New Orleans, March 23–26, 1988. Available as ERIC document ED 297 339.

Wilmer, Henry A. *Practical Jung: Nuts and Bolts of Jungian Psychotherapy*. Illustrated by Henry A. Wilmer. Wilmette, Ill.: Chiron, 1987.

LITERARY CRITICISM

Bartter, Martha A. "Nuclear Holocaust as Urban Renewal," *Science Fiction Studies* 13, pt. 2 (July 1986): 148–58.

Cech, John. "Some Leading, Blurred, and Violent Edges of the Contemporary Picture Book." *Children's Literature: The Annual of the Modern Language Association Division on Children's Literature and the Children's Literature Association* 15 (1987): 197–206.

Franklin, H. Bruce. "The Bomb in the Home: Stories by Japanese and American Women Experts on Nuclearism." Paper presented at the Modern Language Association Conference, New Orleans, December 28, 1988.

MacCannell, Dean. "Baltimore in the Morning . . . After: On the Forms of Post-Nuclear Leadership." *Diacritics* 14, no. 2 (Summer 1984): 33–46.

MYTHOLOGY AND RELIGION

Chernus, Ira. *Dr. Strangegod: On the Symbolic Meaning of Nuclear Weapons*. Columbia: Univ. of South Carolina Pr., 1986.

PHILOSOPHY

Schell, Jonathan. *The Fate of the Earth.* New York: Alfred A. Knopf, 1982.

SCIENCE

Sperry, Roger. *Science and Moral Priority: Merging Mind, Brain and Human Values.* New York: Columbia Univ. Pr., 1983.

Chapter 3. Voices from Hiroshima and Nagasaki

Primary Sources

PICTURE, COMIC, AND ILLUSTRATED BOOKS

Coerr, Eleanor. *Sadako and the Thousand Paper Cranes.* Illustrated by Ronald Himler. New York: G. P. Putnam, 1977.

Lifton, Betty Jean. *A Place Called Hiroshima.* Photographs by Eikoh Hosoe. Tokyo and New York: Kodansha, 1985; distributed by Harper and Row.

Maruki, Toshi. *Hiroshima no Pika.* Illustrated by Emil Antonucci. New York: Lathrop, Lee and Shepherd, 1982.

Mattingly, Christobel. *The Miracle Tree.* Illustrated by Marianne Yamaguchi. San Diego: Harcourt Brace Jovanovich, Gulliver Books, 1986.

Merton, Thomas. *The Original Child Bomb: Points for Meditation to Be Scratched on the Walls of a Cave.* Illustrated by Emil Antonucci. New York: New Directions, 1961.

Nakazawa, Keiji. *Barefoot Gen: A Cartoon Story of Hiroshima.* Illustrated by the author. 3 vols. Philadelphia: New Society Publishers, 1987–89. Originally published Tokyo: Project Gen, 1978–89.

Unforgettable Fire: Pictures Drawn by Atomic Bomb Survivors. Edited by the Japan Broadcasting Corporation (NHK). New York: Pantheon Books, 1981.

FICTION

Booth, Martin. *Hiroshima Joe.* Boston: Atlantic Monthly Press, 1985.

Clarkson, Helen. *The Last Day: A Novel of the Day after Tomorrow.* New York: Dodd, Mead, 1959.

Ibuse, Masuji. *Black Rain.* Originally *Kuroi Ame,* published in *Showa,* January 1965–September 1966. Reprint. Palo Alto: Kodansha International, 1969; New York: Bantam, 1985.

Kundera, Milan. *The Book of Laughter and Forgetting.* Translated from the Czech by Michael Henry Heim. New York: Penguin Books, 1981.

Kunetka, James, and Whitley Strieber. *Warday, and the Journey Onward.* New York: Holt, Rinehart and Winston, 1984.

Lanham, Edwin. *The Clock at 8:16: A Novel about Hiroshima.* Garden City, N.Y.: Doubleday, 1970.

Oe, Kenzaburo, ed. *The Crazy Iris and Other Stories of the Atomic Aftermath*. New York: Grove Press, 1985.

Paulsen, Gary. *Sentries*. New York: Bradbury, 1986.

Swarthout, Glendon. *Bless the Beasts and Children*. New York: Doubleday, 1970.

NONFICTION

Bruckner, Karl. *The Day of the Bomb*. Translated by Frances Lobb. Princeton, N.J.: D. Van Nostrand, 1962.

Goldman, Peter, et al. *The End of the World That Was: Six Lives in the Atomic Age*. New York: New American Library, 1986.

Hersey, John. *Hiroshima*. New York: Knopf, 1946. Originally published in the *New Yorker*, August 31, 1946.

Arata Osada, ed. *Children of Hiroshima*. Tokyo: Publishing Committee for "Children of Hiroshima," 1980; London: Taylor and Francis Ltd., 1981. Originally published as *Gembaku no ko*, 1951.

Sanders, Scott. "At Play in the Paradise of Bombs." *North American Review* 268, no. 3 (September 1983): 55–58.

ART

Maruki, Iri, and Toshi Maruki. *The Hiroshima Murals*. Edited by John W. Dower and John Junkerman. Tokyo: Kodansha International Ltd., 1985.

POETRY

Contemporary American Poetry. Edited by A. Poulin, Jr. Boston: Houghton Mifflin, 1971.

Dickey, William. "Armageddon." In *Writing in a Nuclear Age*. Edited by Jim Schley. *NER/BLQ: New England Review and Bread Loaf Quarterly* 5, no. 4 (Summer 1983). Reprint. Hanover, N.H.: University Press of New England, 1984.

RECORDED INTERVIEWS

Ginsberg, Allan. Interview, June 12, 1988, National Public Radio, WAMC, Albany, N.Y.

Halifax, Joan. *Way of the Warrior*. New Dimensions Radio, P.O. Box 410510, San Francisco, CA 94141–0510.

Secondary Sources

ECOLOGY AND ETHICS

Leopold, Aldo. *A Sand County Almanac*. New York: Oxford Univ. Pr., 1966.

Meeker, Joseph W. *The Comedy of Survival: In Search of an Environmental Ethic*. Los Angeles: International College Guild of Tutors Press, 1980.

EDUCATION AND PSYCHOLOGY

Education for Peace and Disarmament: Toward a Living World. Edited by Douglas Sloan. New York: Teachers College Press, 1983.

LaFarge, Phyllis. *The Strangelove Legacy: Children, Parents, and Teachers in the Nuclear Age*. New York: Harper and Row, 1987.

Lifton, Robert J. *Death in Life: The Survivors of Hiroshima*. New York: Random House, 1967.

Mindell, Arnold. *Coma: Key to Awakening*. Boston: Shambhala, 1989.

Musil, Robert. "Teaching in a Nuclear Age." In *Education for Peace and Disarmament: Toward a Living World*. Edited by Douglas Sloan. New York: Teachers College Press, 1983.

LITERARY CRITICISM AND BIBLIOGRAPHY

Babbitt, Natalie. Review of *Hiroshima no Pika* by Toshi Maruki. *New York Times Book Review*, October 10, 1982, p. 24.

Brians, Paul. *Nuclear Holocausts: Atomic War in Fiction 1895–1984*. Kent, Ohio: Kent State Univ. Pr., 1987.

Briley, Dorothy. "*Hiroshima no Pika*." Paper presented at Simmons College Institute, "Do I Dare Disturb the Universe?" Boston, July 18, 1983. Quoted by Barbara Harrison. "Howl Like the Wolves." *Children's Literature: Annual of the Modern Language Association Division on Children's Literature and the Children's Literature Association* 15 (1987): 79.

Franklin, H. Bruce. "The Bomb in the Home: Stories by Japanese and American Women Experts on Nuclearism." Paper presented at the Modern Language Association Convention, New Orleans, December 28, 1988.

Harrison, Barbara. "Howl Like the Wolves." *Children's Literature: Annual of the Modern Language Association Division on Children's Literature and the Children's Literature Association* 15 (1987): 67–90.

Kingston, Carolyn. *The Tragic Mode in Children's Literature*. New York: Teachers College Press, 1974.

Pines, Maya. "A Garden of Terrors." Review of *The Strangelove Legacy: Children, Parents, and Teachers in the Nuclear Age*, by Phyllis LaFarge. *New York Times Book Review*, March 22, 1987, p. 38.

Schwenger, Peter. "Writing the Unthinkable." *Critical Inquiry* 13, no. 1 (Autumn 1986): 33–48.

MYTH AND RELIGION

Chernus, Ira. *Dr. Strangegod: On the Symbolic Meaning of Nuclear Weapons*. Columbia: Univ. of South Carolina Pr., 1986.

Eisler, Riane. *The Chalice and the Blade: Our History, Our Future*. San Francisco: Harper, 1987.

Schmookler, Andrew Bard. *Out of Weakness: Healing the Wounds That Drive Us to War*. New York: Bantam, 1988.

SOCIOLOGY

Barash, David P., and Judith Eve Lipton. *The Caveman and the Bomb.* New York: McGraw-Hill, 1985.

Chapter 4. The Peace Pilgrim as Hero/Hera

Primary Sources

PICTURE AND ILLUSTRATED BOOKS

Benson, Bernard. *The Peace Book.* Illustrated by the author. New York: Bantam, 1982.

Briggs, Raymond. *When the Wind Blows.* Illustrated by the author. New York: Schocken Books, 1982.

Bydlinski, Georg, and Hans Domenego. *Macht die Erde nicht kaput!* Freiburg, Germany: Herder, 1984.

Kastner, Erich. *Die Konferenz der Tiere* (The Conference of the Animals). Illustrated by Walter Trier. Hamburg: Deutscher Bucherbund, 1949.

Peet, Bill. *The Wump World.* Boston: Houghton Mifflin, 1970.

Ruprecht, Frank. *Jakob's Traum.* Stuttgart: Otto Maier, 1983.

Schmogner, Walter. *Das neue Drachenbuch.* Frankfurt: Insel, 1981.

Dr. Seuss [Theodore Seuss Geisel]. *The Lorax.* New York: Random House, 1971.

Thiele, Colin. *The Sknuks/The Skunks.* Illustrated by Mary Milton. Rigby Publishing, 1977; distributed by Weldon Publishing, 372 Eastern Valley Way, Willoughby, NSW 2068, Australia. Published in German as *Die Ttupak! Die Kaputt!* (Modling, Austria: St. Gabriel, 1977).

FICTION

Langton, Jane. *The Fragile Flag.* New York: Harper and Row, 1984.

Madison, Arnold. *It Can't Happen to Me.* New York: Scholastic, 1981.

Naylor, Phyllis. *The Dark of the Tunnel.* New York: Atheneum, 1985.

Percy, Walker. *The Thanatos Syndrome.* New York: Farrar, Straus, and Giroux, 1987.

Thompson, Julian. *Band of Angels.* New York: Scholastic, 1986.

NONFICTION

Meltzer, Milton. *Ain't Gonna Study War No More: The Story of America's Peace Seekers.* New York: Harper, 1985.

Moore, Melinda, and Laurie Olsen, with the Citizens Policy Center Nuclear Action Youth Project. *Our Future at Stake: A Teenager's Guide to Stopping the*

Nuclear Arms Race. Illustrated with photographs. Philadelphia: New Society Publishers, 1985.

Peace Pilgrim: Her Life and Work in Her Own Words. Compiled by some of her friends. Santa Fe, N. Mex.: Friends of Peace Pilgrim, 1983. Available at no charge from Friends of Peace Pilgrim, 43480 Cedar Avenue, Hemet, CA 92344.

Pirtle, Sarah. *Outbreak of Peace*. Philadelphia: New Society Publishers, 1987.

Steps toward Inner Peace: Suggested Uses of Harmonious Principles for Human Living: A Discourse by Peace Pilgrim. Hemet, Calif.: Friends of Peace Pilgrim, n.d. Available at no charge from Friends of Peace Pilgrim, 43480 Cedar Avenue, Hemet, CA 92344.

DRAMA

Woollcombe, David. *The Peace Child*. Based on *The Peace Book* by Bernard Benson. Washington, D.C.: The Peace Child Foundation, P.O. Box 33168, Washington DC 20033.

POETRY

Hagedorn, Hermann. *The Bomb That Fell on America*. Santa Barbara, Calif.: Pacific Coast Publishing Co., 1946.

Secondary Sources

EDUCATION AND PSYCHOLOGY

Christie, Daniel J., and Linden Nelson. "Student Reactions to Nuclear Education." *Bulletin of the Atomic Scientists* 44, no. 6 (July/August 1988): 22–23.

Jampolsky, G. G. *Children as Teachers of Peace*. Foreword by Hugh Prather. Millbrae, Calif.: Celestial Arts, 1982.

Kath, Ruth. "Nuclear Education in Contemporary German Children's Literature." *The Lion and the Unicorn: The International Scene* 18 (1986): 31–39.

LaFarge, Phyllis. *The Strangelove Legacy: Children, Parents and Teachers in the Nuclear Age*. New York: Harper and Row, 1987.

Macy, Joanna Rogers. *Despair and Personal Power in the Nuclear Age*. Philadelphia: New Society Publishers, 1983.

_____. *Despairwork: Awakening to the Peril and Promise of Our Time*. Philadelphia: New Society Publishers, 1982.

Simon, Roger I. "Empowerment as a Pedagogy of Possibility." *Language Arts* 64, no. 4 (April 1987): 370–82.

Winter, Metta L. "Nuclear Education Update." *School Library Journal* (January 1986): 22–26.

LITERARY CRITICISM

Ball, Patricia M. *The Central Self: A Study in Romantic and Victorian Imagination*. London: Athlone Press, 1968.

Gakov, Vladimir, and Paul Brians. "Nuclear War Themes in Soviet Science Fiction: An Annotated Bibliography." *Science Fiction Studies* 16, pt. 1 (March 1989): 67–84.

Kaminski, Winifred. "War and Peace in Recent German Children's Literature." Translated and adapted by J. D. Stahl. *Children's Literature: Annual of the Modern Language Division on Children's Literature and the Children's Literature Association* 15 (1987): 55–66.

Kath, Ruth. "Nuclear Education in Contemporary German Children's Literature." *The Lion and the Unicorn: The International Scene* 18 (1986): 31–39.

MYTH AND RELIGION

Fox, Matthew. *Original Blessing: A Primer in Creation Spirituality.* Santa Fe, N.Mex.: Bear and Co, 1983.

LaChapelle, Dolores. *Earth Wisdom.* Photographs by Steven J. Meyers. Drawings by Randy LaChapelle. Los Angeles: Guild of Tutors Press, 1978.

Macy, Joanna Rogers. "Learning to Sustain the Gaze." In *Facing Apocalypse.* Edited by Valerie Andrews, Robert Bosnak, and Karen Walter Goodwin. Dallas, Tex.: Spring Publications, 1987.

Watkins, Mary. "In Dreams Begin Responsibilities': Moral Imagination and Peace Action." In *Facing Apocalypse.* Edited by Valerie Andrews, Robert Bosnak, and Karen Walter Goodwin. Dallas, Tex.: Spring Publications, 1987.

REVIEWS

Review of *The Peace Book,* by Bernard Benson, *Booklist* 79, no. 7 (December 1, 1982): 466.

SOCIOLOGY

Protest and Survive. Edited by E. P. Thompson and Dan Smith. Drawings by Marshall Arisman. New York: Monthly Press Review, 1981.

Chapter 5. Scenarios of End-Time

Primary Sources

PICTURE BOOKS

Briggs, Raymond. *When the Wind Blows.* New York: Schocken Books, 1982.

de Brunhoff, Jean. *The Story of Babar.* Translated by Merle Haas. New York: Random House, 1933.

Eco, Umberto. *The Bomb and the General.* Illustrated by Eugenio Carmi. Orlando,

Fla.: Harcourt Brace Jovanovich, 1989. Originally published as *La bomba e il generale* (Italy: Gruppo Editoriale Fabbri-Bompiani, Sonzogno, Etas S.p.A.).

PICTURE BOOK IN VIDEO FORMAT

Briggs, Raymond. *When the Wind Blows*. [Video] With the voices of Sir John Mills, Dame Peggy Ashcroft. Screenplay by Raymond Briggs, based on his illustrated book. Directed by Jimmy T. Murakami. 80 min. International Video Entertainment, 1987. Reviewed in *New York Times*, Sunday, June 19, 1988, Art/Leisure Section, p. 30.

DRAMA

Kopit, Arthur. *The End of the World*. New York: Hill and Wang, 1984.

FICTION

Bromley, Dudley. *Final Warning*. Chicago: Children's Press, 1982.

Bryant, Peter [Peter George]. *Red Alert*. New York: Ace, 1958. Published in England as *Two Hours to Doom*.

Burdick, Eugene, and John Harvey Wheeler, Jr. *Fail–Safe*. New York: McGraw-Hill, 1962.

Clarkson, Helen. *The Last Day*. New York: Dodd, Mead, 1959.

George, Jean Craighead. *Julie of the Wolves*. New York: Harper and Row, 1972.

George, Peter Bryant. *Dr. Strangelove; or How I Learned to Stop Worrying and Love the Bomb*. Reprint, with introduction by Richard Gid Powers. Boston: Gregg, 1979.

Kunetka, James W., and Whitley Strieber. *Warday, and the Journey Onward*. New York: Holt, Rinehart, and Winston, 1984.

Miller, Walter M., Jr. *A Canticle for Leibowitz*. Philadelphia: Lippincott, 1959; Bantam, 1961.

Mowat, Farley. *Never Cry Wolf*. Boston: Little, Brown, 1963.

Paulsen, Gary. *Sentries*. New York: Bradbury, 1986.

Pausewang, Gudrun. *The Last Children of Schevenborn*. Translated by Norman Watt. Saskatoon: Western Producer Prairie Books, 1988. Reprinted in England as *The Last Children* (London: Julia MacRae, 1989). *Die letzten Kinder von Schewenborn, oder sieht so unsere Zukunft aus?* Ravensburg, Germany: Otto Maier, 1983.

———. *Die Wolke*. Ravensburg, Germany: Otto Maier, 1987.

Roshwald, Mordecai. *Level 7*. New York: McGraw-Hill, 1959.

Shute, Nevil. *On the Beach*. New York: William Morrow, 1957.

Strieber, Whitley. *Wolf of Shadows*. New York: Sierra Club Books, 1985; distributed by Knopf.

Vonnegut, Kurt. *Cat's Cradle*. New York: Holt, Rinehart, and Winston, 1963; Dell, 1987.

FILMS

Kubrick, Stanley, and Terry Southern. *Dr. Strangelove, or How I Learned to Stop Worrying and Love the Bomb*. Directed by Stanley Kubrick. 93 min. Color. RCA, 1964.

NONFICTION

U.S. Civil Defense Preparedness Agency. *Your Chance to Live.* sm 3-12, 1972. Washington: GPO, 1973.

Vonnegut, Kurt. "A Letter to the Next Generation from Kurt Vonnegut, the Literary Wit of Our Time." *Time* 131, no. 6 (February 8, 1985): Special Advertising Section, unp.

SPEECHES

Hodgson, Edward S. "Education from Eden: Crucial Lessons from Coral Reefs." Speech given at dinner meeting of Phi Beta Kappa, Desmond Americana, Colonie, New York, April 30, 1988.

BOOK REVIEWS

Paterson, Katherine. Review of *Wolf of Shadows,* by Whitley Strieber, *New York Times Book Review,* December 1, 1985, p. 39.

HISTORY

Weart, Spencer R. *Nuclear Fear: A History of Images.* Cambridge, Mass.: Harvard Univ. Pr., 1988.

Secondary Sources
LITERARY AND FILM CRITICISM

Abrash, Merritt. "Through Logic to Apocalypse: Science Fiction Scenarios for Nuclear Deterrence Breakdown." *Science Fiction Studies* 13, pt. 2 (July 1986): 129–38.

Berger, Harold L. *Science Fiction and the New Dark Age.* Bowling Green, Ohio: Bowling Green Univ. Popular Press, 1976.

Brians, Paul. *Nuclear Holocausts: Atomic War in Fiction: 1895–1984.* Kent, Ohio: Kent State Univ. Pr., 1986.

Dowling, David. *Fictions of Nuclear Disaster.* Iowa City: Univ. of Iowa Pr., 1987.

DuPlessis, Rachel Blau. "Psyche and Wholeness." *Massachusetts Review* 20 (Spring 1979): 77–96.

Ferguson, Frances. "The Nuclear Sublime." *Diacritics* 14, no. 2 (Summer 1984): 4–11.

Franklin, H. Bruce. Introduction to *Countdown to Midnight: Twelve Great Stories about Nuclear War.* Edited by H. Bruce Franklin. New York: Daw Books, 1984.

Nuclear War Films. Edited by Jack G. Shaheen. Foreword by Marshall Flaum. Carbondale: Southern Illinois Univ. Pr., 1978.

Powers, Richard Gid. Introduction to *Dr. Strangelove, or How I Learned to Stop Worrying and Love the Bomb.* Reprint. Boston: Gregg, 1979.

Stableford, Brian. "Man-Made Catastrophes." In *The End of the World.* Edited by Eric S. Rabkin, Martin H. Greenberg, and Joseph D. Olander. Carbondale: Southern Illinois Univ. Pr., 1983.

Wagar, Warren. *Terminal Visions.* Bloomington: Indiana Univ. Pr., 1982.

Wolfe, Gary. "The Remaking of Zero: Beginning at the End." In *The End of the World.* Edited by Eric Rabkin, Martin H. Greenberg, and Joseph D. Olander. Carbondale: Southern Illinois Univ. Pr., 1983.

MYTH AND RELIGION

Eliade, Mircea. *Dreams and Mysteries.* Translated by Philip Mairet. New York: Harper and Row, 1975.

Mielke, Robert. "Imaging Nuclear Weaponry: An Ethical Taxonomy of Nuclear Representation." *Northwest Review: Warnings, an Anthology on the Nuclear Peril* 22, nos. 1, 2 (1984): 164–80.

Perlman, Mike. "When Heaven and Earth Collapse: Myths of the End of the World." In *Facing Apocalypse.* Edited by Valerie Andrews, Robert Bosnak, and Karen Walter Goodwin. Dallas, Tex.: Spring Publications, 1987.

Wasson, Robert G. *Soma, Divine Mushroom of Immortality.* New York: Harcourt Brace Jovanovich, 1971.

PSYCHOLOGY

Erikson, Erik. "A Developmental Crisis of Mankind." Unpublished paper quoted by Robert Lifton, "The Image of the End of the World." In *Facing Apocalypse.* Edited by Valerie Andrews, Robert Bosnak, and Karen Walter Goodwin. Dallas, Tex.: Spring Publications, 1987.

Goleman, Daniel. "Erikson, in His Own Old Age, Expands His View of Life." *New York Times,* June 14, 1988, p. C14.

SCIENCE

Bateson, Gregory. *Steps to an Ecology of Mind: A Revolutionary Approach to Man's Understanding of Himself.* New York: Ballantine Books, 1972.

Gore, Rick. "Extinctions." Photographs by Jonathan Blair. *National Geographic* 175, no. 6 (June 1989): 662–99.

McKibben, Bill. "Reflections: The End of Nature." *New Yorker,* September 11, 1989, pp. 47–105.

Trefil, James. "Stop to Consider the Stones That Fall from the Sky." *Smithsonian* 20, no. 6 (September 1989): 80–92.

SOCIOLOGY

Protest and Survive. Edited by E. P. Thompson and Dan Smith. Drawings by Marshall Arisman. New York: Monthly Press Review, 1981.

SOUND RECORDINGS

Fuller, Robert. *A Better Game Than War*. New Dimensions Radio, P.O. Box 410510, San Francisco, CA 94141-0510; n.d.

Chapter 6. Survivors in an Atomized Eden

Primary Sources

PICTURE BOOKS

Briggs, Raymond. *When the Wind Blows*. New York: Schocken Books, 1982.
Macaulay, David. *Baaa*. Boston: Houghton Mifflin, 1985.

COMIC BOOKS

Ellison, Harlan, and Richard Corben. *Vic and Blood*. New York: St. Martin's Press, 1989.

SHORT STORIES

Ellison, Harlan. "A Boy and His Dog." *New Worlds* (April 1969). Reprint. In *The Beast That Shouted Love at the Heart of the World*. New York: Signet, 1974.
Merril, Judith. "That Only a Mother." In *Astounding Science Fiction* (June 1948). Reprint. In *Isaac Asimov's Science Fiction Treasury*. Edited by Isaac Asimov, Martin Greenberg, and Joseph Olander. New York: Bonanza Books, 1980.

FICTION

Ahern, Jerry. *The Survivalist* Series. New York: Zebra, 1981– .
Atwood, Margaret. *The Handmaid's Tale*. New York: Fawcett, 1986.
Blumenfeld, Yorick. *Jenny, My Diary*. Boston: Little, Brown, 1982.
Carter, Angela. *Heroes and Villains*. New York: Simon and Schuster, 1969. Reprint. Penguin, 1981.
Cook, Paul. *Duende Meadow*. New York: Bantam Books, 1985.
Forman, James. *Doomsday Plus Twelve*. New York: Scribner's, 1984.
Frank, Pat. *Alas, Babylon*. Philadelphia: Lippincott, 1959. Reprint. New York: Bantam, 1960.
Hoban, Russell. *Turtle Diary*. New York: Random House, 1975.
Hoover, H. M. *Children of Morrow*. New York: Four Winds Press, 1973. The sequel is *Treasures of Morrow* (1976).
Huxley, Aldous. *Ape and Essence*. New York: Harper, 1948.

Johnson, Annabel and Edgar. *Danger Quotient*. New York: Harper and Row, 1984.

Kunetka, James, and Whitley Strieber. *Warday, and the Journey Onward*. New York: Holt, Rinehart and Winston, 1984.

Lawrence, Louise. *Children of the Dust*. New York: Harper, 1985.

Malamud, Bernard. *God's Grace*. New York: Farrar, Straus, and Giroux, 1982.

Merril, Judith. *Shadow on the Hearth*. Garden City, N.Y.: Doubleday, 1950.

_____. "That Only a Mother." In *Astounding Science Fiction* (June 1948). Reprint. In *Isaac Asimov's Science Fiction Treasury*. Edited by Isaac Asimov, Martin Greenberg, and Joseph Olander. New York: Bonanza Books, 1980.

Miklowitz, Gloria. *After the Bomb*. New York: Scholastic, 1984.

_____. *After the Bomb: Week One*. New York: Scholastic, 1987.

Naylor, Phyllis. *Dark of the Tunnel*. New York: Atheneum, 1985.

O'Brien, Robert C. *Z for Zachariah*. New York: Atheneum, 1975.

Palmer, David. *Emergence*. New York: Bantam, 1984.

Service, Pamela. *Winter of Magic's Return*. New York: Atheneum, 1985.

Siegel, Barbara, and Scott Siegel. *The Burning Land*. New York: Pocket Books, 1987.

_____. *The Survivors*. New York: Pocket Books, 1987.

_____. *Thunder Mountain*. New York: Pocket Books, 1987.

_____. *Shockwave*. New York: Pocket Books, 1988.

Wyndham, John. *Re-Birth, or the Chrysalids*. New York: Ballantine, 1955. Originally published as *The Chrysalids* (London: Michael Joseph, 1955).

Secondary Sources

BOOK REVIEWS

Dorris, Michael, and Louise Erdrich. "Bangs and Whimpers: Novelists at Armageddon." *New York Times Book Review*, March 13, 1988, pp. 1, 24–25.

Lukas, J. Anthony. "The Rapture and the Bomb." Review of *Blessed Assurance: At Home with the Bomb in Amarillo, Texas*, by A. G. Mojtaibai. *New York Times Book Review*, June 8, 1986, p. 7.

Williamson, Susan H. Review of *Warday, and the Journey Onward*, by James Kunetka and Whitley Strieber. *VOYA* 7 (February 1985): 340.

Zeiger, Hannah. Review of *Children of the Dust*, by Louise Lawrence. *Horn Book Magazine* 62, no. 1 (January/February 1986): 63.

HISTORY

Eisler, Riane. *The Chalice and the Blade: Our History, Our Future*. New York: Harper and Row, 1987.

Weart, Spencer R. *Nuclear Fear: A History of Images*. Cambridge, Mass.: Harvard Univ. Pr., 1988.

LITERARY CRITICISM

Bartter, Martha. *The Way to Ground Zero: The Atomic Bomb in American Science Fiction.* New York: Greenwood Press, 1988.

Bosmajian, Hamida. "Writing for Children about the Unthinkable." *Children's Literature,* 17 (1989): 206–11.

Brians, Paul. "Nuclear Fiction for Children." *Bulletin of the Atomic Scientists* 44, no. 6 (July/August 1988): 24–27.

_____. *Nuclear Holocausts: Atomic War in Fiction, 1895–1984.* Kent, Ohio: Kent State Univ. Pr., 1986.

_____. "Rambo's Relatives." *American Book Review,* March/April 1986, pp. 19–20.

Brians, Paul, and Jane Winston-Dolan. "Nuclear War Fiction by Women Authors." Paper presented at Interface '84: Eighth Annual Humanities and Technology Conference, Marietta, Ga., October 25–26, 1984.

Crow, John, and Richard Erlich. "Mythic Patterns in Ellison's *A Boy and His Dog.*" *Extrapolation: Journal for the Scholarly Study of Science Fiction and Fantasy* 18 (1977): 162–166.

Dowling, David. *Fictions of Nuclear Disaster.* Iowa City: Univ. of Iowa Pr., 1987.

Franklin, H. Bruce. "The Bomb in the Home: Stories by Japanese and American Women Experts on Nuclearism." Paper presented at the Modern Language Association Conference, New Orleans, December 28, 1988.

_____. *War Stars: The Superweapon and the American Imagination.* New York: Oxford Univ. Pr., 1988.

Lenz, Millicent. "Hope Amidst the Ruins: Notes Toward a Nuclear Criticism of Young Adult Literature." *JOYS: Journal of Youth Services in Libraries* 1, no. 3 (Spring 1988): 321–28.

May, Keith M. "Ape and Essence." In *Aldous Huxley.* London: Paul Elek Books, 1972.

Schwenger, Peter. "Writing the Unthinkable." *Critical Inquiry* 13, no. 1 (Autumn 1986): 33–48.

MYTH AND RELIGION

Campbell, Joseph. *The Power of Myth,* with Bill Moyers. Edited by Betty Sue Flowers. New York: Doubleday, 1988.

Chernus, Ira. *Dr. Strangegod: On the Symbolic Meaning of Nuclear Weapons.* Columbia: Univ. of South Carolina Pr., 1986.

SCIENCE

Sheldrake, Rupert. *A New Science of Life: The Hypothesis of Formative Causation.* Los Angeles: J. P. Tarcher, 1981.

Watson, Lyall. *The Dreams of Dragons: Riddles of Natural History.* New York: William Morrow, 1987.

SOCIOLOGY

Mojtaibai, A. G. *Blessed Assurance: At Home with the Bomb in Amarillo, Texas.* Boston: Houghton Mifflin, 1986. Reprint. Albuquerque: Univ. of New Mexico Pr., 1988.

WOMEN'S STUDIES

Griffin, Susan. *Woman and Nature: The Roaring Inside Her.* New York: Harper Colophon, 1978.
Koen, Susan, Nina Swaim, and friends. *Ain't No Where We Can Run: A Handbook for Women on the Nuclear Mentality.* Norwich, Vt.: WAND (P.O. Box 421, 05055), 1980.

Chapter 7. The Quest for Wholeness in a Broken World

Primary Sources
ESSAYS

Haines, John. "Death Is a Meadowlark: Memorials and Consolations from a Work in Progress." In *Writing in a Nuclear Age.* Edited by Jim Schley. Hanover, N.H.: University Press of New England, 1984.
Thompson, E. P. "Overthrowing the Satanic Kingdom," *Protest and Survive.* Edited by E. P. Thompson and Dan Smith. New York: Monthly Review Press, 1981. Reprinted in *The Nuclear Predicament: A Sourcebook,* edited by Donna Gregory. New York: St. Martin's Press, 1986.

POETRY

Heaney, Seamus. Note to "The Birthplace." In *Writing in a Nuclear Age.* Edited by Jim Schley. Hanover, N.H.: University Press of New England, 1984.
Kramer, Aaron. "A Hundred Planets." In Aaron Kramer, "Hiroshima: A 37-Year Failure to Respond." In *Writing in a Nuclear Age.* Edited by Jim Schley. Hanover, N.H.: University Press of New England, 1984.

SHORT STORIES

Matheson, Richard. "Pattern for Survival." *Magazine of Fantasy and Science Fiction* (May 1955). Reprint. In *The Best from Fantasy and Science Fiction,* Fifth Series. Edited by Anthony Boucher. New York: Ace, 1956.

FICTION

Brin, David. *The Postman*. New York: Bantam Books, 1985.

Gee, Maggie. *The Burning Book*. New York: St. Martin's Press, 1983.

Hoban, Russell. *The Mouse and His Child*. New York: Harper, 1976.

———. *Riddley Walker*. New York: Simon and Schuster, 1980.

Ibuse, Masuji. *Black Rain*. Tokyo and Palo Alto: Kodansha, 1969; New York: Bantam, 1985. Originally published as *Kuroi Ame* in *Showa* (January 1965–September 1966). Reprint. *Japan Quarterly* 14, nos. 2–4 (1967).

Johnson, Denis. *Fiskadoro*. New York: Knopf, 1985.

Joyce, James. *Finnegan's Wake*. 1939; London: Faber and Faber, 1975.

McIntyre, Vonda. *Dreamsnake*. Boston: Houghton Mifflin, 1978. The first portion was published in *Analog* (October 1973), under the title "Of Mist, Grass, and Sand."

Miller, Walter M., Jr. *A Canticle for Leibowitz*. Philadelphia: Lippincott, 1959; New York: Bantam, 1961. First published in *Fantasy and Science Fiction* (April 1955, 1956, and 1957).

Paton Walsh, Jill. *The Green Book*. New York: Avon, 1977.

Plath, Sylvia. *The Bell Jar*. London: Heineman, 1963; New York: Bantam, 1971.

Swindells, Robert. *Brother in the Land*. New York: Holiday House, 1984.

Wilhelm, Kate. *Where Late The Sweet Birds Sang*. New York: Harper and Row, 1976.

Secondary Sources

ANTHROPOLOGY

Bateson, Gregory. Quoted in R. Morgan, "Epoch B." *New York Times Sunday Magazine*, February 29, 1976, p. 33.

Brown, G. B., and E. G. Brown, Jr. "Prayer Breakfast." *CoEvolution Quarterly* (Spring 1976), p. 84. On Gregory Bateson.

Lipset, David. *Gregory Bateson: The Legacy of a Scientist*. Boston: Beacon Press, 1982.

BOOK REVIEWS

Hammond, Nancy C. Review of *The Green Book*, by Jill Paton Walsh. *Horn Book Magazine* 58, no. 6 (December 1982): 652–53.

ECOLOGY AND ETHICS

Meeker, Joseph. *The Comedy of Survival: In Search of an Environmental Ethic*. Los Angeles: International College Guild of Tutors Press, 1980.

LITERARY CRITICISM

Bartter, Martha J. *The Way to Ground Zero: The Atomic Bomb in American Science Fiction*. New York: Greenwood Press, 1988.

Bosmajian, Hamida. "Conventions of Image and Form in Nuclear Narratives for Young Readers," *Papers on Language and Literature* 26 (1990): 73–89.

Brians, Paul, and Jane Winston-Dolan. "Nuclear War Fiction by Women Authors." Paper presented at Interface '84, Eighth Annual Humanities and Technology Conference, Marietta, Ga., October 25–26, 1984.

Lake, David J. "Making the Two One; Language and Mysticism in *Riddley Walker*." *Extrapolation* 25 (1984): 157–70.

Morrissey, Thomas J. "Armageddon from Huxley to Hoban." *Extrapolation* 25 (1984): 197–213.

Percy, Walker. "Walter M. Miller, Jr.'s *A Canticle for Leibowitz*: A Rediscovery." *Southern Review* 7, no. 2 (1971): 572–73.

Schwenger, Peter. "Writing the Unthinkable." *Critical Inquiry* 13, no. 1 (Autumn 1986): 33–48.

Schwetman, John W. "Russell Hoban's *Riddley Walker* and the Language of the Future." *Extrapolation* 26 (1985): 212–19.

PSYCHOLOGY

Lifton, Robert J. *The Broken Connection: On Death and the Continuity of Life.* New York: Simon and Schuster, 1979.

_____. *Death in Life: The Survivors of Hiroshima.* New York: Random House, 1967.

MYTH AND RELIGION

Brown, Norman O. "The Apocalypse of Islam." In *Facing Apocalypse*. Edited by Valerie Andrews, Robert Bosnak, and Karen Walter Goodwin. Dallas: Spring Publications, 1987.

Campbell, Joseph. *The Power of Myth*, with Bill Moyers. Edited by Betty Sue Flowers. New York: Doubleday, 1988.

Chapter 8. Gaia as Cosmic Myth

Primary Sources

LETTER

Schweickart, Russell L. Letter to Paul Winter, January 25, 1982. Reprinted in a brochure accompanying "Missa Gaia: Earth Mass," by Paul Winter. Living Music Records, Box 68, Litchfield, CT 06759: 1982. Unpaged.

PICTURE BOOKS

Kastner, Erich. *Die Konferenz der Tiere, nach einer Idee von Jella Lepman* (The Conference of Animals, after an Idea of Jella Lepman). Hamburg, Germany: Deutscher Bucherbund, 1949.

POETRY

Eliot, T. S. "Burnt Norton," in *The Complete Poems and Plays, 1909–1950*. New York: Harcourt, Brace, 1952.

SHORT STORIES

Del Ray, Lester. "Helen O'Loy." *Astounding Science Fiction* 21 (December 1938).

FILMS

E. T.: The Extra-Terrestrial in His Adventure on Earth. Screenplay by Melissa Mathison. Produced by Stephen Spielberg and Kathleen Kennedy. Universal Studios, 1982.

FICTION

Aldiss, Brian. *Helliconia Winter*. New York: Atheneum, 1985. Sequel to *Helliconia Spring* (1982) and *Helliconia Summer* (1983).

Heinlein, Robert. *The Green Hills of Earth*. Chicago: Shasta Publishers, 1951.

Hoban, Russell. *Turtle Diary*. New York: Random House, 1975.

Kotzwinkle, William. *E. T.: The Extra-Terrestrial in His Adventure on Earth*. New York: Berkley Books, 1982.

Mailer, Norman. *Of a Fire on the Moon*. London: Weidenfeld and Nicolson, 1970.

Moffet, Judith. *Pennterra*. New York: Congdon and Weed, 1987.

Service, Pamela. *Winter of Magic's Return*. New York York: Athenum, 1985.

Tolan, Stephanie S. *The Pride of the Peacock*. New York: Charles Scribner's Sons, 1986.

Secondary Sources

ANTHROPOLOGY

Capra, Fritjof. *Uncommon Wisdom: Conversations with Remarkable People*. New York: Bantam Books, 1988. A conversation with Gregory Bateson.

BOOK REVIEWS

Mallon, Thomas. "One Small Shelf for Literature." *New York Times Book Review Section*, July 16, 1989, pp. 1, 26–28.

Ottenberg, Eve. "Big Brain, No Nerve." *The Village Voice* 25, no. 9 (March 3, 1980): 34.

Rothstein, Mervin. "The Painful Nurturing of Doris Lessing's 'Fifth Child.' " *New York Times*, June 14, 1988, p.C21.

ECOLOGY AND ETHICS

Berry, Wendell. "The Futility of Global Thinking." *Harper's Magazine*, September 1989, pp. 16–22.

LITERARY AND FILM CRITICISM

Bamberger, Richard. "Trends in Modern Literature for Children and Young People." C. C. Williamson Memorial Lecture No. 7. Nashville Tenn.: George Peabody College for Teachers, School of Library Science, 1973 (c1974).

Benet's Reader's Encyclopedia. 3d ed. New York: Harper and Row, 1987.

Berger, Alfred I. "Love, Death and the Atomic Bomb: Sexuality and Community in Science Fiction, 1935–55." *Science Fiction Studies* 8 (1981): 280–95.

Brians, Paul. *Nuclear Holocausts: Atomic War in Fiction 1895–1984*. Kent, Ohio: Kent State Univ. Pr., 1987.

Lenz, Millicent. "E. T.: A Cosmic Myth for Space-Age Children." *Children's Literature Quarterly* 8, no. 2 (Summer 1983): 3–5.

Lepman, Jella. *A Bridge of Children's Books*. Translated from the German by Edith McCormick. Foreword by J. E. Morporgo. Chicago: American Library Association, 1969. Originally published as *Die Kinderbuchbrucke* (Frankfurt: S. Fischer, 1964).

Naha, Ed. "Inside E. T." *Starlog* 63 (October 1982): 65.

Seeing Earth: Literary Responses to Space Exploration. Edited by Ronald Weber. Athens: Univ. of Ohio Pr., 1980.

Speculations: An Introduction to Literature through Fantasy and Science Fiction. Edited by Thomas Edward Sanders. New York: Glencoe, 1973.

MYTH

Berg, Colin. "The Art of Return." *Parabola* 12, no. 3 (August 1987): 63–67.

Campbell, Joseph. *The Inner Reaches of Outer Space*. New York: Alfred Van Der Marck Editions, 1985.

———. *Myths to Live By*. New York: Bantam, 1973.

Eisler, Riane. *The Chalice and the Blade: Our History, Our Future*. San Francisco: Harper and Row, 1989.

Lurker, Manfred. *Dictionary of Gods and Goddesses, Devils and Demons*. New York: Routledge and Kegan Paul, 1984.

Stone, Merlin. *Ancient Mirrors of Womanhood: A Treasury of Goddess and Heroine Lore from Around the World*. Illustrated by Cynthia Stone. New Sibylline Books, 1979; Boston: Beacon Press, 1984.

PSYCHOLOGY AND RELIGION

Becker, Ernest. *The Denial of Death*. New York: Free Press, 1973.

Chernus, Ira. *Dr. Strangegod: On the Symbolic Meaning of Nuclear Weapons*. Columbia: Univ. of South Carolina Pr., 1986.

de Chardin, Teilhard. *The Phenomenon of Man*. New York: Harper and Row. 1965.

Fox, Matthew. *Original Blessing: A Primer in Creation Spirituality*. Santa Fe, N. Mex.: Bear and Company, 1983.

_____. *A Spirituality Named Compassion and the Healing of the Global Village, Humpty Dumpty, and Us*. San Francisco: Harper and Row, 1979.

_____ and Brian Swimme. *Manifesto for a Global Civilization*. Santa Fe, N. Mex.: Bear Books, 1982.

Schmookler, Andrew Bard. *Out of Weakness: Healing the Wounds That Drive Us to War*. New York: Bantam, 1988.

SCIENCE

Berger, Alfred I. "Love, Death and the Atomic Bomb: Sexuality and Community in Science Fiction, 1935–55." *Science Fiction Studies* 8 (1981): 280–95.

Ehrlich, Paul R., Carl Sagan, Donald Kennedy, and Walter Orr Roberts. *The Cold and the Dark: The World after Nuclear War*. Foreword by Lewis Thomas. New York: W. W. Norton, 1984.

The Home Planet. Conceived and edited by Kevin W. Kelley for the Association of Space Explorers, with original design concept by Carol Denison. Reading, Mass.: Addison-Wesley, 1988.

Kerr, Richard A. "No Longer Willful, Gaia Becomes Respectable." *Science* 240, no. 4851 (April 22, 1985): 393–95.

Lovelock, James. *Gaia: A New Look at Life on Earth*. New York: Oxford Univ. Pr., 1979.

"What Is Gaia?" Brochure accompanying recording of "Missa Gaia/Earth Mass," with Paul Winter and the Paul Winter Consort. Litchfield, Conn.: Living Music Records, 1982.

Wiley, John P., Jr. "[Gaia] Phenomena, Comment and Notes." *Smithsonian* 19, no. 2 (May 1988): 30–33.

Further Reading

Schneider, Stephen H. "Gaia: A Goddess of the Earth?" *1988: Yearbook of Science and the Future*. Chicago: Encyclopaedia Britannica, Inc., 1987, pp. 28–43.

SOCIOLOGY

Barash, David P., and Judith Eve Lipton. *The Caveman and the Bomb*. New York: McGraw-Hill, 1985.

Earth's Answer: Explorations of Planetary Culture at the Lindisfarne Conferences. Edited by Michael Katz, William P. Marsh, and Gail Gordon. New York: Harper and Row, 1977.

Gottlieb, Annie. *Do You Believe in Magic? The Second Coming of the Sixties Generation*. New York: Time Books, 1987.

Wolfe, Tom. *The Right Stuff*. New York: Farrar, Straus, and Giroux, 1979.

VIDEO

"The Other Side of the Moon." Produced by Lemle Pictures, Inc. South Carolina ETV Network, 1989. Broadcast on PBS, July 1989.

Chapter 9. A Life-Affirming Ethic: Valuing Everything We Touch

Primary Sources

AUTOBIOGRAPHY AND BIOGRAPHY

Lansing, Alfred. *Endurance: Shackleton's Incredible Voyage*. New York: McGraw-Hill, 1959; Carroll and Graff, 1986.

McCarthy, Mary. *Memories of a Catholic Girlhood*. San Diego: Harcourt Brace Jovanovich, 1957.

Scott, Robert Falcon. *Scott's Last Expedition*. Edited by Leonard Huxley. Preface by Clements R. Markham. London: Macmillan, 1913; Dodd, Mead, 1964.

Shackleton, Ernest Henry. *The Heart of Antarctica: Being the Story of the British Antarctic Expedition, 1907–1909*. Philadelphia: Lippincott, 1909.

_____. *Shackleton, His Antarctic Writings (Selections)*. New York: P. Bedrick Books, 1983.

_____. *South*. New York: Macmillan, 1926.

DRAMA

Bolt, Robert. *The Mission*. New York: Penguin, 1986. The basis for the Warner Brothers film of the same name.

ESSAYS

Awiakta, Marilou. "What Is the Atom, Mother? Will It Hurt Us?" *Ms.* (July 1983): 44, 47–48.

Des Pres, Terrence. "Self/Landscape/Grid," in *Writing in a Nuclear Age*. Edited by Jim Schley. Hanover, N.H.: University Press of New England, 1984.

Williams, William Carlos. Quoted in *Writing in a Nuclear Age*. Edited by Jim Schley. Hanover, N.H.: University Press of New England, 1984.

FICTION

Gardner, John. *Grendel*. Illustrated by Emil Antonucci. New York: Knopf, 1971; 1987.

Hoban, Russell. *Turtle Diary*. New York: Random House, 1975.

Hoover, H. M. *Children of Morrow*. New York: Four Winds Press, 1973.

Joyce, James. *Portrait of the Artist as a Young Man*. 1916; New York, Viking, 1964.
LeGuin, Ursula. *Always Coming Home*. Composer, Todd Barton. Artist, Margaret Chodos. Geomancer, George Hersh. New York: Harper and Row, 1985.
_____. *The Word for World is Forest*. New York: Berkley/Putnam, 1972.
McIntyre, Vonda. *Dreamsnake*. New York: Houghton Mifflin, 1978.
O'Brien, Robert C. *Mrs. Frisby and the Rats of NIMH*. New York: Atheneum, 1971.
Service, Pamela. *Winter of Magic's Return*. New York: Atheneum, 1985.
Weston, Susan. *Children of the Light*. New York: St. Martin's Press, 1985.
Wyndham, John. *Re-Birth, or the Chrysalids*. New York: Ballantine, 1965. Originally published as *The Chrysalids* (London: Michael Joseph, 1955).

FILMS

Koyaanisqatsi. PAV Films, 1983. 87 minutes.
Letters from a Dead Man. Script by Konstantin Lopushansky and Viacheslav Rybakov, in collaboration with Boris Strugatsky.
The Mission. Warner Brothers, 1986.

POETRY

Crossley-Holland, Kevin. *Beowulf: A New Translation*. Introduction by Bruce Mitchell. New York: Farrar, Straus, and Giroux, 1968.
Hopkins, Gerard Manley. "Pied Beauty." *Poems of Gerard Manley Hopkins*. Preface and Notes by Robert Bridges. 3d ed. Edited and enlarged with an introduction by W. H. Gardner. London: Oxford Univ. Pr., 1948.
Levertov, Denise. "On the 32nd Anniversary of the Bombing of Hiroshima and Nagasaki." In *Facing Apocalypse*. Edited by Valerie Andrews, Robert Bosnak, and Karen Walter Goodwin. Dallas, Tex.: Spring Publications, 1987.

SOUND RECORDINGS

Fuller, Robert. "A Better Game Than War." Interview. New Dimensions Radio, WRPI, Troy, N.Y., July 31, 1988.
Houston, Jean. "Spiral into Life." New Dimensions Radio, WRPI, Troy, N.Y., June 3, 1988.
It's a Big World. A&M Records, Inc., 1986. AP-6021.
Rastaman Vibration. Island Records, 1976. SR90033-4.
War. Island Records, 1983. 90067-1.
Zenyatta Mondatta. A&M Records, 1980. SP-3720.

Secondary Sources

BOOK REVIEWS

Mesic, Penelope. Review of *Riddley Walker*, by Russell Hoban. *The Bulletin of the Atomic Scientists* (June/July 1982); 49–50.

Perrin, Noel. "Science Fiction: Imaginary Worlds and Real-Life Questions."
New York Times Book Review, April 9, 1989, pp. 37–38.
Vendler, Helen. *New York Times Book Review* (April 28, 1988), pp. 41–45.

ECOLOGY AND ETHICS

Berry, Thomas. *The Dream of the Earth.* San Francisco: Sierra Club Books, 1988.
"Confrontation." Washington, D.C.: Greenpeace USA, n.d. Available from
Greenpeace USA, 1611 Connecticut Avenue NW, Washington, DC 20070.
"Endangered Earth." *National Geographic* 174, no. 6 (December 1988).
McKibben, Bill. "Reflections: The End of Nature." *New Yorker,* September 11,
1989, pp. 47–105.
"Planet Earth." *U.S. News and World Report* 105, no. 17 (October 31, 1988).
"The Planet of the Year." *Time* 133, no. 1 (January 1, 1989).
Shepard, Paul. *The Tender Carnivore and the Sacred Game.* New York: Charles
Scribner's Sons, 1973.
Sperry, Roger. *Science and Moral Priority: Merging Mind, Brain, and Human Values.* New York: Columbia Univ. Pr., 1983.
United Nations General Assembly. *World Charter for Nature.* A/RES/37/7. New
York: United Nations, 1982.

HISTORY

Weart, Spencer R. *Nuclear Fear: A History of Images.* Cambridge, Mass.: Harvard Univ. Pr., 1988.

LITERARY CRITICISM AND BIBLIOGRAPHY

Berlin, James. "Rhetoric and Ideology in the Writing Class." *College English* 50
(1988): 477–94.
Bernstein, Joanne, and Masha K. Rudman. *Books to Help Children Cope with Separation and Loss: An Annotated Bibliography.* Vol. 3. New York: Bowker, 1989.
Brians, Paul. "And That Was the Future: The World Will End Tomorrow." *Futures* August 1988, pp. 425–33.
De Kerckhove. "On Nuclear Communication." *Diacritics* 14 (Summer 1984):
80.
Gakov, Vladimir, and Paul Brians. "Nuclear-War Themes in Soviet Science
Fiction: An Annoted Bibliography." *Science Fiction Studies* 16, pt. I (March
1989): 67–84.
McLaughlin, Becky R. "In the Classroom: How to Combat Nuclear War Using
Female Gender Identity Formation, the Idea as Gift, Pop Music, and
Brecht's 'Alienation Effect.'" Paper presented at the Midwest Modern Language Association Conference, St. Louis, Mo., November 3–5, 1988.
Williams, Raymond. "Alignment and Commitment." *Contemporary Literary
Criticism.* edited by Robert Con Davis. London: Longman, 1986.

MYTH

Chief Seattle. Quoted in Joseph Campbell, *The Power of Myth*, with Bill Moyers. Edited by Betty Sue Flowers. New York: Doubleday, 1988.

Cirlot, J. E. *A Dictionary of Symbols.* 2d ed. Translated from the Spanish by Jack Sage. Foreword by Herbert Read. New York: Philosophical Library, 1971.

Highwater, Jamake. *The Primal Mind: Vision and Reality in Indian America.* New York: Harper and Row, 1981.

LeGuin, Ursula. *Dancing at the Edge of the World: Thoughts on Words, Women, Places.* New York: Grove Press, 1989.

Pearson, Carol S. *The Hero Within: Six Archetypes We Live By.* San Francisco: Harper and Row, 1989.

Stone, Merlin. *Ancient Mirrors of Womanhood: A Treasury of Goddess Lore from Around the World.* Illustrated by Cynthia Stone. Boston: Beacon Press, 1979.

PHILOSOPHY AND RELIGION

Capra, Fritjof. *The Turning Point: Science, Society and the Rising Culture.* New York: Simon and Schuster, 1982; Bantam, 1988.

Dubos, Rene. "Education for the Celebration of Life: Optimism in Spite of It All." In *Education for Peace and Disarmament: Toward a Living World.* Edited by Douglas Sloan. New York: Teachers College Press, 1983.

Fox, Matthew. *The Coming of the Cosmic Christ: The Healing of Mother Earth and the Birth of a Global Renaissance.* San Francisco: Harper and Row, 1988.

Fox, Matthew, and Brian Swimme. *Manifesto for a Global Civilization.* Santa Fe, N.Mex.: Bear Books, 1982.

Hyde, Lewis. *The Gift: Imagination and the Erotic Life of Property.* New York: Random House, 1983.

Keyes, Ken. *The Hundredth Monkey.* Coos Bay, Oreg.: Vision Books, 1982.

Noel, Daniel C. "The Nuclear Horror and the Hounding of Nature: Listening to Images." *Soundings: An Interdisciplinary Journal* 70 (Fall/Winter 1987): 289–308.

Robertson, James. *The Sane Alternative: A Choice of Futures.* Foreword by Hazel Henderson. St. Paul, Minn.: River Basin Publishing Company, 1978.

Stanton, Elizabeth Cady, and the Revising Committee. *The Woman's Bible.* New York: European Publishing Company, 1894; Seattle: Coalition Task Force on Women and Religion, 1974.

PSYCHOLOGY

Becker, Ernest. *The Denial of Death.* New York: Free Press, 1975.

Fox, Matthew, and Brian Swimme. *Manifesto for a Global Civilization.* Santa Fe, N. Mex.: Bear Books, 1982.

Giegerich, Wolfgang. "Saving the Nuclear Bomb." In *Facing Apocalypse.* Edited by Valerie Andrews, Robert Bosnak, and Karen Walter Goodwin. Dallas, Tex.: Spring Publications, 1987.

Gilligan, Carol. *In a Different Voice: Psychological Theory and Women's Development*. Cambridge, Mass.: Harvard Univ. Pr., 1982.

Harman, Willis, and Howard Rheingold. *Higher Creativity: Liberating the Unconscious for Breakthrough Insights*. Los Angeles: J. P. Tarcher, 1984.

Houston, Jean. *Lifeforce: The Psycho-Historical Recovery of the Self*. New York: Delacorte, 1980.

_____. *The Possible Human: A Course in Extending Your Physical, Mental, and Creative Abilities*. Los Angeles: J. P. Tarcher, 1982.

Lifton, Robert J. *The Broken Connection: On Death and the Continuity of Life*. New York: Basic Books, 1979.

Martin, Charles E., Bonnie Crammond, and Tammy Safter. "Developing Creativity Through the Reading Program." *The Reading Teacher* 35 (February 1982): 568–72.

Metzner, Ralph. "Knots, Ties, Nets, and Bonds in Relationship." *Journal of Transpersonal Psychology* 17, no. 1 (1985): 41–45.

Watkins, Mary. " 'In Dreams Begin Responsibilities': Moral Imagination and Peace Action." In *Facing Apocalypse*. Edited by Valerie Andrews, Robert Bosnak, and Karen Walter Goodwin. Dallas, Tex.: Spring Publications, 1987.

_____. *Invisible Guests: The Development of Imaginal Dialogues*. Hillsdale, N.J.: Analytic Press, 1985.

SCIENCE

Brand, Stewart. *II Cybernetic Frontiers*. New York: Random House/Bookworks, 1974.

Gore, Rick. "Extinctions." Photographs by Jonathan Blair. *National Geographic* 175, no. 6 (June 1989): 662–99.

Sheldrake, Rupert. *A New Science of Life*. Los Angeles: J. P. Tarcher, 1981.

_____. *The Presence of the Past: Morphic Resonance and the Habits of Nature*. New York: Times Books, 1988.

Sperry, Roger. *Science and Moral Priority: Merging Mind, Brain, and Human Values*. New York: Columbia Univ. Pr., 1983.

Stableford, Brian. *Future Man*. New York: Crown, 1984.

Trefil, James. "Stop to Consider the Stones That Fall from the Sky." *Smithsonian* 20, no. 60 (September 1989): 81–93.

Van, Jon. "Study Links Ice Ages, Greenhouse Effect." *Chicago Tribune*, August 1, 1989, Sect. 1, p. 3.

SPEECHES

Asimov, Isaac. Address at Rensselaerville Institute, Rensselaerville, N.Y., July 23, 1988.

Index

Italicized page number is the first reference to a title or author in the bibliography

Millicent Lenz is an assistant professor at the School of Information Science and Policy at SUNY Albany, where she teaches courses in literature for children, library materials for young adults, and curriculum and supportive resources. She holds a master's and PhD in English as well as an MLS, and has published articles on children's literature in several journals, including *Catholic Library World*, the *Children's Literature Association Quarterly*, and *Journal of Youth Services in Libraries*. She is also the co-author (with Ramona M. Mahood) of *Young Adult Literature: Background and Criticism* (ALA, 1980).